BROKEN RECORD

BROKEN RECORD

THE INSIDE STORY
OF THE GRAMMY AWARDS

by Henry Schipper

A Birch Lane Press Book
Published by Carol Publishing Group

A Birch Lane Press Book
Published by Carol Publishing Group
Birch Lane is a registered trademark of Carol Communications, Inc.
Editorial Offices: 600 Madison Avenue, New York, N.Y. 10022
Sales & Distribution Offices: 120 Enterprise Avenue, Secaucus, N.J. 07094
In Canada: Canadian Manda Group, P.O. Box 920, Station U, Toronto,
   Ontario M8Z 5P9

Queries regarding rights and permission should be addressed to Carol Publishing Group, 600 Madison Avenue, New York, N.Y. 10022

Carol Publishing Group books are available at special discounts for bulk purchases, for sales promotions, fund raising, or educational purposes. Special editions can be created to specifications. For details, contact: Special Sales Department, Carol Publishing Group, 120 Enterprise Avenue, Secaucus, N.J. 07094

Manufactured in the United States of America
10 9 8 7 6 5 4 3 2 1

Library of Congress Cataloging-in-Publication Data

Schipper, Henry.
   Broken record : the story of the grammy awards / by Henry
Schipper.
      p.   cm.
   ISBN 1-55972-104-9 (cloth) :
   1. Grammy Awards—History. I. Title.
   ML76.G7S3 1992
   781.64′079′73—dc20   92-6129
                                                                CIP
                                                                MN

Acknowledgments

Thank you, members and officers of the National Academy of Recording Arts and Sciences, past and present, along with Grammy winners and other record industry veterans who agreed to be interviewed for this book. This being the first written history of the Grammys, your input was invaluable.

Those interviewed include: Lou Adler, Van Alexander, Steve Allen, George Avakian, Al Bell, Ted Bergmann, Hal Blaine, Harold Bradley, Les Brown, Lew Chudd, Ray Conniff, Hal Cooke, Pierre Cossette, Jim Conkling, Stan Cornyn, Christopher Cross, Joe Csida, Bill Denny, Barry DeVorzon, Jim Ellers, Nesuhi Ertegun, Mick Fleetwood, Bernie Fleischer, Jerry Fuller, Stan Freberg, Vic Garbarini, Al Green, Jimmie Haskell, Bill Hobin, Mary Jarvis, Phil Jones, Paul Keyes, Grelun Landon, Bob Levinson, Al Livingston, Henry Mancini, Johnny Mann, Dave Marsh, Marilyn McCoo, Vaughn Meader, Mike Melvoin, Roger Miller, Walter Miller, Artie Mogul, Mickey Newberry, Robert Oermann, Milt Okun, Nick Perito, John Phillips, George Schlatter, Francis Scott, Paul Shefrin, George Simon, Joe Smith, Glenn Snoddy, Jim Stewart, Billy Taylor, Nino Tempo, Mary Travers, Paul Weston, Jerry Wexler, Bob Yorke, and Frank Zappa.

Publications and periodicals used as source material for this book include: *ASCAP* magazine, *Bam* magazine, *Billboard, Cash Box, Country Music, Daily Variety, Hollywood Reporter, Los Angeles Herald Examiner, Los Angeles Times, New York Times, Pulse, Rolling Stone, USA Today,* and *Variety.*

Record industry pros who provided key assists in the way of photos and information include: Kathy Acquaviva, Diana Baron, Paula Batson, Marie Bonan, Laura Gold, Trish Heimers, Bob Merlis, Lisa Millman, Carolyn Marrujo de O'Hara, Laura Swanson, Sue Satriano.

Thanks to my agent Bert Holtje for his perseverence and encouragement. Likewise to my editor Gail Kinn for working hard on a fast turnaround.

A major debt of gratitude to Michael Ochs, who opened the doors to his vast record and research library.

Ditto for Jeff Graham, who introduced writer and publisher, got the ball rolling, and offered supportive and insightful feedback throughout.

Heartfelt thanks to Mark Rowland, for listening to countless Grammy anecdotes, howling appropriately, and critiquing the manuscript.

And to Jeff Ressner, for his persistent interest and counsel, and for setting up some highly rewarding spin-off assignments.

Finally, I want to thank Shannon Hogan, for her loving friendship . . . and Jessica O'Dwyer, for making things so much buttuh . . .

Dedicated to Lewis, Rose, Jenny, Marcel, and Teddy

Contents

BROKEN RECORD

ONE

All Shook Up: 1957

Was the record industry about to become "a slave to the enthusiasms of teen age girls"? That was the question posed by *Billboard* magazine in the spring of 1957, and it was a question that deeply troubled the men who would start the Grammy Awards.

The National Academy of Recording Arts & Sciences (NARAS), the organization that sponsors the Grammys, was formed in 1957 at the height of a pitched battle over the direction of popular music. Did the future belong to rock 'n' roll, and what *Billboard* called "the pre-shave set," or would "good music," personified by Frank Sinatra, Perry Como, and Doris Day, prevail?

The Grammy fathers, without exception, belonged to the good-music camp. Reared on big band and swing, accustomed to the songwriting artistry of people like Irving Berlin and Jerome Kern, they hated rock 'n' roll, regarded it as a kind of antimusic—lyrically inane, shoddily produced, a mockery of any reasonable set of musical standards.

It wasn't just primitive or sloppy musicianship that Grammy founders reviled in rock. The raw energy and freedom of the music went completely against the grain of the repressed and fearful fifties. The artistry of singers like Crosby, Sinatra, Como, and Cole lay in their ability to sublimate emotion, to transcend, refine, etherealize it. The results were sometimes exquisite, sometimes shallow, but always in keeping with the controlled posture of a generation that came of age during the Depression, fought World War II, then segued into the Cold War. Rock 'n' roll was an antithesis, a yelping breakaway and discovery in youth of vitality and emotion—the end of the fifties in the midst of the fifties. Grammy elders complained about the noise of rock, but that was just a cover. It was the abandon, the shout, the *idea* of a shout, that put them in such a spin, deafened them to the exhilarating and sometimes liberating musicality of Elvis, Chuck Berry, and the rest.

After Elvis, there could be no question about the success of rock. Presley's popularity was astonishing, unprecedented: He single-handedly accounted for *half* of RCA Records' sales in 1956. And it wasn't just Elvis. The first burst of rock produced a fabulous collection of artists, with Jerry Lee Lewis, Little Richard, Chuck Berry, Buddy Holly, the Everly Brothers, Fats Domino, and other future Hall of Famers selling millions of records and knocking the suddenly dated mood vocals of Como and Crosby off the air. By the end of 1957, more than half the records on the *Billboard* charts were rock hits.

Perhaps the Grammys could help stem the tide. The awards, according to a "Grammy Credo" drawn up at the time, would reward "artistry" and "excellence" (buzzwords for people like Sinatra and Ella Fitzgerald) while paying no heed to "sales and mass popularity" (code for top-selling rock and r&b). Teens might make Elvis "the King," but the Grammys would give industry experts a chance to tell the world what *they* thought was good. In a contest based on quality rather than record sales, with mature professionals casting the votes, rock 'n' roll surely wouldn't have a chance.

"We had nothing to do with rock 'n' roll, nor did we care much for it," recalls bandleader Les Brown, an influential member of NARAS during the formative years. "NARAS was founded to reward the good stuff—what we thought was the good stuff—and to challenge the crap."

"Every songwriter who wrote beautiful harmonies and lyrics where 'moon' didn't rhyme with 'town' deplored three-chord tunes and nonrhyming lyrics," concurs NARAS founder and first president, Paul Weston. "When music got in the hands of American teenagers, quality went down the tubes."

The Grammy story began in 1955 when a group called the Hollywood Beautification Committee asked a quintet of record biz executives to figure out who should or should not receive a star on the Hollywood Walk of Fame.

The Walk, a strip then being planned along the famed intersection of Hollywood and Vine, would feature sidewalk stars for some 1,200 performers as part of an earnest plan by Hollywood property owners to clean up Hollywood Boulevard. Tinseltown's most famous street was in danger of losing its tourist trade due to an influx of winos, hookers, and other unsavory transients.

The five record industry chieftains—Paul Weston of Columbia, Lloyd Dunn of Capitol, Sonny Burke of Decca, Jesse Kaye of MGM, and Dennis Farnon of RCA—met every month at the Brown Derby Restaurant in Hollywood to draw up their list. At first they decided that any artist who sold a million singles or 250,000 LPs during his or her career should get a star. But that left some of the industry's best artists out, people like Billie Holiday, Ella Fitzgerald, Bessie Smith, and others whose artistry exceeded their record sales.

The music men, all of whom had strong bonds to the creative side of the business, soon found themselves fantasizing about an award that had nothing to do with sales and everything to do with art, a kind of ideal, pure award, the likes of which the music business—indeed, the entertainment industry as a whole—had never seen.

"Our criteria for the Walk of Fame, we realized, was wrong," Weston concluded. "It may have been right for selecting names to put in cement, but what we really needed was a proper means for rewarding people on an artistic level."

And so the idea and the ideal of the Grammys was born. Weston and his colleagues continued to meet at the Brown Derby long after their Walk of Fame duties were finished, and formulated the vision and structure of what would become the industry's most prestigious awards.

The irony of all this is that the Grammys, born in opposition to the Walk, came to perform a similar function. The Hollywood Beautification Committee created the Walk to clean up an increasingly sleazy

Hollywood Boulevard. NARAS created the Grammys, at least in part, to clean up and gentrify pop. The Walk, it was hoped, would maintain property values in Tinseltown. The Grammys, it was hoped, would maintain musical values—as understood by esteemed elders like Weston and his peers.

NARAS was officially formed on May 28, 1957, in a back room of the same Brown Derby Restaurant in which the Grammys had been conceived two years earlier. The number-one record in the nation at the time, fittingly, was Elvis Presley's "All Shook Up."

Billboard, quick to apprehend the practical function of NARAS and the Grammys, hailed the project as the "greatest public relations effort" ever mounted by the record industry. The Academy's first chairman, Jim Conkling, former president of Columbia Records and future president of Warner Bros. Records, echoed the theme, declaring that "our major aim is to get respect."

With that in mind, NARAS invited some of the most respectable artists in the business to help get the awards off the ground, asking Perry Como, Patti Page, Doris Day, Frank Sinatra, Mitch Miller, Stan Freberg, and Nat King Cole, along with Cole Porter, to serve on a temporary steering committee.

The first NARAS board of governors, elected on June 26 at a meeting in the Beverly Hilton Hotel, likewise attests to the organization's genteel musical range. Jazz sax man Benny Carter, lyricist Sammy Cahn, crooner Nat King Cole, bandleader Stan Kenton, classical conductor Felix Slatkin, and torch singer (and Paul Weston's wife) Jo Stafford were all elected to the board. Weston, meanwhile, was named president of the organization's Los Angeles chapter.

The artists helped give NARAS early credibility, but industry executives like Conkling and Weston, Columbia's West Coast A&R chief, gave it clout. This was no starry-eyed group of outsiders, but a collection of some of the heaviest hitters in the record business. There was Capitol Records vice president Lloyd Dunn, who funneled office supplies from Capitol to NARAS. Francis Scott, a crucial early backer, was head of album A&R at Capitol. Bob Yorke, who helped negotiate the first Grammy TV show, was West Coast chief for RCA.

The Grammy founders' imposing credentials helped them win support from the major labels, but the Grammys were by no means a label-controlled operation. The whole dream behind the awards was to create an independent vehicle, of, by, and for the creative people in the record business. Label interests—that is, promoting "product" —were antithetical to the concept of the Grammys.

NARAS put its idealism on the line from the start. With Weston emphatically leading the way, the Academy quickly formulated its most important and fundamental rule: Only creative members of the industry—recording artists, conductors, songwriters, engineers, and so on—could vote for the awards; publicists, publishers, record promoters, even record company presidents who lacked creative credentials, could not.

"We decided early in the game that we were not going to have any categories of membership that could be influenced for commercial reasons," Conkling explained.

The rule was radical—the Oscars, Emmys, and Tonys were much more liberal in their voting requirements—but Weston and his colleagues knew that if their vision of the Grammys as an honest artistic salute was to have a chance, they had to keep the commercial side of the business at bay.

"Anyone who could say 'TV' could join the Television Academy [sponsor of the Emmys]," Weston explains. "We were determined to make NARAS a creative organization."

Nevertheless, mercenary interests were quick to try and wangle their way into the awards. The head of a supermarket chain that sold records wanted to help pick Grammy nominees. An irate Weston batted the proposal down. Music publishers and song pluggers, notorious for hustling their wares (with payola, if necessary) clamored to get in, but were likewise rebuffed.

In its purist zeal, NARAS even considered barring songwriters from the organization, because of their relationship to publishers and interest in promoting their own copyrights.

"We were worried. They have to promote their product. So we had to say, 'Well, are they pure enough to be in?' " recalls Conkling.

Composer Sammy Cahn, a NARAS board member, protested loudly, pointing out that the record industry wouldn't exist without lyricists, "unless you wanted people humming." The proposal was dropped, and NARAS not only admitted tunesmiths, but created a Song of the Year award.

All told, NARAS came up with twenty-eight categories for the first Grammys, enough to showcase the entire industry and give "everyone a chance" for an award, according to Conkling. Well, almost everyone. Conspicuous by its absence, rather incredibly, was rock 'n' roll, the bad-boy dynamo of the business and the one form of music NARAS didn't want to support or, evidently, even acknowledge.

"The rock movement was new and we just didn't understand it," Conkling would confess ten years later in a *Billboard* interview.

Indeed, the NARAS founders established Grammys for every other conceivable genre and pocket of the business: six for classical, two for jazz, one each for r&b, country, comedy, spoken word, movie sound track, Broadway, and children's recordings. Even waning subgenres like dance band and nonclassical orchestra had their own awards. But rock, pointedly, had none.

NARAS conservatives justified the snub, at least among themselves, by arguing that rock was "a passing fad," according to Nesuhi Ertegun, cofounder of Atlantic Records and NARAS president in 1964–65. "Many people were under the impression it would disappear in two or three years."

The tension between purist and commercial interests expressed itself most clearly in the Grammy Credo, a statement of principles written by pop satirist Stan Freberg and sent to Grammy voters along with their Grammy ballots during the early years of the awards. Freberg, who recorded highly successful parodies of early rock and r&b hits ("a musical trend I personally loathe," he wrote on the back of one of his albums), was an undisguised enemy of rock 'n' roll.

"We shall judge a record on the basis of sheer artistry, and artistry alone," Freberg proclaimed. "A record shall, in the opinion of the Academy, either attain the highest degree of excellence . . . or it shall not receive an Academy award.

". . . Sales and mass popularity are the yardsticks of the record business," he continued. "They are not the yardsticks of this Academy. We are concerned here with the phonograph record as an art form.

"If the industry is to grow, not decline in stature; if it is to foster a greater striving for excellence in its own field; if it is to discourage mediocrity and encourage greatness, we, as its spokesmen, can accept no other Credo."

Freberg's credo was the subject of intense and annual debate within NARAS. On the surface, it seemed just the kind of high-minded affirmation of values an awards show like the Grammys should have, explicitly rejecting commercialism in favor of art. Within the context of the rock-versus-"good music" debate, however, it served to formalize the Academy's antirock, anti-r&b stand. The credo was "a fence," in the words of early rock producer Lou Adler, that kept unwanted forms of music out.

But it was also a principled pledge to make the Grammys something more than a reflection of the *Billboard* charts, and people like Weston and even Ertegun defended it passionately. "There were more man-hours spent on the language of the credo than fighting World Wars I and II," recalls George Avakian, an executive with Warner Bros. Records and NARAS president in 1966–67. "People were trying to define what the Academy stood for."

NARAS knew that its dream of an industrywide award would never be realized if it were just a Los Angeles–based operation. L.A. and New York were the twin centers of the music business, highly competitive and accounting for roughly even shares of studio activity. Of the major labels, Columbia and RCA were based in the Big Apple, and without their participation, the Grammys would be meaningless.

Conkling went to New York and organized a meeting at the Park Sheraton Hotel. Approximately two dozen major industry figures attended, including arranger/conductor Percy Faith, producer John Hammond, and bandleader Guy Lombardo. Despite fears that Los Angeles would dominate the organization, New York launched a chapter on February 5, 1958, the second of seven branches that NARAS would eventually spawn. Lombardo was elected the chapter's first president, though more as a figurehead whose celebrity, it was hoped, would draw members to the fledgling branch.

With credo, categories, and East and West Coast chapters in place, NARAS was about ready to debut its award. Only one detail remained—a name. Someone suggested "The Eddies," in honor of Thomas Edison, inventor of the phonograph, but the idea was scotched. "People would think it was named after Eddie Fisher," Freberg quipped. A relative of Emile Berliner, the inventor who refined Edison's machine, lobbied for the "Berliner Awards," but that name was likewise vetoed. NARAS eventually decided to let the public come up with a name, putting out word of a contest through an Associated Press wire story and offering twenty-five albums to the winner. Almost half of the responses suggested the obvious—Grammy, a nickname for the gramophone. Mrs. Jay Danna's letter from New Orleans had the earliest postmark, and she won the prize. Twenty-five years later, NARAS flew her to Los Angeles to attend the silver anniversary Grammy show.

Capitol Records art director Marvin Schwartz, who would win three of the first five album-art Grammys, designed the actual award, a composite of the Edison, Victor, and Columbia gramophones. The Grammys, a composite of industry idealism and intolerance, were ready to make their bow.

TWO

Volare: 1958

Nominations for the first Grammy Awards, announced March 16, 1959, reflected all the aspirations, pretensions, blind spots, and contradictions of NARAS. The awards were dominated by mainstream, established stars like Frank Sinatra, Peggy Lee, and Perry Como. Sinatra, the ultimate pop artist in the eyes of many Grammy founders, generated no fewer than twelve nominations, three times more than any other star.

There were a few fresh faces: Hollywood composer Henry Mancini garnered four Grammy bids for his jazzy "Peter Gunn" TV theme; Italian crooner Domenico Modugno, "the most popular import since the pizza pie," won Record and Song of the Year honors for his middle-of-the-road (MOR) smash, "Volare"; and David Seville and the Chipmunks chirped their way to three nominations with "The Chipmunk Song," the first of many novelty hits to win Grammy praise.

Nominees for the prestigious Record of the Year award, given to the years top single, were: "Witchcraft" by Sinatra, "Volare" by Modugno, "Fever" by Lee, "The Chipmunk Song" by Seville, and "Catch a Falling Star" by Como.

Eligible records the Grammys ignored included "Johnny B. Goode" by Chuck Berry, "Good Golly Miss Molly" by Little Richard,

"La Bamba" by Ritchie Valens, and "Maybe Baby" by Buddy Holly and the Crickets.

Doris Day, Eydie Gorme, and Andy Williams all drew nominations. Elvis, to no one's surprise, did not, despite his incredible popularity. An item next to *Billboard*'s Grammy coverage noted that Presley's latest single, "I Need Your Love Tonight," had shipped one million copies within two days of its release.

Rock 'n' roll fans weren't the only ones who had cause to complain. The field of nominees for the first Country & Western Performance Grammy included such dubious "country" songs as "All I Have to Do Is Dream" by the Everly Brothers and "Tom Dooley," a folk smash by the Kingston Trio. "Dooley" wound up winning the award.

The r&b field was equally off-key. In a year that produced hits by Chuck Berry, Little Anthony, Little Richard, the Coasters, Clyde McPhatter, and the Platters. NARAS nominated "Belafonte Sings the Blues" by Harry Belafonte, "Patricia" by Perez Prado, "The End" by Earl Grant, "Looking Back" by Nat King Cole, and "Tequila" by a makeshift studio group called the Champs. "Tequila," a 90-proof miscast, won.

The people who attended the first Grammy Awards banquet, held May 4, 1959, in the Grand Ballroom of the Beverly Hilton Hotel in Los Angeles, weren't too disturbed about Grammy's snub of rock and its errant sense of country and r&b. The celebrity-studded throng of 485 constituted a who's who of the music industry's stodgy old guard, with Sinatra, Dean Martin, Sammy Davis, Jr., Peggy Lee, Jo Stafford, Helen Grayco, Gene Autry, Ann Richards, Meredith Willson, and Johnny Mercer all on hand.

The guests paid $15 apiece and dined on chicken squab souvaroff. Entertainment included stand-up comic Mort Sahl and a parody skit called "How South Was My Pacific" starring future Maytag pitchman Jesse White. The atmosphere was informal. Everyone knew everyone, and Weston and his wife, Jo Stafford, roamed the tables drafting friends like Sinatra, Martin, and Lee to present awards. A shortage of Grammy statues—NARAS hadn't expected many *groups* to win—was the evening's biggest glitch.

More than anyone, Sinatra represented the artistry and attitude that NARAS wanted the Grammys to foster and salute. In the midst of one of the most fertile stretches of his career, the self-styled "saloon singer" was a virulent critic of rock, which he once described as "the most brutal, ugly, degenerate, vicious form of expression it has been my displeasure to hear."

"It smells phony," Sinatra railed in a 1957 guest column in *Western World* magazine. "It is sung, played and written for the most part by cretinous goons and by means of its almost imbecilic reiteration and sly, lewd—in plain fact—dirty lyrics, it manages to be the martial music of every sideburned delinquent on the face of the earth."

Endearing himself, no doubt, to "legit" singers everywhere, Sinatra went on to describe the music of Elvis Presley as "a rancid-smelling aphrodisiac."

With an organization composed of reverential colleagues and fans and a dozen nominations for acclaimed singles like "Witchcraft," and albums like *Only the Lonely* and *Come Fly With Me*, Sinatra seemed a shoo-in to sweep the first Grammy awards, to pick up trophy after trophy in a kind of triumphal affirmation of the artistry and "good music" he represented.

Anticipating the moment, Sinatra booked two tables for the night, then sat through one of the rare humiliations of his career, losing in category after category and failing to take home a single vocal award. Twice he lost to the simple-hearted Modugno and his ultralight "Volare," which, to the consternation of Grammy highbrows, won both Record and Song of the Year awards. Mancini's *Peter Gunn* snared the Album of the Year prize. Como won the male vocal award. The only Grammy Sinatra won was a Best Album Cover award for *Only the Lonely*, a consolation prize that did little to console him.

"He was so upset about not winning a music award that he refused to let any of the photographers take our picture that night," Sandra Giles, Sinatra's actress-date later told Sinatra biographer Kitty Kelley. "He wasn't nasty to me, but he was very moody and drank a lot afterwards. . . . Looking back, I guess I should have been grateful that Elvis didn't win anything."

It was Sinatra's very popularity that apparently did him in. Nominated twice for Album of the Year honors (*Only the Lonely* and *Come Fly With Me*) and twice for the Male Vocal Performance award ("Witchcraft," "Come Fly With Me"), he split his own vote, thereby clearing the way for upsets by Modugno and Como.

Surprise stars of the evening were Modugno, Mancini (who would go on to win seventeen trophies over the next six years), and Chipmunks Simon, Theodore, and Alvin, who won a Grammy apiece in the comedy, children's, and engineering categories. Ella Fitzgerald (who took female and jazz female honors for her *Irving Berlin* and *Duke Ellington* songbooks, respectively) and Count Basie (who won dance band and jazz group kudos for his *Basie* LP) were the only other artists to win more than one award.

THREE

High Hopes: 1959

The months following the first Grammy show were hectic ones for NARAS. Generally pleased with their maiden effort, the Grammy governors nonetheless had some serious fine-tuning to attend to, particularly with regard to the twenty-eight Grammy categories.

The main problem, of course, was the glaring and preposterous absence of a category for rock 'n' roll. Grudgingly, and apparently unable to recognize the detested music by name, NARAS created a de facto category for rock: Best Performance by a "Top 40" Artist. Despite the new award, Grammy voters continued to snub rock, giving the first "Top 40" Grammy to Nat King Cole for "Midnight Flyer," a typically smooth Cole croon that was neither rock nor Top 40. The song never dented the *Billboard* charts.

NARAS also created a Best Performance, Folk award, giving the Kingston Trio, misplaced winner of the first country Grammy, a proper home. The Chipmunks' victory in the engineering category, meanwhile, prompted the Academy to create a Best Engineering, Novelty Recording Grammy, clearing the way for "serious" engineers to win the original engineering prize. Finally, NARAS added a new glamour category, Best New Artist of the Year.

Early blunders and pratfalls notwithstanding, the Grammys were now clearly on their feet, receiving front-page coverage from the trade press and grabbing the attention of the record industry, if not the public. But the road ahead would prove rocky.

The Academy itself was on financially shaky ground, living off $100 lifetime memberships cadged from supporters and industry execs, and forced, despite misgivings, to borrow money from the major record companies. But big-label subsidies were a dangerous and potentially compromising way to go, and Grammy boosters knew that the long-term integrity of the awards depended on independent forms of support—specifically, on a network TV deal, which was where the big money and exposure lay.

After the first show, NARAS was eager, even desperate, to go big time, in the manner of the Oscars, Emmys, and Tonys. The Grammy founders had assumed that landing a network deal would be "a lead-pipe cinch," recalls Bob Yorke, an RCA exec and the NARAS activist in charge of lining up a network and sponsor.

As it turned out, all three networks were interested in the show, but only if NARAS promised to deliver marquee artists who could justify a prime-time airing, artists like Sinatra and—Elvis. NARAS, of course, could make no such promises. Aside from the fact that it hated Elvis, the Academy, understandably, wanted the Grammy show to spotlight Grammy winners. The networks, just as understandably, were wary of whom the button-down Grammy voters would pick. Certainly, the chances of Elvis winning an award were nil.

"We met with all the networks many times," Yorke recalls. "Their reaction was quite negative. They were looking for a cheap [special]. We were only interested in putting on a show that represented our awards, that represented excellence, not popularity.

"We wanted a showcase for the industry, to show that it wasn't just churning out unintelligible pop crap, but glorious traditional and classical music, children's records as well as Elvis Presley."

A further complication was the Academy's fussiness about sponsorship of the show. Obsessed with projecting a respectable image that would offset the damage done to the music biz by payola scandals and rock 'n' roll, the Academy rejected a deodorant company, among others, as insufficiently dignified for its blue-blood awards. With finances getting desperate, NARAS finally struck a sponsorship deal with Swiss Watchmakers of America and persuaded NBC to carry the Second Annual Grammy Awards as a one-shot, one-hour special to air November 31, Thanksgiving weekend, 1959.

NARAS knew it had to score big ratings to avoid scrounging for another network and sponsor the next year, and since the key to ratings was celebrities, the Academy did everything it could to make sure its Grammy winners performed on the show. This was tricky, however, since no one was supposed to know who the winners were prior to the telecast. Ella Fitzgerald, Nat King Cole, and the Mormon Tabernacle Choir were all heavy favorites, but NARAS couldn't guarantee them Grammys, and they were disinclined to attend unless they knew they would win. The two-hundred-member Mormon Tabernacle Choir, in particular, was not about to fly to Los Angeles on the mere chance that it *might* win an award.

Desperate to land a few stars, the Academy did something it has never done again. According to Conkling, it peeked at the award results, confirmed that Ella, Cole, and the MT Choir had in fact won, and leaked that info to the performers. Fitzgerald and the MT Choir performed on the show.

The show was set to air November 31, and NARAS announced nominations for the second Grammys on October 5, barely four months after its first awards. Almost immediately, the Grammys were plunged into a controversy every bit as threatening to their long-term existence as the Academy's precarious finances.

Once again, Mancini, Sinatra, and Ella were the leading nominees, along with a charismatic newcomer by the name of Bobby Darin. But the big news, for those in the music industry, wasn't who was nominated, but the fact that one label, RCA, totally dominated the competition, drawing over one hundred nominations, more than all the other record labels combined.

Something, obviously, was amiss, and charges of bloc voting—whereby a record label organizes all of its NARAS members to vote along company lines—began to fly. Four days after the Grammy nominations were announced, Columbia Records president Goddard Lieberson sent a stinging letter to Conkling blasting the Grammys for their "shocking" nominations and deriding the awards as nothing more than a "popularity poll" influenced by "electioneering and lobbying."

Coming from Lieberson, one of the most distinguished figures in the industry, the charges were very serious indeed, and could not be brushed aside as mere sour grapes, even though Columbia had fared poorly in the first two Grammy votes. Indeed, bloc voting, which threatened to make a sham of the Academy's vaunted ideals, had afflicted the first Grammy show. Capitol Records was the main culprit and beneficiary, primarily in the lower-profile classical categories. The first Classical Performance, Orchestral Grammy, for example, went to Capitol's Hollywood Bowl Symphony Orchestra, a studio ensemble conducted by Felix Slatkin, for its recording of a relatively lightweight piece called *Gaiété Parisienne*. The album was chosen over a powerhouse field that included performances by Bruno Walter, Leonard Bernstein, Eugene Ormandy, and the Boston Symphony Orchestra.

Capitol and RCA were the main bloc-voting labels in the early Grammy years, because they had more members in NARAS than any other company. In its zeal to establish a membership base and raise funds through membership dues, NARAS had actively recruited the labels, perhaps naively thinking that Grammy ideals would temper any mercenary impulses label partisans might have.

While Columbia was standoffish, with Lieberson and label A&R chief Mitch Miller wary of the West Coast-born-and-based awards, RCA and Capitol encouraged their staffers to join the Academy and then immediately set about hustling for awards, allegedly sending memos to their employees reminding them to vote the party line.

"In the beginning there was a great deal of bloc voting," recalls George Avakian, an executive with Warner Bros. who served as president of NARAS in 1966–67. "Capitol put on a big drive for two or three years . . . and swept with mediocre recordings. Another record company sent out a memo . . . and suddenly they got a hell of a lot of awards. Later, Columbia put on a counterdrive.

"We talked on this subject for endless hours, until I was ready to fall on the floor and faint," Avakian continues, noting that NARAS was appalled and irate about what was happening.

"We discussed all kinds of ways of preventing it. We sent notices to the record companies telling them, 'Hey, cut it out.' We tried to embarrass them on a personal level. We told the Capitol guys they weren't playing fair."

At one point NARAS even debated the idea of devaluing the votes of bloc-voting labels, Avakian says, so that a vote from RCA, for example, would only be worth half as much as a vote from Decca, but the solution seemed more drastic than the problem and was dropped.

One thing the Academy did do in the wake of Lieberson's attack was launch an intensive membership drive in the hope of enlarging the voting pool, so that no single label could make a huge splash.

Also, NARAS elders, including CBS's own John Hammond, met with Lieberson and convinced him that the Academy's heart, at least, was in the right place, that the idea of the Grammys was honest and sound, and that the only way to iron out the operational warps was by having all the industry's major players involved. Columbia staffers began joining NARAS, and it wasn't long before Columbia product began racking up nominations and awards. Indeed, in 1962, Columbia won nearly twice as many Grammys as either RCA or Capitol.

All of which prompted *Billboard* to write a May 5, 1962, front-page editorial urging NARAS members to "vote carefully" and to give conscientious consideration to all the nominees.

"The Naras executives have done their part. . . . The end result of their vision can only enhance our industry—both creatively and financially. . . . Don't muff it," the paper implored.

Ironically, the star of the second Grammys didn't record for RCA, Capitol, Columbia, or any of the major labels. Bobby Darin, whose cool, suggestive reading of "Mack the Knife" won the Record of the Year award, recorded for Atlantic, a leading independent that enjoyed tremendous success in r&b and, to a lesser extent, r&r.

Indeed, twenty-three-year-old Darin was himself something of a rock 'n' roller, having scored a Top 5 hit in 1958 with the effervescent "Splish Splash," a feat he duplicated a year later with his own teen ballad, "Dream Lover." Grammy voters were so enamored of Darin's "Mack the Knife" that they overlooked his rock 'n' roll past—literally—naming Darin Best New Artist of 1959, despite the fact that he had recorded "Splish Splash" the year before. The oversight was logical enough: Since rock 'n' roll did not officially exist as a Grammy category, Darin's career did not *really* begin until he moved on to better things.

Although Sinatra, Ella Fitzgerald, and Duke Ellington all won big at the second Grammys, Darin was the night's most buzzed-about star. The Darin who sang "Mack the Knife" seemed tailor-made for Academy tastes—a younger Sinatra, a pop-jazz singer with a subtle, contemporary edge that bridged the worlds of stylish crooning and pop cool, attracting both older and younger fans. Comparisons to Sinatra were inevitable and lent the second Grammys a degree of dramatic tension, since Darin and The Voice were vying for many of the same awards.

The two dueled to a draw: "Mack the Knife" bested Sinatra's "High Hopes" for Record of the Year, while Sinatra's *Come Dance With Me* won the Album of the Year prize. Sinatra also won a Vocal Performance, Male Grammy (likewise for *Come Dance with Me*), offsetting Darin's Best New Artist award. After the show, the rivalry flared. When asked how it felt to match Sinatra, Darin reportedly replied: "I hope to surpass Frank Sinatra in everything he does."

Although Darin claimed he was misquoted, Sinatra was not appeased. "I'm a saloon singer," he disdainfully responded when queried by reporters about the quote. "Bobby Darin does my prom dates." Later, newspapers around the country ran a picture of Sinatra and Rat Packer Dean Martin using a picture of Darin for a dart board. On the level of soap opera, at least, the Grammys were on their way.

FOUR

This Masquerade: Jazz

Musicologists hoping to re-create the jazz scene of the late fifties and early sixties would be ill-advised to use the Grammys as a guide. Grammy voters, their hearts and ears attuned firmly to the big band past, hailed Ella Fitzgerald, Duke Ellington, and Count Basie as the era's biggest stars, while lavishing praise on "classy" white-bread lightweights like Henry Mancini and André Previn.

While Fitzgerald, Ellington, and Basie were still going strong as mainstream jazz stars—many consider Ellington among the greatest composers America has ever produced—they are hardly the artists that come to mind when thinking of the cool-jazz, hard-bop, and free-form innovations of the late fifties. One of the greatest periods in the history of modern jazz, the era was teeming with important and enduring figures—Miles Davis, Dexter Gordon, John Coltrane, Ornette Coleman, Charles Mingus, Lee Morgan, Sonny Rollins, Art

Blakey, Horace Silver, Thelonieus Monk, and Cecil Taylor, to name a few. None of the above, with the exception of Davis, who won a Grammy for jazz composition in 1960 for *Sketches of Spain*, received so much as a Grammy nomination during the awards' first few years.

And who did win Grammy nominations? The likes of Larry Elgart, Ray Anthony, Perez Prado, Warren Covington, Matty Matlock, Urbie Green, Jonah Jones, and the Four Freshmen, most of whom are not even listed in recent jazz encyclopedias and guides.

Jones, a middling sax player with a theatrical flair, was actually the leading Grammy jazz nominee in 1958, apparently thanks to bloc voting on his behalf by Capitol Records. Jones pulled down four 1958 bids with his *Baubles, Bangles and Beads* and *Jumpin' With Jonah* LPs, winning the Best Jazz Performance, Group trophy the following year for the enthusiastically titled *I Dig Chicks*.

Swinging hipsters the Four Freshmen, also likely beneficiaries of Capitol's esprit de corps, were even more preposterous nominees, nabbing an award in group jazz for their *Four Freshmen in Person* LP in 1958, a year that produced such unnominated gems as Miles Davis and Gil Evans's *Porgy and Bess*, Sonny Rollins's *Freedom Suite*, and Ornette Coleman's *Something Else*.

The irony about the Academy's supersquare and sometimes absurd predilections was that NARAS elders deeply valued and identified with jazz, albeit of the big band and swing variety that shaped their collective sensibilities in the thirties and forties. Indeed, many of the NARAS founders boasted solid jazz credentials. Paul Weston, the organization's guiding light, was a respected composer and arranger who perfected his chops with the Tommy Dorsey band in the forties. Francis Scott, a NARAS founder and president in 1965–66, played saxophone and fronted his own swing orchestra. George Avakian, another early NARAS president, produced jazz albums for Decca Records while still attending Yale.

Not surprisingly, many Grammy dons had a hard time swallowing the bop revolution and an even harder time dealing with the avant-garde explorations of people like Coltrane and Coleman. Their allegiance to retro jazz came through in the very categories they created, with two dying genres—dance band and nonclassical orchestra—getting their own awards.

In 1960, the square tendencies bubbling up in the Grammy nominations spilled over into the awards, as Mancini and Previn, jazz artists by only the politest of standards, became Grammy jazz stars. Mancini, who won the 1958 Album of the Year Grammy with his jazz-flavored *Peter Gunn* LP, claimed the 1960 Best Jazz Performance, Large Group award for his "Blues and the Beat." Pianist Previn, appealing to the classical, "good music" pretensions of NARAS middlebrows, landed Jazz Performance Solo honors two years straight, winning in 1960 for *West Side Story* and in 1961 for his *Previn Plays Harold Arlen* album.

You didn't have to hang out at Birdland to know that Previn, gifted though he was, was not the greatest jazz soloist of his time, or that Henry Mancini did not front the hottest band in the land. The NARAS nominees and winners were so obviously out of tune with the leading edge of contemporary jazz that the Academy appointed a jazz nominations committee in hopes of producing a better mix of artists. Things improved immediately, although not without a fight.

"That was a hell of a battleground," recalls pianist Billy Taylor, a member of the committee in the early sixties, who eventually resigned from NARAS because of its backward and commercial jazz tastes. "We used to argue about Coltrane, but we were such a minority. The [rest of the committee] listened to us politely, then went about the business at hand."

Eventually, Coltrane and artists like Mingus, Thelonious Monk, Dizzy Gillespie, Bill Evans, Miles Davis, and even free-jazz trailblazer Ornette Coleman drew nominations, but, through the sixties and early seventies, Davis and Evans were the only ones to win awards. Mingus, nominated for Best Original Jazz Composition in 1963 for "The Black Saint and the Sinner Lady," lost, somehow, to TV quipster Steve Allen and his "Gravy Waltz" (cowritten with Ray Brown).

Despite the pop success of crossover artists like Herb Alpert and Stan Getz, jazz was sliding into a Grammy—and, indeed, industry-wide—black hole during the mid-sixties, squeezed increasingly into the margins by the commercially explosive sounds of rock, r&b, and country. NARAS deleted its big band award in 1964 and its prize for jazz composition in 1967, whittling the jazz field to just two categories while expanding country to six, r&b to four, and creating a field of five "contemporary" Grammys to encompass rock 'n' roll.

Ironically, Grammy jazz taste was more contemporary than ever during these years, albeit along commercial soul-jazz lines. Ramsey

Lewis won the Instrumental Jazz Performance, Small Group prize in 1965 for his chart-topping "The In Crowd." Crossover guitarist Wes Montgomery followed in 1966 with "Goin' Out of My Head." Cannonball Adderley won in '67 for "Mercy, Mercy, Mercy," and Montgomery scored again with his posthumous "Willow Weep for Me."

Rock-jazz "fusion," the great commercial hope for jazz at the turn of the decade, made a big Grammy splash in 1969, as Blood, Sweat & Tears dominated the nominations and won three awards. The eleven-man ensemble, featuring horns, a big beat, brawny arrangements, and the rumbling vocals of David Clayton-Thomas, received Album of the Year honors for its eponymous debut disc.

A more ferocious form of fusion—Miles Davis's landmark *Bitches Brew*—knocked the jazz world on its collective ear in 1970. Fusion represented a way back into the marketplace for jazz, a marketplace riddled with glossy melodic or simplistic funk compromise. Davis's electrified assault was something else, a firestorm of rich-funk-jazz aggression and brilliance that challenged rather than accommodated pop taste. Davis's most commercially successful record, *Bitches Brew* won the Jazz Performance, Large Group Grammy in 1970.

Jazz spawned a couple of Grammy controversies in the early seventies, the first of which involved trumpet giant Louis Armstrong, who in 1972, a year after he died, won the Bing Crosby Lifetime Achievement Grammy. No one begrudged Satchmo the award, but some, like legendary rock producer Phil Spector, found it insulting to honor the great Armstrong on the altar of the less-great Crosby, who, Spector wrote, "parlayed a pleasing personality and a very minor talent into a multimillion-dollar career. . . . Will the Academy see fit to present Dylan with 'The Kate Smith Award' next year?" Spector sarcastically asked in a letter to the *Los Angeles Times*.

The barb apparently hit home. NARAS didn't hand out another career salute until 1984, at which time it dropped Der Bingle's name from the honor, which it rechristened—effective retroactively—the Lifetime Achievement Award. (Lucky for NARAS that Spector hadn't been paying attention in 1967, when Ella Fitzgerald received her Bing Crosby award—presented by, would you believe, Pat Boone.)

Another jazz flare-up occurred in 1973 when no jazz performers or presenters were asked to participate in the ninety-minute Grammy TV show.

According to Los Angeles critic Leonard Feather, NARAS managing director Christine Farnum rationalized the jazz snub by noting that the Grammys didn't feature "Hawaiian music" or "square dance music" on the awards show, either.

The Grammys gave Feather and jazz fans reason to cheer in 1974, as Charlie Parker won, posthumously, his only Grammy, a Jazz Performance by a Soloist award, for an album titled *First Recordings*. Parker's daughter Kim accepted the award. "This is very weird," she said. "Bird's still getting awards and somebody else is still getting his money."

Also at the '74 awards, Stevie Wonder turned one of his five Grammys over to Duke Ellington's son, explaining, "Mr. Ellington contributed more music than I ever could in a thousand years." Two years later, Wonder would score a number-one hit—and numerous Grammy nominations—with "Sir Duke," an r&b-pop valentine to Ellington.

In 1976, after years of complaint, NARAS created a Jazz Vocal Performance award, so that singers would no longer have to compete against—and invariably lose to—instrumentalists. Instead, they competed against and lost to Ella Fitzgerald. The Grammy's first vocal queen immediately reclaimed her crown, after a fourteen-year exile, with her *Fitzgerald & Pass . . . Again* LP, then proceeded to win the vocal prize in 1979, '80, '81, and '83.

Perhaps because of Fitzgerald's dominance, NARAS created separate Jazz Vocal Performance, Male and Female Grammys in 1980, adding a Vocal Performance, Group award in 1981. Suddenly, the jazz field was bulging, with seven awards, more than country, gospel, r&b, or rock 'n' roll. The new categories quickly spawned new stars. Manhattan Transfer, a sleek quartet with airtight, high-flying harmonies, won the first four group vocal awards, kicking off the skein in 1980 with a tour-de-force piece of vocal bop called "Birdland." The group made its biggest Grammy splash in 1985 with *Vocalese*, an album that generated no fewer than twelve nominations and three awards. Three years later, it broke into the Grammy mainstream, winning a Pop Vocal Performance prize for *Brasil*. To date, the quartet has won seven awards.

Vocal acrobat Bobby McFerrin, meanwhile, took over the male-jazz field, winning four straight Grammys between 1985 and 1988. McFerrin was the surprise star of the 1988 awards, winning Record and Song of the Year honors for his calypso-ish pop mantra, "Don't

Worry, Be Happy," and becoming the first jazz-pop artist since George Benson in 1976 to win a major award. He has amassed nine Grammy trophies thus far.

The eighties also brought a new wave of instrumentalists to the Grammy fore, most notably trumpet wunderkind Wynton Marsalis, a rigorous virtuoso who established himself as a Grammy star at the age of twenty-two when he became the first artist in Grammy history to win a jazz *and* classical soloist award. Marsalis nabbed the 1983 jazz salute with his *Think of One* LP and the classical with *Haydn: Concerto for Trumpet and Orchestra in E-Flat Major.* A four-time soloist champ, Marsalis has so far amassed eight awards, two of them in the classical field.

Recent years have also yielded long-overdue Grammys to a couple of jazz music's most illustrious stars. John Coltrane, snubbed by conservative NARAS voters in the fifties and sixties, finally won a solo award, posthumously, in 1981 for his *Bye Bye Blackbird* reissue. And Sarah Vaughan, one of the most astonishing virtuosos in jazz and a Grammy nominee all the way back in 1959, finally broke Ella Fitzgerald's vocal monopoly, winning a jazz Grammy in 1982 with *Gershwin Live!*

Other late arrivals to the Grammy ball include hard-bop drummer Art Blakey, winner of the 1984 group prize with *New York Scene*, expatriate sax man Dexter Gordon, who won top solo honors in 1987 with his *Other Side of Round Midnight* LP, and longtime Basie Band vocalist Joe Williams, who claimed a vocal prize in 1984 with *Nothing But the Blues.*

The award to Williams, ironically, drew the ire of jazz fans and jazz members of NARAS, not because Williams didn't deserve his Grammy, but because he wasn't allowed to accept his trophy during the live Grammy telecast. Indeed, as they had done in 1973, the NARAS TV producers delivered a no-jazz show, with neither performances, presenters, nor recipients from jazz on the three-hour telecast. Older jazzophiles within the Academy were particularly incensed over the fact that the Grammy show did include an unusually audacious and lengthy pop-rock segment, featuring a nine-minute jam by Prince and the Revolution.

"This year, we had eight untalented people dominating the entire show," vibist Terry Gibbs seethed in the *Los Angeles Times.* "We have Cyndi Lauper with whatever color hair she has this particular night, and Prince with his sissy whatever-you-want-to-call-it. Now, after putting on four no-talent freak acts, why not make the fifth act, say, Ella Fitzgerald? Sneak in Dizzy Gillespie. Do something classy."

Before the night was over, partisans were circulating a petition at post-Grammy parties mandating the inclusion of jazz in all future telecasts. With jazz guardian Leonard Feather once again leading the way, a number of members resigned in protest from the Academy and attempted to form a jazz organization to launch their own awards.

"I've decided I'd rather contribute to the blind than to the deaf," explained drummer Shelly Manne, who turned on his NARAS card in 1984. Ouch.

The jazz community's ruffled feathers (and Feather) settled somewhat after NARAS pledged to be more sensitive to jazz. The Academy lived up to its pledge in 1985, featuring a nine-minute jazz jam— longest performance of the night—on that year's Grammy show. Soloists included Dizzy Gillespie, Buddy Rich, Sarah Vaughan, Herbie Hancock, and Joe Williams.

The irony of Grammy's periodic jazz flaps is that NARAS, relatively speaking, has been good to jazz, certainly more so than to rock 'n' roll, which didn't even have a Grammy category between 1967 and 1979. Despite parochial blunders and blinders in the early years, NARAS elders have consistently esteemed jazz. To date, no fewer than thirty-three jazz recordings have been inducted into the Grammy Hall of Fame, nearly a third of the overall total, and thirteen jazz artists have received the prestigious Lifetime Achievement Award, likewise close to a third of those honored.

Miles Davis, John Coltrane, Sarah Vaughan, and Art Tatum are among the recent honorees.

FIVE

Button-Down Mind: 1960–63

The early sixties were a strange, deceptively sleepy period in popular music. Rock 'n' roll seemed to be petering out, all its biggest stars in limbo or gone. Elvis was in the army, Buddy Holly was dead, Little Richard was a born-again preacher, Chuck Berry was in jail for having sex with a minor, and Jerry Lee Lewis had derailed his career by marrying a minor—his fifteen-year-old third cousin, Myra Gale.

It was possible, for one last, long moment to imagine, as Paul Weston and his Grammy confreres undoubtedly did, that rock really had been a passing fad, that refined, adult-oriented pop had weathered the storm, that the good old days of tasteful crooning and "Sing Along With Mitch" were back.

In fact, the transitional period between Elvis and the Beatles, between the first and second comings of rock, was not so barren as it seemed. Phil Spector was building his majestic "Wall of Sound," scoring hit after hit with girl groups like the Chiffons, the Crystals, and the Ronettes. Roy Orbison emerged as a major star. The Everly Brothers, Ricky Nelson, Dion, the Four Seasons, and Gene Pitney all created lasting work.

On the soul front, Sam Cooke, James Brown, Otis Redding, Wilson Pickett, Curtis Mayfield, Jerry Butler, and Jackie Wilson were on a collective roll. Motown Records, meanwhile, had started cranking out the hits—"Money" by Barrett Strong, "Shop Around" by Smokey Robinson and the Miracles, "Please Mr. Postman" by the Marvelettes, "Fingertips" by Little Stevie Wonder, and "Heat Wave" by Martha and the Vandellas. None of which brought home any Grammy awards.

Grammy voters were tuned into another world, a world rooted in the politely swinging past more than the present or future, a world of denial in which Sinatra reigned supreme, Mancini was a glamorous star, Steve Lawrence and Eydie Gorme were the last word in talent and charm, and Robert Goulet was a rising heartthrob. Given the stagnation to which rock had seemed to succumb, the Grammy world could celebrate its own renaissance without guilt or doubt.

Indeed, there were many things to celebrate. Old-fashioned melody and strings seemed to be making a comeback. Percy Faith's "Theme From *A Summer Place*," the top-selling record of 1960, according to *Billboard*, won the Record of the Year Grammy, while Ernest Gold's "Exodus," another instrumental theme, took the Song of the Year prize. Henry Mancini and Johnny Mercer teamed up for "Moon River," winning Record and Song of the Year Grammys in 1961. Two years later they encored with "Days of Wine and Roses," which likewise won the song and record awards. Tony Bennett, meanwhile, proved that male bel canto singers could still find an audience; his signature reading of "I Left My Heart in San Francisco" led to Record of the Year and Solo Vocal Performance, Male Grammys in 1962.

A major event for Grammy regulars in 1961 was the return of Judy Garland. The definitive torch singer of her time, Garland bounced back from a personal and professional slide with a wildly acclaimed concert at Carnegie Hall—"probably the greatest evening in show-business history," according to liner notes to the concert LP. Garland's *Judy at Carnegie Hall* won the Album of the Year Grammy, along with three other awards.

Though they scorned such emerging subgenres as girl groups and surf music, the Grammys weren't entirely oblivious to industry trends. The year 1962 marked the Grammy discovery of Peter, Paul and Mary, soft-focus folkies who brought the Greenwich Village scene into the mainstream, impressing NARAS pros with their pretty harmonies and ultraclean sound. PP&M won vocal group and folk Grammys in '62 for "If I Had a Hammer," repeating the feat in 1963 with Bob Dylan's "Blowin' in the Wind."

Comedy records, an increasingly important part of the business with artists like Bill Dana, Allan Sherman, Bob Newhart, Vaughn Meader, and others enjoying unprecedented sales, also left a mark on the Grammys. Newhart's *Button Down Mind*, an intimate and sardonic guide through the psyche of a Madison Avenue Everyman, won the 1960 Album of the Year salute, one of only two nonmusical records ever to win that award. Newhart also won Best Comedy Performance and Best New Artist laurels. Two years later, Meader's *The First Family*, a gentle parody of JFK *en famille*, which sold a then incredible five million copies, garnered the album and comedy album prizes.

But the biggest and the best news of this period was the arrival of a new singer who must have made Academy old-timers feel that the future really was theirs. Twenty-one-year-old Barbra Streisand may have been young enough to identify with rock 'n' roll, but her phenomenal, fourteen-karat voice was strictly legit, a voice in the grand tradition of the show-tune and torch singers. And yet Streisand was contemporary, an Ethel Merman of the sixties, fresh, unpredictable, overloaded with personality and talent, immensely attractive to both old and young MOR fans. Her debut *Barbra Streisand Album*, featuring over-the-top covers of "Cry Me a River" and "Happy Days Are Here Again" along with a plucky, little-girl reading of "Who's Afraid of the Big Bad Wolf," wowed and heartened Grammy voters, who rewarded Streisand with 1963 honors for Album of the Year and Best Vocal Performance, Female.

With Bobby Darin and Peter, Paul and Mary representing the outer edge of Grammy taste, the Academy's relationship to rock 'n' roll wended a twisted path through the early sixties. The Academy killed its rock-oriented Top 40 category in 1960, replacing it with a softer-sounding Best Performance by a Pop Single Artist prize. Ray Charles's "Georgia on My Mind" won the award that year, making "The Old Payola Roll Blues"—a Stan Freberg satire that depicted rock as a payola-infested musical joke—the closest thing to a rock record to dent the 1960 awards.

But, really, this was going too far. A growing contingent within NARAS pressured for change, and the organization finally established a Best Rock and Roll Recording Grammy in 1961. Recognizing its own backwardness in the field, the Academy appointed a special panel of rock experts to help sort out the nominees: Lou Adler (who produced early hits by Jan and Dean and, later, Carole King and the Mamas and the Papas), Nick Venet (who signed the Beach Boys), and Jimmie Haskell (house arranger for Imperial Records).

"Every time they came to an artist they were unfamiliar with they came to us, and there were a lot of them," recalls Adler, who says the Academy's overtures toward rock were halfhearted.

"Paul Weston and Margaret Whiting came to me and said they wanted someone to represent the music that was happening at the time. It was very, very frustrating. They didn't relate to, understand, or accept the music. They thought the songs were nonsense. I remember Weston and Jo Stafford. They were very nice people, but narrow-minded. I remember walking away feeling they just didn't want us. It was very token."

Indeed, Grammy's rock 'n' roll choices didn't improve much, despite the input from Adler et al. Chubby Checker's "Let's Twist Again" was the high point for rock fans during these years, winning the 1961 rock award. Bent Fabric, a piano noodler from Denmark, won the following year with a playful instrumental called "Alley Cat," preferred by Grammy cognoscenti over the Four Seasons' "Big Girls Don't Cry," the Drifters' "Up on the Roof," Sam Cooke's "Twistin' the Night Away," Neil Sedaka's "Breaking Up Is Hard to Do," and Mary Wells's "He Beat Me to the Punch."

Nino Tempo & April Stevens's warbling remake of "Deep Purple," a chestnut from the thirties, won in 1963. Two of the "rock 'n' roll" nominations that year were startling, even by Grammy standards— "Teen Scene" by Chet Atkins, and "The Shelter of Your Arms" by Sammy Davis, Jr. But the field was not entirely bizarre: Sam Cooke was nominated for "Another Saturday Night."

Tempo thought he had no chance against the legendary soulster Cooke. "Be sure you dress well when you walk up to get the award," he told Cooke when the two ran into each other after the nominations were announced. "There's no way we can compete with you."

The year 1963 was critical for NARAS. The organization was once again in desperate financial straits. After one airing in 1959, NBC dropped the Grammy show, and for the next four years the Academy had to scrounge for survival in the absence of a big-bucks TV deal. The take from the Grammy banquet in Los Angeles was barely enough for office supplies—$9,000 in 1961 and similar amounts in subsequent years.

In 1962, the Grammys bailed themselves out with an unexpectedly successful premium LP, *Go With the Greats*, featuring tracks by Nat King Cole, Perry Como, Ella Fitzgerald, Judy Garland, Paul Weston, Jo Stafford, and other Grammy faves. Chevrolet distributed the record as a freebie with each car it sold, and the Grammys netted an estimated $100,000. But later efforts to duplicate the record's success failed, and once again NARAS was forced to go a-begging to the record companies for subsidies, to the tune of $20,000 to $25,000 apiece from Capitol, Columbia, and RCA, according to NARAS's Francis Scott.

A network deal was vitally important, but landing one, once again, proved difficult. Apparently, the NBC Grammy special in 1959 hadn't left much of an impression, even at NBC. According to producer Ted Bergmann, who made the rounds pitching the Grammy show, the network didn't know what the Grammys were when he proposed the show in 1963. "What is that, the Grandma Awards?" Bergmann remembers a befuddled exec asking.

Since the Grammys weren't prestigious enough to guarantee performances by nominees, Bergmann formulated an after-the-fact Grammy show. "The Best on Record" would be built around taped performances and would air months after the Grammys were announced. What was lost in drama would, theoretically at least, be made up in celebrity and entertainment value.

Bergmann lined up Timex as a sponsor, and NBC agreed to take the show if NARAS could guarantee appearances by Sinatra, Bing Crosby, and Bob Hope. George Simon, executive director of the Academy's New York chapter and a former jazz critic who had written Sinatra's first review—a rave that Sinatra never forgot—put in a call to Old Blue Eyes. And Les Brown, bandleader for Bob Hope and West Coast NARAS honcho, pulled strings to get Hope and Crosby. "They all said yes," Brown recalls, "and we got the show."

"The Best on Record" had a star-crossed launch. Set to bow on November 24, 1963, the special disappeared in television's "black weekend" following the assassination of President Kennedy in Dallas on November 22. Ironically, it was rescheduled for December 8, as a last-minute fill-in for a documentary about the Bay of Pigs, Kennedy's botched attempt to overthrow Cuba's Fidel Castro. That show had also been canceled because of the assassination; NBC was unwilling to explore a subject that presented the martyred president in an unseemly light.

Kennedy's murder had one other effect on the first "Best on Record." Winner of that year's Album of the Year Grammy was none other than Kennedy impersonator Vaughn Meader, who had taped a Kennedy parody for the show. This, of course, had to be cut. Although Meader reportedly offered to "do a serious tribute to the memory of the president," and despite irate pleadings on his behalf by Shelley Berman, Meader was replaced by Diahann Carroll, who sang a medley from *No Strings*, a Richard Rodgers Broadway show.

Artists appearing on the telecast were almost entirely from the "old school"—Steve Lawrence and Eydie Gorme, Peter Nero, Tony Bennett, Henry Mancini, Connie Francis, Bob Newhart, Eddy Arnold, Dean Martin, Andy Williams, and, for the "younger generation," the New Christy Minstrels.

Most TV critics, middle-aged and sharing the Grammy affinity for "classy" entertainment, offered enthusiastic reviews. But the Grammy's warped reflection of the contemporary music scene did not go entirely unnoticed.

"It [the show] was a bland, banal, and utterly false picture of the record business and everyone concerned with it should be ashamed of himself," scolded Ralph J. Gleason of the *San Francisco Chronicle*, expressing sentiments that would be echoed, with increasing frequency and rancor, in coming years.

SIX

Help! 1964—66

The arrival of the Beatles in 1964 antiquated NARAS overnight. Insist as they might that the group was just another teen infatuation, Grammy graybeards could harbor no more serious illusions about the future of pop. The charts belonged to the Fab Four, the British Invasion in general, and their revived and inspired American counterparts—and not only the charts, but the true voice and spirit of the times. The Beatles closed the door on the fifties and rushed headlong into the sixties with a bracing yeah, yeah, yeah to life that rang through their voices, their songs, and the rock spirit that once again took over pop's center stage.

Grammy voters, of course, did not succumb to Beatlemania. The Academy continued to nurture its own—people like Sinatra, Streisand, Mancini, Ray Conniff—while searching out and applauding the milder breezes of post-Beatles pop—Herb Alpert, Petula Clark, Roger Miller, and the New Vaudeville Band. But the assured insularity of the Academy's early years was over, giving way to a subtle air of resignation and change.

The Beatles' conquest of America was swift. Their first U.S. single, "I Want to Hold Your Hand," was released on January 25, 1964. One week later, it was number one, pushing Bobby Vinton's "There, I've Said It Again" off the top and staying there for seven weeks, at which time another Beatles song, "She Loves You," took over, holding the top spot for two weeks—until the group's "Can't Buy Me Love" replaced it. On April 4 the Beatles became the only group in *Billboard* history to own the entire Top 5, with "Can't Buy Me Love," "Twist and Shout," "She Loves You," "I Want to Hold Your Hand" and "Please Please Me." The Beatles accounted for no fewer than fourteen of the trade mag's top one hundred hits that week, four more than the previous record, held by Elvis at the height of his career.

Grammy folk had extremely mixed feelings about the Beatles, alternately praising, patronizing, snubbing, and insulting them from year to year. The boys won two awards in 1964, taking Best New Artist honors along with Best Performance by a Vocal Group trophy for "A Hard Day's Night." The new artist salute seemed badly dated by the time it was announced on April 14, 1965; the Beatles, developing with breathtaking speed, were already working on *Help!* and contemplating *Rubber Soul.*

Though they won a pair of Grammys, the Beatles had a way to go before they also won the respect of the Academy, as anyone watching the May 18, 1965, "Best on Record" show could see and hear.

"Nobody really knows what makes a hit . . . though I have a personal hunch that it doesn't hurt if you're a Beatle or a Chipmunk or something like that," quipped host Steve Allen, who specialized in condescending put-downs of rock 'n' roll. "For people, it's a little bit tougher." Later, brilliantine-headed Robert Goulet picked up the theme, singing the praises of performers with "normal haircuts," while black comic Godfrey Cambridge sarcastically (and accurately) lamented the fact that white singers, "particularly the English singers, sound more colored than I do."

Despite the compulsive jabs, NARAS featured the Beatles on the 1965 show in a segment shot at London's Twickenham Studios, where the group was filming *Help!* Boston Pops maestro Arthur Fielder, who had recorded a symphonic version of "I Want to Hold Your Hand," introduced "the new longhairs" (prior to the Beatles, "longhair" was synonymous with classical music), whom he praised as "that very exciting, interesting group."

At Twickenham the Beatles performed "I'm So Happy Just to Dance With You," then gathered around Peter Sellers, who gave them their Grammy trophies.

"Thank you very much, Peter," McCartney said, as his mates

looked bemusedly at their statues and tried to suppress grins. "It's a great pleasure for us too, I'm sure."

In 1964, NARAS organized a Nashville chapter, and the country capital quickly established itself as a power center in the Grammy world, launching an intense membership drive and exerting immediate and dramatic influence on the awards.

That influence was all too evident in 1965, when three Nashville acts—the Statler Brothers, Roger Miller, and the Anita Kerr Singers—beat the Beatles for Grammy Awards. Incredibly, the Statlers' woebegone country hit, "Flowers on the Wall," knocked off "Help!" to win the Best Contemporary (R&R) Performance Group award, while Miller's "King of the Road" topped "Yesterday" for contemporary (R&R) record and male vocal honors.

A bigger shocker—and the worst Grammy embarrassment in the history of the awards—came when the Anita Kerr group, a little-remembered, treacly pop choral outfit, topped the Beatles and "Help!" for Best Performance by a Vocal Group honors with an album called *We Dig Mancini*.

Joe Smith, an executive with Warner Bros. Records, Kerr's label at the time (and now chairman of Capitol-EMI), was sitting with Kerr during the Grammy ceremonies in Los Angeles when she won the award. "I wanted to put my head in my hand and quietly slink away," he recalls, still incredulous about the event. "Anita came back to the table after picking up the [Grammy] and I had to kiss her and congratulate her. I turned to the stage so that I didn't have to talk too much about it.

"It was a joke. How could it be? Anita versus the Beatles. A nice album versus a change in the direction of popular music. I figured the old Academy members were fighting the new music, and she was one of them. She came out of Nashville and had a big contingency there.

"Mo Ostin [WB's president] was there, too. We looked at each other and rolled our eyes. We couldn't say what a bullshit miscarriage of justice it was, because Anita was at the table. . . . But I knew then that I could never take any of the rock aspects of the Grammys seriously until things changed."

Kerr, whose group won the vocal group Grammy *again* in 1966 (knocking off the Beach Boys' "Good Vibrations," the Mamas and the Papas' "Monday, Monday," and the Association's "Cherish"), was one of the most popular and best-known members of NARAS. She was active in all three major Grammy towns—New York, Los Angeles and Nashville—maintaining homes in L.A. and Nashville, and serving as vice president of the Nashville Grammy chapter in 1964.

But it wasn't just Kerr's personal popularity that cost the Beatles a Grammy in 1965. Many Grammy granddads honestly thought *We Dig Mancini* was a better record than "Help!"—an opinion some, like "Best on Record" bandleader Les Brown, hold to this day. "We wouldn't think of voting for the Beatles in those days," recalls Brown, who has since recorded "Yesterday," "Michelle," and other Beatle standards. " 'Help!' was an awful record, and the Anita Kerr Singers were a very good singing group. Music-wise, they had every reason to win."

Esteemed jazz critic and onetime NARAS officer Leonard Feather, who would rail against the awards regularly for slights against jazz, applauded the Grammy Beatle snub of 1965: "American musical tastes are finally creeping upward," he wrote in the March 26, 1966, *Los Angeles Times*. "Any organization that presents 47 Grammys for 'artistic merit' without once acknowledging the Beatles can't be all bad."

Grammy voters made it up to the Beatles in 1966, tapping "Michelle" for the prestigious Song of the Year prize. It was the first time in the history of the awards that NARAS picked a truly contemporary song instead of retro-mood tunes like "Shadow of Your Smile" and "What Kind of Fool Am I?" Surprisingly, Grammy voters chose "Michelle" over four songs that were much more in line with past choices—"Somewhere, My Love," "The Impossible Dream" "Strangers in the Night," and "Born Free"—and the win seemed to betoken a liberal shift in the Academy. In addition, Paul McCartney won a rock 'n' roll solo vocal Grammy for "Eleanor Rigby."

With two more trophies to their credit, the Beatles once again appeared on the "Best on Record" show. By May 1967, when the telecast aired, the group's *Revolver* was already out, and *Sgt. Pepper* was just three months away. "Best on Record" writer Mort Lachman, however, was still playing to the aging Grammy gallery with mop-top jokes that betrayed a startling ignorance of the Beatles' growth. Liberace, of all people, introduced the band as "somewhere in between" Richard Burton and Twiggy. "I'm referring to the Beatles, the singers with the hair umbrellas," he continued, pausing for a trademark grin. "I first met them when they were working in a little cellar club in Liverpool and, fortunately, a talent scout spotted them before the *exterminator* did."

The tone of the telecast improved briefly as the Beatles, on film, offered a darkly hallucinogenic version of "Strawberry Fields Forever," lip-syncing the song around a skeletal tree strung with cobwebs. After the song, NARAS hastened to serve the Beatles up the way it liked them, lounge-lizard style, as Brylcreemed crooner John Gary took the stage to sing "Michelle."

Torch chanteuse Vikki Carr introduced Gary as a singer who, unlike the Beatles, "achieved success without growing a beard," adding that his version of "Michelle" was "one of the most memorable" around. Indeed—the performance was unforgettably bad. Accompanied exclusively by strings, on a set bedecked with flowers, Gary sang "Michelle" in a desensitized tenor that made it sound as if it were being channeled through an alien and unfriendly culture. A doe-eyed Claudine Longet look-alike, the Grammy vision of Michelle, hovered in the background.

Gary was able to wangle the spot because his manager, Joe Csida, was president of NARAS's New York chapter, a position that afforded him considerable influence with the organization. Csida laughingly acknowledges that a lounge star like Gary was not exactly the right person for the Beatles song. "I thought it was very funny. But I was eager to have it happen. The exposure was very good."

If the Grammys were ambivalent about the Beatles, they were quite sure about what they thought of the Rolling Stones. They hated the Stones, hated them the way a cultural academy always hates outsiders from the street. The Stones were yin to the Beatles' yang, a kind of outlaw opposition—jaunty, angry, anarchic—that reflected and fed the rumbling undercurrents of the sixties. From the Grammy point of view, Mick Jagger and his mates were the enemy, the dread, degenerate beast that Grammy voters always suspected lurked in the heart of rock 'n' roll—primitive, lawless, and very, very loud.

"The Rolling Stones were anathema to these people," Nesuhi Ertegun, president of NARAS in 1964–65, recalls. "They were rebels, revolutionaries who were part of our music, but [the people in NARAS] tried to ignore them, push them away, pretend they didn't exist."

"I hated them," confesses Les Brown, who produced a variety

show in Hollywood in the early sixties on which the Stones performed. "They made my band sound like a string quartet."*

NARAS didn't bother to disguise its feelings about the Stones. Host Steven Allen kicked off the 1965 "Best on Record" show by enthusing about "the feeling of power" a record player brings. "Sometimes I put on the Rolling Stones just so I can turn 'em off." Obviously, a majority of Grammy voters did likewise. The World's Greatest Rock 'n' Roll Band, with over twenty Top 10 hits to its credit, has never won a Grammy. Indeed, the group never even got a nomination until 1978. "Satisfaction," one of the seminal records of the sixties, was completely ignored.

Surprisingly, the Stones, who were never half so hostile as they seemed, took the Grammy slights to heart. According to John Phillips of the Mamas and the Papas, Jagger was beside himself when the Ms and Ps won a group vocal Grammy in 1966 while the Stones were once again ignored.

"There's no fuckin' justice," Jagger railed while cruising around L.A. with Phillips. "We've made fifteen albums and have never been nominated for a Grammy. And you come along and make one album and win. . . . They hate us; they think we're weird."

Bob Dylan was another artist who didn't quite cut it with Grammy voters. Maybe that's because Dylan's "Ballad of a Thin Man," with its withering refrain—"You *know* something's happening, but you don't know what it is, do you, Mr. Jones"—was a good description of NARAS during this time. Pop music was in the throes of a revolution, Dylan was leading the charge, and the Academy stubbornly pretended he didn't exist.

NARAS did give two Grammys to Peter, Paul and Mary in 1963 for their soft cover of Dylan's "Blowin' in the Wind," but the songwriter who liberated both the form and content of the pop song, making it the most poetically charged medium of the sixties, had to wait until

---

* Brown's animus against the Stones remains strong to this day. He recalls with relish the time Stones guitarist Keith Richards approached Brown's own guitarist, Barney Kessel, whom Richards greatly admired. "I have all your records, Mr. Kessel, and I'd appreciate it if you'd tune my guitar." "I will," Kessel replied, "if you promise that after I tune it, you'll weld it."

1979 to win his first Grammy,* a rock vocal salute for his born-again single, "Gotta Serve Somebody." Dylan drew three folk nominations during the sixties, the first in 1962 for his eponymous Bob Dylan album, another in 1964 for *The Times They Are A-changing'*, and a third in 1968 for *John Wesley Harding*. He lost, respectively, to "If I Had a Hammer" by Peter, Paul and Mary, "We'll Sing in the Sunshine" by Gale Garnett, and "Both Sides Now" by Judy Collins.

Ironically, Dylan hinted at the changes in store for pop, changes the Grammys would long try to deny, at a NARAS seminar held at New York University in 1964. "Songs are becoming too conscious," the budding symbolist said while sitting on a panel that included Elvis's producer Steve Sholes and lounge crooner John Gary. "Next I'll be singing songs out of my unconscious, and then I won't be having any repertoire problems at all."

In 1965, the year Dylan put rock on the leading edge of contemporary culture with *Highway 61 Revisited* and "Like a Rolling Stone," the Grammy snub was so egregious it prompted *Variety* to chide NARAS with a "Razzberries for Grammy" headline and a story questioning the judgment of an electorate that failed to give "the single most influential figure in the pop field" a single mention.

Clearly, the gulf that separated the Grammys from a large part of pop reality did not narrow after the Beatles exploded in 1964. Between 1964 and 1966, the British Invasion and the revitalized American scene produced one of the most exciting and creative periods in the history of pop. The Grammys opened up only a little, just enough to maintain a comfortable distance from the cutting edge, honoring secondary sixties stars like Herb Alpert and Petula Clark while continuing to heap awards on Mancini, Sinatra, and Eydie Gorme.

"Welcome to the award show that dares to be similar," cracked 1966 Grammy host Bob Hope, gently twitting the Academy for its tenacious conservation.

In 1964, the year of the Beatles, Grammy center stage belonged to jazz saxophonist Stan Getz, who teamed with Astrud Gilberto on "The Girl From Ipanema," an alluring pop hit that triggered a bossa nova craze and won the Record of the Year award. Gilberto's strikingly understated, sexy reading of the song was very sixties, a

---

* Dylan won a Grammy in 1972, along with seven other artists, for his participation on *The Concert for Bangla Desh*, which won the Album of the Year award.

kind of vocal without makeup that turned the big-voice jazz-pop tradition inside out.

Getz also won Album of the Year and Instrumental Jazz Performance honors for *Getz/Gilberto*, his bossa nova collaboration with Joao Gilberto. Getz was the first artist to win both Record and Album of the Year Grammys.

Louis Armstrong also enjoyed the Grammy limelight in 1964, winning Best Vocal Performance, Male kudos for his raspishly expressive "Hello, Dolly!" This must have been a sweet moment for many Grammy members; the sixty-four-year-old Satchmo's long-shot hit, the first million seller of his fifty-year career, proved that you didn't have to be young to top the charts. Indeed, it was "Pops" who finally knocked the Beatles off the *Billboard* throne after a record-setting two-month-plus reign. "Dolly!" written by Jerry Herman for the musical of the same name, also won the 1964 Song of the Year Grammy.

Henry Mancini continued his stylish roll in 1964, composing the enduringly comic "Pink Panther Theme" and racking up his fifteenth, sixteenth, and seventeenth Grammys. Barbra Streisand, meanwhile, more than lived up to her promise, taking Broadway by storm with *Funny Girl* and establishing herself as Grammy queen with a Best Vocal Performance, Female award for "People" in '64 and *My Name is Barbra* the following year.

Of all the Grammy vets and pets to do well, however, none did better or buoyed the spirits of NARAS more than Frank Sinatra. After strolling through a series of mediocre records in the early sixties, Sinatra returned to top form in 1965 with *September of My Years*, an exceptionally honest album in which he sang the song of his own twilight with a kind of virile resignation that must have hit home with his aging contemporaries in the Academy. It was time for Sinatra and the old guard to pass the torch, personally, professionally, historically, but this was a hell of a swan song—beautifully shaded, bittersweet, nostalgic, and proud. NARAS thanked and honored Sinatra with Album of the Year and Best Vocal Performance, Male awards.

Sinatra enjoyed even greater success in 1966, winning a then-unprecedented third Album of the Year prize with *Frank Sinatra: A Man and His Music*, as well as Record of the Year and male vocal kudos for "Strangers in the Night."

Other big Grammy winners during this period included modish-looking trumpeter Herb Alpert and his Tijuana Brass and country crossover star Roger Miller. Alpert, who enjoyed a string of instrumental hits with a brisk, clean, Latin-flavored pop-jazz hybrid that was quickly dubbed "Ameriachi," won five Grammys in 1964 and 1965, including Album of the Year honors for *A Taste of Honey*.

Miller, country's first crossover superstar, won more Grammys than anyone else, a record-setting five in 1964 and six in 1965, most of them in the newly expanded country field. As *Billboard* pointed out, Miller "dang near" won all the '64 country awards with "Dang Me," his first big hit, and pulled off another near-sweep the following year with his hobo anthem, "King of the Road." Miller even had a hand in the 1965 female country Grammy, which went to Jody Miller (no relation) for "Queen of the House," a distaff response to Miller's song.

The Grammys loosened up noticeably in 1966, despite wins by people like Eydie Gorme (female vocal honors for "If He Walked into My Life") and Ray Conniff (choral group kudos for "Somewhere My Love"). A bona fide hippie group, the Mamas and the Papas, won the Contemporary (R&R) Group Vocal award with "Monday, Monday"; the Beatles' "Michelle" took home Song of the Year honors; the "Batman Theme," high sixties camp, won the Best Instrumental Theme Grammy; and Wes Montgomery's soulful jazz version of "Goin' Out of My Head" landed a jazz soloist award.

But while NARAS and the Grammys were inching into the sixties, the sixties were about to shift into overdrive, into counterculture, acid rock, feedback, Woodstock. Grammy voters were hardly prepared to keep pace. The Grateful Dead and the Doors had about as much chance of winning a Grammy as Abbie Hoffman and Timothy Leary had of landing a Senate seat. For NARAS, which had come to represent a kind of Silent Majority of pop, a whole new set of radical challenges—and conservative reactions—was at hand.

SEVEN

Both Sides Now: 1967–70

Woody Herman and Frank Zappa—an odd couple, indeed—performed at Grammy ceremonies in New York's Waldorf-Astoria on February 14, 1967. Herman was a Grammy favorite, a big band star who would accumulate nine jazz Grammys before he died in 1987. Zappa? Zappa was the freakiest of all the freaks in the sixties cultural revolution, a sinister-looking longhair provocateur, the last person one would expect straitlaced NARAS to ask to entertain at its annual ball.

But NARAS was tired of getting flak for being out of step with the times. The organization's New York board thought that Zappa and his group, the Mothers of Invention, who had received good reviews during a celebrated three-month stand at Manhattan's Garrick Theatre, might bring some credibility to the awards and possibly loosen up Academy old-timers who closed their ears to the period's weirder sounds. The Academy got more than it bargained for.

Unbeknownst to NARAS, Zappa hated the Grammys, regarding the award show as a self-congratulatory farce run by industry insiders who had nothing to do with the era's most artistically deserving work. The evening having been booked, however, Zappa resolved to put a lid on his feelings. But his hostilities came rushing to the surface when he found a copy of the Grammy Credo alongside his silverware: "We, the National Academy of Recording Arts & Sciences . . . shall judge a record on the basis of sheer artistry, and artistry alone," the credo, written by Stan Freberg, declared. ". . . Sales and mass popularity are the yardsticks of the record business. They are not the yardsticks of this Academy."

"I started howling when I read that," Zappa recalls. "The National Academy of Recording Arts & Sciences was not about art, and it never was. I grew up listening to Stan Freberg, who I like, and I thought, Stan, how could you do this?"

Zappa abruptly changed his performance plans. Woody Herman's band was playing "Satin Doll" as an intro to the awards, and Zappa decided to "mutilate the song, put it through a fun-house mirror." As he led the Mothers, dressed in freak clothes, through their twisted version, band members dismembered baby dolls and offered arms and legs to the tuxedo-and-gown crowd.

The performance was a kind of karmic nightmare for NARAS, bringing to life the organization's worst fantasies about degenerate rock 'n' roll and freak culture. When the New York chapter met the Monday after the awards to discuss the show, "there was a lot of talk about [how] disgusting [Zappa's] behavior was," recalls Nick Perito, a NARAS board member who produced a number of New York Grammy dinners.*

"Everyone rolled their eyes in the back of their heads and said, 'What a schmuck, what a tasteless dope.' . . . The idea [in inviting Zappa] had been to lend some energy to a prestigious affair. He turned it into a barroom."

Ah, the sixties . . . NARAS had a tough time in the sixties, especially the decade's culminating, apocalyptic years. By 1967 the Grammys were ten years old, but the world, especially the world of popular music, seemed to have time-warped into another dimension. NARAS, a conservative organization to begin with (created to *conserve* musical values of the past), suddenly found itself in the most radical of times. Music that would have been inconceivable in the late fifties—the

---

* Prior to 1971, Grammy winners were announced simultaneously at dinners held in New York, Los Angeles, and other Grammy chapter cities. After 1971, the awards were announced live on the Grammy telecast.

psychedelic brilliance of *Sgt. Pepper's Lonely Hearts Club Band*, the feedback revelations of Jimi Hendrix, the tripped-out virtuosity of Cream, the whole tribal communion of Woodstock—was taking over, hijacking popular culture, forging a counterculture.

NARAS and the Grammys seemed irrelevant. Despite continual efforts to recruit younger professionals into the organization, the limits of Grammy taste remained narrow. Of the dozens of artists to perform at the 1969 Woodstock festival, only two—Crosby, Stills & Nash and Blood, Sweat & Tears (who hardly count)—won an award that year. The list of sixties artists who never won a Grammy seems all-encompassing: the Doors, Janis Joplin, Jimi Hendrix, Jefferson Airplain, the Grateful Dead, Cream, the Who, Credence Clearwater, Santana, Van Morrison, the Byrds, the Rolling Stones, Rod Stewart, Led Zeppelin, and many more. Bob Dylan didn't win a solo Grammy until 1979. Eric Clapton won his first in 1990.

"Do you *know* what a Jefferson Airplane is?" one Academy staffer asked, half seriously, when producer Ted Bergmann tried to book the group for the 1968 "Best on Record" show.

Ignorance, as they say, is bliss, and Grammy voters, according to Stan Cornyn, an Academy board member at the time, never fretted too much about the music they ignored.

"When you're in your own club you don't expect a lot of homeless to be there to make you feel tense. There was about as much tension there as in a country club," he recalls.

The Grammy country club did not, presumably, subscribe to *Rolling Stone*. The magazine was withering in its scorn for NARAS and the awards, which it dismissed as "the sitting spittoon" of the record industry.

Despite all the omissions, the spirit of the sixties still seeped through. NARAS would've been the laughingstock of the industry if it hadn't given the Beatles' *Sgt. Pepper's Lonely Hearts Club Band* the Album of the Year award for 1967. The other nominees were *It Must Be Him* by Vikki Carr, *My Cup Runneth Over* by Ed Ames, *Ode to Billie Joe* by Bobbie Gentry, and *Francis Albert Sinatra & Antonio Carlos Jobim* by Sinatra and Jobim. It should be noted that NARAS was hardly enthralled with *Sgt. Pepper*. The album won a second Grammy as Best Contemporary Album, but lost twice in vocal group categories to the Fifth Dimension's "Up, Up and Away."

Sgt. Pepper was pretty much the Beatles' last hurrah as far as

NARAS was concerned. The group would win only one more Grammy—a 1970 Best Original Score salute for *Let It Be*—despite a final run of albums that included *Magical Mystery Tour*, *The White Album*, and *Abbey Road*. Ironically, a "Mission Impossible/ Norwegian Wood" medley by the Alan Copeland Singers found favor with the Academy, winning the 1968 Contemporary Pop Chorus Award.

To the end, NARAS couldn't resist patronizing the Beatles with feeble barbs. "The grooviest thing in England at the moment is a giant scavenger hunt—everybody's running around London trying to find John Lennon some clothes and a kimono for poor Yoko," chirped Beatle wannabe Davy Jones of the Monkees on the 1969 telecast. It was a sight only the Grammys would dare to present—using a Monkee to make fun of a Beatle.

Simon & Garfunkel, with their attractive voices and well-turned songs, were one group with sixties credibility that Grammy voters really liked. The duo made a good first impression in 1968, winning Record of the Year and Contemporary Pop Group Vocal honors with "Mrs. Robinson," along with a Best Original Score Grammy (for Simon) for *The Graduate*.

In 1970, S&G rewrote the Grammy record book with "Bridge Over Troubled Water," a song that betokened the end of the tempestuous sixties with its message of healing and reconciliation. NARAS voters loved the message, heaping an unprecedented six Grammys on the duo, including Record, Album, and Song of the Year awards, the first-ever sweep of the top three statues.

Other quasi-Woodstock Grammy winners included *Hair*, the Broadway hippie smash, which won the Best Score From an Original Cast Show Album Grammy in 1968; Judy Collins, winner of the 1968 Folk Performance Grammy with "Both Sides Now"; Joni Mitchell, who won the same award with "Clouds" in 1969; and Crosby, Stills & Nash, hailed as Best New Artists of 1969. Also, Jose Feliciano won the 1968 Contemporary Pop Male Vocal Grammy for his jazzy cover of the Doors' "Light My Fire." The Doors themselves never got a Grammy nomination.

Indeed, from the point of view of a Doors fan, the Grammys offered an emasculated version of the sixties, celebrating artists who were able to sublimate or alchemize the explosive energy of the times into likeable, middle-of-the-road pop.

The Fifth Dimension, for example, enjoyed great Grammy success with "Up, Up and Away" in 1967, an effervescent hit written by a twenty-one-year-old college dropout named Jimmy Webb that won five Grammys, including Record and Song of the Year awards. Two years later, the group, which had already established itself as Vegas headliners, adopted a hippie persona and cut the anthemic "Aquarius/ Let the Sunshine In" medley from *Hair*, once again generating Record and Song of the Year awards.

Glen Campbell was another big winner, a golden-haired good old boy who gave the Grammys a safe "contemporary" sound. Campbell grabbed three statuettes in 1967 for "By the Time I Get to Phoenix" (also written by Jimmy Webb), and one more for "Gentle on My Mind." The following year, Grammy voters embarrassed themselves badly, giving Campbell's *By the Time I Get to Phoenix* LP the Album of the Year Grammy over Simon & Garfunkel's *Bookends* and the Beatles' *Magical Mystery Tour*.

The contemporary female sound was provided by Bobbie Gentry, a sultry, weirdly charismatic singer whose "Ode to Billie Joe" earned her three 1967 Grammys, including Best New Artist and Best Vocal Performance, Female awards.

One group that NARAS members, including the older crowd, got genuinely excited about was Blood, Sweat & Tears, a jazz-rock ensemble that used horns and wasn't afraid to include "Variation on a Theme by Erik Satie" on its debut *Blood, Sweat & Tears* album. The group dominated the 1969 nominations, landing ten and winning three awards, including Album of the Year.

Old-style Grammy favorites continued to win the occasional award. Henry Mancini took consecutive instrumental arrangement honors in 1969 and 1970 for his themes to *Romeo and Juliet* and *Z*, jacking his Grammy tally up to twenty awards. Percy Faith spun his choral version of *Romeo and Juliet* into a 1969 Grammy as well.

Peggy Lee, a nine-time Grammy bridesmaid, won her first and only female vocal award, scoring in 1969 with her deadly "Is That All There Is?" Elvis Presley also won his first Grammy during this period, though it wasn't a rock award. Ironically, The King landed Best Sacred Performance honors in 1967 for "How Great Thou Art."

Rock 'n' roll continued to be the one form of music NARAS couldn't bring itself to embrace. For years, the Academy debated creating a "contemporary" field of awards to recognize younger artists, and in 1965 it did so, replacing the Best Rock and Roll Recording Grammy with four Contemporary (R&R) awards.

Two years later, however, as "rock 'n' roll" was maturing into "rock," NARAS removed the R&R subhead from the awards. Once again, rock was in Grammy exile, despite the fact that there were now forty-eight categories, including five for country, two for gospel, and one choral award.

The contemporary categories, meanwhile, simply duplicated the general categories again and again. In 1967, the Xerox became complete: Bobbie Gentry won the female vocal and contemporary vocal award, Glen Campbell did likewise on the male side, the Fifth Dimension's "Up, Up and Away" was named both best song and contemporary song, and on and on.

"The membership was older, and a lot of people did not relate to rock 'n' roll," Barry DeVorzon, a songwriter and NARAS board member who fought for the contemporary awards, explains. "Even when we established contemporary categories, they'd always vote for the wrong goddamned song."

In order to avoid a repeat of the '67 mess, NARAS dropped its general awards (best male, female, and group vocal) in 1968, thereby making the newly named "contemporary-pop" awards, in effect, general. The Grammys were back where they had started in 1958. Despite withering criticism from the rock press, NARAS persisted without any rock Grammys until 1979—twenty-one years after the awards had begun—when it finally created four rock prizes.

By the late sixties, popular music was the hottest force in pop culture, but the Grammys were still the weakest of the major awards shows— less prestigious, less glamorous, less of an event both inside and outside the industry than the Oscars, the Emmys, or the Tonys. NARAS elders were sure this was because their Grammy telecast, "The Best on Record," was an after-the-fact, taped review of the Grammys rather than a live show. There were no dramatic moments, no celebrity arrivals, no fashions to ogle, no speeches to mock—just performances, and then often by people like Eydie Gorme, John Gary, the Swingle Singers, and Henry Mancini.

Between 1963 and 1968, "The Best on Record" generated a measly $225,000 for NARAS in rights fees. Ratings were good, but not great, grooved at around twelve million homes per telecast, which was solid for a variety show but weak compared to the sixteen to twenty million reached by the Oscars and Emmys.

"For this reason, NARAS has not been able to demand and receive rights remuneration comparable to the other two academies," "Best on Record" producer Ted Bergmann informed NARAS in 1968. "As a matter of fact, NARAS has been forced to waive its contractual increases in rights money because there has been no significant increase in audience size, and it's doubtful that NARAS will be able to look forward to any further increase in income from the show unless this condition is remedied."

NARAS was convinced that the remedy to improving its market share, increasing its rights fees, and elevating its stature as an awards show was to go live. But a live show was much more difficult and costly to produce, and no one at NBC believed the Grammys had the clout with either the industry or the public to justify the switch. Who would come? Who would watch?

"All the NARAS directors met with the man from the network," DeVorzon recalls. "We appealed to him: 'Why can't we have a live show?' He told us, 'No way; you're not important enough.' He shot down the whole idea."

Bergmann in particular was opposed to taking the Grammy show live, mainly because he didn't think NARAS could get Grammy-nominated artists to attend and perform. Though contractually obligated to book stars on "The Best on Record," "NARAS could never deliver the artists, even though they won Grammys," Bergmann says, "because the acts didn't consider the Grammys very important. We had a tough time getting them there to tape sessions. The idea of getting all the artists in town for one night scared me. . . . They wouldn't turn up."

NARAS board members like DeVorzon disagreed and clamored for a live telecast. In 1968, Bergmann proposed a compromise in which the most prestigious Grammy—the Record of the Year award—would be announced on the show. The ploy proved awkward and controversial. Academy members angrily booed during Grammy ceremonies in Los Angeles when they found out the Record of the Year winner was being saved for the telecast.

Tensions between NARAS and "The Best on Record" peaked during the taping for the 1969 show. DeVorzon had submitted a written critique of the show to the Grammy board of trustees in August, panning the telecast for its "low budget" look, its weak writing, lighting, and camera work, and its overall lack of "dignity" and "creative direction." The board sent DeVorzon to work with Bergmann and "Best on Record" director George Schlatter as a production liaison. According to Bergmann, when DeVorzon tried to advise Schlatter on how to format the show, Schlatter erupted: "I know how to direct and you don't; so stay out of the way."

A spat between Bergmann and NARAS president Irving Townsend was apparently more serious. Townsend, an executive for CBS Records, wanted the 1969 "Best on Record" to include an extended feature on the Moog synthesizer, a technological breakthrough that was generating considerable excitement in the music biz as a result of Walter Carlos's *Switched-on Bach* LP. The album, which won three Grammys, including Classical Album of the Year, happened to belong to CBS.

The problem with doing a special on the Moog, of course, was that it was a telegenic yawn, and Bergmann and Schlatter decided "to brush it off" with a short tribute by Henry Mancini. According to Bergmann, Townsend pressured for a longer piece, at one point showing Bergmann a telegram he had received from CBS president Clive Davis. "Davis told Townsend, in effect, that 'it behooves you, as an officer of CBS and NARAS, to see to it that the Moog synthesizer, for which CBS Records has received a Grammy, gets on the show,' " Bergmann recalls.

Bergmann held his ground—"No record company was going to dictate what we put on the show"—but his days as producer of the Grammy Awards were numbered.

Shortly after the '69 awards, DeVorzon pitched the show to producers Burt Sugarman and Pierre Cossette. The pair were convinced they could find a sponsor and network for a live Grammy telecast, and agreed to put money for one year's rights to the show—about $125,000—in escrow so that NARAS would stay afloat if the venture failed.

Bergmann says that when he met the NARAS board for contract talks, Townsend told him he could continue to produce the Grammys, but only if it was live, if NARAS was given complete creative control, and if Schlatter was dismissed. "Get yourself another boy," Bergmann replied, and Sugarman and Cossette took over the show.

EIGHT

Dang Me: Country

When the Grammys were launched in the late 1950s, most of the kingpins of the music industry regarded "country 'n' western," as it was then called, as a backwater of the record business, a kind of hayseed form of folk, of dubious artistic merit and limited commercial clout.

New York and Los Angeles were the twin capitals of the record world, where most of the industry's classical, jazz, show-tune, TV-and-film, pop, and other important records were cut. NARAS, which quickly sprouted chapters on both coasts, thought it had the business pretty well covered when the Grammys debuted in 1959.

Alas, the music pros who made up the Academy weren't too familiar with country, a fact that became painfully obvious when nominations for the first Country & Western Performance Grammy were announced. The rock-oriented Everly Brothers drew a bid with "All I Have to Do Is Dream," while collegiate folkies the Kingston Trio were nominated for "Tom Dooley," the decade's biggest folk smash.

"Dooley" won, and NARAS officials wiped egg off their faces all the way to Nashville, to which they hastened in hopes of bringing the country capital—and a few knowledgeable country pros—into the Grammy fold. *Daily Variety* announced the formation of a "hillbilly music" chapter in early 1960. It expired after six months, the victim of NARAS snobbery on the one hand and Nashville vainglory on the other.

Nashville honchos, led by publishing magnate Wesley Rose, wanted to use the Grammys to help break country out of its regional straitjacket and into the pop mainstream. To that end, they angled for what NARAS officials felt was an unreasonably high profile within the organization. "They thought half the TV show should be theirs," one NARAS officer at the time recalls.

NARAS, for its part, was unwilling to accept its country brethren on equal terms. "We looked at them as hillbillies," concedes Jim Conkling, first chairman of the Academy and one of the early emissaries to Nashville. Indeed, NARAS refused to give the Nashville chapter any immediate representation or vote on the Academy board.

Insulted by the Academy's tokenism, Nashville eventually told the members of NARAS "they could take their game and go play somewhere else," according to Bill Denny, a onetime country music publisher who was involved in the early Grammy talks. After six months, the Grammys were a dead issue in Nashville, and the Grammy country award was once again in the hands of East and West Coast "experts" who knew little or nothing about the country field.

To its credit, NARAS navigated the country waters reasonably well during the early sixties, avoiding a repeat of the "Tom Dooley" debacle and saluting a string of pop-oriented crossover hits—"The Battle of New Orleans," recorded by Johnny Horton in 1959, "El Paso" by Marty Robbins in 1960, "Big Bad John" by Jimmy Dean in 1961, "Funny Way of Laughin' " by Burl Ives in 1962, and "Detroit City" by Bobby Bare in 1963.

In addition, Grammy voters toasted Ray Charles in 1962 for his daring country cover of "I Can't Stop Loving You," the first crossover performance of a country tune by a major r&b star. Charles's million-selling *Modern Sounds in Country & Western Music* LP proved that country songs—"oatunes," as *Variety* called them—could succeed in pop and even r&b markets. With Patsy Cline and Jim Reeves pioneering a softer country sound and likewise enjoying widespread pop success, country was poised on the brink of a phenomenal period of growth and change.

By 1964 the major recording studios were scurrying to set up offices in Nashville and the "mossbacks in [Naras] realized that country was more than backwood fiddle and yodeling," recalls George Avakian, Academy president in 1966–67. NARAS resolved to bring what had become the third-biggest force in pop music into the Grammy fold.

To that end, a delegation of Grammy emissaries—Avakian, Conkling, and Warner Bros. vice president Hal Cooke—went to Nashville to try once again to launch a chapter. The delegation met with Rose, head of the giant Rose/Acuff publishing house and one of the shrewdest and most powerful men in Nashville.

It was Rose, Avakian says, who "put the kibosh" on the first Grammy-Nashville linkup, confident that NARAS would eventually return to Nashville on bended knee and that country would be able to dictate its own terms. Which is exactly what happened. Bargaining from strength, Nashville persuaded NARAS to establish six country awards, a stunning concession that suddenly gave country more awards than r&b, rock 'n' roll, and jazz combined, and created a kind of country "Grammys within the Grammys." Added were awards for country album, single, song, new artist, and male and female vocal.

"This was the deal Rose was waiting for," Avakian says. "He could feel Nashville was being accepted on terms closer to its own estimate of itself."

Nashville made its presence felt immediately. "King of the Road" Roger Miller became the first country artist to dominate the Grammys, winning no less than eleven trophies between 1964 and 1965. Two of Miller's wins, moreover, came in noncountry fields, with "King of the Road" beating the Beatles' "Yesterday" twice for Contemporary (R&R) Vocal and Contemporary (R&R) single awards.

Miller wasn't the only Nashville artist to beat the Beatles in 1965. The big shocker was the success of the Anita Kerr Singers, a Nashville-based jingles group, which knocked "Help!" to win the Best Performance by a Vocal Group prize with an album called *We Dig Mancini*.

Kerr was a vice president of the Nashville NARAS chapter, and undoubtedly benefited, as did the Statlers and Miller, from bloc voting by her Nashville peers.

Bloc voting, usually by major record labels, had plagued the Grammys since their inception in 1958, but Nashville, a chapter with a cause, raised the practice to truly alarming heights. To a degree,

NARAS had only itself to blame. In its zeal to recruit Nashville, NARAS intimated that bloc voting could give the fledgling chapter extra clout and enable it to have an immediate impact on the awards.

"We actually came right out and said, between the lines, you can do a lot of bloc voting," Avakian recalls. "In the early days, a relatively small number of votes carried a hell of a lot of weight, so people could really gang up . . . and that was one of the arguments we took [to them]."

Nashville, to be sure, didn't need much prodding. The chapter jumped "from birth to instant manhood," in the words of producer and publisher Bud Killin, beefing up its active membership from under fifty in March of 1964 to a hundred by May. In 1966, recruitment went into high gear, as Nashville signed up every eligible country artist, producer, and A&R person in sight, foraged the gospel community for another hundred votes, then went all the way to Memphis and r&b stronghold Stax Records, picking up forty-eight additional members. By 1968, the Nashville roll call was 551 names long. With a total NARAS membership of around two thousand, Nashville could really make a difference, and did.

Anita Kerr won another Grammy in 1966, beating the Mamas and the Papas' "Monday, Monday," the Beach Boys' "Good Vibrations," and the Association's "Cherish" for vocal-group honors with her version of "A Man and a Woman," a sixties classic if ever one there wasn't.

That same year, a black, blind street singer by the name of Cortelia Clark, utterly unknown outside of Nashville, where he sang for small change, won the folk Grammy, beating the likes of Pete Seeger, Peter, Paul and Mary, Leadbelly, Ravi Shankar, and Mimi and Richard Fariña.

Just to show it wasn't a fluke, Nashville hauled in the folk award again in 1967, with John Hartford winning for "Gentle on My Mind."

Nashville, clearly, was going for any Grammy it could get— "ganging up," to use Avakian's phrase—and achieving particular success in the smaller categories, where a bloc of votes could dominate. Country artists began winning an unnatural number of awards for Best Album Notes, for example, with John O. Loudermilk winning in 1967 for *Suburban Attitudes in Country Verse*, and Johnny Cash winning in '68 for *Johnny Cash at Folsom Prison*, and again in '69 for *Nashville Skyline* by Bob Dylan.

Confessions of a Broken Man by Porter Wagoner, meanwhile, won Best Album Cover Photography in 1966, getting the nod over Dylan's *Blonde on Blonde*, among others.

"[Nashville] was suddenly getting awards hand over fist," Avakian recalls. "It was beginning to seem like muscle was what was getting awards. Whoever could get the most members in there could get the most for their people."

"Nashville wanted to put themselves on the map, and this was one way to do it," adds Nesuhi Ertegun, cofounder of Atlantic Records and NARAS president in 1964–65. "They took full advantage of the Academy in a very intelligent way, when people here [in New York] and in L.A. were half asleep."

Nashville had its greatest Grammy impact in 1967, when it helped make country-based singers Glen Campbell and Bobbie Gentry Grammy superstars. Campbell won four awards, including Best Vocal Performance, Male for "By the Time I Get to Phoenix," while Gentry took home three, including Best New Artist and Best Vocal Performance, Female honors for "Ode to Billie Joe."

Gentry was the first, and, with Debby Boone, one of only two country-flavored artists to win the Best New Artist salute.

Nashville continued to lobby effectively within NARAS, which created two gospel awards (eventually increased to seven) in 1967. Elvis Presley promptly won his first Grammy—in the Best Sacred Performance category—for his version of "How Great Thou Art."

Despite its flagrant shenanigans, Nashville, like its r&b and rock 'n' roll counterparts, has had cause to complain about Grammy mistreatment and neglect. Country artists have been virtually locked out of the three most prestigious Grammy categories—the Record, Song, and Album of the Year awards.

Campbell's *By the Time I Get to Phoenix* is the only Nashville-linked album to win the LP award. No country disc has ever won the Record of the Year prize. "The Battle of New Orleans" by Jimmy Driftwood (1959); "Little Green Apples" by Bobby Russell (1968); and "Always on My Mind" by Johnny Christopher, Mark James, and Wayne Carson (1982) are the only country tunes to win the Song of the Year prize.

Country giants who have never won a Grammy include Patsy Cline, Bob Wills, Roy Acuff, Buck Owens, and Kitty Wells—though Wells and Acuff, as well as Hank Williams, have received Lifetime

Achievement Grammys. "Your Cheatin' Heart" by Hank Williams, "Blue Yodel (T for Texas)" by Jimmie Rodgers, "Crazy" by Patsy Cline, and "Cool Water" by the Sons of the Pioneers are the only country songs to date inducted into the Grammy Hall of Fame, a shrine erected in 1973 to honor recordings released before 1958, the year the Grammys were born.

NINE

The Way We Were: 1971–76

The death of sixties rock came, quite literally, with the death of Jimi Hendrix in August 1970, followed by the death of Janis Joplin a month later, and the formal dissolution of the Beatles in December. When Jim Morrison of the Doors was found dead of an overdose in Paris six months after this, the musical obit of the era was complete.

But the sixties cast a long shadow over the pop music landscape. Artists like Neil Young, Joni Mitchell, the individual Beatles, the Rolling Stones, Elton John, Sly Stone, Randy Newman, Carole King, Van Morrison, James Taylor, and many others struggled with the changes, indeed the trauma, wrought by the death of Woodstock and the failure of the counterculture dream. From the howling recognitions of Lennon's early post-Beatles work, to the resonant comforts of Carole King's *Tapestry*, to the ironic, sharply etched details of Joni Mitchell's *Court and Spark*, to the raucous, debauched honesty of the Stones' *Exile on Main Street*, pop was teeming with rich fallout chronicling the end of one era and the emergence of another.

But if the sixties died hard, the seventies were not to be denied. Long-repressed commercial impulses within the music biz, held in check by counterculture scorn, returned to the fore, tentatively at first but with growing confidence and success, until, by the middle of the decade, pop was once again more product than culture. Mellow—the toothsome mellow of the Carpenters and the posthippie mellow of Seals & Crofts, Bread, and similar groups—served as the transitional sound, softening pop standards and paving the way for the return of silly-little-love-songs and formula schlock. By the middle of the decade, syrupy tunes like Olivia Newton-John's "I Honestly Love You" and the Captain and Tennille's "Love Will Keep Us Together" were topping the charts and, need we add, winning Grammy Awards.

"You got to scrape that shit right off your shoes," Mick Jagger urged in the Stones' 1972 *Exile on Main Street*, and anyone who listened to pop radio knew what he was talking about.

The Grammys, of course, were only too glad to say good-bye to the sixties, that barefoot, buzz-saw decade that liberated popular music from the aesthetics of "good taste" to which may NARAS members adhered. The seventies, from the start, were much more palatable, with people like Carole King, James Taylor, and a battalion of singer-songwriters offering acoustic, friendly balm in place of Woodstock's electric hue and cry.

King really set the tone with *Tapestry*, a soothing, soulful set of songs about friendship and romance that generated four Grammy Awards, including a rare sweep of the Record ("It's Too Late"), Song ("You've Got a Friend"), and Album (*Tapestry*) of the Year prizes. In addition, King and *Tapestry* won the Pop Vocal Performance, Female Grammy, while James Taylor won the male vocal prize for his version of "You've Got a Friend." An instrumental cover of King's *Smackwater Jack* by Quincy Jones won the Pop Instrumental Performance award.

Roberta Flack was the 1972–73 Grammy queen, wowing NARAS voters with her meltingly sensuous, quiet storm of a voice and spawning Record and Song of the Year honors two years running, in 1972 with "The First Time Ever I Saw Your Face," and the following year with "Killing Me Softly With His Song." Flack is the only artist in Grammy history to generate that particular double double.

A Grammy tradition of paying tribute to superstar humanitarian causes began in 1972, when NARAS gave *The Concert for Bangla Desh* the Album of the Year prize. Organized by ex-Beatle George Harrison, the concert featured performances by Dylan, Eric Clapton, and Leon Russell and was coproduced by Phil Spector, all of whom won their first Grammys for their work on the benefit LP.

While all the individual Beatles were active and commercially successful after the breakup of the group, Paul was the Grammy favorite, picking up a Best Arrangement Accompanying Vocalist(s) award with wife Linda in 1971 for "Uncle Albert/Admiral Halsey" and a pop group vocal nod with Wings in 1974 for "Band on the Run." NARAS voters preferred McCartney, the softest Beatle, even while he was in the group, giving him a Solo Vocal Performance award for "Eleanor Rigby" in 1966 and picking "Michelle," the quintessential McCartney song, as 1966 Song of the Year, the only Beatle tune to ever win that honor.

Lennon, a much more prickly, discomfitting soloist, drew a complete Grammy blank until he was murdered in 1980, having won neither awards nor nominations for his harrowing masterpiece, *John Lennon/Plastic Ono Band*, or his much sweeter, chart-topping *Imagine* LP. His only solo Grammy was posthumous—a 1981 Album of the Year award for *Double Fantasy*.

NARAS did give the Beatles a Trustees Award in 1972, saluting the boys "for their outstanding talent, originality and music creativity that have done so much to express the mood and tempo of our times and to bridge the culture gap between several generations." Perhaps the Academy was trying to apologize for having chosen Anita Kerr, the Statler Brothers, Roger Miller, the Fifth Dimension, and Glen Campbell over the Beatles while they were still a group.

The biggest Grammy winner between 1973 and 1976 was Stevie Wonder, the onetime boy genius who came of age with an astonishing series of albums that generated no fewer than fifteen awards, including three Album of the Year prizes. Wonder, who wrote, arranged, produced, sang, and played a half-dozen instruments on the LPs, won five Grammys in 1973 with *Innervisions* and *Talking Book*, five more the following year with *Fulfillingness' First Finale*, and, after a one-year recording hiatus, another five in 1976 with *Songs in the Key of Life*.

Against the pallid landscape of mid-seventies pop, Wonder's artistry dazzled. But his Grammy success masked the fact that the Academy's taste was sinking into the commercial mire. Olivia Newton-John won Record of the Year honors in 1974 with her ultrasaccharine "I

Honestly Love You," a tearjerker of a song that managed to beat four good records—"Help Me" by Joni Mitchell, "Don't Let the Sun Go Down on Me" by Elton John, "Midnight at the Oasis" by Maria Muldaur, and "Feel Like Makin' Love" by Roberta Flack.

What could one make of an organization that picked the worst nominee for its most prestigious award? "Sham, Sham, Sham" scolded *Rolling Stone* magazine in a headline for one of its numerous scathing Grammy critiques. But NARAS was unfazed. The Record of the Year winner in 1975 was the gooey *Love Will Keep Us Together* by the Captain and Tennille. Other records released that year included *Blood on the Tracks* by Dylan, *Born to Run* by Bruce Springsteen, *Fame* by David Bowie, *Miracles* by Jefferson Starship, *No Woman, No Cry* by Bob Marley, and *For the Love of Money* by the O'Jays, none of which received a Grammy nomination, much less an award.

From the point of view of rock fans, certainly, the Grammy definition of pop was abominably soft. For four years in a row, Song of the Year honors went to easy-listening standards—"The Way We Were" in 1974, "Send in the Clowns" in 1975, "I Write the Songs" in 1976, and "You Light Up My Life" and "Evergreen" (a tie) in 1977.

The early seventies were shaky years for NARAS on the TV front, as the Academy made the leap from its after-the-fact "Best on Record" show to a live awards telecast that, it hoped, would put the Grammys on a par with the Oscars and the Emmys in terms of TV ratings and pop-culture prestige.

True to its word, NBC dropped the Grammy show when NARAS insisted on the live broadcast. But ABC picked it up after new producers Pierre Cossette and Burt Sugarman secured Andy Williams as host and Chevrolet as sponsor. The first live Grammy show, expanded to ninety minutes, aired on March 16, 1971, from the Palladium in Hollywood. A hanging TV light exploded, showering the wife of ABC Records president Howard Stark with sparks, but other than that, things proceeded smoothly, if blandly.

The talent lineup wasn't as scintillating as it might have been. Half of the performers were from Nashville, and the other half included MOR softies like the Osmond Brothers, Anne Murray, and the Carpenters. But Cossette did score one monumental coup—a surprise appearance by Paul McCartney. The ex-Beatle picked up the group's last Grammy, a Best Original Score award for *Let It Be.* Accompanied by his wife, Linda, and dressed in a blue suit and gym shoes, McCartney received his Grammy from, of all people, John Wayne.

McCartney's appearance made for a promising start, but a crisis of major proportions was looming, NARAS, determined to spotlight its chapter cities, told Cossette that the 1972 telecast had to emanate from New York, and the 1973 show from Nashville. ABC had no problem with the Big Apple—the '72 Grammy Awards aired live from Manhattan's Felt Forum—but the network was unwilling to take the show south.

"They figured we'd have nothing but shit-kickers in Nashville," explains Cossette, "and they didn't want that. They didn't want to change the image of the show."

Indeed, ABC flatly told Cossette that if NARAS insisted on the country setting, it would drop the show. Cossette pleaded with the Academy to change its mind, but to no avail, and, to Cossette's horror, ABC passed on its option.

Suddenly, Cossette, who had split with Sugarman and was now handling the Grammys solo, had a contract with NARAS to produce a show that both ABC and NBC had killed, a contract that guaranteed NARAS $125,000 regardless of whether the show aired. The Head of programming at CBS, Bob Wood, scoffed at Cossette when he pitched the program to him.

"You want me to tell my people we're buying a show that two networks have dropped?" a disbelieving Wood asked.

With production deadlines for the Grammys drawing near, Cossette grew desperate and badgered Wood, a longtime pal, about the show. He finally swayed him when he barged into Wood's bedroom one morning and hopped into bed with the TV exec and his wife.

"You've got to buy this show," Cossette pleaded, hamming it up. "Otherwise I'll have to borrow money. I'll have to sell my house, I mean, Jesus Christ, you've gotta help!!"

"Buy the show from Pierre," Mrs. Wood laughingly instructed.

"Well, you must be desperate," Wood finally said. "I'll stick my neck out for you."

To this day, CBS carries the Grammy Awards.

Interestingly, the Grammys' main competition, the American Music Awards, were born out of ABC's decision to scotch the Grammy show and CBS's decision to pick it up. After watching the 1973 Grammys notch a whopping 53 percent audience share, according to Cossette, ABC decided to make up for its blunder, by starting a new music awards show.

The AMAs, hosted by Dick Clark, were launched the very next year, heavily promoted—"You'd think it was *Roots*," says Cossette—and broadcast weeks before the Grammys in order to undercut its more established rival. The strategy worked. The AMAs have prospered and regularly trounce the Grammys in the ratings war.

But CBS and NARAS have had reason to celebrate as well. After the Nashville show, Cossette signed a five-year, ten-special Grammy deal, with the network calling for five Grammy shows and five spin-off programs. The pact guaranteed NARAS $1.75 million, more than the organization made in its first fifteen years.

TEN

Just the Way You Are: 1977–82

As the seventies unfolded, the boring sentimentalism and studio slickness of mainstream pop triggered a host of reactions, the most commercially successful of which was disco. If the middle of the road, as represented by the schmaltz of Barry Manilow or the born-again romanticism of Debby Boone, was lifeless and dull, disco at least offered some intensity.

Derided as a form of antimusic, the logical last extension of the synthetic seventies, disco's relentless beat nevertheless provided a kind of flattened, almost military passion, a trancelike seventies sublimation that made it the after-hours addiction of choice for millions of music fans.

Sociology aside, disco produced some very strong artists and records—"I Will Survive" by Gloria Gaynor, "Don't Leave Me This Way" by Thelma Houston, and "Last Dance" by Donna Summer, to name a few. When the Bee Gees' *Saturday Night Fever* exploded through the first half of 1978, selling an unprecedented twenty-five million copies and winning the Grammy Album of the Year award, disco was the dominant, hottest sound around.

But would it last? That was the question NARAS, along with the rest of the industry, was pondering. Grammy voters began giving Grammys to disco as early as 1975, when "Fly, Robin, Fly" by Silver Convention won an r&b instrumental award. Almost immediately, disco pros began stumping for a special category. The Academy snuffed the idea for three years, fearful that disco was a fad that would fade as suddenly as it had arrived.

Disco diva Donna Summer railed at the Grammy establishment for slighting the genre when she accepted a Rhythm and Blues Vocal Performance, Female Grammy in 1979 for "Last Dance."

"Disco has sold millions and millions of records and has rejuvenated this industry," she told reporters backstage at the Shrine Auditorium in Los Angeles. "If there are categories for things like gospel and classical, why aren't there categories for disco?"

The phenomenal success of *Saturday Night Fever* finally convinced NARAS that disco was here to stay, and the Academy created a Best Disco Recording Grammy in 1979. Unfortunately, NARAS conservatives had been right this time. The bottom fell out of disco almost as soon as NARAS decided to give it an award, and one year later, a red-faced Grammy board of governors terminated the prize.

Gloria Gaynor and her "I Will Survive" anthem won the one and only disco award, topping a strong field that included "Bad Girls" by Donna Summer, "Boogie Wonderland" by Earth, Wind & Fire, and "Don't Stop 'Til You Get Enough" by Michael Jackson.

If disco was the escapist response to the banalities of MOR pop, punk, which was born in lower-class England and quickly took root in New York's Lower East Side, was an almost violently combative alternative. Punk was ugly and primitive by design, a scathing negation of everything from the pop foppery of Rod Stewart and Elton John, to the overblown productions of Chicago and Boston, to the passive, too-pretty laments of the Eagles, Linda Ronstadt, and Jackson Browne. Though it never achieved the mass success of disco, punk was hugely influential, hurling a tonic rage into pop's sterile emotional mix and spawning a host of prickly, more accessible artists like Elvis Costello and the Talking Heads.

The one-chord nihilism of groups like the Sex Pistols and the Ramones, of course, had no chance of winning any Grammy Awards, but even the artier New Wavers were snubbed. Costello did win a Best New Artist nomination in 1978, but lost to A Taste of Honey, a one-hit group whose disco-ish "Boogie Oogie Oogie" impressed NARAS more than Costello's brilliant but barbed *My Aim Is True*. The choice did much to discredit the Grammys for a new generation of fans, and prompted *Rolling Stone*'s Dave Marsh to contend that NARAS members wouldn't know a good record "if it bit them on the ass."

Grammy's ongoing credibility problems had a lot to do with the fact that Andy Williams was still host of the Grammy TV show. By the mid-seventies, Williams was an MOR dinosaur with a dwindling audience of middle-age fans. He represented the music industry about as much as Ray Conniff or Jim Nabors did—i.e., not at all. Yet, Williams was entrenched as Grammy host, the image and symbol of the awards. This was largely due to his relationship with Grammy producer Pierre Cossette. The two were close pals and business partners—Cossette produced Williams's popular TV variety series in the sixties for CBS. Moreover, Cossette felt he owed Williams a Grammy debt, since the singer had agreed to host the Grammys in 1971, when he was a big star and Cossette needed a name in order to persuade Chevrolet to sponsor the show.

But it was obvious from the start that Williams would be a problem. Though he wore Nehru jackets and an occasional string of beads, Williams, a smooth, romantic crooner in the tradition of Bing Crosby, had absolutely no connection to the rock-pop-soul-r&b-jazz-country of the sixties or seventies. It wasn't long before people within the Academy itself began to clamor for a change.

"For years the NARAS trustees wanted Andy removed," recalls Bernie Fleischer, first vice president of NARAS in 1977 and a member of the organization's all-important television committee. "Everybody [on the TV committee] was saying, 'How long are we going to be stuck with Andy Williams? He was great years ago, but he doesn't reflect the music business today.'"

Cossette was able to deflect the calls for a new host by insisting that only an experienced, coolheaded pro like Williams could handle a complex technical production like the Grammys, that NARAS would be courting prime-time disaster if it opted for someone else. Indeed,

Williams got a chance to prove himself in a crisis during the 1976 awards, when a satellite feed of Stevie Wonder performing in Lagos, Nigeria, went awry. "Stevie, can you *see* us?" a flustered Williams cried. After the show, the members of the NARAS TV committee voted unanimously to dump Williams, and this time they were not to be denied.

In the scramble to pick a successor, a number of intriguing candidates emerged, none more intriguing or surprising than the Thin White Duke himself, David Bowie. Cossette favored Bowie, whom he describes as "the Fred Astaire of our time," and NARAS seriously pondered offering him the job. "He would have been a radical departure," concedes TV committee member Mike Melvoin (later NARAS president), "but the impulse was to make the show contemporary." CBS, unfortunately, was not about to put its multimillion-dollar special in the hands of Ziggy Stardust, and the idea was scotched.

Eventually, NARAS (or CBS) settled on John Denver, who was about as middle-of-the-road as Andy Williams, but more contemporary—by a hair. Anyway, he was younger. Denver took over in 1977 and helmed the show into the eighties, giving up the wheel twice to Kenny Rogers (1979 and 1985) and once to Paul Simon (1981).

With punk on the left and disco on the right, the Grammys cruised down pop's great middle of the road, casting kudos on supersofties like Debby Boone, Anne Murray, and Barry Manilow while also embracing a number of easy-on-the-eardrums hipsters like Fleetwood Mac, the Eagles, and Billy Joel.

In 1977, Grammy voters were particularly hip, at least with regard to the Album of the Year award. Nominees included three *Rolling Stone* magazine cover groups—Fleetwood Mac, the Eagles, and Steely Dan. Fleetwood Mac's *Rumours*, deservedly, won the award. A seventies pop masterpiece, the album was tense, sleek, exhilarating, and incredibly popular, selling more than twenty million copies worldwide.

The Eagles, meanwhile, wound up winning two Grammys, including the Record of the Year award for "Hotel California," the decade's most seductive cautionary tale. The Eagles' win may well have resulted from a split vote by conservative Grammy members, who had three mushy nominees from which to choose—Debby Boone's "You Light Up My Life," Crystal Gayle's "Don't It Make My Brown Eyes

Blue," and Barbra Streisand's "Evergreen." The Eagles won a second Grammy in the Best Arrangement for Voices category for "New Kid in Town."

Despite her loss, 1977 was a good Grammy year for Streisand, who won for the first time since 1965, nabbing Pop Vocal Performance, Female and Song of the Year honors for "Evergreen" a tune she cowrote with Paul Williams. "You Light Up My Life" by Joe Brooks also received a 1977 Song of the Year Grammy, the only time in Grammy history that two nominees tied for a major award. "This song was turned down by every firm that is out there tonight. Some turned it down twice. . . . This is so sweet," Brooks exulted, while picking up his award.

The talent lineup for the 1977 Grammy show was unusually bland, with Debby Boone, Ronnie Milsap, Crystal Gayle, Shaun Cassidy, Dancing Machine, and John Denver representing the pop field. Pierre Cossette needed at least one hot group for the show. The Bee Gees, Fleetwood Mac, and the Eagles had all been nominated for major awards, but neither the Bee Gees nor Fleetwood Mac would perform. The Eagles, who lived in Malibu, a short limo ride from the Shrine, were Cossette's last best hope.

Eagles manager Irving Azoff told Cossette the group would be happy to perform, but on one condition: that Cossette guarantee in advance that they'd won.

"I know you know, Pierre. There's no way you don't know, and you gotta tell me," Azoff insisted, according to Cossette. "I can't put 'em up there and have them lose."

"Irving," Cossette protested, "I can't tell you, because I don't know."

"You know what?" Azoff returned. "I'm gonna keep them in Malibu."

A few days later, Azoff proposed a compromise. If Cossette arranged a secret dressing room for the Eagles, so that no one would know they were at the Shrine, the boys would take the stage if they won the award. If they lost, their fans would never know they cared enough to go to the show.

Cossette ran the idea by Bernie Fleischer, a key member of the NARAS TV committee and president of the Los Angeles chapter of the Academy.

"Tell them to go *fuck* themselves," Fleischer said. "They're obviously too good for the show."

After another few days, Azoff once again called Cossette. The Eagles had changed their minds, he said. They would perform after all, without a Grammy guarantee. A jubilant Cossette immediately booked them for the night's climactic spot, just before the presentation of the Record of the Year award. But Azoff, notorious for his tough and sometimes punitive managerial style, was apparently stringing Cossette along. The Eagles never showed, and a scrambling Cossette had to improvise a finish midway through the show.

As it turned out, the Eagles and "Hotel California" won the prestigious Record of the Year prize. Immediately after the awards, a furious Azoff accosted Cossette.

"He couldn't wait to find me," Cossette remembers. " 'You son of a bitch, why didn't you *tell* me,' he cried. He still didn't believe I didn't know."

The Eagles' seeming "snub" of the Grammys dominated coverage of the awards in both the *Los Angeles Times* and *Rolling Stone*, with the group coming off like hipper-than-Grammy heroes who couldn't relate to the concept of the awards.

"Eagles Give Grammys the Bird," *Rolling Stone* sneeringly announced, explaining that the group was "wary of award shows" and didn't "want to endorse them by participating."

"The whole idea of a contest to see who is 'best' just doesn't appeal to us," singer-drummer Don Henley told the *Times*. "It's all a matter of personal taste."

Of course, 1978 was the year of the Bee Gees and *Saturday Night Fever*, the top-selling album of the seventies. The Grammys succumbed to the disco craze along with everyone else. The Bee Gees, who had won a Pop Vocal Performance, Group Grammy in 1977 for "How Deep Is Your Love," won five more awards in '78, including Album of the Year kudos for *Saturday Night Fever*.

Amazingly, *Fever* had to beat out another sound track, *Grease*, which was coproduced by Bee Gee Barry Gibb and featured *Fever* star John Travolta. The Bee Gees' surge also kept the Rolling Stones from cashing in their first Grammy nomination, an Album of the Year bid for *Some Girls*.

Billy Joel was the other big Grammy winner of 1978, nabbing both Record and Song of the Year awards with "Just the Way You Are," a hip Hallmark card of a song that launched Joel on a three-year

Grammy roll. The singer-songwriter, whose pouty, black-jacket style masked a strong affinity for old-fashioned melody and form, picked up Album of the Year and Pop Vocal Performance, Male Grammys in 1979 for *52nd Street*, along with a Rock Vocal Performance, Male award in 1980 for *Glass Houses*.

Did somebody say *rock*? Yes, indeed. The Grammy boycott of rock finally ended in 1979, with the establishment of male, female, group, and instrumental rock Grammys. The long exile of rock was over, in part because of mounting criticism inside and outside NARAS, but also because punk had displaced rock as the industry's scorned, illegitimate sound.

Certainly, Grammy taste in rock was . . . porous. Bruce Springsteen recharged rock 'n' roll through the late seventies and early eighties, but didn't win a Grammy until 1984. He was nominated for his *The River* LP in 1981, but lost, pathetically, to soap opera rocker Rick Springfield and "Jessie's Girl." Maybe some of the older Grammy voters got the names confused. A defensive Springfield bristled when reporters asked him if he felt uncomfortable beating The Boss for the rock 'n' roll prize. "I think I deserve the award; what can I tell you?" he said.

One lifelong Grammy loser who finally won an award was Bob Dylan. He notched the very first Rock Vocal Performance, Male prize with his born-again "Gotta Serve Somebody." Dylan's burning sermon of a song must have finally made fans out of conservative Grammy voters in Nashville, Memphis, Atlanta, and other gospel strongholds. Dylan, who performed the song on the 1979 Grammy telecast wearing a white tux with an old-fashioned stand-up collar, drew a standing ovation from the Grammy crowd when he picked up his award.

"I didn't expect to win, and I want to thank the Lord," he said.

If Dylan's win and the creation of rock categories signaled a new spirit in the Academy, that signal was quickly scrambled in 1980 when NARAS heaped a stunning five Grammys on Christopher Cross, an innocuous popster with a made-for-Muzak sound who swept the Record, Song, and Album of the Year awards with his *Sailing* single and LP. In the long history of Grammy goofs, the coronation of so mild a talent as Cross was one of the most embarrassing, and seriously called into question Grammy standards and taste.

"(Cross's) wins achieved something that once seemed impossible," wrote Robert Hilburn of the *Los Angeles Times*. "They made the Grammy voting look even more conservative than usual."

Cross, who had been playing fraternity parties the year before, also snagged Best New Artist and Arrangement Accompanying Vocalist honors, becoming the gaudiest first-time Grammy winner in the history of the awards, bigger than the Beatles, Streisand—anyone. This was truly a Cross the Grammys would have to bear for a long time.

Grammy voters redeemed themselves somewhat in 1981 when they gave John Lennon and Yoko Ono's *Double Fantasy* the Album of the Year award. The record, a loving portrait of Lennon and Ono's relationship and family life as they entered their forties, had been climbing up the charts when Lennon was assassinated in the lobby of his exclusive New York co-op, on December 8, 1980.

With intense security protecting them at every point, Ono and five-year-old Sean Lennon attended Grammy ceremonies at the Shrine, arriving through a secret entry minutes before the award was announced. The Grammy was Lennon's first since leaving the Beatles a decade before. Ono fought back tears as the Grammy crowd gave her what was probably the most emotional ovation in the history of the awards.

"Both John and I were always proud and happy that we were a part of the human race . . . and that we made good music for the earth and for the universe," she said.

The Lennon victory overshadowed major Grammy triumphs for Kim Carnes, who nabbed Record and Song of the Year honors (the latter shared with Jackie De Shannon) with her gin-soaked, alluring "Bette Davis Eyes," and Quincy Jones, winner of five lower-profile Grammys for *The Dude*.

Alas, in 1982, the Grammy studio aesthetic brought it to another sad, if only too logical, pass. An actual studio group, Toto, dominated the awards, winning Record of the Year honors for the hit single "Rosanna" and Album of the Year kudos for *Toto IV*. Only Grammy technocrats, with their exaggerated sense of craft, could hail as the industry's best act a group like Toto, as formulaic as it was proficient. "Toto-ly awful," one music fan wrote to the *Los Angeles Times*, voicing an opinion, one may safely presume, shared by many outside the Academy.

The Toto landslide, coming on the heels of the Christopher Cross sweep, really exposed the weaknesses of the Academy's collective musical values and once again made the Grammys something of a laughingstock within the industry. Chagrined NARAS officers mounted yet another membership drive aimed at bringing younger blood into the organization. The efforts eventually paid off, but immediate salvation would come from another source, from an artist the Grammys had long ignored but would soon apotheosize—from Michael Jackson.

ELEVEN

Respect: R&B

Rhythm & blues spooked the founders of the Grammys almost as much as rock 'n' roll. Rude, rough, earthy, and sexual, "race music," as it was once called, boogied all over the highbrow, "quality"-pop standards of the Grammy crowd.

Stan Freberg, the man who wrote the Grammy Credo and set the tone and terms of NARAS taste at the start of the awards, hated r&b, especially doowop, which he once described on an album cover as "a musical trend I personally loathe."

Indeed, Freberg made a living ridiculing r&b in popular parody versions of songs like "The Great Pretender" and "Sh-Boom" ("On your mark, get set, mumble!" he screamed at the start of the latter song), lampooning what he felt were the yowling vocals and moronic simplemindedness of such hits.

"The Chords, the Penguins . . . were terrible, terrible r&b groups," Freberg, who hasn't changed his tune, maintained in a recent interview. "They sang out of tune, the songs were dumb, you couldn't understand the lyrics.

"The people I idolized—Frank Sinatra, Peggy Lee, Count Basie— spent all this time in the studio making the best possible high-fidelity records they could. It sounded to me like the new stuff was recorded through a Dixie cup."

Worst of all, the "new stuff" was beginning to dominate the market and affect industry tastes. According to Freberg, a producer once grew exasperated with Sammy Davis, Jr., because he delivered his lyrics *too* clearly. "Can you give me more of a *black* sound?" the session chief implored.

"I'm-doing-the-best-that-I-can," a frustrated Davis replied.

Grammy aversion to r&b was evident in 1958, the year the awards began. The first slate of Best Rhythm & Blues Performance nominees had little to do with rhythm & blues. An impromptu L.A. studio band called the Champs drew a bid for their south-of-the-border hit "Tequila." Pop crooners Nat King Cole ("Looking Back") and Harry Belafonte (*Belafonte Sings the Blues*) were also nominated, along with Perez Prado ("Patricia") and Earl Grant ("The End"). "Tequila," which must've been what Grammy voters were drinking at the time, won the award.

NARAS sobered up by 1960, assembling a truly great field of R&B nominees, including Hank Ballard ("Finger Poppin' Time"), Jackie Wilson ("Lonely Teardrops"), Muddy Waters ("Got My Mojo Working"), Bo Diddley ("Walkin' and Talkin' "), Etta James ("All I Could Do Was Cry"), and Ray Charles ("Let the Good Times Roll").

Charles was the Grammy's first big r&b star, winning nine trophies between 1960 and 1966 and four consecutive r&b nods from 1960 to 1963. In 1960 alone, Charles won four awards, including the Best Vocal Performance, Male prize for "Georgia on My Mind."

Charles instantly legitimated the Grammys on the r&b front. He had virtually invented soul in the fifties, with such fervent, gospel-driven hits as "What'd I Say" and "I Got a Woman," and his stature as an r&b artist was second to none.

And yet Charles's success masked a conservative, antisoul bias among Grammy voters. Younger artists like Sam Cooke, James Brown, Otis Redding, and Jackie Wilson, to say nothing of Motown's emerging stable of stars, went unnoticed. In 1962, the year of "Locomotion" by Little Eva, "He's a Rebel" by the Crystals, "Twistin' the Night Away" by Sam Cooke, and "Green Onions" by Booker T and the MGs, NARAS gave Charles the r&b Grammy for a *country* song, "I Can't Stop Loving You," which the academicians presumably decided belonged in the r&b field because Charles was black.

Charles didn't have a hit in 1964, and, without the cover of a Brother Ray tune, the Academy's lurking antipathy toward r&b came to the fore. Nancy Wilson, a black nightclub singer who was about as r&b as Eydie Gorme, won the Best Rhythm & Blues Recording Grammy with a record called "How Glad I Am," a preposterous choice in a year that produced "My Guy" by Mary Wells, "Dancin' in the Street" by Martha & the Vandellas, "Walk on By" by Dionne Warwick, and "Baby Love" by the Supremes (the latter two were nominated for the r&b prize).

Wilson herself was befuddled by the award, telling NARAS during Grammy ceremonies in New York that "she had recorded a pop record and was surprised—but delighted—to find it in the r&b category," according to *Billboard*.

It's possible that many NARAS voters had never heard of Martha & the Vandellas or the Supremes. According to Nesuhi Ertegun, co-founder of pioneering r&b label Atlantic Records and NARAS president in 1964–65, members of the NARAS board drew a blank when it came to such r&b stars as Percy Sledge and Otis Redding.

"It's hard to believe, but [they] had no idea who those people were," Ertegun recalls. "Or, if they did know, they would say, 'Oh, this is horrible.' "

When Ertegun lobbied to create new r&b categories—a single award covered the r&b field until 1965—he says he was rebuffed by NARAS conservatives, who argued that r&b "was not good music, and we should not glorify it by giving awards."

"They felt it would cheapen the Academy to recognize the existence of that kind of music," Ertegun explains. " 'Why pay any attention to it?' they said. 'No one will know it existed in a couple years.' "

Some NARAS officers sided with Ertegun on behalf of r&b, he notes. George Simon, executive director of the New York chapter, was "extremely helpful, whatever his own tastes." Likewise were John Hammond, Columbia's famed talent scout who discovered Billie Holiday and Aretha Franklin (as well as Bob Dylan and Bruce Springsteen), and NARAS officers George Avakian, Francis Scott, and Bob Yorke.

But the overall resistance to r&b at NARAS was so stiff that Ertegun's own colleagues at Atlantic thought he "was a jerk" for working with the organization.

"Forget about them, they'll never understand," Jerry Wexler, the Atlantic A&R chief who produced Ray Charles, Aretha Franklin, and Otis Redding, admonished. "It's a lost cause. The opposition is too strong."

Ironically, Wexler provided the spark that finally got NARAS to increase its r&b categories, blasting the organization in an open letter to NARAS president Scott after the 1965 awards for brushing off r&b with a single award while handing out five trophies to country stars.

"R&b is basic and is certainly the strongest precursor of rock 'n' roll and contemporary Top 40 music," Wexler wrote, chastising NARAS for its "weird alignment of categories."

The letter generated front-page press in the music trades and brought the r&b controversy within the Academy to a head. It was obvious that r&b was not, as some of the old-timers would have it, a passing fad. Indeed, soul was emerging as one of the hottest and truest sounds of the sixties, breaking down historic barriers in radio and the charts and enjoying unprecedented pop success. With Wexler's scolding ringing in their ears, NARAS governors created two new r&b Grammys in 1966—Best Rhythm & Blues Solo Vocal Performance, and Best Rhythm & Blues Group. A year later, the solo category was split into male and female r&b awards.

After the Nancy Wilson gaffe in 1964, red-faced NARAS voters did their homework. The 1965 field of soul nominees was hip and hardcore: "Shotgun" by Junior Walker, "Shake" by Otis Redding, "In the Midnight Hour" by Wilson Pickett, "My Girl" by the Temptations, and "Papa's Got a Brand New Bag" by James Brown.

Amazingly, "Papa's Got a Brand New Bag," the grittiest and blackest nominee—a record that provided a metaphor for the budding black-power movement—won the award. Brown's victory marked a turning point. NARAS was learning from its mistakes, and, with occasional lapses, would henceforth acquit itself admirably in the r&b field.

Despite his win, Brown was, alas, deemed too funky to appear on the Grammy TV show. Few black artists and no soul stars, with the exception of Ray Charles, had performed on "The Best on Record." Producer George Schlatter hoped to "liven up" the awards by putting Brown on the 1966 show, but was overruled.

"[Brown] was too controversial for the Academy," Schlatter recalls. "You could just get it so hip, but not James Brown."

Having taken a giant step forward in 1965, NARAS took a half step back in '66, returning to the safe haven of Ray Charles, who won Rhythm & Blues Vocal Performance and Best Rhythm & Blues Recording Grammys for "Cryin' Time," a beery country lament that didn't belong in the r&b category and probably won with help from Nashville's burgeoning bloc of votes. Charles's honky-tonk hit knocked off a great r&b field, identical in both categories—"Uptight" by Stevie Wonder, "When a Man Loves a Woman" by Percy Sledge, "It's a Man's World" by James Brown, and "Love Is a Hurtin' Thing" by Lou Rawls.

NARAS righted itself in 1967 when it discovered Aretha Franklin, the unrivaled queen of soul who would win eight consecutive r&b vocal Grammys between 1967 and 1974, the greatest winning streak in the history of the awards. Franklin kicked off her roll with "Respect," a sexual, racial, and political battle cry of a song that won Best Rhythm & Blues recording as well as Rhythm & Blues Vocal Performance.

Otis Redding, in 1968, got his first and only Grammy wins, as "Dock of the Bay," a song he recorded three days before he was killed in a plane crash in Madison, Wisconsin, claimed song and male vocal awards. Ironically, Redding didn't think of "Dock of the Bay," with its yearning tranquility, as an r&b tune, but as a kind of folk-soul offshoot that he hoped would reach beyond his r&b audience.

Perhaps the worst Grammy blind spot of the sixties involved Motown Records, the most important and popular force in black music for most of the decade. Motown brought soul into the pop mainstream with artists like the Supremes, Marvin Gaye, Stevie Wonder, Smokey Robinson, Martha & the Vandellas, Mary Wells, Tammi Terrell, and the Four Tops, none of whom won a Grammy during their sixties heyday. Holland-Dozier-Holland, the Motown songwriting team most responsible for the label's sound, produced twenty-eight Top 20 hits between 1963 and 1966, including twelve number-one songs, but likewise disappeared without a trace in the Grammy r&b void.

Indeed, Motown landed but a single Grammy during the sixties, finally getting an r&b nod in 1968 when the Temptations won for "Cloud Nine." According to Phil Jones, a Motown exec at the time, label chairman Berry Gordy was acutely aware of the Grammy snub.

"We started looking for Grammys in about 1964 with the Supremes. We never got zip. He [Gordy] was always grumbling about it, wondering, Why don't we ever win?"

After NARAS gave Nancy Wilson the r&b Grammy in 1964 for

"How Glad I Am," "blue smoke" was emanating from Motown head-quarters, Jones recalls.

"Marvin Gaye's 'Pride and Joy' couldn't get nominated, and that won. Come on . . . I think the whole black music industry must have said, 'Jesus Christ, don't they know we're here?' "

"I used to call [NARAS's New York chapter executive director] George Simon and take his head off. That poor man got more grief from me. He'd just say, 'Well, you have to get involved.' "

Motown did get involved. In 1964, Jones says he and fellow exec Barney Ales attended Grammy ceremonies in New York "to let 'em know we're alive." Later, Motown tried "to organize [the NARAS] Chicago chapter," attending meetings in Chi-town and at one point busing some thirty NARAS members into Detroit to visit label head-quarters in hopes of turning them into "Motown enthusiasts [who would] vote for us."

At the same time, Motown made sure all its eligible staffers joined NARAS—about twenty-five or thirty artists, musicians, producers, and so on—and voted for Motown acts. The campaign netted a handful of nominations, including "Heat Wave" by Martha & the Vandellas, "My Girl" by the Temptations, "Uptight" by Stevie Wonder, "I Second That Emotion" by Smokey Robinson and the Miracles, and "I Heard It Through the Grapevine" by Marvin Gaye, but the Tempta-tions' "Cloud Nine" was the only Motown song that came up a winner.

"What the fuck you gotta do to win a Grammy?" an exasperated Gaye complained to Jones in 1971 after losing once again, this time with "What's Going On," regarded by many as his greatest work. Gaye would have to wait until 1982, the year before he died, before bagging a Grammy win. Smokey Robinson got his first Grammy in 1987. Lamond Dozier, of the Holland-Dozier-Holland team, finally broke through in 1988 as cowriter, with Phil Collins, of "Two Hearts." The Supremes, Diana Ross, the Four Tops, and the Jackson Five have never won a Grammy.

It wasn't just Motown that was getting the Grammy shaft. Black artists as a whole were having a harder time than their white counter-parts in striking Grammy gold, especially in the most prestigious categories.

Indeed, none of the great r&b songs of the sixties and most of the seventies, including "Respect," "Dock of the Bay," and "Papa Was a

Rolling Stone," were deemed worthy of Song of the Year nominations, and r&b artists rarely pulled Record or Album of the Year nods.

Gloria Gaynor's "I Will Survive" and "After the Love Has Gone" by Earth, Wind & Fire finally broke the song barrier in 1979. Isaac Hayes's "Theme From Shaft," meanwhile, made him the first r&b nominee since Ray Charles in 1961 to penetrate the Record and Album of the Year enclaves. The big three Grammys were reserved for pop, mostly white pop, much of it patently inferior to its ghettoized competition.

In 1973, an ex-deejay by the name of Chuck Mann decided that NARAS wasn't giving r&b its due and organized the Soul and Blues Awards Show as an r&b alternative to the Grammys.

"The Grammys started in the fifties and haven't progressed very much," Mann told the Los Angeles Times. "[They] are still confining blacks to certain limited categories, and the whole thing needs changing. I would like to see them restructure their categories."

Mann's project quickly fizzled, perhaps partly because of Stevie Wonder's stunning crossover success at the 1973 Grammys. Wonder dominated the awards in the mid-seventies, winning fifteen trophies, including five r&b nods and three Album of the Year awards between 1973 and 1976. He was the first black artist since Ray Charles*, in 1960, to win both pop and r&b Grammys.

Other r&b stars of the seventies were Earth, Wind & Fire, *the* crossover band of the decade, and winner of six r&b Grammys between 1975 and 1982. Also Natalie Cole, daughter of 1959 "Top 40" Grammy winner Nat King Cole. Ms. Cole broke an important Grammy barrier in 1975 when she became the first black singer to win the Best New Artist award. Cole broke Aretha Franklin's hammerlock on the female r&b Grammy that same year, winning with "This Will Be (an Everlasting Love)."

Black artists enjoyed unprecedented crossover Grammy success in the early 1980s, as Michael Jackson, Tina Turner, and Lionel Richie all won major awards with hugely popular records that seemed to promise a new era of color-blind pop.

---

* Gladys Knight & the Pips also turned the trick in 1973, nabbing Pop Vocal Performance, Group honors for "Neither One of Us (Wants to Be the First to Say Goodbye)," and R&B Vocal Performance, Group kudos for "Midnight Train to Georgia."

Jackson was the all-conquering hero of the 1983 Grammys, racking up an unprecedented eight trophies, including Record and Album of the Year salutes along with Rock, Pop, and Rhythm & Blues Vocal Performance nods.

Ironically, Turner, who won the 1984 record, song, and pop vocal honors with "What's Love Got to Do With It," along with a rock vocal Grammy for "Better Be Good to Me," failed to win an r&b prize. As did Lionel Richie, whose *Can't Slow Down* took home the 1984 Album of the Year Grammy.

Prince, a funkier, more erotically explicit artist, didn't get nominated for the major Grammys, despite the enormous success of his *Purple Rain* sound track, which sold nine million records and spent twenty-four weeks atop the *Billboard* charts. The Purple One did win two r&b Grammys, however, nabbing the Best New Rhythm & Blues Song of the Year prize in 1984 for "I Feel for You" (performed by Chaka Khan), and r&b group honors (with The Revolution) in 1986 for "Kiss."

The eighties were good for veteran r&b stars. Marvin Gaye, who wanted to attack Lou Rawls physically after losing to him twice in the 1970s, won his first Grammy in 1982, receiving r&b vocal and instrumental kudos for his comeback hit, "Sexual Healing."

James Brown, meanwhile, won his first Grammy since 1965, taking r&b vocal honors in '86 with "Living in America." Aretha Franklin, enjoying her hottest record in over a decade with "Freeway of Love," took home r&b song and female vocal Grammys in '85. And Gladys Knight & the Pips scored their first Grammys since 1973—"Midnight Train to Georgia" and "Neither One of Us (Wants to Be the First to Say Goodbye)"—winning 1988 r&b group honors with "Love Overboard."

Ironically, the Grammy elders of the eighties, many of whom came of age listening to Motown and Aretha, succumbed to some of the same conservatism that afflicted the first generation of NARAS honchos. Rap, the most important r&b offshoot of the eighties and one of the industry's hottest sounds, didn't get a single r&b award until the decade was nearly over, giving way for the most part to *Big Chill* favorites from the sixties.

Like the graybeards who founded the Grammys and thought r&b was a passing fad, many NARAS voters no doubt figured rap would eventually disappear. To its credit, NARAS eventually decided the hard-core subgenre was here to stay and created a rap category within the r&b field in 1988, making sure that rappers would get at least one award. Rap's more street-oriented artists were less than impressed. Grammy voters "are tight-collar stuffed shirts at least four or five years behind the music," Chuck D of Public Enemy told *USA Today* after receiving a nomination for "Fight the Power" in 1989. Tone Lōc, nominated for "Funky Cold Medina," agreed. "I don't think [Grammy voters] have the insight into rap to know what's really happening. They only know about the mainstream. . . . I don't think they're ready for N.W.A."

In 1990, NARAS sliced the rap Grammy in two, creating rap solo and rap duo/group awards. "U Can't Touch This" by M.C. Hammer took home the solo prize, while "Back on the Block" by Ice-T, Melle Mel, Big Daddy Kane, and Kool Moe Dee won the group salute.

TWELVE

Thriller: 1983–87

The Grammys turned a major corner in 1983, the year of Michael Jackson. For once, the awards were in sync with, and even part of, an electrifying pop surge. Jackson's *Thriller*, released at the end of 1982, ignited a national case of Michaelmania that had antecedents in only the Beatles and Elvis. But where the Grammys had scorned Elvis and patronized the Beatles, they embraced Jackson, providing a climactic salute to his extraordinary pop artistry and appeal.

Jackson's *Thriller*, of course, was the pop triumph of the eighties. Propulsive, melodramatic, strangely charismatic, the album spent thirty-seven weeks on top of the *Billboard* charts, generating a record six Top 10 singles—"Billie Jean," "Beat It," "Thriller," "Wanna Be Startin' Somethin'," "Human Nature," and "P.Y.T. (Pretty Young Thing)." To date, the LP has sold an incredible forty-two million copies worldwide, some seventeen million more than *Saturday Night Fever*, the second-best-selling album of all time.

Jackson dominated the Grammys as no other artist had in the history of the awards. It wasn't just the number of trophies he won—a record-setting eight—but the way he won them. *Thriller*, of course, nabbed the Album of the Year prize, while "Beat It" won the Record of the Year award. Most impressive, however, was the fact that Jackson scored a first-ever crossover sweep, winning rock, pop, and rhythm & blues vocal awards for "Beat It," *Thriller*, and "Billie Jean," respectively. In addition, "Billie Jean" was named Best New Rhythm & Blues Song, and Jackson and coproducer Quincy Jones drew Producer of the Year kudos. Finally, Jackson nabbed Best Recording for Children honors for his narration of *E.T. The Extra-Terrestrial*.

"This is the award I'm most proud of," the whispery-voiced singer told the Shrine Auditorium crowd. "It's not just for kids, it's for everybody."

The only artist to beat Jackson was Sting, whose artfully ambiguous "Every Breath You Take" knocked off "Billie Jean" and "Beat It" for Song of the Year honors. In a normal year, Sting would have been the big Grammy star. The songwriter-lead singer for the Police won four awards, including Rock and Pop Vocal Performance by a Group, for "Every Breath."

Jackson dominated even the commercial breaks of the '83 Grammys, starring (for a $6 million endorsement fee) in a series of hugely hyped Pepsi spots that premiered during the three-hour telecast. Interest in the ads was morbidly heightened by the fact that Jackson had suffered second- and third-degree burns on his scalp when a special-effects bomb set his pomaded hair on fire during the filming of the blurbs. Both Pepsi and the Grammys enjoyed through-the-roof ratings.

Indeed, when NARAS and CBS sat down to negotiate a new contract after the 1983 show, the Academy and Cossette were in the driver's seat. Jackson "gave us a very strong hand," recalls 1984–85 NARAS president Mike Melvoin. "After Michael Jackson, we realized that we were, for the moment, and potentially, the Super Bowl of music." Confident that NBC would be happy to take the show if CBS balked, NARAS asked for—and got—a robust licensing-fee hike from CBS, which hastened to sign a new seven-year Grammy deal.*

While Jackson's transcendent success did much to redeem Grammy credibility after the Christopher Cross and Toto debacles, NARAS was moving internally to avoid similar pratfalls in the future. In 1984, Melvoin launched a new drive to bring younger members into the

---

* The value of the Grammys as prime-time network product continued to soar during the eighties and into the nineties. According to trade reports, CBS agreed to pay an eye-popping $60 million in 1992 for the right to carry the Grammys through 1997.

fold. Melvoin, a respected jazz composer and keyboardist, was the first NARAS president since Nesuhi Ertegun in 1965 to have solid ties to and proven sympathies with rock 'n' roll, having played on Lennon's "Imagine," the Beach Boys' "Good Vibrations," and the Jackson Five's "ABC." For good measure, Melvoin's daughter Wendy was lead guitarist in Prince's group, the Revolution.

By the end of Melvoin's term in '85, NARAS membership was up 20 percent, and, for the first time in Academy history, a plurality of the NARAS electorate said rock was the music they identified with the most. According to NARAS research, 34.2 percent of its members were rock-oriented, 33.9 were primarily into pop, while 22.9 listed jazz, 15.4 country, and 15.3 r&b as their favorite genre.*

The new demographics had an immediate impact in 1984. Prince, Bruce Springsteen, and Tina Turner, the year's most acclaimed and popular stars, all won Grammys, and Turner and Prince performed on the show. Once again, the Grammys provided an emotional capper for one of the year's biggest stories—the stirring comeback of Tina Turner, whose cynical but lilting "What's Love Got to Do With It" won Song and Record of the Year awards.

Turner was the darling of the '84 Grammys, also winning pop female vocal honors for "What's Love Got to Do With It" along with the rock vocal prize for "Better Be Good to Me." The Grammy tribute was personal as well as artistic, a heartfelt recognition of the tough road Turner had traveled—walking away from an abusive marriage to Ike Turner in 1976, then working six nights a week out of the limelight for years before returning to the top. "I've been waiting so long for this," Turner told the Grammy crowd, which cheered her with standing ovations that seemed to salute her character as well as her career.

Springsteen, whose *Born in the U.S.A.* album and tour were both megahits, won his first Grammy in 1984, nabbing Rock Vocal Performance, Male honors for "Dancing in the Dark." *Born in the U.S.A.* was nominated in both Record and Album of the Year categories, but lost to Turner and Lionel Richie (*Can't Slow Down*), respectively.

Though he won only one award, Springsteen was, at the time, the biggest star in the world, and everyone, *everyone*, wanted to shake

* Totals exceed 100 percent because some NARAS members listed more than one area of "prime interest."

his hand—even ousted Grammy host Andy Williams, who begged longtime pal and Grammy producer Pierre Cossette to arrange a meeting with The Boss after the '84 show.

The moment the last award was announced, Cossette ran to Springsteen and, under the pretext of avoiding the mob, steered him and his mom through the Shrine Auditorium catacombs into an officer where Williams was waiting. Cossette was nervous that Springsteen would see through the setup, but, as it turned out, he had nothing to fear.

"Springsteen walks in and says, '*Andy!* Jesus Christ, man,' and he hugs him and tells him that the first song he performed in public was 'Moon River,' " Cossette recalls.

"Mrs. Springsteen was even more impressed. 'Oh God, Andy Williams!' she swooned."

Prince, pop's purple provocateur, did not have a tête-à-tête with Andy Williams, but he did win three Grammys during the '84 awards—rock vocal performance and original score kudos for his hugely successful *Purple Rain* album, and a best rhythm & blues song nod for "I Feel for You," which was recorded by Chaka Khan.

Strangely, Prince's biggest hit, "When Doves Cry," didn't draw a single nod, a fact that pained Melvoin and other contemporary-minded members of NARAS. "We bit the big one when 'When Doves Cry' didn't get a Record of the Year nomination," Melvoin recalls. "I was dumbfounded, because 'When Doves Cry' is a Swiss watch of a record—well made in every regard."

The snub almost kept a miffed Prince from performing on the Grammy show, but at the last minute, partly as a favor to Melvoin's daughter Wendy, partly as a calculated career move, he changed his mind. The result was a sizzling, eight-and-a-half-minute jam, the hottest in the history of the Grammy telecast, which ended with Prince leading the Revolution down the center aisle and through the Shrine Auditorium crowd.

The *Los Angeles Times*'s Robert Hilburn enthused after the show, "1984 may go down as the year in which rock 'n' roll was finally welcomed to the Grammy club." He noted that Prince, Springsteen, and Best New Artist winner Cyndi Lauper "were almost constant subjects of attention during the three-hour-plus program."

It was also the year NARAS presented rock icon Chuck Berry with his first Grammy, a Lifetime Achievement Award. The tribute showed how far NARAS had come since the early days when Academy founders had scoffed at the likes of Berry, Elvis, and other pioneering rock stars. Thirty years after he first hit the charts with "Maybelline," Berry was hailed as "a composer and performer whose talents inspired the elevation of rock 'n' roll to one of music's major art forms."

"It's about time they gave me something; I do deserve something," Berry told a reporter backstage during the show, before gushing: "Man, I wouldn't give this up for anything. . . . Ain't it something!"

Despite the changes, the Grammy sensibility was still very much mainstream. Springsteen and Prince may have garnered Album of the Year nominations, but crossover smoothie Lionel Richie won the award with *Can't Slow Down*. A year later, Phil Collins, another pop softie, won the Album of the Year title, along with male pop vocal honors, for his *No Jacket Required* LP.

And Grammy voters were still very much capable of completely humiliating themselves, which they did by nominating actress-singer wannabe Pia Zadora for, of all things, the 1984 female rock vocal prize. Zadora's record, "Rock It Out," was in the same category as Tina Turner's "Better Be Good to Me."

"When it showed up in the nominations, the TV committee, which met that day, looked at each other in utter shock and disbelief," Melvoin recalls. "We didn't know whether to laugh or cry."

Zadora got the nomination, Melvoin says, because there were so few entries in the female rock category that virtually every eligible record was nominated.

"Gentlemen, if we don't take membership outreach seriously," Melvoin warned, "we will be stabbed in the heart, just like this, every time."

The year 1985 was the year of the pop charity. "We Are the World," a superstar anthem written by Michael Jackson and Lionel Richie and recorded by a chorus of virtually every important pop star, raised over $50 million for famine-wracked Africa and triggered a rash of similar, if less spectacularly successful, projects.

"We Are the World" was recorded on January 28, the night of the American Music Awards, with artists taking a limo ride across town from the AMAs to A&M Studio in Hollywood to cut the song. The AMAs, Grammys' glitzy competitor, gained considerable legitimacy and prestige from its association with the extraordinary project. The Grammys angled for a more spectacular tie-in, nearly arranging to premiere "We Are the World" on the February 26, 1985, show, but a final mix wasn't ready in time.

A year later, Grammy voters, who had given George Harrison's *Concert for Bangla Desh* the Album of the Year Grammy in 1972, were even more supportive of "We Are the World" (on which NARAS prez Melvoin played synthesizer); the disc won song, record, pop group vocal, and video honors.

Producer Quincy Jones, accepting the Record of the Year salute with Jackson and Richie, thanked "the generation that changed 'I, Me, My' to 'We, You, Us.' " Jackson, sounding slightly bizarre, thanked God "for picking Lionel and myself to write 'We Are the World.' "

In 1986 NARAS continued to make amends for past sins, honoring the Rolling Stones, the group that early NARAS members despised above all others, with a Lifetime Achievement Award. To this day, the Stones have never won a Grammy, despite the fact that they "poured the foundation for modern pop and rock . . . and lyrically awakened the senses and consciousness of America and the world," in the words of NARAS, whose consciousness, at last, was also awakened.

It didn't take Grammy voters nearly so long to sing the praises of U2, the broodingly majestic rock band from Ireland that shot to supergroup status in 1987 with *The Joshua Tree*. The record, which sold over five million copies, won Album of the Year and Rock performance by a Group Grammys. U2 smuggled a quart of beer into Radio City Music Hall and guzzled throughout the show, but turned serious when accepting the awards. "We set out to make soul music, which is not about being black or white, or the type of instruments you play," lead singer Bono explained. "It's a decision to reveal or conceal."

Just to show how quickly the worm can turn, Michael Jackson made Grammy headlines once again—this time as the biggest *loser* of the '87 awards. *Bad*, Jackson's first album since *Thriller*, drew four nominations, but lost in every category. Making matters worse, Jackson, expecting a big night, attended the show and delivered an over-the-top rendition of his hit "Man in the Mirror." Throughout the night cameras zoomed in on the singer, seemingly on the verge of tears, as he lost award after award.

The experience was so unpleasant that, a year later, Jackson reportedly huddled in his limo outside the Shrines' back door, unwilling to enter unless he won Record of the Year honors for "Man in the Mirror." He lost, this time to Bobby McFerrin and "Don't Worry, Be Happy."

NARAS, if not Jackson, seemed to take McFerrin's advice to heart. Already one could sense that the sparkle and zip of recent Grammy shows, the energy that had started building with Jackson's *Thriller*, were petering out. Eternally centrist, the Grammys were drifting into a new realm of predictability and blandness—a kind of yuppie middle of the road. A new wave of industry pros, baby-boomer engineers, singers, musicians, lyricists, etc., who had cut their teeth on sixties pop and rock and roll, were joining the Academy, melding with the old regime. And the names were getting hipper: Steve Winwood, Linda Ronstadt, Paul Simon—*especially* Paul Simon. But the armchair sensibility, the reverence above all for craft and polish and platinum records, were the same.

Already the new demographics were producing curious, if inevitable, results. Paul Simon's *Graceland* may have been a worthy choice for the Album of the Year Grammy in 1986, but only the peculiar mix of Grammy voters could have sustained the tribute for an extra year, naming the "Graceland" single Record of the Year in 1987. Nothing against the single, but it was practically an oldie by the time of the awards, and was only eligible in 1987 on a technicality.* It was not a good sign.

Indeed, an old Grammy ghost provided the highlight of the 1987 show. Little Richard, yet another seminal rocker who never got a Grammy nod, stepped up the to the podium with postpunk crooner David Johansen to announce the winner of the Best New Artist award.

Suddenly, one of the true wildmen of rock confronted the Grammys on national TV for snubbing him throughout this career. "You'all never gave ME nothing'," Richard scolded, as a startled Johansen helplessly looked on. "And I am the *architect* of rock 'n' roll. I am the *originator*."

The tirade was playful, but with a sharp and unpredictable edge. There was no way of telling where Richard's rant was going, whether Richard himself knew, and for a long half minute, the global Grammy

---

* The *Graceland* album was released during the 1986 Grammy eligibility year, but the "Graceland" single, despite heavy radio play, wasn't released until 1987.

telecast careened in his hands. "And the winner is . . . STILL ME!" Richard screamed, enjoying himself immensely as Cossette, NARAS, and CBS executives squirmed.

Finally, Richard reined himself in and opened the envelope. Jody Watley was the winner—if anyone still cared.

THIRTEEN

Don't Worry, Be Happy: 1988–Present

NARAS made a couple of long-overdue moves after the 1987 awards, creating two new categories, one for heavy metal-hard rock, another for rap. Though rap had long been on the cutting edge of r&b and metal accounted for a hefty piece of the rock 'n' roll pie, not a single artist from either genre had ever won a Grammy award.

Both categories produced immediate controversies. NARAS picked a credible crop of heavy-metal nominees, including Metallica and Jane's Addiction, two of the year's biggest acts. But NARAS also nominated Jethro Tull, a rock dinosaur—the group's lead instrument was a flute!—that only NARAS squares could have placed in the contemporary hard rock-metal scene. Naturally, they gave Tull the award, drawing boos from the Shrine Auditorium crowd that could be heard nationwide.

"Our voting membership will be light in [this] category for the first few years," a sheepish-sounding NARAS president Mike Greene explained to reporters backstage. "Our membership is growing . . . but it has a ways to go."

Hoping to avoid future embarrassments, the Grammy trustees created separate categories for hard rock and heavy metal after the '88 show. In 1989, Metallica ("One") became the first bona fide metal act to win an award.

Meanwhile, a number of rappers, including nominees L.L. Cool J and D.J. Jazzy Jeff & The Fresh Prince, called a rap boycott of the '88 Grammys because the rap award was not set for presentation on the telecast.

"You go to school for twelve years, they give you your diploma, and they deny you that walk down the aisle," Fresh Prince protested during a press conference the day of the show. The Prince and Jazzy Jeff wound up winning the award with their loopy "Parents Just Don't Understand."

U2's Grammy wins in 1987 convinced some that NARAS had finally turned over a new leaf, put its stodgy, antirock past behind it. The *Los Angeles Times*'s Robert Hilburn, who had taken NARAS to task regularly for fifteen years, hailed the "remarkable transformation" of the awards. *Billboard* columnist Paul Grein, writing in *Pulse* magazine, went even further, describing the Grammys as "positively . . . hip."

Celebrations of hipness, alas, proved premature. Cutting-edge folkie Tracy Chapman drew six nominations and was expected to dominate the 1988 awards. But the singer, who looked like a sharecropper's daughter and sang stark tunes about poverty and depression, was too radical for the Grammy mainstream, which rejected her for the three biggest awards—Record, Song, and Album of the Year. Chapman did manage to win Best New Artist, Contemporary Folk Recording, and Pop Vocal Performance, Female honors, the latter for her grim, poignant hit, "Fast Car."

More palatable to Grammy taste was vocal acrobat Bobby McFerrin, whose quasi-novelty, mood elevator song "Don't Worry, Be Happy" provided a nifty alternative to Chapman's work. The tune, used by George Bush in his 1988 presidential campaign, copped Record and Song of the Year Grammys. "I think happiness, as opposed to worrying, is a very strong issue," a testy McFerrin told reporters backstage at the Shrine when asked to compare his music to Chapman's.

NARAS leaders, if not voters, did their best to give the '88 Grammys an irreverent, pro-rock edge. Performers on the telecast included such out-of-the-mainstream artists as Sinead O'Connor, who showcased a fresh tattoo on her shaved skull, and heavy-metal band Metallica, a group that must have had NARAS elders from the early days gaping at their TV screens.

"That song, of course, was written by Steve Allen," quipped host Billy Crystal, after Metallica's performance, tweaking the old-timers who used to guffaw at Allen's rock put-downs when *he* hosted the Grammys in the early sixties.

How things had changed. In his televised speech, NARAS president Mike Greene went so far as to pay tribute to heavy metal as "the art form that is keeping the rebellious essence of rock 'n' roll alive."

Unfortunately, Grammy's "schizophrenic struggle between hip and stodgy sensibilities," as *USA Today* put it, continued in 1989. To the delight of all, Bonnie Raitt emerged as the surprise star of the show, winning four awards, including Album of the Year honors for her *Nick of Time* LP.

Raitt's wins gave the '89 Grammys a deserved glow. Here was an artist whose entire career had been marked by loyalty—through considerable thick and thin—to her bluesy muse, who had never sold out, even after Warner Bros. Records dropped her in 1986 because she wasn't selling millions of albums. Raitt's Grammy grand slam, like Tina Turner's triple win in 1984, showcased the awards at their best, as a kind of court of last recourse, where artistic and even personal justice are occasionally served.

"This means so much for the kind of music that we do," Raitt said in accepting the prize for best album. "It means that those of us who do rhythm and blues are going to get a chance again."

Raitt's emotionally satisfying wins masked the fact that conservatives and hit-oriented members of the Academy were once again having their way. Maintaining a long tradition of reverence for schlock ballads, Grammy voters picked Bette Midler's "Wind Beneath My Wings" as both Song *and* Record of the Year. Midler herself could hardly believe that she had won the latter award.

"I am stunned, flabbergasted," she gasped, no doubt echoing the more harshly rendered reactions of many others.

Other dubious choices included Michael Bolton, whose soaring, Ray Charles-cloned middle-of-the-road ballad, "How Am I Supposed to Live Without You," beat Prince and Roy Orbison for the Pop Vocal Performance, Male prize.

And then, of course, there was Milli Vanilli, the ultimate Grammy fiasco. No one knew at the time that the West German dance duo were musical fakes, literally—that they had lip-synced their way through every note of *Girl You Know It's True*, their debut album that sold over seven million copies.

What was obvious, however, despite the gaudy record sales, was that this act personified all the worst tendencies of post-MTV pop. Contrived, image-driven, marketing-born-and-bred, anyone could see that Rob Pilatus and Fab Morvan had the most tenuous claim on musical talent, regardless of whether or not they actually sang their songs.

As a smash act, the duo were legitimate winners and performers on Dick Clark's American Music Awards, which honor the most *popular* artists and records of the year. But they had no business at all being on the Grammys, which are supposed to honor excellence, and only excellence, in music. It didn't take a Vladimir Horowitz to know that musical excellence was not what Milli Vanilli was all about.

Indeed, only weeks before the Grammy show, *Rolling Stone* magazine voted Milli Vanilli Worst Band of the Year. Undaunted, NARAS invited the duo to perform live on the telecast, which they did, lip-syncing their hit, and Grammy voters rewarded them with the coveted, if wildly miscast, Best New Artist of the Year trophy.

For once, Grammy members would pay, and pay dearly, for their voting sins. In November, just as ballots for the 1990 Grammys were being sent out, the Milli Vanilli scandal broke. Naturally, every news account referred to Rob and Fab as the "Grammy-winning pair."

Unfazed, and acknowledging no error on the part of the Academy, NARAS president Mike Greene adopted a righteously aggrieved tone in responding to the hoax.

"The people who serve on the awards and nominations committee do not take very kindly to being shucked and jived about something like this," he told the *Los Angeles Times*.

One week later, the NARAS board, handling the crisis by emergency conference call, voted to rescind Milli Vanilli's Grammy, the first time the Academy had ever taken back an award.

"I hope this action signals loudly and clearly to producers, record companies, and packagers that the Academy cares deeply about this issue," Greene intoned, wagging his finger rhetorically at those who had presumably duped NARAS into giving Milli Vanilli its Grammy and having the duo lip-sync on the Grammy show.

"I hope this revocation will make the industry think long and hard before anyone ever tries to pull something like this again."

No sooner did the Milli Vanilli crisis die down than a new one flared. If the lip-syncing poseurs were the first act ever to forfeit a Grammy, Sinead O'Connor was the first artist to reject one.

The rejection notice came in the form of a scathing letter sent to Greene in January 1991, blasting the Grammys for their "false and materialistic values." O'Connor, whose acclaimed *I Do Not Want What I Have Not Got* LP had just received four 1991 Grammy nominations, said she would neither perform on the Grammy show nor accept any awards.

"They [the Grammys] acknowledge mostly the commercial side of art," she wrote. "They respect mostly commercial gain, since that is the main reason for their existence."

Later, just days before the Grammy show, and despite widespread hostility to her moralistic stand, O'Connor slammed the Grammys again, sounding almost repulsed by the award.

"I wouldn't want it near me," she told late-night host Arsenio Hall. "As far as I'm concerned, it represents everything I despise about the music industry."

Ouch.

O'Connor's attack did not "shake the conscience of the industry," as she had hoped. Nor did it seriously afflict the Grammys. Still, it had to hurt, hitting NARAS in an area that had always been a bit inflated—its organizational ego, its idealized sense of itself.

After all, the Grammys were supposedly founded on a commitment to artistic rather than commercial values. Remember Stan Freberg's Grammy Credo? "Sales and mass popularity are the yardsticks of the record business," it declared. "They are not the yardsticks of the Academy."

And yet, here was a widely admired performer, one whose credibility lay in her artistry, not her record sales, accusing the Grammys of being, in effect, a corrupt and bankrupt awards show.

Mike Greene tried to defuse O'Connor's attack with a respectful, if patronizing, response. "We applaud that Sinead feels so strongly about these issues and believe that her convictions only add to the seriousness of her work. . . .

"But I'm afraid that Sinead may not be properly informed about the difference between the overtly commercial aspects of popularity contests as opposed to the Grammys, which are voted on by the creative community."

The only thing O'Connor needed to be "informed about" in order to feel justified in her remarks was the 1991 Grammy nominees. Megahits dominated the major categories—inevitable perhaps, given their vast exposure, but a sign nonetheless of Grammy values. Four of the five Album of the Year nominees—*Please Don't Hurt 'Em Hammer* by M.C. Hammer, . . . *But Seriously* by Phil Collins, and eponymous debut albums by Mariah Carey and Wilson Phillips— sold more than three million records. The fifth, *Back on the Block* by Quincy Jones, sold over two million.

Despite her remarks, O'Connor won a Grammy, for Best Alternative Music Performance.

"If they send it to her, she'll send it back," the singer's publicist told reporters backstage after the award was announced.

By the time the actual 1991 telecast rolled around, the awards seemed somewhat anticlimactic. Or maybe just dull. Grammy favorite Quincy Jones was the big winner, collecting a ridiculous six awards, the second-largest haul in Grammy history, for his slick compendium of black styles and sound, *Back on the Block*.

Ridiculous because *Back on the Block* had no business being regaled with such lavish praise. Maybe one Grammy, or two, but Album of the Year, plus five other trophies? Grammy voters were indulging themselves, embracing an old standby in a year of lackluster nominees.

Jones, of course, is in many ways the consummate Grammy artist, a studio maestro with an equal-opportunity ear, savvy and slick with everything from jazz to r&b to pop. Clearly, despite all the infusions of new blood and the recruitment of younger members, the old guard in NARAS, the studio-oriented core of engineers, producers, and industry pros, was still very strong. The Grammys have always been, and probably always will be, their awards.

With his wins, Jones passed Henry Mancini as the most honored nonclassical artist in Grammy lore, with twenty-five statuettes. Consider it for a moment: Quincy Jones, a low-profile, background industry figure, renowned more for his melting-pot, middle-of-the-road production skills than for anything else, excellent in his own limited arena but mediocre when held up against the musical giants of the last thirty-three years—this is the man Grammy voters have chosen to reward again and again, beginning all the way back in 1963, above all others? This, to go by his sheer number of awards, is the transcendent musical genius of our time?

Quincy Jones. Twenty-five Grammys. Number one in the Grammy pantheon. That one fact condenses the whole Grammy story, the warp and weirdness and, to some extent, the curious integrity and honesty of the awards. Sinead O'Connor only got it half right. Sure, record sales make a difference with the seven thousand-plus Grammy voters, most of whom make their living in a hit-oriented business that measures talent in platinum and gold. But for every Milli Vanilli that exposes the mercenary side of Grammy taste, there's a Quincy Jones or Bobby McFerrin to expose the quirkier, sincerely conservative side, the side that appreciates and respects and understands musical craft more than content.

Of course, that's not the whole picture. The Grammys have honored many great artists and records through the years. NARAS is a pluralistic society, with numerous factions and a consensus that shifts from year to year, depending on the crop of records. A crossover hit from any "respectable" part of the musical universe (rap, hard rock, heavy metal, etc. are the underclass) can win a Grammy by picking up votes outside its natural support group.

Which is how hipper, baby-boom favorites like U2 or Bonnie Raitt won their awards.

But the strongest, most deeply rooted and influential faction, the one that limits the range of Grammy taste and ghettoizes anything outside the mainstream, is that represented by the Quincy Jones vote. It used to be the Henry Mancini vote.

Grammy founders should be proud. The old-fashioned sense of pop excellence they sought to foster through the awards, as a bulwark against rock 'n' roll, has survived. So has rock, of course. NARAS failed to roll back music history. But within its own universe, and according to its own terms, it has maintained its standard of "excellence," its mission of "quality control," for better, and, as we have seen, for worse.

A peculiar Grammy sideshow in recent years has been the practice—perhaps the strategy—of giving Lifetime Achievement Grammys (more properly called Lifetime Grievance Grammys) to artists whose records and careers Grammy voters have largely or completely ignored.

The Rolling Stones, Chuck Berry, Jimi Hendrix, James Brown, Paul McCartney, John Lennon, Motown Records founder Berry Gordy (whose legendary label won just one Grammy during the entire sixties) . . . and Bob Dylan.

Dylan's grievance against the Grammys, as previously discussed, is particularly acute. *The Freewheelin' Bob Dylan*; *The Times They Are A-Changin'*; *Another Side of Bob Dylan*; *Bringing It All Back Home*; *Highway 61 Revisited*; *Blonde on Blonde*; *John Wesley Harding*; *Nashville Skyline*; *Self Portrait*; *New Morning*; *Blood on the Tracks*; *Desire*—none of these albums, nor any singles from these albums, have won a Grammy.

The sudden race to honor Dylan, McCartney, Lennon, et al. stems not just from a desire to make amends for past crimes or to gain belated credibility with those artists' fans. Always under the gun to deliver high ratings, the Lifetime Achievement Award enables NARAS to invite the most legendary names in pop to perform on the show.

Indeed, NARAS' lust for ratings has produced some grotesque, inexcusable moments—asking Richard Gere, for example, a hot name on the strength of the movie *Pretty Woman*, to handle the 1991 Lennon tribute, which he delivered without sincerity, understanding, or heart.

Jack Nicholson, on the other hand, was an inspired choice to introduce and raise a toast to Bob Dylan, summing him up as an artist who "has been, and still is, a disturber of the peace"—which is, of course, exactly why Grammy voters had shunned him throughout his career.

Dylan, letting bygones be bygones, took the stage and delivered a disturb-the-peace, withering rendition of "Masters of War," the only meaningful reference during the entire three-hour Grammy extravaganza to the fact that a war in the Persian Gulf was in fact being waged while Grammys were being handed out.

He then turned to the Shrine Auditorium crowd, packed with thousands of tuxedo-clad members of the Academy, and offered this elliptical comment: "It's possible to be so defiled in this world that even your mother and father won't know you. But God will always believe in your own ability to mend your own ways."

FOURTEEN

A Star Is Born

All stars are not created equal, especially in the universe of the Grammys. More than 1,200 artists and groups won a Grammy between 1958 and 1991, but only 150 have won more than three awards. The twenty-six profiles that follow offer a cross section of the biggest winners, Grammy perennials like Barbra Streisand, Aretha Franklin, and Michael Jackson, as well as some of the most interesting one-hit wonders, Grammy flash in the pans such as Vaughn Meader, Cortelia Clark, and Domenico Modugno.

Ella Fitzgerald

Billie Holiday broke your heart and Sarah Vaughan astonished your ears, but Ella Fitzgerald won all the awards. Especially Grammys. From 1958, the year the Grammys began, through the early sixties, Ella was the unrivaled queen of the Grammy ball, crowned time and again as the female and jazz vocalist of the year over the likes of Vaughan, Peggy Lee, Lena Horne, and other aspirants to the throne.

Second only to Henry Mancini as a Grammy winner in the early years, Fitzgerald has to date amassed thirteen trophies, more than any other nonclassical female recording artist except Aretha Franklin, who now has fifteen.

Ella's popularity has hardly been undeserved. Blessed with perfect pitch and exact diction, a dizzying talent for improvisation, and a cool, masterful sense of time, she was and remains a consummate jazz-pop singer. And yet, there has always been something a bit safe about Ella, something too respectable, the perfect classy artist for the cultivated, middle-brow Grammy crowd. For years, Fitzgerald symbolized the virtues and the limitations of the Grammys, and her monopoly of the female vocal awards galled many outside NARAS.

Though she began her career in the late thirties as a big band singer with Chick Webb's band and was not averse to scatting in bop clubs with the likes of Dizzy Gillespie as swing began to fade, Fitzgerald was angling for a broader, more durable base by the time the Grammys were launched in 1958. Guided by impresario Norman Granz, she starred in Granz's uptown-oriented "Jazz at the Philharmonic" concerts, sang in symphonic contexts, and embarked on a series of ambitious albums that would establish her as the interpreter par excellence of the great American book of songs, as composed by the likes of Jerome Kern, Cole Porter, and Irving Berlin.

Grammy voters were quick to reward her. Ella won two Grammys in 1958, nabbing the first Vocal Performance, Female award for her *Ella Fitzgerald Sings the Irving Berlin Song Book* and the Jazz Performance, Individual salute with her *Duke Ellington Song Book*.

Fitzgerald repeated the following year, this time winning the female vocal Grammy for "But Not for Me" and the jazz trophy for *Ella Swings Lightly*. The ritual continued in 1960 with her "Mack the Knife" single and *Mack the Knife/Ella in Berlin* LP, both winning major awards.*

One singer who surely grew weary of Ella's Grammy monopoly was Peggy Lee, a perennial Grammy also-ran who was nominated against Fitzgerald five times between 1958 and 1962—with "Fever," "Alright, Okay, You Win," "I'm Gonna Go Fishing," *Latin à la Lee*,

---

* In 1960, NARAS created separate male and female vocal categories for both albums and single tracks, i.e., Best Male Vocal/Album, Best Male Vocal/Single, etc. The following year the Academy cut back to one male and one female vocal category, in which both albums and singles were eligible to compete. And so it has remained. Albums and singles compete against each other in all the vocal categories; pop, country, r&b, rock, jazz, and general.

and "I'm a Woman"—and lost every time. (The tradition continued some thirty years later, when Ella's *All That Jazz* knocked off Lee's *The Peggy Lee Songbook—There'll Be Another Spring* for the 1990 jazz vocal prize.)

It took Judy Garland, armed with the most acclaimed record of her career, *Live at Carnegie Hall*, to break the Fitzgerald spell at last, beating Ella's recording of "Mr. Paganini" for the Best Vocal Performance, Female prize of 1961.

But Fitzgerald returned in 1962, winning back the award with *Ella Swings Brightly*, before fading in the mid-sixties as a singer by the name of Barbra Streisand came to the Grammy fore.

With the disappearance of jazz vocal categories in 1961, and the whittling of jazz categories overall to just two in 1967, Fitzgerald no longer had a fair Grammy field in which to compete. But when NARAS reinstituted a Jazz Vocal Performance award in 1976, Ella was there to reclaim her crown, winning with *Fitzgerald & Pass . . . Again*.

She began a new streak in 1979 when she won for *Fine and Mellow*, then repeated the next year with *A Perfect Match/Ella & Basie*, and again in 1981 with *Digital III at Montreux*. Her most recent awards came in 1983 for *The Best Is Yet to Come* and in 1990 for *All That Jazz*.

Topping it all off, Ms. Grammy received a Lifetime Achievement Grammy in 1967 (the fourth person, after Bing Crosby, Frank Sinatra, and Duke Ellington, to get the award) for her "superb musicianship" and "unfailing integrity." Her 1938 recording of "A-Tisket A-Tasket" with Chick Webb & his Orchestra was named to the Grammy Hall of Fame in 1986.

Domenico Modugno

Critics still make fun of NARAS for giving its first Record and Song of the Year Grammys to romantic Italian crooner Domenico Modugno for his 1958 hit "Nel Blu Dipinto di Blu," better known as "Volare."

An open-hearted, sentimental ballad that has inspired lounge lizards—and lounge lizard parodies—around the world, "Volare" seems more embarrassing in retrospect than it did at the time. In the stale waters of late fifties middle-of-the-road pop, the song, with its strange title (literal translation: "The Blue Painted in Blue") and uninhibited Italian flavor and feel, had a quasi-exotic appeal. Modugno's recording exploded across the United States, selling two and a half million discs, more than any other record that year.

Cover versions were released by everyone from Dean Martin and Nelson Riddle to the McGuire Sisters and Jesse Belvin. At one point, *Billboard* reviewed seven different versions of the song in the same issue, while announcing the imminent release of three more. Combined sales of "Nel Blu Dipinto di Blu" in 1958 alone passed the eight million mark.

Grammy voters were caught up in the phenomenal popularity, choosing "Volare" over two classic recordings for both Record and Song of the Year—Peggy Lee's "Fever" and Frank Sinatra's "Witchcraft." The fact that "Volare" had been recorded by artists from every major label and that label-oriented members of NARAS could therefore feel they were voting for "their" song doubtless contributed to its success.

Modugno, "a descendent of Italian gypsy royalty," according to the liner notes of the *Volare* LP, was born on January 9, 1928, in Polignana à Mare, Italy. A high-school dropout, he went to Rome with a guitar, five dollars in his pocket, and the desire to become a film star. After a stint in the military, Modugno studied acting (with Sophia Loren), and eventually landed a part as a balladeer in *Il Mantello Rosso* (*The Red Cloak*). His acting was okay, but his singing was better, and Modugno was quickly signed to perform on a radio series hosted by Italian comic Walter Chiari.

"Nel Blu Dipinto di Blu (Volare)," inspired by a painting on the back of a cigarette pack, describes a dream of a man painting his hands blue and singing as he flies through "the blue painted in blue" (*volare* means "to fly"). Written by Modugno and his friend Franco Migliacci (who had the dream), "Nel Blu" won Italy's San Remo song festival in 1958, sold nearly a million copies in Italy, and rocketed Modugno on a career that would establish him as "the music genius of Italy," with sales of twenty million records by 1965.

"Although he scored a second, smaller U.S. hit with "Ciao Ciao Bambina" in 1959 and continued to sell millions of records in Italy and Europe, Modugno's first Grammy triumphs were his last. He never won another award or received another nomination.

"Nel Blu Dipinto di Blu," however, has proven to be a song "with legs," as they say in the movie biz. After the first deluge of covers died down, Bobby Rydell recorded what proved to be the most popular English version of the song, taking it to number four on the *Billboard* charts in 1960. Al Martino scored a hit with "Volare" in 1975. And in 1988, thirty years after Modugno's Grammys, the song once again caught the Academy's ear, with Henry Mancini drawing a Best Instrumental Arrangement Accompanying Vocals nomination for his work on a Luciano Pavarotti recording of the tune.

Henry Mancini

By the mid-sixties, Henry Mancini owned so many Grammys that when "Best on Record" producer George Schlatter needed trophies to dress the set of the Grammy TV show, he sent a truck to Mancini's house and hauled away the composer's supply. Many of the awards passed out on the early Grammy shows belonged to Mancini.

The actual awards had been distributed months earlier, at Grammy ceremonies in New York, Los Angeles, and other Grammy chapter cities. "The Best on Record" was an after-the-fact Grammy show, in which Mancini's trophies were handed out as props.

" 'You'll get 'em back, don't worry about it,' George would tell me," a chuckling Mancini recalls. "I guess I'm lucky I have them now."

Mancini, one of Hollywood's most polished, alluring composers, has no fewer than twenty trophies lined up in a "Grammy shrine" in his Encino, California, home. Only one other nonclassical artist has won more, Quincy Jones, who finally passed Mancini in 1990 and now has twenty-five.

Mancini racked up the bulk of his collection some twenty-five to thirty years ago. He won the first Album of the Year Grammy in 1958 with *Music From Peter Gunn* and dominated the awards for the next six years with songs like "Charade," "Moon River," "The Pink Panther," and "Days of Wine and Roses." By 1964 he had amassed forty-four nominations and seventeen awards.

A more unlikely pop kingpin would be hard to imagine. Balding, slightly stooped, and shy, Mancini was barely known outside film-composing circles when his throbbing, jazzy "Peter Gunn" theme emerged as one of the surprise hits of 1958. The record sold over a million copies and became the first TV theme and jazz-based LP to top the charts.

"Peter Gunn," which netted five nominations (including a treatment by Ray Anthony that drew a Best Performance by a Dance Band bid), also won the first Grammy arrangement award. The theme has proven to be a Grammy favorite through the years. Mancini's encore *More Music From Peter Gunn* picked up six Grammy nominations in 1959, a synthesizer version of "Gunn" by Emerson, Lake & Palmer won a Rock Instrumental nomination in 1981, and a New Wave treatment by Art of Noise (featuring Duane Eddy) won the Rock Instrumental award in 1987.

"Peter Gunn" kicked off a phenomenal Grammy roll for Mancini. In 1960 he won two awards (Best Arrangement and Best Performance by an Orchestra) for "Mr. Lucky," another TV detective theme, as well as a Best Jazz Performance, Large Group trophy for his *Blues and the Beat* LP. The next year brought a whopping five awards, including Record and Song of the Year honors for "Moon River," which Mancini composed in a single octave so that Audry Hepburn could sing the tune in *Breakfast at Tiffany's*. The *Breakfast* score won the Sound Track of the Year Grammy.

Mancini won just one Grammy—Best Instrumental Arrangement, for "Baby Elephant Walk"—in 1962, but came back strong in '63, snagging three for "Days of Wine and Roses," including (once again) Record and Song of the Year salutes. "The Pink Panther," which Mancini describes as "tippytoe music for David Niven," kept things purring in 1964, making off with three instrumental awards.

Mancini, son of an Aliquippa, Pennsylvania, steelworker, won his first award in 1937 (at the age of thirteen), as flutist in the Pennsylvania All-State Band. He subsequently studied at the Juilliard School of Music and, after a military hitch during World War II, landed work as pianist-arranger with the Glenn Miller Band.

In 1952 Mancini went to work for Universal Studios, contributing to more than a hundred pictures over the next six years, including *The Glenn Miller Story* and Orson Welles's *Touch of Evil*.

A chance encounter with director Blake Edwards outside the Universal barbershop in 1958 proved serendipitous for both men. Edwards was working on a new TV detective series, *Peter Gunn*, and he asked Mancini if he would be interested in writing the theme. Mancini took his cue for the music from the show's name. "When you say 'Peter Gunn,' it almost throws you into something with some drive to it," he observes. The theme, with its dangerous, blaring sound, was a perfect match for the private eye melodrama of Edwards's show, and the director credited Mancini with being half responsible for the success of "Peter Gunn." Before long, Mancini was drawing fully one-third of the show's fan mail.

"Peter Gunn" created a sensation in scoring circles, liberating composers from traditional, quasi-classical sounds and stimulating a rush of copycat themes. Mancini himself received an offer from MCA to do an 1870s *Western* using a "Peter Gunn"–style jazz-rock theme. "I said, 'Well, do you think it would fit?' They said, 'Yeah, sure, you know, it's *big*.' They wanted it just like 'Peter Gunn.' It would have been a laughable anachronism. I had to turn it down."

Since 1964, Mancini has won only three Grammys, landing an instrumental arrangement award for the "Love Theme From *Romeo and Juliet*" in 1969, and instrumental arrangement and contemporary instrumental performance kudos in 1970 for his "Theme From Z."

Mancini continues to generate nominations—seventy-one to date (second behind Quincy Jones, who has eighty). His most recent was an instrumental arrangement nod for *Monster Movie Music Suite* in 1990.

Duke Ellington

"We do love you madly," a beaming Duke Ellington told the Academy, along with a national prime-time TV audience, after receiving a Lifetime Achievement Grammy during the 1966 "Best on Record" show.

The feeling, obviously, was mutual. Between 1958, the first year of the Grammys, and 1974, the year of Ellington's death, the Academy gave the Duke nine awards, more than any other jazz performer. Two posthumous awards have since brought his total to eleven, which makes him the second-leading jazz winner in Grammy annals, behind Ella Fitzgerald, who has thirteen awards.

In addition to the Lifetime Achievement salute, Grammy officers have given Ellington a Trustees Award and placed four Ellington recordings—*Black and Tan Fantasy*, "Mood Indigo," "Take the 'A' Train," and "Black, Brown and Beige"—in the Grammy Hall of Fame. Benny Goodman is the only other artist with four records in that shrine.

If anyone deserved a perpetual Grammy toast, it was Edward Kennedy "Duke" Ellington. Regarded by many as the greatest figure in the history of jazz and one of the giants of twentieth-century music, Ellington had already produced a fabulous body of work by the time the Grammys were launched in 1958.

The most graceful, sophisticated, and painterly of composers, he worked both large and small, knocking off countless mini-master-pieces—"Satin Doll," "Prelude to a Kiss," "Mood Indigo," "Don't Get Around Much Anymore," and "Sophisticated Lady" are a few—while at the same time redefining the limits and substance of jazz with a vast output of suites, tone poems, concertos, and full-blown symphonic and sacred works.

As a bandleader, Ellington was without peer, putting together some of the greatest units of all time and drawing exquisitely expressive work from soloists like Ben Webster, Barney Bigard, Johnny Hodges, Cootie Williams, Harry Carney, and, later, Paul Gonsalves and Clark Terry.

The Grammys, of course, came along too late for many of Ellington's greatest recordings, but there was still plenty to celebrate and reward. *Anatomy of a Murder*, the Duke's first film score, won three Grammys in 1959, taking home Best Sound Track Album, Musical Composition, and Performance by a Dance Band honors.

In 1965 Duke's *Ellington '66* won an Instrumental Jazz Performance, Large Group award. The following year he nabbed a Jazz Composition Grammy for *In the Beginning God*. In 1967 came another salute for a large group instrumental with *Far East Suite*, and Ellington took home the same prize in '68 for *And His Mother Called Him Bill*.

In the seventies, Ellington won four more instrumental awards, beginning with *New Orleans Suite* in 1971, *Toga Brava Suite* in 1972, the posthumous *Ellington Suites* in 1976, and *At Fargo, 1940 Live* in 1979.

In 1966, Ellington became the third person to receive a Lifetime Achievement Grammy (following Bing Crosby in 1962 and Frank Sinatra in '65). The inscription on the prize read: "To Duke Ellington, for his tremendously high standards of musicianship and creativity maintained through his entire career as composer, pianist, arranger, and conductor, and for his artistic integrity and dedication to the music that has influenced and inspired countless peoples throughout the world."

Vaughn Meader

When John Fitzgerald Kennedy was assassinated on November 22, 1963, few people were more directly or traumatically affected than Album of the Year Grammy winner Vaughn Meader.

Meader had rocketed to fame the year before with *The First Family*, an irreverent, enormously popular album featuring impersonations of the president, wife Jackie, children Caroline and John-John, and even brother Bobby in a variety of behind-the-scenes settings. The record sold upward of five million copies, receiving five Grammy nominations and two awards.

The day after JFK died, *The First Family* was pulled from record stores around the country, Meader's nightclub and TV bookings were canceled, and a scheduled appearance on the premier "Best on Record" Grammy show, initially set to air November 24, two days after the assassination, was cut.

"They dug two graves when they shot the president," Lenny Bruce told a Greenwich Village audience shortly after the assassination, "one for Kennedy and one for Vaughn Meader."

Meader's success in the year and a half before Kennedy's death was truly phenomenal. Riding Kennedy's enormous popularity, *The First Family* landed a spot in the *Guinness Book of World Records* as the fastest-selling album of all time, ringing up 1.6 million in sales in two weeks, 3.6 million in a month, and 5.5 million after a year. (Those numbers were surpassed a year later, fittingly enough, by the *BBC Tribute to John F. Kennedy*, which sold four million copies in six days and won Best Documentary/Spoken Word Grammy in 1964.)

Meader's *The First Family* was so successful, it drew the bemused attention of JFK himself, who quipped: "I listened to Mr. Meader's record, but I thought it sounded more like Teddy than it did me."

Grammy voters, along with the rest of the country, fell in love with Meader's affectionate parodies. One of only two comics to win an Album of the Year Grammy (Bob Newhart turned the trick in 1960), Meader knocked off some tough competition, including Ray Charles's

Modern Sounds in Country & Western Music, Tony Bennett's *I Left My Heart in San Francisco*, the Stan Getz/Charlie Byrd *Jazz Samba* collaboration, and another highly popular comedy LP, Allan Sherman's *My Son the Folksinger*. Meader won the 1962 Comedy Performance Grammy as well.

Meader was just another struggling young comic in Greenwich Village when he began improvising JFK impressions in early 1962. An extended routine built around a Kennedy press conference landed him a spot on a summer TV series called "Celebrity Talent Scouts"; Meader stole the show. Among those watching was TV gag writer Bob Booker, who quickly pitched Meader the idea of expanding his routine to include Kennedy's glamorous family and putting the whole thing on record.

Every major label turned the project down, frightened by the then-daring concept of presidential satire. An executive at CBS Records scornfully told Booker he "wouldn't touch that with a ten-foot pole," Meader recalls. When *The First Family* sold its first million, Booker sent the exec a ten-foot pole.

Meader finally landed a deal with Cadence Records, a small independent label willing to take a chance. Auditions were held to cast Jackie, while radio actors were hired for the other roles. The album was recorded at Fine Recording Studios in New York before a live studio audience that belly-laughed throughout the show. They might not have laughed so hard had they known what the real JFK was saying while Meader and his colleagues clowned. The album was cut on October 22, 1962, the night of the president's tense Cuban missile crisis speech detailing a nuclear Mexican standoff between the United States and the Soviet Union.

Meader, who was a Young Democrat and a Kennedy supporter, recorded a follow-up album, *The First Family, Volume II*, six months later, which also did well. A JFK Christmas parody of "The Night Before Christmas" ("not a creature was stirring, not even a security guard"), with a B-side gripe session between Santa and JFK, was poised for release when the president was shot.

"It would have sold a few million and it was a guaranteed Grammy single, no question," Meader avers. "MGM printed a couple hundred deejay copies to be sent out November 22. They never went out."

Ironically, on the day Kennedy was shot, Meader was scheduled to perform for the Wisconsin State Democratic Party in Milwaukee. A cabbie at the airport asked him if he'd heard the news about Kennedy. Meader thought he was joking: "I heard millions of Kennedy jokes. I said, 'No, how does it go?' Then I heard it on the radio."

Meader took the cab back to the airport and returned to New York, where he fell into "deep hibernation" as his career flamed out. After two months, he tried a comeback, without Kennedy routines, but couldn't get booked. "Everything I did was Kennedy-associated," he later told *Daily Variety*. "I was a reminder of a more tragic day."

Meader mounted a number of satirical political revues in the mid-sixties, but nothing clicked. Like millions of other Americans, he was profoundly disillusioned by the Kennedy assassination, and in 1967 he dropped out, giving his possessions away and moving to the Haight-Ashbury hippie ghetto in San Francisco. "When the sixties hit, I found myself at loose ends, and I embraced it, the Beatles, 'Strawberry Fields.' It was incredible."

Increasingly political, Meader helped organize entertainment for various Yippie gatherings, and disgustedly called it quits as a stand-up comic after a crowd in Chicago clamored for jokes about booze and broads. "This was 1968, just after the Democratic National Convention, and I started yelling, 'Don't you people know what's going on?' I was supposed to play for a week. They asked me not to come back, and that was when I decided to get out of comedy."

For the next few years, Meader, who commanded $5,000 a night during the heydey of *The First Family*, drifted from coast to coast, changing his name and appearance repeatedly, living at various times in a tepee, a log cabin in Maine, an L.A. commune, and a houseboat, and working as a piano player in ski lodges and as a federal program assistant in Louisville, Kentucky.

In 1971 he combined psychedelia and religion in an album called *The Second Coming*, which traced the adventures of Jesus in Harlem and Judas (as an agent) in Hollywood. The record got good reviews, but no airplay or Grammy bids.

In 1974, Meader came full circle, starring in *The Walls Come Tumbling Down*, a one-man play about a man obsessed with the Kennedy assassination. It opened in L.A. and closed after a week. "It felt strange. It wasn't something I wanted to do," he says.

The fifty-three-year-old Meader now lives with his fourth wife in

Hallowell, Maine, near the town of his birth, and fronts a rock 'n' roll revival band called Class Reunion.

"I love it," he enthused to an AP reporter on the twenty-fifth anniversary of JFK's death, describing Maine as his "slow-lane home."

Peter, Paul and Mary

When Mary Travers of Peter, Paul and Mary first heard Bob Dylan's "Blowin' in the Wind," she was so excited she played it for everyone she knew, including her mom.

"But he can't *sing*," Mery Travers complained.

"But listen to the *words*," protested her daughter.

A few months later, when Peter, Paul and Mary recorded their prettier, softer version of the song, everyone, including Travers's mom, fell in love with Dylan's work.

"We translated Dylan for the world," Travers maintains.

Like Travers's mother, Grammy voters didn't care much for Dylan, waiting until 1979 to give him his first solo award; but they swooned over Peter, Paul and Mary's "translation" of "Blowin' in the Wind." The song won two Grammys in 1963, snagging Best Folk Recording and Best Performance by a Vocal Group prizes.

Ironically, Peter, Paul and Mary might never have recorded "Blowin' in the Wind" if the Chad Mitchell Trio, which cut it first, had been able to release its version of the song. But Belafonte Enterprises, the CM3's record company, refused to issue the single, objecting to the lyric, "How many deaths will it take till he knows that too many people have died?"

"You can't have a pop song with the word *death* in it," a label executive assured Milt Okun, musical director for both the Mitchell Trio and Peter, Paul and Mary. "I thought Chad Mitchell was more correct for the song," says Okun, "but they literally wouldn't let us [the CM3] put it out."

Five months later, Peter, Paul and Mary cut their version, which, in addition to winning two Grammys, sold three hundred thousand copies in two weeks, an unheard-of figure for a folk release, and went on to become Warner's best-selling record to that time.

The Peter, Paul and Mary–Bob Dylan connection went beyond

"Blowin' in the Wind." The group was the brainchild of Dylan manager Albert Grossman, who felt the era of Kingston Trio/Brothers Four–style folk groups, with their clean-cut, collegiate look and sound, was drawing to a close and that the time was right for something sexier, more bohemian, more politically charged.

Peter Yarrow, Paul Stookey, and Mary Travers, three Greenwich Village folkies, had the right look—"two rabbis and a hooker," according to a Warners executive—but needed a lot of work on their sound. Under Okun's direction they rehearsed seven days a week for seven months before making their bow at New York's Bitter End in 1961.

The performance was well received, although Vanguard Records owner Manny Sullivan, who sat with Okun, made sarcastic comments throughout the set. Okun, who had his own doubts about the group, was so embarrassed he couldn't bring himself to tell Sullivan he "was responsible for what we were hearing." Afterward, he advised Grossman "to get Peter and Paul to shave off their beards and get Mary some decent clothes."

But Grossman knew he was on to something, and a few months later Warner Bros. (despite last-minute misgivings about Stookey's and Yarrow's goatees), signed PP&M. Their eponymous first album quickly rose to the top of the charts.

Peter, Paul and Mary were an immediate hit with Grammy voters, winning top folk and group vocal honors for "If I Had a Hammer" in 1962 and becoming perennial Grammy nominees (*Album 1700* in 1967, *Late Again* in '68, *Day Is Done* in '69) until they disbanded in 1970. The group won a fifth and final trophy in 1969, for *Peter, Paul & Mommy*, a children's album.

When they broke up, NARAS acted as if all of folk music had died. The Academy eliminated the Best Folk Performance Grammy, keeping it on the shelf until 1979.

Barbra Streisand

Barbra Streisand was a Grammy godsend when she burst onto the scene in 1963 and finally gave NARAS members someone other than Ella Fitzgerald to cheer about in the female vocal categories. There was nothing wrong with Fitzgerald, of course, except for the fact that she seemed to be the only female singer Grammy voters esteemed and had therefore become a symbol of the conservative, predictable predilections of the Grammy crowd.

Streisand was fresh, exciting, contemporary, a torch singer of the sixties who could make show tunes matter for a new generation of fans. A mere twenty-one when she shot to the top with her debut *Barbra* LP, Streisand sounded like she'd been belting out standards for four or five past lives. Her voice was outrageously good, both in terms of power and richness of tone, and her theatrical way with a tune, her ability to be "a great actress in each song," in the words of composer Jule Styne, made her the best in the business the moment she arrived.

Styne, a songwriter many older Grammy voters greatly admired, pronounced the young Streisand "one of the greatest singers of our time."

The Grammys certainly wasted no time in heaping Barbra with awards. The Brooklyn diva won 1963 Album of the Year honors for *The Barbra Streisand Album*, beating *The Days of Wine and Roses* by Andy Williams, *The Singing Nun* by the Singing Nun, *I'm a Woman* by Peggy Lee, *The World of Miriam Makeba* by Miriam Makeba, and *Bach's Greatest Hits* by the Swingle Singers.

That debut album also netted Streisand the first of six female vocal Grammys in 1963, landing Best Vocal Performance honors ahead of *Blame It on the Bossa Nova* by Eydie Gorme, along with offerings from the Singing Nun, Makeba, and Peggy Lee.

In 1964 Streisand won a second Best Vocal Performance Grammy with "People," an instant standard from the Broadway hit *Funny Girl*. In 1965 she won the award for the third consecutive time, nailing the prize with her *My Name Is Barbra* LP.

Streisand's name was Barbara, with an *a*, when she was born in 1942 in the tough Williamsburg section of Brooklyn. Her father, an English and philosophy teacher, died when she was a year old, and Streisand was raised by her mother. "We weren't *poor* poor, but we didn't have anything," she told an interviewer after she became a star.

Acting, not singing, was young Streisand's passion, and when she finished high school in 1959 at the age of sixteen, she headed for Manhattan, determined to make it on Broadway. Streisand's mother pleaded with her to study typing and stenography—"Just in case"—

but she refused. "I knew I had talent, and I was afraid that if I learned to type I would become a secretary," she explained in 1964.

According to the Streisand legend, she sang in public for the first time while competing in a talent contest sponsored by a Greenwich Village bar. She won, and soon found herself performing at the Blue Angel, a showcase for up-and-coming talent, where producer David Merrick saw her and immediately cast her as Miss Marmelstein, the Jewish ugly ducking in the Broadway musical *I Can Get It for You Wholesale*.

By the time the play closed in December 1962, Streisand was the subject of bidding wars on every entertainment front. In short order, she signed a recording contract with CBS Records, a network TV deal with CBS, and landed the part of Fanny Brice in *Funny Girl*, the show that put her over the top as a full-fledged star.

After winning four Grammys in three years, Streisand tailed off in the late sixties and early seventies, drawing scattered nominations but no awards. "The Way We Were," her big 1973 hit, generated Song of the Year honors for Marilyn and Alan Bergman, but Babs herself won nothing. Streisand made up for this disappointment in 1977, winning two Grammys for "Evergreen" (from *A Star Is Born*), which nabbed Song of the Year and Pop Vocal Performance, Female salutes. Streisand cowrote "Evergreen" with Paul Williams, with whom she subsequently exchanged lawsuits in a battle over credit for the tune. When the two reached the Grammy podium to accept the award, Williams thanked his doctor for giving him "some incredible Valiums" to help him make it through the night.

Streisand snagged her seventh Grammy in 1980, winning pop duo honors with Barry Gibb for the disco-ish "Guilty," and her most recent win came in 1986, when she notched female vocal honors for *The Broadway Album*, a record that was tailor-made for the NARAS old-line constituency. The album beat Madonna's "Papa Don't Preach" and Dionne Warwick and Friends' "That's What Friends Are For," among others.

Streisand told the Shrine Auditorium audience she had a feeling she would win, since Grammy ceremonies were held on February 24 and twenty-four was her lucky number. "I was born on the twenty-fourth, I gave birth on the twenty-fourth, and I won my first Grammy twenty-four years ago," she said. "With a little bit of luck, I'd like to see you twenty-four years from now."

Herb Alpert

Mix the Grammys and the early sixties, and what do you get? Herb Alpert and the Tijuana Brass. In 1965, a year that saw the release of "Like a Rolling Stone" by Bob Dylan, "Satisfaction" by the Rolling Stones, "California Dreamin' " by the Mamas and the Papas, and "In the Midnight Hour" by Wilson Pickett, Grammy voters gave Alpert's "A Taste of Honey" the Record of the Year award.

Given the ever-present Grammy yen to celebrate the likes of Robert Goulet and Eydie Gorme, Alpert was a progressive choice. His "Ameriachi" sound, a brisk, infectious blend of simplified jazz, south-of-the-border frills, and a hint of rock, was a kind of mod gallop for the decade, and just about everyone enjoyed the ride. By the end of 1965, Alpert had three million-selling albums on the charts and a continuous flow of instrumental singles—seventeen by 1968—that sold well despite the radically shifting waters of sixties pop.

Alpert had two big Grammy years, 1965 and 1966, when he won a total of five awards. A leading nominee in 1965 with six bids, Alpert's "A Taste of Honey" nabbed Record of the Year, Instrumental Arrangement, and Instrumental Performance, Non-Jazz wins. In 1966, he pulled five more nominations, including Album and Record of the Year bids for *What Now My Love*. The disc lost in the big categories, but won another set of instrumental arrangement and performance awards.

Alpert, an ex-army bugler, cast about for a long time, looking for an individual style. He finally found it in 1962, when he began experimenting with two tape recorders in his Los Angeles garage, overdubbing himself from recorder to recorder, and building up an interesting sound. The technique was particularly effective with "Twinkle Star," a song, written by a friend, that had a nice Spanish flair. Alpert added the roaring *olés!* of a Tijuana bullfight crowd, which he recorded by suspending a microphone in the stadium, and changed the name of the song to "The Lonely Bull."

The record, which he produced himself for two hundred dollars, sold over a million copies and launched his career. Even a savvier businessman than artist, Alpert and his partner, Jerry Moss, used the profits to start their own record company, A&M Records, an enormously successful independent label that sold millions of records by the TB and spin-off Latin groups like the Baja Marimba Band, Sergio Mendes and Brasil '66, and Chris Montez.

Since the sixties, Alpert has won one more Grammy, nabbing Pop Instrumental Performance honors in 1979 for his best-selling disco-jazz hit, "Rise." Alpert's wife, Lani Hall, meanwhile, added a Latin Pop Performance Grammy to the family collection with *Es Facil Amar* in 1985. And A&M records, of course, has sustained Alpert's Grammy touch, via such winning artists as the Carpenters, the Police, Carole King, the Captain and Tennille, and Quincy Jones.

The Mamas and the Papas

It was 1965, and the Beatles were performing at the Hollywood Bowl. Four feverish fans, unable to get tickets, drove their 1958 Buick convertible high into the Hollywood Hills and listened, longingly, dreamily, to the sounds of the Fab Four and the screams of the crowd below.

"I guarantee you before the year is over, we'll play the Hollywood Bowl," John Phillips told wife Michelle, Cass Elliot, and Dennis Doherty, otherwise known as the Mamas and the Papas. "And before the year's out," he added, "we'll win a Grammy award."

Phillips's prediction, fantastic as it must have seemed at the time, was right on the mark. Within a year, the Mamas and Papas had topped the charts with a string of hits, performed at the Hollywood Bowl (opening for Sonny and Cher), and won a Grammy, the first hippie group to draw praise from the conservative NARAS crowd.

"Monday, Monday," their winning song, took the Best Contemporary (R&R) Group Performance award, beating "Good Vibrations" by the Beach Boys, "Cherish" by the Association, "Guantanamera" by the Sandpipers, and "Last Train to Clarksville" by the Monkees. The song also received nominations for Record of the Year, Best Contemporary (R&R) Recording, and Best Performance by a Vocal Group, but lost in each category, to Frank Sinatra's "Strangers in the Night," the New Vaudeville Band's "Winchester Cathedral," and the Anita Kerr Singers' "A Man and a Woman," respectively.

The Mamas and the Papas were able to succeed where nearly all other counterculture artists failed because of their pristine harmonies

and sparkling sound. Ragged looks and long hair image notwithstanding, the quartet featured exceptional vocalists who logged fourteen-
hour-a-day rehearsals perfecting their arrangements and songs.
Group leader Phillips drew his inspiration from Norman Luboff, an
esteemed choral arranger from the fifties (and a 1960 Grammy winner), whose records he studied as a child and whom he credits for
making the Mamas and the Papas "musically sound."

Not that anyone would ever mistake the Mamas and the Papas,
visually or musically, for the Norman Luboff Choir. In storybook
hippie style, the foursome dropped acid the first time they met, sang
all night, and then spent months in the Virgin Islands, slowly con-
suming a quart of liquid LSD, sleeping on the beach, and honing
their sound.

"If the Academy had known what we were really like, they never
would have nominated us at all," Phillips notes. "But the squeaky-
clean harmonies, the dedication to music came through and overrode
everything."

"Monday, Monday," ironically, almost never made it onto *If You
Can Believe Your Eyes and Ears*, the group's debut album. Phillips,
who wrote the song in half an hour, had to plead with the other
members of the group and producer Lou Adler, all of whom "hated
it," to record the tune, and prevailed only because they needed a final
cut to round out the LP.

"After we recorded it, everyone said, 'Gee, it doesn't sound bad
after all,' " Phillips recalls.

"To this day I have no idea what the song means. People on the
street stop me and say, 'Monday, Monday—it's a girl, right?' I say
right. They say, 'It's a day of the week, right?' I say right. I have no
idea. Denny [Doherty] said what we need is a universal song that
appeals to everyone. I picked on 'Monday.' "

"Monday, Monday" was the group's second single, passing "California Dreamin' " on its way to the top of the charts and selling a sizzling
150,000 copies the day it was released. Although the Mamas and the
Papas launched six top ten hits in the fifteen-month period between
February 1966 and May 1967, they came unglued as a group by the
end of '67 and never won another Grammy nomination or award.

Twenty-one years later, Phillips, sans other Mamas and Papas,
garnered a songwriting nomination for "Kokomo," the Beach Boys'
hit from the movie *Beach Party*, which he cowrote with Bruce

Johnson, Mike Love, Terry Melcher, and Scott Mackenzie. The song was nominated in the Best Song Written Specifically for a Motion Picture or Television category, but lost to "Two Hearts" by Phil Collins and Lamont Dozier.

Cortelia Clark

The Grammys do not generally stir one's sense of pathos, but the story of Cortelia Clark is an exception. Clark won the Grammy for Best Folk Recording in 1966, an improbable, indeed astonishing feat, given the fact that he was a blind, black, utterly obscure street singer from Nashville who won the award over the likes of Pete Seeger; Peter, Paul and Mary; Leadbelly; Mimi and Richard Fariña; and Ravi Shankar.

Fifty-nine-year-old Clark, a fixture in downtown Nashville with his beat-up guitar, blind man's cane, and tin cup, won his Grammy with an aptly titled album called *Blues in the Street*, which presented him on location, busking for change in downtown Nashville amid the sounds of passing traffic and clanking coins.

The album, produced for $1,007, heralded Clark as Nashville's own "authentic, original street singer." It sold a minuscule number of copies, and RCA dropped Clark from its roster one week before he won his award. His victory seemed like a Cinderella story, with NARAS cast as the Fairy Godmother.

"The Grammy isn't presented to the one with the most sales, and it has nothing to do with whether a recording artist is well known," Clark's young manager, Mike Weesner, reminded a reporter following the award. "It is presented, simply, to the best."

Theoretically, Weesner was right. In reality, the quality of Clark's work had little, if anything, to do with his win. It's doubtful that many people in NARAS outside of Nashville knew who Clark was or listened to his record. Nashville members of the Academy, however, undoubtedly voted for Clark as they voted for all their favorite sons—en masse—and the solid bloc from the organization's third-largest chapter was enough to put the unknown bluesman over the top.

The Grammy win was not, alas, enough to change the fortunes of Cortelia Clark. Without the money to rent, let alone buy, a tuxedo,

Clark didn't even attend the Nashville Grammy bash. The day after he was voted Folk Artist of the Year, he was back on the street, singing the blues and trying to raise a few bucks. Briefly, Clark was famous—the busker who won a Grammy—and UPI, AP, *Newsweek*, and CBS-TV all ran stories. "I really am pleased," Clark told reporters. "I hope now that they'll let me record some more." But Nashville, despite giving him its Grammy vote, didn't take Clark seriously enough to offer him another contract, and he never recorded again. In 1969, barely three years after he became a Grammy star, Clark died when the kerosene stove in his trailer home exploded, covering him with third-degree burns.

Cortelia Clark was born in Chicago in 1907, blind in one eye. In an interview with RCA producer Felton Jarvis that kicks off *Blues in the Street*, Clark says he came to Nashville when he was eleven and worked in a broom factory until cataracts and a failed eye operation left him totally blind. Taught by another blind man the rudiments of guitar, Clark roamed the Southwest during the Depression years, then returned to Nashville and staked out his post on Fifth Avenue, three blocks from the Grand Ole Opry, at the start of World War II.

Clark was "discovered" by Mike Weesner, an aspiring record producer who had grown up in Nashville and watched and listened to Clark many times as a child. Weesner convinced RCA's Jarvis, one of the biggest producers in Nashville and whose artists included Elvis Presley, to sign Clark to a recording contract.

RCA recorded *Blues in the Street* in a single afternoon, using two mikes. The album is primitive, rough, but compelling. Scraping raw chords off his guitar, Clark shouts his largely improvised blues in a singsong voice that seems to stumble and feel its way along. He is not a "great" artist, and yet there is something so real about what he does, his rude, spawning musicality, so basic to the process of the blues, that there ought to be a place for him and others like him in the Grammys—and not just as a bittersweet fluke.

Though few people outside Nashville remember Clark and his moment of Grammy fame, his story and name have not altogether died. Country crooner Mickey Newberry wrote a song called "Cortelia Clark" that pays tribute to the bluesman's hard life and death. The song, Newberry says, is one of his most popular, requested by fans in concerts around the world.

Simon & Garfunkel

Simon & Garfunkel were one sixties group the Grammys admired, but the feeling wasn't altogether mutual. Asked to perform "Mrs. Robinson" on the 1968 "Best on Record" Grammy show, the duo balked, not sure the association would go over well with their fans.

Hoping to change their minds, "Best on Record" producer Ted Bergmann showed Simon & Garfunkel a *Newsweek* story lauding the pair as one of the few contemporary groups that could claim both counterculture and "establishment" fans.

"They went crazy when they saw that," Bergmann recalls. "They screamed, 'We don't want to be identified with the fucking establishment!' "

Simon & Garfunkel finally agreed to tape "Mrs. Robinson," Grammy Record of the Year for 1968, but only on condition that they retain production control. They ultimately turned in an antic, homemade music video that showed them romping through Yankee Stadium ("Where have you gone, Joe DiMaggio?"), running the bases, and swinging baseball bats to the strains of the song.

"Mrs. Robinson," written for the movie *The Graduate*, was Simon & Garfunkel's first Grammy hit. It beat "Hey Jude" by the Beatles, "Harper Valley P.T.A." by Jeannie C. Riley, "Honey" by Bobby Goldsboro, and "Wichita Lineman" by Glen Campbell for the Record of the Year prize. The song also won the Contemporary Pop Group Vocal award, once again beating "Hey Jude," along with "Child Is Father to the Man" by Blood, Sweat & Tears, "Fool on the Hill" by Sergio Mendes, "Goin' Out of My Head/Can't Take My Eyes off You" by the Lettermen, and "Woman, Woman" by Gary Puckett & the Union Gap. In addition, *The Graduate*, with songs by Simon and scoring by Dave Grusin, nabbed the Best Original Score Grammy.

Two years later, Simon & Garfunkel scored an even bigger Grammy triumph, with "Bridge Over Troubled Water," their anthemic, pop-spiritual smash, which won six awards, including Song, Record, and Album of the Year trophies. (Carole King and Christopher Cross are the only other artists in the history of the Grammys to sweep the top three awards.) "Bridge Over Troubled Water" also won Grammys for Best Arrangement Accompanying Vocalists, Best Engineering, and Best Contemporary Song. Once again, Simon & Garfunkel rolled over a powerful Beatles song—"Let It Be"—en route to their awards, beating out the Beatles' farewell ode for both Record and Song of the Year honors.

Simon & Garfunkel's feelings about NARAS and the Grammys softened a bit by 1970, and they attended that year's awards dinner in Los Angeles, albeit with halfhearted interest and limited enthusiasm.

According to *Rolling Stone* critic Jon Landau, who wrote a scalding review of the Grammys after the 1970 show, Simon & Garfunkel "looked very sorry they'd come" to the ceremony.

"They were being used," Landau charged, "as had everyone else who appeared on the program, to justify the existence of the wretched people who put this thing on in the first place. And if they hadn't known it before they came they surely knew it by then."

Perhaps. The duo, who would shortly break up, left before all the awards they had a shot at winning were announced. Later that night, "Bridge Over Troubled Water" coarranger Jimmie Haskell brought three new trophies to Simon & Garfunkel's hotel and phoned them from the lobby to tell them the news.

"That's nice," a blasé Simon said. "Could you leave them at the desk?"

Simon & Garfunkel split up not long after the '70 Grammys and never received another Grammy nomination or nod. But "Bridge Over Troubled Water" won again in 1971, with Aretha Franklin taking an r&b vocal prize for her rendition of the song.

Since their breakup, both Simon and Garfunkel have pursued solo careers, although only Simon has continued as a Grammy star. In 1975 he won a second Album of the Year Grammy with *Still Crazy After All These Years*, which also landed a Pop Vocal Performance, Male award. Eleven years later, Simon garnered the 1986 Album of the Year Grammy with *Graceland*, joining Frank Sinatra and Stevie Wonder as the only artists in Grammy history to win the award three times.

A year later, the "Graceland" single, released during the 1987 Grammy eligibility year, won the Record of the Year prize.

Glen Campbell

When Glen Campbell came to longtime pal and Columbia Records A&R exec Jerry Fuller with a demo of his new album, Fuller imme-

In the year of *Sgt. Pepper*, Glen Campbell and Bobbie Gentry dominated the 1967 Grammy Awards. PHOTO COURTESY JASPER DAILEY.

Joni Mitchell (right), one of the very few Woodstock artists to win a Grammy, with the Top Folk Recording award she won in 1969 for *Clouds*. PHOTO COURTESY JASPER DAILEY.

Singers with an attitude: Marvin Gaye and Jerry Lee Lewis, together backstage at the 1982 awards. Neither had ever won a Grammy. Gaye won two that night for "Sexual Healing." PHOTO COURTESY JASPER DAILEY.

Grammy voters hated most of the important young artists of the sixties. Simon & Garfunkel were an exception, winning big in 1968 with music from *The Graduate* and sweeping in 1970 with *Bridge Over Troubled Water*. PHOTO COURTESY JASPER DAILEY.

Is there a valet in the house? Henry Mancini, Grammy winner emeritus, parks his car outside the 1975 awards. PHOTO COURTESY JASPER DAILEY.

Until 1986, the Shrine Auditorium was as close as Elton John ever got to a Grammy. Here he sits strawhatted during a rehearsal for the 1988 telecast. PHOTO COURTESY JASPER DAILEY.

Reborn as an artist and a star after leaving Ike, Tina Turner capped a spectacular comeback in 1984 with four Grammys, including Record of the Year, for "What's Love Got to Do With It?" PHOTO COURTESY JASPER DAILEY.

No Grammys for Dylan, Springsteen, Bowie, or Marley in 1975, but pop softies Captain & Tennille won big, snagging Record of the Year honors for "Love Will Keep Us Together." PHOTO COURTESY JASPER DAILEY.

Stevie Wonder didn't win anything in the sixties (Motown Records as a label won one Grammy), but he dominated the mid-seventies, winning fifteen awards in four years. Backstage at the 1973 telecast, Wonder is flanked by Chuck Berry (right), and Little Richard (far left), neither of whom has ever won a Grammy. PHOTO COURTESY JASPER DAILEY.

Peggy Lee lost five times to Ella Fitzgerald before winning for the first and, to date, only time in 1969 with "Is That All There Is?" PHOTO COURTESY JASPER DAILEY.

Kris Kristofferson nabbed three of the five country Song of the Year nominations in 1971. He won with "Help Me Make It Through the Night." PHOTO COURTESY JASPER DAILEY.

Paul McCartney (here with his wife Linda) picked up the Beatles' last Grammy, a Best Movie Score salute for *Let It Be,* at the Palladium in Los Angeles in 1970. PHOTO COURTESY JASPER DAILEY.

Grammy royalty, 1970. Left to right: Quincy Jones, Richard and Karen Carpenter, and Glen Campbell. PHOTO COURTESY JASPER DAILEY.

Aretha Franklin put together the longest winning streak in Grammy history, taking home eight consecutive R&B awards between 1967 and 1974. This backstage shot was taken at the 1975 show. PHOTO COURTESY JASPER DAILEY.

Bob Dylan won his solo Grammy in 1979 for "Gotta Serve Somebody." PHOTO COURTESY JASPER DAILEY.

Country outlaw Willie Nelson was too maverick for Grammy's Nashville voters—until he became a mainstream star in the mid-seventies. Since then, he's won five awards. PHOTO COURTESY JASPER DAILEY.

Grammy host Andy Williams (right) never won a Grammy, but he did model the trophy for photographers backstage at the 1975 awards. PHOTO COURTESY JASPER DAILEY.

The Grammys + the sixties = Herb Alpert (left). The mod trumpeter won five awards in 1965-66. PHOTO COURTESY A&M RECORDS.

Henry Mancini with the Beatles. In the world of the Grammys, Mancini was the bigger star. PHOTO COURTESY HENRY MANCINI.

Obscure, blind street singer Cortelia Clark of Nashville is the unlikeliest Grammy winner of all time. Clark beat out Pete Seeger, Leadbelly, Mimi and Richard Farina, Ravi Shankar, and Peter, Paul & Mary for the Best Folk Grammy of 1966. Bloc voting by Nashville put him over the top. PHOTO COURTESY MRS. FELTON JARVIS.

Was this group better than the Beatles? Grammy voters thought so. They picked Anita Kerr Singers' *We Dig Mancini* over the Beatles' *Help* for the Best Vocal Group Award in 1965. PHOTO COURTESY WARNER BROS. RECORDS.

Grammy voters disliked Dylan but loved clean-cut folkies Peter, Paul & Mary, whose cover version of Dylan's "Blowin' in the Wind" won two Grammys in 1963. PHOTO COURTESY WARNER BROS. RECORDS.

diately tabbed "By the Time I Get to Phoenix," a sweetly sorrowful song by rising writer Jimmy Webb, as the obvious single.

"We're not going to release it as a single," Campbell informed Fuller. "We've decided on something else."

Why?

"Because Pat Boone has already recorded and released it."

Fuller got on the phone with Al De Lory, Campbell's producer and the man behind these decisions.

"You're not going to tell me you're afraid of Pat Boone," Fuller sarcastically drawled. Boone hadn't had a hit since 1962 and couldn't have been less a threat to Campbell, whose star was on the rise.

The challenge sufficed to make De Lory and Campbell change their minds.

"I shamed them into making the best move of Campbell's career," Fuller bemusedly recalls.

Indeed he did, and indeed it was. "By the Time I Get to Phoenix" was an across-the-board hit, popular in pop, country, easy-listening, and Top 40 formats, and Glen Campbell, the clean-cut, fair-haired singer with the "aw shucks" style and all-American smile, was a big-time star.

The Grammys played a big role in Campbell's rise to the top, giving the industry stamp of approval to his talent and success via a host of 1967 nominations and four awards. The crossover appeal of "By the Time I Get to Phoenix" generated both Best Male Vocal Performance and Contemporary Male Vocal Performance salutes.

In addition, Campbell's recording of "Gentle on My Mind," released a year before "Phoenix," was revived (Phoenix-like) on the coattails of the latter song's success and won Best Country & Western Male Vocal and Best Country & Western Recording Grammys. The song itself, written by John Hartford, won the Country & Western Song of the Year award. Interestingly, "Phoenix" was also nominated for the Song of the Year Grammy, but lost to "Up, Up and Away," another Jimmy Webb tune.

Demographically, Campbell was ideally positioned to emerge as a Grammy star. Born on a farm in Delight, Arkansas, the seventh son of a seventh son, he played guitar for a country-swing band in his teens, and his Southern roots assured him of solid support from the increasingly populous Nashville branch of NARAS.

Moreover, a seven-year apprenticeship as a Hollywood studio

guitarist made Campbell a favorite with Los Angeles Grammy members (the organization's largest voting bloc) as well. From 1960 to 1967 Campbell established himself as one of the most versatile, highly regarded session men in the business, playing for everyone from Nat King Cole, Frank Sinatra, and Eydie Gorme to the Champs and Nino Tempo. At one point, Campbell even toured with the Beach Boys, standing in for Brian Wilson, who was holed up writing songs.

When Campbell accepted the first of his 1967 Grammys, "he thanked all the people he had backed up on guitar for their votes," noted the *Los Angeles Times*.

Campbell's golden Grammy touch continued in 1968, this time with embarrassing results. *By the Time I Get to Phoenix* won *again*, nabbing the prestigious Album of the Year honor (thank you, Nashville). The album was released after the single and was therefore eligible for the '68 awards.

Phoenix, a thoroughly average album in a year teeming with great ones, was chosen over Simon & Garfunkel's *Bookends*, the Beatles' *Magical Mystery Tour*, and such unnominated works as Aretha Franklin's *Lady Soul*, Big Brother & the Holding Company's *Cheap Thrills*, the Jimi Hendrix Experience's *Electric Ladyland*, Bob Dylan's *John Wesley Harding*, and the Byrds' *Sweetheart of the Rodeo*.

Another Campbell hit, "Wichita Lineman," picked up a slew of 1968 nominations but came away with only an engineering award.

Campbell has yet to win another Grammy, though he has logged occasional nominations through the years. "Rhinestone Cowboy," a 1975 hit, drew record, song, and pop male vocal bids, but failed to cash in on any of them.

Bobbie Gentry

"We've just bought a master from a new singer, and she's got a B side that we need to cover so we won't be embarrassed. Arrange it any way you like. No one will ever hear it."

In such fashion did Capitol Records producer Kelly Gordon call arranger Jimmie Haskell and ask him to provide instrumental backing for a then-unknown song called "Ode to Billie Joe" by a then-unknown singer named Bobbie Gentry.

Haskell listened to the strangely absorbing ode (flip side of a long-forgotten Gentry tune called "Mississippi Delta") and decided that Gentry "had written a little movie," with a full-blown cast of characters and an enigmatic story of backwoods suicide and romance. He arranged the tune accordingly, underscoring Gentry's vocals with sparse, evocative instrumentation, "interesting and weird sounds that had not been used on pop records before."

The record Haskell turned in was over seven minutes long and so strangely compelling that Capitol decided, after whittling it down to the still-unheard-of length of four minutes, fifty-six seconds, to release it as the single instead of "Mississippi Delta."

Capitol's decision was handsomely rewarded. "Ode to Billie Joe" seemed to catch the whole country in its obsessive, trancelike tale, selling 750,000 copies in three weeks and three million overall. Both song and singer mesmerized Grammy voters as well: Gentry garnered eight nominations and three awards, and she was hailed as Best New Artist of 1967, beating out Jefferson Airplane, Harpers Bizarre, the Fifth Dimension, and Lana Cantrell.

Gentry's other Grammys came in the Best Female Vocal and Best Contemporary Female Vocal fields. NARAS preferred "Billie Joe" to Aretha Franklin's "Respect," Dionne Warwick's "Alfie," Petula Clark's "Don't Sleep in the Subway," and Vikki Carr's "It Must Be Him" in the first category. Gentry knocked off Franklin's "A Natural Woman" and Warwick's "Say a Little Prayer,"along with "It Must Be Him," and "Don't Sleep in the Subway," to win the second prize. Haskell, meanwhile, won a Best Arrangement Grammy for his work on the record.

With her larger-than-life features, sultry yet aloof manner, and barefoot-Vegas glamour, Gentry seemed as mysterious and unusual as her song. Born Roberta Lee Streeter in Chickasaw County, Mississippi, she lived in the heart of the Mississippi Delta until she was thirteen, when she moved with her mother to Palm Springs. She changed her name to Gentry while still in high school after seeing the film *Ruby Gentry*, starring Jennifer Jones.

Gentry studied philosophy at UCLA and music at the Los Angeles Conservatory of Music. In 1966 she was performing with her own vocal and dance group in Las Vegas. She submitted a demo of

"Mississippi Delta" to Capitol in hopes of landing a songwriting deal. The label was so impressed it signed her to a recording contract.

Though the mystery of what exactly Billie Joe McCallister threw off the Tallahatchie Bridge has long puzzled fans of "Ode to Billie Joe," according to Gentry, the song is "a study in unconscious cruelty."

"Everybody has a different guess about what was thrown off the bridge—flowers, a ring, even a baby," she says in Fred Bronson's *Billboard Book of Number One Hits*, ". . . but the real message of the song, if there must be a message, revolves around the nonchalant way the family talks about the suicide. They sit there eating their peas and apple pie and talking, without even realizing that Billie Joe's girlfriend is sitting at the table, a member of the family."

A 1976 movie based on the song, starring Robby Benson and Glynnis O'Connor, suggested that Billie Joe tossed his girlfriend's rag doll into the river and killed himself during a crisis of sexual identity.

One of many Best New Artist Grammy winners who failed to live up to the promise of that award, Gentry recorded haphazardly through the seventies and has yet to score another hit or Grammy nod.

Roger Miller

For two years, from 1964 to 1965, "King of the Road" Roger Miller was also king of the Grammys. The first Nashville artist to dominate the awards, Miller came out of nowhere in '64 to steal the show, nabbing five trophies with a sad-sack country blues called "Dang Me" and an ode to moonshine called "Chug-A-Lug."

A year later he did even better, hauling home a record six awards, five of them for his immensely popular "King of the Road." The mark stood for eighteen years, until Michael Jackson "beat it" in 1983.

Most of Miller's Grammys came in the country categories, newly expanded from one to six in 1964. Miller virtually swept the field, winning Best Country & Western Song, Single Album, and Vocal Performance, Male awards in '64 and '65. the only Grammys he lost were the ones he wasn't eligible for—Best New Country & Western Artist of 1965 (he won in '64), and female vocal honors. And he almost *did* win the latter award in 1965, nabbing a kind of proxy salute via

Jody Miller's "Queen of the House," a female answer to "King of the Road."

Miller also won rock'n' roll Grammys for "King of the Road" in 1965, beating "Yesterday" by the Beatles for the Best Contemporary (R&R) Single and Vocal Performance, Male. Though Miller can't be blamed, the wins were preposterous. Miller was no rock'n' roller, and 1965 was a year that saw the release of such landmark rock tracks as "Satisfaction" by the Rolling Stones and "Like a Rolling Stone" by Bob Dylan, neither of which were even nominated by the antirock Grammy crowd.

Miller, a Nashville free spirit whose good-old-boy charm belied an openness and interest in everything from rock to Broadway to jazz, was at least aware of the Rolling Stones. "I considered myself part of what the Stones were doin' and part of what Steve Lawrence was doin'," he says. "I worked the whole board."

It all came together with "King of the Road," a wry everyman hit that Miller wrote after driving past a billboard in Davenport, Iowa, on which he saw the words that became the song's opening line: "Trailers for sale or rent . . ."

"Those were just words that I liked," he recalls. "I had no story, no details, no hook line. I just started thinkin' about those words, and a few days later, in Boise, Idaho, I sat down and wrote the song. It's about a hobo walking along. He was a train catcher, years ago. I guess you'd call him homeless now."

The record sold half a million copies in eighteen days, nearly three million overall, and has been covered by over three hundred artists. It garnered the most nominations of any Grammy song in 1965, eight, including Record and Song of the Year.

Though it failed to win either of those awards, "King of the Road" does hold the distinction of being the only Grammy record to inspire a chain of motels. Launched by Miller and a group of backers in 1969, King of the Road Enterprises opened motels in Tennessee, Georgia, and South Carolina.

Miller, whose songs evince a bemused soulfulness born of hard times, was only too familiar with the royal life of the road. Raised by an uncle on a dirt-poor cotton farm near Erick, Oklahoma, he dropped out of school in the eighth grade and drifted through the Southwest, chopping cotton, washing dishes, herding and dehorning cattle, even riding rodeo bulls.

Miller joined the army when he turned seventeen, and his guitar playing and singing landed him an assignment entertaining the troops in a Special Services country band. The experience prompted Miller to try his luck in Nashville, where he worked as a bellhop before catching on as a fiddler with Minnie Pearl.

By the early sixties, Miller had written a handful of country hits and performed on "The Tonight Show," but his bank account was discouragingly low, and he decided to go to Hollywood to give acting a try. In order to raise money for the trip, Miller cut an album for Smash Records—eighteen songs in a single afternoon for an $1,800-dollar advance. The session produced "Dang Me" and "Chug-a-Lug," each of which would quickly sell a million copies and turn Miller into country's biggest crossover star.

Miller quit the music business three times before striking it rich, and he was anything but blasé about his Grammy awards. In 1965 he insisted on carrying all six of his trophies out of the awards dinner to his waiting limousine. Tottering after an evening of triumph and champagne, Miller stumbled and dropped his cargo, breaking a number of awards.

"It's not a pretty story," Miller says, with his quiet, ironic drawl, "but it's one that really had to be told."

Miller has continued to write and record into the eighties, but hasn't won a Grammy since "King of the Road." He did win a Best Cast Show Album nomination in 1985, however, for his score to *Big River*, a Broadway musical based on *Huckleberry Finn* that won seven Tony Awards.

Carole King

With Carole King, the Grammys finally got hip. King won four Grammys in 1971, including Record, Album, and Song of the Year, and, as *Newsday* rock critic and frequent Grammy basher Robert Christgau conceded, "only a sorehead" could complain.

King was not merely popular—the Grammys specialized in honoring popular but lightweight artists like Glen Campbell and the Fifth Dimension—she was one of the most resonant artists of her time, bringing a toned-down but soulful counterculture sensibility into the mainstream. Her enormously successful *Tapestry* LP (still the all-time best-selling album by a female artist, with over fifteen million sales) was a perfect transition from the messianic sixties to the home-spun seventies—at once a retreat into the spheres of friendship and romance and an eloquent affirmation of posthippie values.

The Grammys were thrilled with the change. Having squirmed miserably through the post-Beatles pop apocalypse without once recognizing Bob Dylan, the Rolling Stones, Jimi Hendrix, and count-less other seminal stars, they embraced King with delight and relief.

"They [NARAS members] were very, very happy that they could give Carole King those Grammys," recalls Lou Adler, who produced *Tapestry* and released the record on his own Ode label. "When all that softness came back, they settled back in their chairs. . . ."

Tapestry, of course, won the Album of the Year Grammy, beating *All Things Must Pass* by George Harrison, *Shaft* by Isaac Hayes, and the original cast recording of *Jesus Christ, Superstar*.

In winning Record of the Year plaudits for "It's Too Late," King competed against herself via James Taylor's cover of "You've Got a Friend." Other nominees were "My Sweet Lord" by George Har-rison, "Theme From Shaft" by Isaac Hayes, and "Joy to the World" by Three Dog Night.

"You've Got a Friend," meanwhile, won Song of the Year honors, besting "Help Me Make It Through the Night" and "Me & Bobby McGee" by Kris Kristofferson, and "I Never Promised You a Rose Garden" by Joe South.

Her fourth award came in the Pop Vocal Performance, Female category, where *Tapestry* topped a strong field that included "Me & Bobby McGee" by Janis Joplin (Joplin never won a Grammy), and "The Night They Drove Old Dixie Down" by Joan Baez.

Although King won her first and last Grammys with *Tapestry* in 1971, she might well have nabbed other awards had Grammy voters in the early sixties not been so disdainful of teen-oriented r&b and rock 'n' roll. Among the great songwriters of pop-rock's early years, King and then-husband Gerry Goffin penned such classics as the Shirelles' "Will You Love Me Tomorrow," the Crystals' "He's a Rebel," the Drifters' "Up on the Roof," and Bobby Vee's "Take Good Care of My Baby." One King-Goffin song received a Grammy nomi-nation—"The Locomotion," by Little Eva (King's baby-sitter)—but lost the 1962 r&b award to Ray Charles's "I Can't Stop Loving You."

Roberta Flack

Creamy-voiced Roberta Flack was mistress of the Grammys in 1972 and 1973 when she became the only person in the history of the awards to win Record of the Year honors two years in a row. Her 1972 winner, "The First Time Ever I Saw Your Face," also generated a Song of the Year Grammy for Ewan MacColl, while her follow-up "Killing Me Softly With His Song" did the same for tunesmiths Norman Gimbel and Charles Fox.

Flack was the first solo black artist to win Record of the Year, the most prestigious of all Grammys, and is still the only woman to do so twice.

It took Grammy voters two years to discover "The First Time Ever I Saw Your Face," a song that folksinger Ewan MacColl wrote for his bride, Peggy Seeger (daughter of Pete), and that Flack recorded in 1969 on her largely ignored *First Take* LP.

One person the album impressed was actor-director Clint Eastwood, who was looking for just the right romantic song for a scene in his 1971 film noir about a deejay, *Play Misty for Me*. Eastwood remembered Flack's "First Time" and decided to use it for the film. The exposure prompted Atlantic Records to release it as a single, and the song took off, hitting number one on *Billboard's* pop chart and staying there for six weeks.

It's doubtful that "First Time" would have gone to the top if Atlantic had released it in 1969. The tender, devotional feeling of the song, along with Flack's luscious sensuality, were too soft for the late sixties. By 1972, however, it was on the mark, mellowing the hot soul thrust of the sixties and anticipating the quiet-storm sensibility of the new decade.

Ironically, when Flack won the Record of the Year Grammy for "The First Time Ever I Saw Your Face," one of the records she beat was "American Pie" by Don McLean. (Other nominees were "Alone Again (Naturally)" by Gilbert O'Sullivan, "Song Sung Blue" by Neil Diamond, and "Without You" by Nilsson). It was McLean's poignant elegy-history of rock 'n' roll that inspired singer Lori Lieberman to write the outline for "Killing Me Softly With His Song," which songwriters Gimbel and Fox would later polish and Flack turn into her next Grammy winner and number-one hit.

Indeed, "Killing Me Softly" was the number-one song in the

country when Flack won her Grammys for "The First Time" on March 3, 1973. A year later, "Killing Me Softly" kept Stevie Wonder from utterly overwhelming the 1973 awards (he won five Grammys), beating "You Are the Sunshine of My Life" in Record and Song of the Year contests. Other 1973 Record of the Year nominees were "Bad, Bad Leroy Brown" by Jim Croce, "Behind Closed Doors" by Charlie Rich, and "You're So Vain" by Carly Simon.

In addition to her Record of the Year Grammys, Flack has won two pop vocal awards, nabbing top duo honors with Donny Hathaway in 1972 for "Where Is the Love," and the female vocal prize in '73 for "Killing Me Softly." She has since received scattered nominations but no awards.

Stevie Wonder

When Paul Simon accepted his 1975 Album of the Year Grammy for *Still Crazy After All These Years,* the first person he thanked was Stevie Wonder, "for not recording an album this year."

Simon was kidding, but seriously. From *Talking Book* in 1973 to *Songs in the Key of Life* in 1976, Wonder was without question the most fecund, imaginative artist in pop, and the dominating figure of the Grammy Awards.

Three times in four years Wonder won five Grammys. Three times in four years he won Album of the Year honors, the only person to pull a triple play with such speed and one of only three artists (Sinatra and Simon are the others) to do it at all. To date, Wonder has won seventeen Grammys, third best on the all-time nonclassical list, behind Quincy Jones and Henry Mancini.

NARAS, which snubbed all Motown artists in the sixties, ignored Little Stevie Wonder for the first ten years of his career, spurning everything from "Fingertips," the hot harmonica call-and-response classic he recorded when he was twelve, to "Signed, Sealed, Delivered," "My Cherie Amour," "For Once in My Life," and other sixties soul-pop standards Wonder wrote and recorded as a teen.

By the time the twenty-three-year-old prodigy released *Innervisions* in 1973, both he and Motown were fed up with Grammy neglect. Determined to generate the kind of press that would bring Wonder's work to the attention of Grammy members, Motown hired outside publicists to supplement its own efforts. The combined campaign, including a "Hear It Like Stevie" listening party, at which guests previewed the album wearing blindfolds, paid off. *Innervisions* drew major media attention and seven Grammy nominations, more than any other work that year.

Wonder almost wasn't around to enjoy his long-overdue Grammy success. On August 6, 1973, while he was touring South Carolina, a truck hauling logs screeched to a stop in front of Wonder's car, sending its cargo through the singer's windshield. Wonder was in a coma for a week, and lucky to be alive by the time the Grammys were held on April 4, 1974.

The close call made his Grammy victories especially sweet. When *Innervisions* was named Album of the Year, Wonder brought his mother, two brothers, and a sister to the Grammy stage and thanked the Academy for "making this the sunshine of my life."

Innervisions beat Roberta Flack's *Killing Me Softly With His Song* (winner of Song and Record of the Year Grammys) for the Album of the Year award. Other nominees were *There Goes Rhymin' Simon* by Paul Simon, *The Divine Miss M* by Bette Midler, and *Behind Closed Doors* by Charlie Rich.

Wonder also took home Pop Vocal Performance, Male honors in '73 for "You Are the Sunshine of My Life" and Rhythm & Blues Vocal Performance, Male honors for "Superstition," which also won the Best Rhythm & Blues Song prize.

The leading nominee of the 1974 Grammys as well, with eight, Wonder won his second straight Album of the Year award, this one for *Fulfillingness' First Finale*, knocking off Paul McCartney (*Band on the Run*), Joni Mitchell (*Court and Spark*), Elton John (*Caribou*), and John Denver (*Back Home Again*). In accepting the award, Wonder thanked an odd list of personal heroes—Elijah Muhammad and Jack Benny, to name a few.

Once again, Wonder notched pop and r&b vocal awards, with "Fulfillingness' First Finale" taking the former and "Boogie on Reggae Woman" the latter. Wonder's gritty "Living for the City," meanwhile, was named best r&b song, over a field that included one of his own songs, "Tell Me Something Good." The following year, Ray Charles won an r&b vocal Grammy for his version of "Living for the City."

Wonder negotiated a new recording contract with Motown in

1975, one that gave him a then-unprecedented 20 percent of all royalties and a $13 million guarantee over the next seven years. The deal was a steal for Motown. Although he took two years to record his next album, *Songs in the Key of Life* was another masterpiece, a three-disc LP of breathtaking originality and range.

The album brought Wonder his third Album of the Year Grammy, chosen by NARAS over *Silk Degrees* by Boz Scaggs, *Breezin'* by George Benson, *Framptom Comes Alive* by Peter Frampton, and *Chicago X* by Chicago. In addition, *Songs in the Key of Life* drew male pop vocal honors, while "Sir Duke," Wonder's salute to Duke Ellington, won the male r&b vocal award. Capping off his incredible mid-70s roll, Wonder bagged the Producer of the Year prize.

Wonder added to his Grammy tally in 1985, notching a fourth r&b vocal award with *In Square Circle*. A year later he logged a group vocal trophy for "That's What Friends Are For," an AIDS charity record Wonder cut with Dionne Warwick, Gladys Knight, and Elton John.

Fleetwood Mac

If the Grammys gave an Album of the Decade award, Fleetwood Mac's *Rumours* would certainly have been a strong contender for the seventies prize. The Bee Gees' *Saturday Night Fever* put the country in a party-till-you-drop disco mode. The Eagles' *Hotel California* offered hipper-than-thou commentary on fast-lane seventies culture. But *Rumours* cut deeper, provided a more intimate, personal sound track, one that tapped into and helped define both the sleekness and soulfulness of the times.

Rumours, which won the Album of the Year Grammy in 1977 (beating *Hotel California*, among others), was a spectacular success, spending over seven months atop the *Billboard* charts and launching four Top 10 songs—"Dreams," "You Make Loving Fun," "Go Your Own Way" and "Don't Stop." None of these hits, strangely, received Grammy nominations.

The extraordinary success of *Rumours* was matched, curiously enough, by the hellish circumstances under which it was made. The album took over a year to complete, in large part because Fleetwood

Mac's two couples—Christine and John McVie and Lindsay Buckingham and Stevie Nicks—were in the throes of breaking up, a
situation that lent the album an intense charge while turning the
recording process into a rock 'n' roll version of "Days of Our Lives."

"It was a pretty bizarre situation," recalls drummer Mick Fleetwood. "John and Christine were horribly unhappy. Stevie and Lindsay were impossible around each other. My marriage was going down
the tubes. . . . People from the outside did not expect us to finish
that album.

"*Rumours*, in retrospect, turned out to be a very truthful docu-
ment of what was going on," he adds. "We weren't planning on airing
our dirty laundry in public, but we made the album as we went along,
quite literally, writing a lot of the songs in the studio, and, I think,
[the honesty] humanized everything."

Grammy voters were certainly impressed. *Rumours*, the first and
only Grammy winner for Fleetwood Mac, nabbed the Album of the
Year prize against a field of *Aja* by Steely Dan, *Hotel California* by
the Eagles, *Star Wars* by the London Symphony Orchestra and John
Williams, and *JT* by James Taylor. The album was also nominated for
the Pop Vocal Performance, Group award, but lost to the Bee Gees'
"How Deep Is Your Love." A bid in the engineering category also fell
short, losing to Steely Dan's *Aja*.

It had taken Fleetwood Mac ten years and myriad incarnations to
finally gain the Grammy spotlight. The band began in England in
1967 as a roots-oriented folk-blues group. A strong pop-rock turn in
the early seventies brought moderate success. But things changed
dramatically with the addition of Lindsay Buckingham and Stevie
Nicks in 1974.

Mick Fleetwood discovered the duo one afternoon when a studio
engineer in Van Nuys happened to play a tape of an obscure album
called *Buckingham Nicks*. Fleetwood was so impressed that when
guitarist Bob Welch abruptly left the band a few months later, he
asked Buckingham and Nicks, sight unseen, to join the group.

The chemistry of the new lineup was magical, combining the
earthiness of the old Fleetwood Mac with the airier, more harmoni-
cally oriented sound of Buckingham-Nicks.

"It was a weird combination that clicked," Fleetwood recalls, "and
all of us knew we were on to something quite special."

So special, in fact, that Fleetwood went to Warner Bros. president Mo Ostin after the revamped band recorded its first LP and asked to be dropped from the label if Ostin didn't share Mac's enthusiasm for the new sound.

"I was frightened Warner Bros. was just gonna think of this as another Fleetwood Mac album, that it was just gonna do all right. I said to Mo, 'I just want you to know when you listen to this album, how much it means to us. It's something really different, and if you don't think so, let us off the label.' "

The *Fleetwood Mac* LP yielded three hits ("Over My Head," "Rhiannon," and "Say You Love Me") and sold four million copies, more than any other Warner record up to that time. Like many fine albums, it failed to draw any Grammy nods, though it did set the stage for the Grammy salute to *Rumours* in 1977.

Despite numerous hits and multiplatinum sales from *Tusk* (1979), *Mirage* (1982), and *Tango in the Night* (1987), Fleetwood Mac has yet to receive another Grammy nomination or award.

Billy Joel

For a while in the middle and late seventies, Billy Joel seemed like a hip, middle-of-the-road alternative to disco and punk. Brash, street-smart, but musically old-fashioned, he represented an almost defiant assertion of classic pop values in the midst of drum-machine monotony and primitivist squall.

Joel was a made-to-order Grammy star, a seventies hero to those in the music industry who cherished a nicely turned line and a well-constructed song. The fact that he wore a leather jacket and struck a belligerent pose only made his hip-sounding mainstream standards more credible.

Joel was born to immigrant Jewish parents in Hicksville, Long Island, on May 9, 1949. His Alsatian-born father returned to Europe soon after his birth, and Joel was raised by his mother, who worked as a secretary and started him on classical piano lessons at the age of four.

When he quit twelve years later, Joel had discovered Elvis and the Beatles and was helping his mom meet mortgage payments by playing with a band called the Hassles. An amateur boxer—Joel won twenty-two of twenty-eight fights—he never finished high school.

In 1972, Joel cut *Cold Spring Harbor*, his first solo LP. A bitter legal fight over songwriting and performance profits drove Joel underground—he played in an L.A. cocktail lounge for a year and a half under the name of Bill Martin—until Columbia Records came to the rescue, signing him in 1973.

Joel's first record for CBS, *Piano Man*, was a hit, and he encored with two well-received albums, *Streetlife Serenade* and *Turnstiles*. His big breakthrough came in 1977 when he teamed with producer Phil Ramone, a savvy veteran (and former Grammy official in New York) to cut *The Stranger*. The record sold four million copies and spun off four hit singles, including "Just the Way You Are."

Grammy voters loved the song, choosing it over Neil Diamond's "You Don't Bring Me Flowers," an MOR powerhouse, for the 1978 Song of the Year prize. "Just the Way You Are" also beat "Stayin' Alive" by the Bee Gees, "Three Times a Lady" by Lionel Richie, and "You Needed Me" by Randy Goodrum (recorded by Anne Murray).

"Just the Way You Are" once again bested "Stayin' Alive" and "You Needed Me," as well as "Feels So Good" by Chuck Mangione and "Baker Street" by Gerry Rafferty, in winning the 1978 Record of the Year award.

A year later, NARAS voters picked Joel's *52nd Street* for Album of the Year honors over *Bad Girls* by Donna Summer, *Breakfast in America* by Supertramp, *The Gambler* by Kenny Rogers, and *Minute by Minute* by the Doobie Brothers. Perhaps worried about the effect of so many Grammy accolades on his street-singer image, Joel reportedly spurned an invitation to the '79 awards because they were "too Vegasy."

By 1980, critics had begun to turn on Joel and his strenuous, sometimes strained style of Tin Pan Alley rock, but he managed to eke out another Grammy with *Glass Houses*. The album knocked off Bruce Springsteen's "Devil With a Blue Dress/Good Golly Miss Molly" medley and Jackson Browne's "On the Boulevard," among others, to win the Rock Vocal Performance, Male award.

Joel has continued to churn out hits but has yet to win another Grammy, though he did receive a raft of nominations in 1989 for the song "We Didn't Start the Fire" and one bid in 1990 for his *Storm Front* LP.

The Bee Gees

The year was 1978 and America was running a white-hot *Saturday Night Fever*. The John Travolta film about working-class disco culture was the surprise hit of the year, and the sound track, featuring six cuts by the Bee Gees, was a monster, triple-disc LP that sold twenty-five million copies (second only to Michael Jackson's *Thriller* on the all-time sales list), and topped the *Billboard* charts for twenty-four weeks.

It's hard to imagine how ubiquitous a triumph *Saturday Night Fever* was. For months the record seemed to dominate every radio station, every jukebox, every party, putting the whole country in a trancelike, if slightly cartoonish, disco mode. The Bee Gees sounded "like mechanical mice with an unnatural sense of rhythm," *Village Voice* critic Robert Christgau wrote with bemused appreciation, pondering the group's hold on the land.

The Grammys weren't really into disco—NARAS resisted establishing a disco award until 1979, then killed it after a single year—but there was no getting around *Saturday Night Fever*. The LP generated five awards, walking away with Album of the Year honors, the first sound track to do so since *Music From Peter Gunn* in 1958.

Its huge commercial success notwithstanding, *Fever*'s Grammy triumphs could not be taken for granted. Although the sound track was released in late 1977, it missed the deadline for the '77 awards.* By the time the 1978 Grammys were handed out on February 15, 1979, *Saturday Night Fever* was fifteen months old. Incredibly, the Bee Gees were still on their phenomenal, *Fever*-fueled roll, topping the charts through early '79 with follow-up disco hits like "Too Much Heaven" and "Love You Inside and Out."

In winning the Album of the Year prize, *Saturday Night Fever* beat the Rolling Stones' *Some Girls*, Jackson Browne's *Running on Empty*, and Barry Manilow's *Even Now*.

Ten different artists—the Bee Gees, David Shire, Yvonne Elliman, Tavares, Kool & the Gang, K.C. & the Sunshine Band, MFSB, Walter Murphy, Trammps, and Ralph MacDonald—and sixteen pro-

* The Grammy eligibility year is October 1 through September 30. In other words, for a record to have been eligible for, say, the 1977 awards, it would have had to have been released between October 1, 1976 and September 30, 1977.

ducers collected Album of the Year Grammys for *Saturday Night Fever*, the biggest crowd of winners to take a Grammy bow until 1985, when forty-five artists and producer Quincy Jones nabbed song and Record of the Year honors with *We Are the World*.

The Bee Gees had a hand in all five *Fever* Grammys, winning Best Pop Vocal Performance, Group laurels in 1977 for "How Deep Is Your Love," the same award the following year for the entire *Fever* sound track, Producer of the Year honors (with Albhy Galuten and Karl Richardson) in 1978, and a Best Arrangement for Voices award for "Stayin' Alive," also in '78.

Hit-makers since the sixties, with more number-one records to their credit than everyone but the Beatles, Elvis, and Michael Jackson, the Brothers Gibb never won a Grammy prior to *Saturday Night Fever*. As a group, they have yet to win another, although Barry Gibb shared a Pop Performance, Duo award with Barbra Streisand in 1980 for "Guilty."

Christopher Cross

In 1980, Texas-born singer-songwriter Christopher Cross won five Grammys—and he's been apologizing ever since.

Cross had the misfortune to have had an excess of good fortune, more than most critics thought he deserved. He not only won the Best New Artist prize (beating the Pretenders, among others), but he swept the three most prestigious awards—Song, Record, and Album of the Year. Cross's ultralight hit, "Sailing," nabbed the first two honors, while his debut, eponymous LP was deemed best album of 1980. As if all that weren't enough, Cross also won a Best Arrangement Accompanying Vocalist salute for "Sailing."

Cross is the only Grammy rookie to bag the top three awards, joining Simon & Garfunkle and Carole King as the only artists overall to turn the trick. But while few people objected to the Simon or King sweeps, Cross's astonishing success drew howls of ridicule from pop-rock critics across the land.

Cross was an extremely conservative Grammy choice for 1980. In a year that produced *London Calling* by the Clash, *The River* by Bruce Springsteen, *Off the Wall* by Michael Jackson, *Dirty Mind* by Prince, *Los Angeles* by X, *Remain in Light* by the Talking Heads, and *Hotter than July* by Stevie Wonder, it seemed preposterous to heap every major award on someone as bland as Cross. The Cross landslide was like a reactionary mandate by the industry pros, a rejection of everything radical and daring that had happened during the year in favor of escapist melody and easygoing craft.

Critics from coast to coast were beside themselves. The *Los Angeles Times*'s Robert Hilburn blasted NARAS for hitting a "new low in conservatism." Even Bill Murray of "Saturday Night Live" got into the act, working a few bars from "Sailing" into his parody of "lounge lizard" acts.

It wasn't Cross's fault that Grammy voters thought he was better than Springsteen, Michael Jackson, and Prince. But that hardly mattered. Cross had the good luck/bad luck to win too many awards at a time when pop battle lines were being drawn, and he came to symbolize the blindly conservative and commercial aspects of the Grammys. It hardly seemed fair. There was something innocent and pure about the creation of "Sailing," Cross's dreamy, much-maligned hit. The song seemed to stream out of his unconscious one afternoon as he strummed his guitar in Bayside, Texas, where he gigged seven nights a week at local clubs for two years.

"I was picking around the guitar, looking for something that worked," Cross recalls, "and I came up with a little progression. I just started singing along, without really thinking about what I was singing, just hoping it was intelligent. And I was very lucky. I kept playing this pattern, almost like a mantra, and I managed to get into a place, a groove, to get lost in it, and the words just sort of came out as one glob.

"When I finished the first verse and turned off the recorder, I was in a cold sweat. I thought, Something wonderful just happened, I'm a genius, and I walked around the room panting, real pleased with myself."

With good reason. A demo of "Sailing" helped win Cross a Warner Bros. recording contract, and two years later it went to number one on the *Billboard* charts, providing some melodic counterpoint to the four-on-the-floor monotony of heavy metal, disco, and punk thrash.

Despite the success, no one was more astonished or overwhelmed than Cross by his jackpot on Grammy night.

"I was convinced by all my friends that I had a good shot at the Best New Artist award, and I went to the awards excited and hopeful for that," he remembers. "When they announced before the TV show that we won the best-arrangement Grammy, I was sitting on top of the moon. Harry Belafonte and Herb Alpert gave me the award, and I was so enamored being next to those guys. I remember staring and thinking, God, there's Herb Alpert. I remember winning and him whispering, 'Here, I think you'll wanna have this.' "

By the time Cross made his final trip to the Shrine stage and accepted the trophy for best LP from Diana Ross, he was "numb" and virtually speechless. He vividly remembers receiving a standing ovation from the celebrity-packed house.

"I looked down at the crowd—so many famous faces. Billy Joel was in the front row. I didn't know him, but he was the one who stood up first . . . and the crowd followed. That stood out for me, that he stood up to applaud me."

Despite his elation, Cross, who has struggled in recent years, had a premonition on Grammy night that there might be a dark side to winning so many awards. When an acquaintance suggested that such acclaim early in his career might be "the worst thing that could ever have happened," Cross was furious, though the remark "struck a chord that was haunting."

"At this point in my career, past illusion and facade, I have to say it was true what she said. People talk about the storm of success—take it from me, it's a hurricane. For me to win five Grammys right off the bat was a big burden. Don't get the wrong impression: I wouldn't trade my Grammys for the world. But at first the Grammys meant everything to me, then nothing. Now I'm proud, but I don't put so much stock in them that they can ruin my life."

Cross followed up his 1980 Grammy conquest with four nominations in 1981 for "Arthur's Theme," which he cowrote with Peter Allen, Burt Bacharach, and Carole Bayer Sager. In the running for best record, song, male pop vocal, and sound track song, the record failed to take home any awards.

Cross has yet to win another nomination or award.

Toto

The Grammys drew a coast-to-coast chorus of boos in 1982 when a rock-by-numbers studio group called Toto racked up five awards, including Record of the Year honors for the hit single "Rosanna" and Album of the Year kudos for *Toto IV*.

Five Grammys for Toto, a group that one critic panned as "state of the bland"? Somebody find Dorothy! The praise seemed, well— excessive. Toto was a fairly creative formula band with good hooks and a smooth, well-crafted sound, but the same could be said of any number of groups, including Chicago, Asia, Men at Work, and the Human League, to name a few.

Suddenly, Toto was a Grammy supergroup, the first band in the history of the awards to win Record and Album of the Year tributes the same year. All this at a time when Bruce Springsteen, Elvis Costello, Prince, and the Talking Heads had yet to win their first awards.

Even members of NARAS were dismayed, and plans were quickly formulated, amid dire warnings that the Grammys were in danger of falling hopelessly out of step, to launch a new membership recruitment drive in hopes of bringing hipper, younger members into the Academy. For 1982, however, the damage had already been done. In addition to winning Album and Record of the Year Grammys, Toto won the Producer of the Year award. Keyboardist David Paich won a Vocal Arrangement for Two or More Voices trophy for "Rosanna," while Paich, Jeff Porcaro, and Jerry Hey copped an Instrumental Arrangement Accompanying Vocals salute, also for "Rosanna."

In winning top album honors, *Toto IV*, which yielded the hit single "Africa" as well as "Rosanna," knocked off *The Nightfly* by Donald Fagen, *American Fool* by John Cougar, *The Nylon Curtain* by Billy Joel, and *Tug of War* by Paul McCartney.

Record of the Year honors for "Rosanna," meanwhile, came at the expense of "Always on My Mind" by Willie Nelson, "Ebony & Ivory" by Paul McCartney and Stevie Wonder, "Steppin' Out" by Joe Jackson, and "Chariots of Fire" by Vangelis.

One possible reason for Toto's grandiose Grammy success was the fact that the band consisted of veteran studio musicians whose collective contacts included many members of NARAS.

"If everyone they've met in a studio during the last few years votes for them, it'll be a runaway," the *Los Angeles Times*'s Robert Hilburn gloomily predicted a few days before the awards, "even though there's a disheartening lack of depth or daring in the group's music."

Prior to its 1982 Grammy haul, Toto had drawn a single nomination, for Best New Artist of 1978. It lost that award (along with Elvis

Costello) to Taste of Honey. Since 1982, Toto has failed to generate
any new Grammy nominations or awards.

Ray Charles

The Grammys achieved credibility in the r&b field when they began
heaping awards on The Genius, Ray Charles, in 1960. Charles won
nine Grammys over the next six years, including four consecutive
r&b awards, the longest Grammy winning streak up to that time.

NARAS had much to atone for, having bestowed the very first r&b
Grammy on "Tequila," a garage-rock classic by the all-white Champs
in 1958. Moreover, Grammy voters hadn't even nominated Ray's call-
and-response classic "What'd I Say" for r&b honors in 1959, while
giving bids to such dubious offerings as "Big Hunk of Love" by Elvis
and "Guess Who" by Jesse Belvin.

NARAS made amends in a big way in 1960, giving Charles four
awards, including three non-r&b nods. Charles's "Georgia on My
Mind" won the Best Vocal Performance Single, Male prize as well as
Best Performance by a Pop Single Artist honors, while his *Genius of
Ray Charles* LP took home the Best Vocal Performance Album, Male
award.

Charles's "Let the Good Times Roll," meanwhile, was named Best
Rhythm & Blues Performance of the year.

Brother Ray was one soul singer musically snooty Grammy voters
had to respect. Screamers like Little Richard and James Brown could
be dismissed as too primitive, but Charles's raw yet nuanced elo-
quence was undeniable. Sinatra, the most venerated of Grammy
stars, dubbed him "The Genius," and the moniker rang true.

Charles's genius, of course, had a lot to do with pain and his ability
to improvise the pathos of his life into his songs. Born in Depression-
wracked Georgia, he lost both his sight and his parents as a child,
studied music at the St. Augustine School for the Blind, and kept
himself from starving at the age of fifteen by hustling jazz gigs in
Florida and Georgia.

At age seventeen he asked a friend to look at a map and locate the
farthest place away from where he was; that done, Charles hopped a
Greyhound bus for Seattle, and kept afloat playing local clubs while

fashioning himself into a discreetly bluesy crooner in the mold of Nat King Cole and Charles Brown.

In 1953, Charles began experimenting with a different voice—his own—and the results were electrifying. Songs like "I Got a Woman" and, later, "What'd I Say" virtually created modern soul, bringing gospelish fervor to r&b themes and inspiring the careers of countless stars.

Ironically, by the time the Grammys crowned him r&b king, Charles was branching out, cutting highly successful pop and country records and taking a backseat, r&b-wise, to younger soulsters like James Brown, Sam Cooke, and Otis Redding, who carried into the sixties the urgent, profane sound Charles had pioneered.

Indeed, Charles was a decidedly conservative choice in 1963, the year Grammy voters picked "Busted," one of his lesser efforts, over a spectacular field of soul nominees—"Fingertips" by Little Stevie Wonder, "Heat Wave" by Martha & the Vandellas, "Da Doo Ron Ron" by the Crystals, "Be My Baby" by the Ronettes, and "Up on the Roof" by the Drifters.

In 1962 Charles threw the record industry, and the Grammy governors, a big curve by recording a country album, *Modern Sounds in Country & Western Music*. No black artist had ever tested the country market before, and Charles's own label, ABC, was horrified by the idea. The album turned out to be an enormous hit, ABC's first platinum seller, with a single, "I Can't Stop Loving You," that sold three million copies.

Grammy officials didn't know what to do. "I Can't Stop Loving You" was obviously country. Yet, Ray Charles was obviously black, Mr. R&B. The song was ultimately placed, against the evidence of one's ears, in the r&b field, where it won. "A Funny Way of Laughin' " by Burl Ives wound up nabbing the country award.

All told, Charles has won eleven Grammys. "Hit the Road Jack" took the Best Rhythm & Blues Recording award in 1961. "Crying Time" pulled the same award, along with an r&b vocal performance record salute, in 1966. Charles won his sixth r&b vocal Grammy in 1975 for his remake of Stevie Wonder's Grammy-winning "Living for the City." His most recent triumph came in 1990, when he snared the r&b duo award with Chaka Khan for "I'll Be Good to You."

Charles has generated many nominations through the years, most notably a 1968 r&b vocal bid for "Eleanor Rigby." John Lennon and

Paul McCartney were so honored by Charles's cover that they paused before flying to India to meet Maharishi Mahesh Yogi to send the ultimate soul man a telegram: "Ray Charles's genius goes on and on," the two Beatles wrote. "We love your heart and soul."

Aretha Franklin

When Aretha Franklin recorded "Respect" in 1967, producer Jerry Wexler knew something extraordinary had happened. Otis Redding wrote the song and enjoyed a modest hit with it early in 1966, but Aretha turned it into more than a hit. In her hands, "Respect" became a hot command, a song that kicked into the sixties at every level—personal, sexual, racial, political—and made people move with a defiant authority that perfectly expressed its time and gave a deep new definition to soul.

"Aretha added another dimension to the song," Wexler explained to *Rolling Stone* magazine in 1988. "It was . . . a very interesting mix: an intuitive feminist outcry, a sexual statement, an announcement of dignity, and a minority person making a statement of pride without sloganeering.

"Before we put that record out," Wexler added, "Otis came into the studio and I played it for him. He looked at me with a big grin and said, 'That girl done stole my song.'"

"Respect" won two Grammys in 1967—Best Rhythm & Blues Recording and Best Rhythm & Blues Vocal Performance, Female— and launched Aretha on a Grammy roll that would bring her eight consecutive r&b vocal salutes, the longest winning streak in the history of the awards. Aretha's hold on the female r&b Grammy wasn't broken until 1975, when Natalie Cole won the award.

Overall, Franklin has won fifteen Grammys, tied with John Williams for fourth best among pop artists, behind Henry Mancini, Quincy Jones, and Stevie Wonder.

Franklin might never have become Lady Soul if she had stayed with Columbia Records, the label that signed her in 1960 and spent years foolishly trying to turn her into a black Streisand, soaking her vocals in strings and shackling her with material like "Swanee" and "Rock-a-Bye Your Baby With a Dixie Melody."

When Franklin switched to Atlantic, a label founded on r&b, she quickly found her voice, and the results were spectacular. Beginning with "I Never Loved a Man the Way I Love You" in 1967, Franklin turned out nine Top 10 hits in little over a year—"Respect," "Baby I Love You," "A Natural Woman," "Chain of Fools," "Since You Been Gone," "Think," "The House That Jack Built," and "I Say a Little Prayer for You."

Aretha's breakthrough record, as both soul queen and Grammy star, was "Respect," which beat "Try a Little Tenderness" by Otis Redding, "Soul Man" by Sam & Dave, "Skinny Legs and All" by Joe Tex, and "Dead End Street" by Lou Rawls to win the top r&b record prize. Franklin knocked off "I Heard It Through the Grapevine" by Gladys Knight, "The Queen Alone" by Carla Thomas, "Tell Mama" by Etta James, and "You'll Go to Hell" by Nina Simone in winning the vocal prize.

In 1968 Franklin won her second r&b vocal Grammy with "Chain of Fools." Her streak continued in 1969 with "Share Your Love With Me," followed by "Don't Play That Song" in 1970, "Bridge Over Troubled Water" in '71 (which beat Janis Joplin's posthumous *Pearl*), *Young, Gifted & Black* in '72, "Master of Eyes" in '73, and "Ain't Nothing Like the Real Thing" in '74.

Franklin didn't always deserve to win, and she knew it. "Master of Eyes," a mediocre effort, beat Ann Peebles's memorable "I Can't Stand the Rain" in part, no doubt, on the strength of Franklin's name. In 1972, Franklin gave her Grammy for *Young, Gifted and Black* to Esther Phillips, whose "From a Whisper to a Scream" would have been a worthier choice.

Not that Franklin was blasé about her Grammy wins. When she accepted her 1974 award for "Ain't Nothing Like the Real Thing," she looked at presenter David Bowie and squealed, "I'm so happy I could kiss David Bowie." (Bowie was so mortified by the affectionate insult, according to one biographer, that when his girlfriend played an Aretha record days later, he broke it in half.)

Franklin continued to pull Grammy nominations throughout the seventies, but didn't win another trophy until 1981, when she notched her ninth R&B Vocal Performance, Female nod for "Hold On I'm Comin'." Four years later, she topped that category for the tenth time, winning with "Freeway of Love." In 1987 Franklin won two awards, sharing r&b duo honors with George Michael for "I

Knew You Were Waiting (for Me)," and bagging femme r&b prize number eleven with her *Aretha* LP.

Earth, Wind & Fire

"All 'n' All," you'd have to say Earth, Wind & Fire was the "Shining Star" of the Grammys for much of the 1970s. The trailblazing rock-funk ensemble racked up six r&b trophies in seven years, including four R&B Vocal Performance by a Group Grammys, more than any other band in the history of the awards.

Good as its Grammy tally was, Earth, Wind & Fire deserved better. The band couldn't break out of Grammy's r&b ghetto despite the fact that it was the decade's number-one crossover act, immensely popular with rock, pop, soul, and even jazz fans. In a year when "Love Will Keep Us Together" by the Captain and Tennille won the Record of the Year Grammy, "Shining Star" wasn't even nominated for the award.

Ironically, the group was founded on the notion that a black group could transcend music-biz categories and walls. The ensemble was formed in 1970 by Maurice White, drummer with the Ramsey Lewis Trio, who became fascinated with metaphysics and occult spirituality after a tour of Egypt and decided to form a group that could translate his newfound vision into musical terms.

Earth, Wind & Fire's initial lineup cut two albums for Warner Bros., unfocused jazzscapes that didn't make much of an impact. But when White switched to Columbia and retooled the band, bringing brothers Fred and Verdine aboard along with singer Philip Bailey, the outfit found its groove.

And what a groove it was. Earth, Wind & Fire lived up to all aspects of its elemental name, blending intense rhythms, vibrant horns, and urgent fly-away vocals in an exuberant, quasi-religious swirl that was highly original yet true to White's jazz-r&b roots— idiosyncratic and vastly appealing.

The group's commercial and Grammy breakthrough came in 1975 with *That's the Way of the World*, a sound track for a movie of the same name that featured Earth, Wind & Fire playing themselves as an up-and-coming rock 'n' soul band. The album's chart-topping hit, "Shining Star," brought the band its first group-vocal Grammy, knocking off an undistinguished field of "Cut the Cake" by the Average White Band, "Fire" by the Ohio Players, "Get Down Tonight" by K.C. and the Sunshine Band, and "How Long" by the Pointer Sisters.

Earth, Wind & Fire notched an r&b vocal nomination in 1976 for "Gratitude," and a Best Rhythm & Blues Song bid in 1977 for "Best of My Love," but failed to win another Grammy until 1978, when it won r&b vocal prize number two with its *All 'n' All* LP.

"Runnin'," a track from the album, won the R&B Instrumental Performance award, while White landed a Best Arrangement Accompanying a Vocalist Grammy for "Got to Get You Into My Life."

The group repeated itself in 1979, winning vocal kudos for "After the Love Has Gone" and instrumental honors for "Boogie Wonderland." "After the Love" was nominated for Record and Song of the Year Grammys but lost in both contests to the Doobie Brothers' "What a Fool Believes." The song, written by David Foster, Jay Graydon, and Bill Champlin, did win the r&b song Grammy.

Earth, Wind & Fire won its last Grammy to date in 1982, nabbing its fourth r&b vocal prize for "Wanna Be With You," a song that shared the award with "Let It Whip" by Dazz Band. Earth, Wind & Fire broke up in 1983, re-formed four years later, and has yet to win another nomination or award.

Marvin Gaye

When Marvin Gaye accepted a Grammy in 1983 for his comeback hit, "Sexual Healing," he puckered up and kissed the trophy. The gesture was heartfelt. Gaye, one of soul's most stylish and creative stars and a hit-maker for twenty years, had never before won the award.

Gaye's kiss that night signaled the end to a volatile and bitter grudge he had held against the Grammys for snubbing him for so many years, often in favor of Lou Rawls, a middle-of-the-road "quality" singer who won two r&b Grammys in head-to-head competition with Gaye.

In 1971 Gaye thought he had a surefire Grammy winner with *What's Going On*, his first self-produced and self-written album and a deeply felt, socially conscious work that drew raves from critics and spawned three million-selling singles: "Mercy, Mercy Me," "Inner

City Blues (Wanna Make Me Holler)," and the title track. The album was a stunner, a song cycle that broke open the form and content of soul, mixing themes of poverty, Vietnam, and the environment with introspective passion and concern.

What's Going On made almost no impression at all on the Academy. A single cut, "Inner City Blues," drew a single nomination, for Rhythm & Blues Performance, Male. NARAS voters chose Lou Rawls's "A Natural Man" instead, a smooth bedroom and nightclub hit that had neither the artistic reach nor the commercial success of Gaye's work.

Gaye, who longed for the industrywide approbation a Grammy confers, was bitter and frustrated by the loss.
"I knew it was my time," he told biographer David Ritz. "But it wasn't. I felt deeply hurt by the whole affair. I felt like I was swindled and I was made at Lou. . . . If I hadn't watched myself I could have wound up fighting him. That's how pissed I was. I thought I'd turned out a great work and the Grammys didn't even give me the time of day. Politics, that's what it was, Hollywood games. I refused to play those games and I suffered."

Gaye's Grammy frustrations continued in 1976, when he was nominated twice but once again came away empty-handed. Gaye's "I Want You" lost the R&B Vocal Performance, Male award to Stevie Wonder's "I Wish," while "After the Dance" lost the R&B Instrumental Performance prize to George Benson's "Theme From Good King Bad."

In 1977, Rawls once again got the best of Gaye when *Unmistakably Lou* beat *Let's Get It On* for the r&b male vocal Grammy. Gaye, who was in the Shrine Auditorium as the award was announced, had to beat down an impulse—a very powerful impulse—to "punch him [Rawls] out on national TV."

"God intervened on Rawls's behalf and kept me in my seat," he told Ritz.

Gaye's self-restraint and patience finally paid off in 1983, exactly twenty years after he first hit the charts with "Hitchhike" and "Pride and Joy." "Sexual Healing," a huge comeback hit that seemed to remind everyone how great Gaye was, won r&b vocal and instrumental Grammys. When Gaye took the stage to receive his long-overdue awards, he was met with standing ovations from the industry-packed Shrine Auditorium crowd.

Grammy producers and network executives held their collective breath, however, as Gaye performed "Sexual Healing" on the show. There was some concern that Gaye would strip down to a G-string and deliver an X-rated version of the erotic song. Gaye behaved himself. One wonders what would have happened if he had lost again.

Gaye never won another Grammy. His "Midnight Love" single was nominated for r&b vocal honors in 1984 but lost in the Michael Jackson avalanche to "Billie Jean." A month after the 1984 awards, and barely a year after his only Grammy wins, Gaye was dead, shot by his father during a family dispute.

Michael Jackson

The Michael Jackson Awards, otherwise known as the Grammys, were held on February 24, 1984, a full fifteen months after the release of Jackson's hypersuccessful *Thriller*. Incredibly, the album was still riding the *Billboard* charts and spinning off hit singles. The title cut went Top 10 the week of the awards.

"It's a pleasure doing the Michael Jackson Show," Mickey Rooney cracked near the start of the telecast. Rooney was anticipating the obvious—a Jackson sweep of spectacular proportions. With fans screaming "We love you, Michael" from the balcony and a record sixty million viewers tuning in, Jackson made trip after trip to the Shrine steps, each time greeted by a standing ovation that seemed to certify his status as conquering hero-pied piper of pop.

All told, *Thriller* generated eleven nominations and grabbed eight Grammys, two more than Roger Miller, the previous record holder, had won in 1965. *Thriller*, of course, was named Album of the Year, while "Billie Jean" won the Record of the Year award.

Jackson would likely have won the Song of the Year Grammy as well if he hadn't been competing against himself with two strong nominations—"Beat It" and "Billie Jean"—which split the Jackson vote and cleared the way for Sting to win with "Every Breath You Take."

Sting stung Jackson twice, the second time as part of the Police, whose "Every Breath You Take" beat "The Girl Is Mine," Jackson's duet with Paul McCartney, for the Pop Vocal Performance by a Duo or Group prize.

Jackson more than evened the score, beating the Police's *Synchronicity* for Album of the Year. Other nominees were the *Flashdance* sound track, *An Innocent Man* by Billy Joel, and *Let's Dance* by David Bowie.

Jackson busted the Police again in the Record of the Year contest, knocking off "Every Breath You Take," along with "All Night Long" by Lionel Richie, "Flashdance" by Irene Cara, and "Maniac" by Michael Sembello.

Among the many victims of Jackson's landslide was Prince, a first-time nominee and two-time loser. Prince's "1999" succumbed to *Thriller* in the Pop Vocal Performance, Male race, while the Purple One's "International Lover" was jilted in favor of "Billie Jean" in the Rhythm & Blues Vocal Performance contest.

Jackson's dominance was nowhere more evident than in the R&B Song of the Year race, where he placed three cuts from *Thriller*—"Billie Jean," "P.Y.T. (Pretty Young Thing)," and "Wanna Be Startin' Somethin'." "Billie Jean" won.

Strangely, none of Jackson's acclaimed music videos, which had so much to do with generating Michaelmania, were nominated for video awards, although "The Making of Thriller" won in '84.

Jackson, wearing a Sgt. Pepper–style jacket with gold epaulets and brocade, attended the awards with Brooke Shields and child actor Emmanuel Lewis of the TV series "Webster." He invited CBS Records head Walter Yetnikoff to the stage for one award, and brought sisters La Toya and Rebbie with him for another.

Although chastened by Katharine Hepburn for wearing sunglasses weeks earlier during the American Music Awards, Jackson wore dark shades his first half-dozen trips to the stage. He took them off on the seventh, looked into the camera, and said, "Katharine, this is for you."

Despite leading the Jackson Five to countless hits in the early 1970s, Michael Jackson never won a Grammy as part of that group. Indeed, he had won but a single award before hitting his *Thriller* jackpot, nabbing Rhythm & Blues Vocal Performance honors in 1979 for "Don't Stop 'Til You Get Enough" from his ten-million-selling *Off the Wall* album.

Jackson's Grammy record since *Thriller* has been spotty. He won

Song of the Year honors (with Lionel Richie) for "We Are the World" in 1985, but his long-awaited follow-up LP, *Bad*, was a Grammy turkey, drawing five nominations but no awards.

Jackson did win again in 1989, bagging Music Video, Short Form honors for "Leave Me Alone." Michael's "Moonwalker" was nominated for the long form award, but he lost to sister Janet Jackson and "Rhythm Nation."

Tina Turner

Tina Turner was, undeniably, the star of the 1984 Grammys, not just because she won the most awards, but because her victories capped off an incredibly gutsy, storybook comeback that lent the Grammys an unusual glow.

Turner had won a Grammy once before—seemingly a lifetime ago—when she was still part of Ike & Tina Turner, the marital and musical collaboration that launched her as an r&b-rock 'n' roll queen. The pair nabbed top Rhythm & Blues Vocal Performance by a Group honors in 1972 for their fired-up version of "Proud Mary."

By 1976, however, Turner's career was on the ropes, the victim in large part of her deteriorating relationship with Ike. Turner told *USA Today* that she walked away from the eighteen-year marriage after a final, violent scene, hitting the road with little more than the clothes on her back.

Turner spent the next eight years touring, paying off debts, and slowly rebuilding her career. She scored a modest hit with a remake of Al Green's "Let's Stay Together" in 1982, but her big break came a year later, when she met British songwriter Terry Britten, who offered her a new tune called "What's Love Got to Do With It."

Though she hated it at first, the song, with its cynical, broken-hearted charm, was tailor-made for Tina, who turned it into the bedroom anthem of the eighties and one of the biggest hits of 1984.

The affection and support for Turner in the Shrine Auditorium on Grammy night was palpable. Three times she took the stage to accept awards, and three times an audience that included Stevie Wonder, Hall & Oates, Cyndi Lauper, and Leonard Bernstein welcomed her with emotional standing Os. Bernstein even rushed his own Lifetime

Achievement Award acceptance speech "in order to leave more time for Tina," who was going to perform.

Turner had lip-synced a performance of "Private Dancer" on the American Music Awards a few weeks before, but she sang for real on the Grammys, despite a severe cold. She wept backstage after receiving her awards. "This is the greatest single moment in my career," she said.

Indeed it was. "What's Love Got to Do With It," walked away with two of the industry's biggest prizes—Record and Song of the Year Grammys—beating Bruce Springsteen's "Dancing in the Dark" for the first award. In addition, the song brought Turner the Pop Vocal Performance, Female trophy, while her follow-up hit, "Better Be Good to Me," won the Rock Vocal Performance prize. Turner became the third black artist to win a rock-vocal Grammy, joining Michael Jackson and Donna Summer.

Turner's emergence as the star of the Grammys was particularly impressive, given her competition. Bruce Springsteen, Prince, Cyndi Lauper, and Lionel Richie all had three or more nominations and any one of them could have been the night's big winner.

Turner's first Grammy nomination had come all the way back in 1961, when she and Ike drew a Best Rock and Roll Recording nod for "It's Gonna Work Out Fine." The song lost to "Let's Twist Again" by Chubby Checker. In 1969 Tina snagged an R&B Vocal Performance, Female nomination for "The Hunter," losing to perennial R&B queen Aretha Franklin and "Share Your Love With Me."

Since 1984, Tina has been a Grammy regular, riding the momentum of her big Grammy year to female rock vocal victories in 1985 ("One of the Living," from the movie *Mad Max: Beyond Thunderdome*), 1986 ("Back Where You Started"), and 1988 (*Tina Live in Europe*). The latter award exposed the sleepy Grammy voting habits of some NARAS members, who reflexively chose Turner and her mediocre *Live in Europe* LP over worthier offerings by Melissa Etheridge, Toni Childs, and Sinead O'Connor.

Quincy Jones

Producer-arranger-composer-instrumentalist Quincy Jones is the Henry Aaron of the Grammy Awards, a low-key, phenomenally durable and consistent pro who has delivered a steady, if unspectacular stream of hits for three decades and quietly accumulated more nominations and awards—eighty and twenty-five at last count—than any other pop artist. Like Aaron chasing Ruth, he finally passed longtime Grammy champ Henry Mancini, who has seventy-one nominations and twenty awards, last year.

As his trophies attest, Jones is the quintessential Grammy artist, a consummate studio craftsman who studied classical composition in Paris before delving into pop, funk, and soul. His ability to meld diverse influences into an assortment of pop modes has made him the producer of choice in the eighties and nineties for an extraordinary range of stars. He is best known for his work with Michael Jackson— Jones produced *Thriller*, the best-selling album of all time—but he has supervised sessions for countless and varied artists, including Lena Horne, Frank Sinatra, George Benson, and Donna Summer.

Despite his success, Jones remains a kind of backstage Grammy superstar, largely because most of his victories have come in the nonglamour arranger-producer categories. He is the only three-time winner of the prestigious Producer of the Year award, which he won most recently for *Back on the Block* in 1990.

Jones's most celebrated Grammy moment, of course, came during the 1983 Grammys, when he hit a grand slam as coproducer of Michael Jackson's *Thriller*. His trophies that year included Producer, Album, and Record of the Year Grammys, all of which he shared with Jackson.

Jones deserved his *Thriller* wins, and not just for the work he did layering Jackson's dazzling vocal tracks. When the final draft of the album was in the can, Jones gave it a long last listen, decided it came up a little short, and told Jackson he had to write "some stronger material." Jackson responded with "Beat It" and "Billie Jean," the album's biggest hits.

Great as his *Thriller* success was, Jones has enjoyed bigger Grammy years twice. In 1981, he won five wards with *The Dude*, an exceptionally polished album that combined Latin funk with soul ballads by James Ingram and Patti Austin. In 1990, Mr. Q hauled in six more statuettes, including Album of the Year honors, for *Back on the Block*, a survey of black sounds from bebop to rap.

Jones enjoyed another major moment in the Grammy limelight in 1985, when he won two awards, again as a producer, for "We Are the

World," the superstar sing-along that raised millions for famine victims in Africa and nabbed Record of the Year and Best Music Video Short Form Grammys. Virtually every pop-rock-r&b artist of note took part in the session, including Bruce Springsteen, Bob Dylan, and Michael Jackson. Jones was perhaps the only producer in town with sufficient prestige to hang a sign outside the studio at A&M Records instructing participants: "Leave your egos at the door."

Jones won his first Grammy in 1963 for his arrangement of "I Can't Stop Loving You," recorded by the Count Basie Band.

In 1989 he received a NARAS Trustees Award for lifetime contributions to the recording field.

Queen of the Grammys, Ella Fitzgerald. She won her first award in 1958, the year the Grammys were born, and her most recent in 1990 PHOTO COURTESY FRANKLIN AGENCY.

Frank Zappa and the Mothers of Invention, the ultimate Grammy nightmare, performed at the 1967 Grammy dinner in New York. Note the doll, which Zappa dismembered and passed out to a horrified tux-and-gown crowd. PHOTO COURTESY WARNER BROS. RECORDS.

Brother Ray Charles dominated the early R&B awards, winning four consecutive Grammys between 1960 and 1963. PHOTO COURTESY ATLANTIC RECORDS.

Roberta Flack is the only woman to win Record of the Year Grammys twice, in 1972 ("The First Time Ever I Saw Your Face") and 1973 ("Killing Me Softly With His Song"). PHOTO COURTESY WARNER BROS. RECORDS.

Steve Martin, getting a laugh out of his 1977 Best Comedy Recording Grammy for *Let's Get Small*. PHOTO COURTESY RICHARD CREAMER.

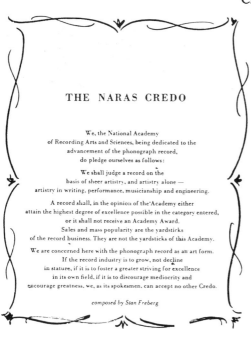

THE NARAS CREDO

We, the National Academy of Recording Arts and Sciences, being dedicated to the advancement of the phonograph record, do pledge ourselves as follows:

We shall judge a record on the basis of sheer artistry, and artistry alone — artistry in writing, performance, musicianship and engineering.

A record shall, in the opinion of the Academy either attain the highest degree of excellence possible in the category entered, or it shall not receive an Academy Award.

Sales and mass popularity are the yardsticks of the record business. They are not the yardsticks of this Academy.

We are concerned here with the phonograph record as an art form. If the record industry is to grow, not decline in stature, if it is to foster a greater striving for excellence in its own field, if it is to discourage mediocrity and encourage greatness, we, as its spokesmen, can accept no other Credo.

composed by Stan Freberg

The Grammy credo, by Stan Freberg, as published in *Billboard* magazine in 1968.

The Grammys were a breeze for guitarist George Benson (below) once he switched from jazz to pop. Benson's *Breezin'* LP generated three trophies in 1976. By 1983 he had won eight awards. PHOTO COURTESY WARNER BROS. RECORDS.

Country plucker Chet Atkins (above) has been a Grammy favorite since the sixties, winning eight country awards. Strangely, Chet's first nomination came in the rock 'n' roll category, for an obscure single called "Teen Scene." PHOTO COURTESY RCA RECORDS.

Hip at last—or so it seemed in 1987 when Grammy voters named U2's *Joshua Tree* Album of the Year. PHOTO COURTESY ISLAND RECORDS.

Bill Cosby is a very funny fellow: so say Grammy voters, who gave him six consecutive comedy Grammys between 1964 and 1969. PHOTO COURTESY WARNER BROS. RECORDS.

Tracy Chapman was too depressing for Grammy voters in 1988. She won three awards, but lost in the big three categories—Record, Song, and Album of the Year. PHOTO COURTESY ELEKTRA/ASYLUM.

It took Bonnie Raitt twenty years to win a Grammy, but in 1989 she won four, including Album of the Year honors for *Nick of Time*. PHOTO COURTESY WARNER BROS. RECORDS.

Metal for the aged. In 1988, NARAS gave the first heavy metal/hard rock Grammy to sixties dinosaur Jethro Tull (above). The resulting catcalls struck home. The following year, Metallica (below) won the heavy metal prize and performed on the Grammy show. TOP PHOTO COURTESY CHRYSALIS RECORDS. BOTTOM PHOTO COURTESY ELEKTRA ENTERTAINMENT.

One Grammy favorite no one can argue with was Duke Ellington, the leading jazz winner of all time. PHOTO COURTESY WARNER BROS. RECORDS.

Boychik comic Allan Sherman (right) won the Best Comedy Recording Grammy in 1963 for *Hello Mudduh, Hello Faddah*. PHOTO COURTESY WARNER BROS. RECORDS.

We love you just the way you are is what Grammy voters seem to say to Billy Joel, giving him Record and Song of the Year honors in 1978. PHOTO COURTESY SONY MUSIC.

Forget the Beatles, the Stones, the Hollies, the Kinks, the Zombies, et al. The British invasion hit the Grammy's in the petite form of Petula Clark, winner of the Best Rock and Roll award in 1964 and 1965. PHOTO COURTESY ED THRASHER.

Grammy maestro Quincy Jones, the leading nonclassical Grammy winner of all time, has twenty-five awards. PHOTO COURTESY WARNER BROS. RECORDS.

Best New Artist of the Year, duo Milli Vanilli, had to give back the 1989 Grammy after admitting to lip-synching their entire debut album, *Girl You Know It's True*.

Bob and Steve, Dylan and Wonder, backstage at the Grammy Awards.

"Everything I despise about the music industry"--that's what the awards represent to Sinead O'Connor (left), the first artist to reject a Grammy, spurning the 1990 Best Alternative Music Performance prize for her aptly titled "I Do Not Want What I Have Not Got." PHOTO COURTESY CHRYSALIS RECORDS.

Carole King (below) at the piano with the Grammys she won in 1971 for *Tapestry*. The album spawned Record, Song, and Album of the Year awards.

Grammy Winners

1ST ANNUAL (1958) GRAMMY WINNERS
Announced on May 4, 1959
Eligibility Year: January 1, 1958 through December 31, 1958

1. **RECORD OF THE YEAR**
   NEL BLU DIPINTO DI BLU
   (VOLARE)
   Domenic Modugno (Decca)

2. **ALBUM OF THE YEAR**
   THE MUSIC FROM PETER
   GUNN
   Henry Mancini (RCA)

3. **SONG OF THE YEAR**
   NEL BLU DIPINTO DI BLU
   (VOLARE)
   Domenico Modugno (Decca)

4. **BEST VOCAL
   PERFORMANCE, FEMALE**
   ELLA FITZGERALD SINGS
   THE IRVING BERLIN SONG
   BOOK
   Ella Fitzgerald (Verve)

5. **BEST VOCAL
   PERFORMANCE, MALE**
   CATCH A FALLING STAR
   Perry Como (RCA-Victor)

6. **BEST PERFORMANCE BY AN
   ORCHESTRA**
   BILLY MAY'S BIG FAT BRASS
   Billy May (Capitol)

7. **BEST PERFORMANCE BY A
   DANCE BAND**
   BASIE
   Count Basie (Roulette)

8. **BEST PERFORMANCE BY A
   VOCAL GROUP OR CHORUS**
   THAT OLD BLACK MAGIC
   Louis Prima and Keely Smith
   (Capitol)

9. **BEST JAZZ PERFORMANCE, INDIVIDUAL**
ELLA FITZGERALD SINGS
THE DUKE ELLINGTON
SONG BOOK
Ella Fitzgerald (Verve)

10. **BEST JAZZ PERFORMANCE, GROUP**
BASIE
Count Basie (Roulette)

11. **BEST COMEDY PERFORMANCE**
THE CHIPMUNK SONG
David Seville (Liberty)

12. **BEST COUNTRY & WESTERN PERFORMANCE**
TOM DOOLEY
The Kingston Trio (Capitol)

13. **BEST RHYTHM & BLUES PERFORMANCE**
TEQUILA
The Champs (Challenge)

14. **BEST ARRANGEMENT**
THE MUSIC FROM PETER GUNN
(Henry Mancini)
Arranged by Henry Mancini
(RCA)

15. **BEST ENGINEERED RECORD, CLASSICAL**
DUETS WITH A SPANISH GUITAR
(Laurindo Almeida & Salli Terri)
Engineer: Sherwood Hall, III
(Capitol)

16. **BEST ENGINEERED RECORD, OTHER THAN CLASSICAL**
THE CHIPMUNK SONG
David Seville
Engineer: Ted Keep (Liberty)

17. **BEST ALBUM COVER**
ONLY THE LONELY
(Frank Sinatra)
Art Director: Frank Sinatra
(Capitol)

18. **BEST MUSICAL COMPOSITION FIRST RECORDED AND RELEASED IN 1958 (OVER 5 MINUTES)**
CROSS COUNTRY SUITE
Composer: Nelson Riddle (Dot)

19. **BEST ORIGINAL CAST ALBUM, BROADWAY OR TV**
THE MUSIC MAN
Meredith Wilson (Capitol)

20. **BEST SOUND TRACK ALBUM, DRAMATIC PICTURE SCORE ORIGINAL CAST**
GIGI—Sound Track
Andre Previn (MGM)

21. **BEST PERFORMANCE, DOCUMENTARY, SPOKEN WORD**
THE BEST OF THE
STAN FREBERG SHOWS
Stan Freberg (Capitol)

22. **BEST RECORDING FOR CHILDREN**
THE CHIPMUNK SONG
David Seville (Liberty)

23. **BEST CLASSICAL PERFORMANCE, ORCHESTRAL**
GAIETE PARISIENNE
Felix Slatkin cond.
Hollywood Bowl Symphony
Orch. (Capitol)

24. **BEST CLASSIAL PERFORMANCE INSTRUMENTAL (WITH CONCERTO SCALE ACCOMPANIMENT)**
TCHAIKOVSKY: CONCERTO
NO. 1. IN B-FLAT MINOR,
OP 23
Van Cliburn, Pianist; Kiril
Kondrashin (RCA)

25. **BEST CLASSICAL PERFORMANCE, INSTRUMENTALIST (OTHER THAN CONCERTO SCALE)**
SEGOVIA GOLDEN JUBILEE
Andrés Segovia (Decca)

26. **BEST CLASSICAL PERFORMANCE, CHAMBER MUSIC (INCLUDING CHAMBER ORCHESTRA)**
BEETHOVEN QUARTET 130
Hollywood String Quartet
(Capitol)

27. **BEST CLASSICAL PERFORMANCE, VOCAL SOLOIST (WITH OR WITHOUT ORCHESTRA)**
OPERATIC RECITAL
Renata Tebaldi (London)

28. **BEST CLASSICAL PERFORMANCE, OPERATIC/CHORAL**
VIRTUOSO
Roger Wagner Chorale (Capitol)

2ND ANNUAL (1959) GRAMMY WINNERS
Announced on November 29, 1959
Eligibility Year: January 1, 1959 through August 31, 1959

1. **RECORD OF THE YEAR**
MACK THE KNIFE
Bobby Darin (Atco)

2. **ALBUM OF THE YEAR**
COME DANCE WITH ME
Frank Sinatra (Capitol)

3. **SONG OF THE YEAR**
THE BATTLE OF NEW ORLEANS
Composer: Jimmy Driftwood
(Columbia)

4. **BEST VOCAL PERFORMANCE, FEMALE**
BUT NOT FOR ME
Ella Fitzgerald (Verve)

5. **BEST VOCAL PERFORMANCE, MALE**
COME DANCE WITH ME
Frank Sinatra (Capitol)

6. **BEST PERFORMANCE BY A DANCE BAND**
ANATOMY OF A MURDER
Duke Ellington (Columbia)

7. **BEST PERFORMANCE BY AN ORCHESTRA**
LIKE YOUNG
David Rose and his Orchestra
with Andre Previn (MGM)

8. **BEST PERFORMANCE BY A CHORUS**
BATTLE HYMN OF THE REPUBLIC
Mormon Tabernacle Choir
Richard Condie, conductor
(Columbia)

9. **BEST JAZZ PERFORMANCE, SOLOIST**
ELLA SWINGS LIGHTLY
Ella Fitzgerald (Verve)

10. **BEST JAZZ PERFORMANCE, GROUP**
I DIG CHICKS
Jonah Jones (Capitol)

11. **BEST CLASSICAL PERFORMANCE, ORCHESTRA**
DEBUSSY: IMAGES FOR ORCHESTRA
Boston Symphony Orch., Charles Munch, conductor (RCA)

12. **BEST CLASSICAL PERFORMANCE, CONCERTO OR INSTRUMENTAL SOLOIST (FULL ORCHESTRA)**
RACHMANINOFF: PIANO CONCERTO No. 3
Van Cliburn, Pianist; Kiril Kondrashin cond. (RCA)

13. **BEST CLASSICAL PERFORMANCE, OPERA CAST OR CHORAL**
MOZART: "THE MARRIAGE OF FIGARO"
Erich Leinsdorf cond. Vienna Philharmonic Orch. (RCA)

14. **BEST CLASSICAL PERFORMANCE, VOCAL SOLOIST (WITH OR WITHOUT ORCHESTRA)**
BJOERLING IN OPERA
Jussi Bjoerling (London)

15. **BEST CLASSICAL PERFORMANCE, CHAMBER MUSIC (INCLUDING CHAMBER ORCHESTRA)**
BEETHOVEN: SONATA NO. 21, IN C, OP .53 (WALDSTEIN); SONATA NO. 18, IN E-FLAT, OP. 31, NO .3
Artur Rubinstein, Pianist (RCA)

16. **BEST CLASSICAL PERFORMANCE, INSTRUMENTAL SOLOIST (OTHER THAN FULL ORCHESTRAL ACCOMPANIMENT)**
BEETHOVEN: SONATA NO. 21, IN C, OP.53 (WALDSTEIN); SONATA NO. 18, IN E-FLAT, OP. 31, NO. 3
Artur Rubinstein, Pianist (RCA)

17. **BEST MUSICAL COMPOSITION FIRST RECORDED AND RELEASED IN 1959 (5 MINUTES)**
ANATOMY OF A MURDER
Composer: Duke Ellington (Columbia)

18. **BEST SOUND TRACK ALBUM—BACKGROUND SCORE FROM MOTION PICTURE OR TV**
ANATOMY OF A MURDER (Motion Picture)
Duke Ellington (Columbia)

19. **BEST SOUND TRACK ALBUM, ORIGINAL CAST, MOTION PICTURE OR TELEVISION**
PORGY AND BESS—Motion Picture Cast
Andre Previn and Ken Darby (Columbia)

20. **BEST BROADWAY SHOW ALBUM**
GYPSY
Ethel Merman (Columbia)
REDHEAD
Gwen Verdon (RCA)

21. **BEST COMEDY PERFORMANCE—SPOKEN WORD**
INSIDE SHELLEY BERMAN
Shelley Berman (Verve)

22. **BEST COMEDY PERFORMANCE—MUSICAL**
THE BATTLE OF KOOKAMONGA
Homer and Jethro (RCA)

23. **BEST PERFORMANCE— DOCUMENTARY OR SPOKEN WORD (OTHER THAN COMEDY)**
A LINCOLN PORTRAIT
Carl Sandburg (Columbia)

24. **BEST PERFORMANCE BY "TOP 40" ARTIST**
MIDNIGHT FLYER
Nat "King" Cole (Capitol)

25. **BEST COUNTRY AND WESTERN PERFORMANCE**
THE BATTLE OF NEW ORLEANS
Johnny Horton (Columbia)

26. **BEST RHYTHM AND BLUES PERFORMANCE**
WHAT A DIFFERENCE A DAY MAKES
Dinah Washington (Mercury)

27. **BEST FOLK PERFORMANCE**
THE KINGSTON TRIO AT LARGE
The Kingston Trio (Capitol)

28. **BEST RECORDING FOR CHILDREN**
PETER AND THE WOLF
Peter Ustinov, narr.; von Karajan cond. Philharmonia Orch. (Angel)

29. **BEST ARRANGEMENT**
COME DANCE WITH ME
(Frank Sinatra)
Arranged by Billy May (Capitol)

30. **BEST ENGINEERING CONTRIBUTION—CLASSICAL RECORDING**
VICTORY AT SEA, VOL. 1
(Robert Russell Bennett)
Engineer: Lewis W. Layton (RCA)

31. **BEST ENGINEERING CONTRIBUTION—NOVELTY RECORDING**
ALVIN'S HARMONICA
(David Seville)
Engineer: Ted Keep (Liberty)

32. **BEST ENGINEERING CONTRIBUTION—OTHER THAN CLASSICAL OR NOVELTY**
BELAFONTE AT CARNEGIE HALL
Engineer: Robert Simpson (RCA)

33. **BEST ALBUM COVER**
SHOSTAKOVICH: SYMPHONY NO. 5
(Howard Mitchell)
Art Director: Robert M. Jones (RCA)

34. **BEST NEW ARTIST OF 1959**
BOBBY DARIN (Atco)

SPECIAL NATIONAL TRUSTEES AWARDS FOR ARTISTS & REPERTOIRE CONTRIBUTION

1. **RECORD OF THE YEAR**
MACK THE KNIFE
Bobby Darin
A&R Producer: Ahmet Ertegun (ATCO)

2. **ALBUM OF THE YEAR**
COME DANCE WITH ME
Frank Sinatra
A&R Producer: Dave Cavanaugh (Capitol)

3RD ANNUAL (1960) GRAMMY WINNERS
Announced on April 12, 1961
Eligibility Year: September 1, 1959 through November 30, 1960

1. **RECORD OF THE YEAR**
THEME FROM A SUMMER PLACE
Percy Faith (Columbia)

2. **ALBUM OF THE YEAR**
BUTTOM DOWN MIND
Bob Newhart (Warner Bros.)

3. **SONG OF THE YEAR**
THEME FROM EXODUS
Composer: Ernest Gold

4. **BEST VOCAL PERFORMANCE SINGLE RECORD OR TRACK— FEMALE**
MACK THE KNIFE
Ella Fitzgerald (Verve)

5. **BEST VOCAL PERFORMANCE—ALBUM—FEMALE**
MACK THE KNIFE—ELLA IN BERLIN
Ella Fitzgerald (Verve)

6. **BEST VOCAL PERFORMANCE SINGLE RECORD OR TRACK—MALE**
GEORGIA ON MY MIND
Ray Charles (ABC)

7. **BEST VOCAL PERFORMANCE—ALBUM—MALE**
GENIUS OF RAY CHARLES
Ray Charles (ABC)

8. **BEST PERFORMANCE BY A BAND FOR DANCING**
DANCE WITH BASIE
Count Basie (Roulette)

9. **BEST ARRANGEMENT**
MR. LUCKY
Henry Mancini (RCA)

10. **BEST PERFORMANCE BY AN ORCHESTRA**
MR. LUCKY
Henry Mancini (RCA)

11. **BEST PERFORMANCE BY A VOCAL GROUP**
WE GOT US
Eydie Gorme/Steve Lawrence (ABC)

12. **BEST PERFORMANCE BY A CHORUS**
SONGS OF THE COWBOY
Norman Luboff Choir (Columbia)

13. **BEST JAZZ PERFORMANCE, SOLO OR SMALL GROUP**
WEST SIDE STORY
Andre Previn (Contemporary)

14. **BEST JAZZ PERFORMANCE, LARGE GROUP**
BLUES AND THE BEAT
Henry Mancini (RCA)

15. **BEST CLASSICAL PERFORMANCE, ORCHESTRA**
BARTOK: MUSIC FOR STRINGS, PERCUSSION AND CELESTE
Fritz Reiner cond. Chicago Sym. (RCA)

16. **BEST CLASSICAL PERFORMANCE, VOCAL OR INSTRUMENTAL CHAMBER MUSIC**
CONVERSATIONS WITH THE GUITAR
Laurindo Almeida (Capitol)

17. **BEST CLASSICAL PERFORMANCE, CONCERTO OR INSTRUMENTAL SOLOIST**
BRAHMS: PIANO CONCERTO NO. 2 IN B-FLAT
Sviatoslav Richter (Leinsdorf cond. Chicago Sym.) (RCA)

15. **BEST CLASSICAL PERFORMANCE, INSTRUMENTAL SOLOIST OR DUO (OTHER THAN ORCHESTRAL)**
THE SPANISH GUITARS OF LAURINDO ALMEIDA
Laurindo Almeida (Capitol)

19. **BEST CLASSICAL PERFORMANCE, VOCAL SOLOIST**
A PROGRAM OF SONG
Leontyne Price (RCA)

20. **BEST CLASSICAL OPERA PRODUCTION**
PUCCINI TURANDOT—Erich Leinsdorf cond. Rome Opera House Chorus & Orch.
Tebaldi, Nilsson, Bjoerling, Tozzi (RCA)

21. **BEST CONTEMPORARY CLASSICAL COMPOSITION**
ORCHESTRAL SUITE FROM TENDER LAND SUITE
Composer, Aaron Copland (RCA)

22. **BEST CLASSICAL PERFORMANCE, CHORAL (INCLUDING ORATORIO)**
HANDEL THE MESSIAH
Sir Thomas Beecham cond, Royal Philharmonic Orch. & Chorus (RCA)

23. **BEST SOUND TRACK ALBUM OR RECORDING OF MUSIC SCORE FROM MOTION PICTURE OR TELEVISION**
EXODUS
Composer: Ernest Gold (RCA)

24. **BEST SOUND TRACK ALBUM OR RECORDING OF ORIGINAL CAST FROM MOTION PICTURE OR TELEVISION**
CAN CAN (Frank Sinatra, Original Cast)
Composer: Cole Porter (Capitol)

25. **BEST SHOW ALBUM (ORIGINAL CAST)**
THE SOUND OF MUSIC (Mary Martin)
Composers: Richard Rodgers, Oscar Hammerstein (Columbia)

26. **BEST COMEDY PERFORMANCE (SPOKEN WORD)**
BUTTON DOWN MIND STRIKES BACK
Bob Newart (Warner Bros.)

27. **BEST COMEDY PERFORMANCE (MUSICAL)**
JONATHAN AND DARLENE EDWARDS IN PARIS
Jonathan and Darlene Edwards (Jo Stafford and Paul Weston) (Columbia)

28. **BEST PERFORMANCE— DOCUMENTARY OR SPOKEN WORD (OTHER THAN COMEDY)**
F.D.R. SPEAKS (Franklin D. Roosevelt)
A&R Producer, Robert Bialek (Wash.)

29. **BEST PERFORMANCE BY A POP SINGLE ARTIST**
GEORGIA ON MY MIND
Ray Charles (ABC)

30. **BEST COUNTRY & WESTERN PERFORMANCE**
EL PASO
Marty Robbins (Columbia)

31. **BEST RHYTHM AND BLUES PERFORMANCE**
LET THE GOOD TIMES ROLL
Ray Charles (Atlantic)

32. **BEST FOLK PERFORMANCE**
SWING DAT HAMMER
Harry Belafonte (RCA)

33. **BEST ALBUM CREATED FOR CHILDREN**
LET'S ALL SING WITH THE CHIPMUNKS
David Seville (Ross Bagdasarian) (Liberty)

34. **BEST ENGINEERING CONTRIBUTION—CLASSICAL RECORDING**
SPANISH GUITARS OF LAURINDO ALMEIDA
Engineer: Hugh Davies (Capitol)

35. **BEST ENGINEERING CONTRIBUTION, POPULAR RECORDING**
ELLA FITZGERALD SINGS THE GEORGE AND IRA GERSHWIN SONG BOOK
Engineer: Luis P. Valentin (Verve)

36. **BEST ENGINEERING CONTRIBUTION, NOVELTY**
THE OLD PAYOLA ROLL BLUES (Stan Freberg)
Engineer: John Kraus (Capital)

37. **BEST ALBUM COVER**
LATIN A LA LEE (Peggy Lee)
Art Director: Marvin Schwartz (Capitol)

38. BEST NEW ARTIST OF 1960
BOB NEWHART (Warner Bros.)

39. BEST JAZZ COMPOSITION OF MORE THAN FIVE MINUTES DURATION
SKETCHES OF SPAIN
Miles Davis and Gil Evans
(Columbia)

SPECIAL NATIONAL TRUSTEES AWARDS FOR ARTISTS AND REPERTOIRE CONTRIBUTION

1. RECORD OF THE YEAR
THEME FROM A SUMMER PLACE
A&R Producer: Ernest Altschuler
(Columbia)

2. ALBUM OF THE YEAR
BUTTON DOWN MIND
A&R Producer: George Avakian
(Warner Bros.)

4TH ANNUAL (1961) GRAMMY WINNERS
Announced on May 29, 1962
Eligibility Year: December 1, 1960 through November 30, 1961

1. RECORD OF THE YEAR
MOON RIVER
Henry Mancini (RCA)

2. ALBUM OF THE YEAR
JUDY AT CARNEGIE HALL
Judy Garland (Capitol)

3. ALBUM OF THE YEAR, CLASSICAL
STRAVINSKY CONDUCTS, 1960: LE SACRE DU PRINTEMPS; PETROUCHKA
Igor Stravinsky cond. Columbia Symphony (Columbia)

4. SONG OF THE YEAR
MOON RIVER
Composers: Henry Mancini and Johnny Mercer (RCA)

5. BEST INSTRUMENTAL THEME OR INSTRUMENTAL VERSION OF SONG
AFRICAN WALTZ
Composer: Galt MacDermott
(Roulette)

6. BEST SOLO VOCAL PERFORMANCE, FEMALE
JUDY AT CARNEGIE HALL
(Album)
Judy Garland (Capitol)

7. BEST SOLO VOCAL PERFORMANCE, MALE
LOLLIPOPS AND ROSES
(single)
Jack Jones (Kapp)

8. BEST JAZZ PERFORMANCE, SOLOIST OR SMALL GROUP (INSTRUMENTAL)
ANDRE PREVIN PLAYS HAROLD ARLEN
Andre Previn (Contemporary)

9. BEST JAZZ PERFORMANCE, LARGE GROUP
WEST SIDE STORY
Stan Kenton (Capitol)

10. BEST ORIGINAL JAZZ COMPOSITION
AFRICAN WALTZ
Composer: Galt MacDermott
(Roulette)

11. **BEST PERFORMANCE BY AN ORCHESTRA—FOR DANCING**
UP A LAZY RIVER
Si Zentner (Liberty)

12. **BEST PERFORMANCE BY AN ORCHESTRA—FOR OTHER THAN DANCING**
BREAKFAST AT TIFFANY'S
Henry Mancini (RCA)

13. **BEST ARRANGEMENT**
MOON RIVER
Henry Mancini, Arranger (RCA)

14. **BEST PERFORMANCE BY A VOCAL GROUP**
HIGH FLYING
Lambert, Hendricks and Ross (Columbia)

15. **BEST PERFORMANCE BY A CHORUS**
GREAT BAND WITH GREAT VOICES
Johnny Mann Singers (Si Zentner Orch.) (Liberty)

16. **BEST SOUND TRACK ALBUM OR RECORDING OR SCORE FROM MOTION PICTURE OR TELEVISION**
BREAKFAST AT TIFFANY'S
Henry Mancini (RCA)

17. **BEST SOUND TRACK ALBUM OR RECORDING OF ORIGINAL CAST FROM MOTION PICTURE OR TV**
WEST SIDE STORY
Johnny Green, Saul Chaplin, Sid Ramin, and Irwin Kostal (Columbia)

18. **BEST ORIGINAL CAST SHOW ALBUM**
HOW TO SUCCEED IN BUSINESS WITHOUT REALLY TRYING
Composer: Frank Loesser (RCA)

19. **BEST COMEDY PERFORMANCE**
AN EVENING WITH MIKE NICHOLS AND ELAINE MAY
Mike Nichols and Elaine May (Mercury)

20. **BEST DOCUMENTARY OR SPOKEN WORD RECORDING (OTHER THAN COMEDY)**
HUMOR IN MUSIC
Leonard Bernstein cond. New York Philharmonic (Columbia)

21. **BEST ENGINEERING CONTRIBUTION—POPULAR RECORDING**
JUDY AT CARNEGIE HALL (Judy Garland)
Engineer: Robert Arnold (Capitol)

22. **BEST ENGINEERING CONTRIBUTION, NOVELTY**
STAN FREBERG PRESENTS THE UNITED STATES OF AMERICA
Engineer: John Kraus (Capitol)

23. **BEST ALBUM COVER**
JUDY AT CARNEGIE HALL (Judy Garland)
Art Dir: Jim Silke (Capitol)

24. **BEST RECORDING FOR CHILDREN**
PROKOFIEV: PETER AND THE WOLF
Leonard Bernstein cond. New York Philharmonic (Columbia)

25. **BEST ROCK AND ROLL RECORDING**
LET'S TWIST AGAIN
Chubby Checker (Parkway)

26. **BEST COUNTRY & WESTERN RECORDING**
BIG BAD JOHN
Jimmy Dean (Columbia)

27. **BEST RHYTHM AND BLUES RECORDING**
HIT THE ROAD JACK
Ray Charles (Am-Par)

28. **BEST FOLK RECORDING**
BELAFONTE FOLK SINGERS AT HOME AND ABROAD
Belafonte Folk Singers (RCA)

29. **BEST GOSPEL OR OTHER RELIGIOUS RECORDING**
EVERYTIME I FEEL THE SPIRIT
Mahalia Jackson (Columbia)

30. **BEST NEW ARTIST OF 1961**
PETER NERO (RCA)

31. **BEST CLASSICAL PERFORMANCE, ORCHESTRA**
RAVEL: DAPHNIS ET CHLOE
Charles Munch cond. Boston Sym. Orch. (RCA)

32. **BEST CLASSICAL PERFORMANCE, CHAMBER MUSIC**
BEETHOVEN: SERENADE, OP.8/KODALY: DUO FOR VIOLIN & CELLO, OP.7
Jascha Heifetz, Gregor Piatigorsky, William Primrose (RCA)

33. **BEST CLASSICAL PERFORMANCE, INSTRUMENTAL SOLOIST (WITH ORCHESTRA)**
BARTOK: CONCERTO NO. 1 FOR VIOLIN AND ORCHESTRA
Isaac Stern (Ormandy cond. New York Philharmonic) (Columbia)

34. **BEST CLASSICAL PERFORMANCE, INSTRUMENTAL SOLOIST OR DUO WITHOUT ORCHESTRA**
REVERIE FOR SPANISH GUITARS
Laurindo Almeida (Capitol)

35. **BEST OPERA RECORDING**
PUCCINI: MADAME BUTTERFLY
Gabriele Santini cond. Rome Opera Chorus & Orch. (Capitol)

36. **BEST CLASSICAL PERFORMANCE, CHORAL**
BACH: B MINOR MASS
Robert Shaw Chorale, Robert Shaw cond. (RCA)

37. **BEST CLASSICAL PERFORMANCE, VOCAL SOLOIST**
THE ART OF THE PRIMA DONNA
Joan Sutherland (Molinari-Pradelli cond. Royal Opera House Orch.) (London)

38. **BEST CONTEMPORARY CLASSICAL COMPOSITION (Tie)**
DISCANTUS
Composer: Laurindo Almeida (Capitol)

MOVEMENTS FOR PIANO AND ORCHESTRA
Composer: Igor Stravinsky (Columbia)

39. **BEST ENGINEERING CONTRIBUTION—CLASSICAL RECORDING**
RAVEL: DAPHNIS ET CHLOE
(Munch cond. Boston Sym. Orch.)
Engineer: Lewis W. Layton (RCA)

40. **BEST ALBUM COVER, CLASSICAL**
PUCCINI: MADAME BUTTERFLY
(Santini cond. Rome Opera Chorus & Orchestra)
Art Director: Marvin Schwartz (Angel)

5TH ANNUAL (1962) GRAMMY WINNERS
Announced on May 15, 1963
Eligibility Year: December 1, 1961 through November 30, 1962

1. **RECORD OF THE YEAR**
I LEFT MY HEART IN SAN FRANCISCO
Tony Bennett (Columbia)

2. **ALBUM OF THE YEAR**
THE FIRST FAMILY
Vaughn Meader (Cadence)

3. **ALBUM OF THE YEAR, CLASSICAL**
Columbia Records Presents VLADIMIR HOROWITZ
Vladimir Horowitz (Columbia)

4. **SONG OF THE YEAR**
WHAT KIND OF FOOL AM I
Composers: Leslie Bricusse and Anthony Newley (London)

5. **BEST INSTRUMENTAL THEME**
A TASTE OF HONEY
Composers: Bobby Scott and Ric Marlow (Reprise)

6. **BEST SOLO VOCAL PERFORMANCE, FEMALE**
ELLA SWINGS BRIGHTLY WITH NELSON RIDDLE
Ella Fitzgerald (album) (Verve)

7. **BEST SOLO VOCAL PERFORMANCE, MALE**
I LEFT MY HEART IN SAN FRANCISCO
Tony Bennett (album) (Columbia)

8. **BEST JAZZ PERFORMANCE, SOLOIST OR SMALL GROUP (INSTRUMENTAL)**
DESAFINADO
Stan Getz (Verve)

9. **BEST JAZZ PERFORMANCE, LARGE GROUP INSTRUMENTAL**
ADVENTURES IN JAZZ
Stan Kenton (Capitol)

10. **BEST ORIGINAL JAZZ COMPOSITION**
CAST YOUR FATE TO THE WINDS
Composer: Vince Guaraldi (Fantasy)

11. **BEST PERFORMANCE BY AN ORCHESTRA—FOR DANCING**
FLY ME TO THE MOON BOSSA NOVA
Joe Harnell (KAPP)

12. **BEST PERFORMANCE BY AN ORCHESTRA OR INSTRUMENTALIST WITH ORCHESTRA—NOT FOR JAZZ OR DANCING**
THE COLORFUL PETER NERO
Peter Nero (RCA)

13. **BEST INSTRUMENTAL ARRANGEMENT**
BABY ELEPHANT WALK
(Henry Mancini & Orch.)
Arranger: Henry Mancini (RCA)

14. **BEST BACKGROUND ARRANGEMENT**
I LEFT MY HEART IN SAN FRANCISCO
(Tony Bennett)
Arranger: Marty Manning (Capitol)

15. **BEST PERFORMANCE BY A VOCAL GROUP**
IF I HAD A HAMMER
Peter, Paul and Mary (Warner Bros.)

16. **BEST PERFORMANCE BY A CHORUS**
PRESENTING THE NEW CHRISTY MINSTRELS
The New Christy Minstrels (Columbia)

17. **BEST ORIGINAL CAST SHOW ALBUM**
NO STRINGS
Composer: Richard Rodgers
(Capitol)

18. **BEST CLASSICAL PERFORMANCE, ORCHESTRA**
STRAVINSKY: THE FIREBIRD BALLET
Igor Stravinsky, Columbia Sym.
(Columbia)

19. **BEST CLASSICAL PERFORMANCE, CHAMBER MUSIC**
THE HEIFETZ-PIATIGORSKY CONCERTS WITH PRIMROSE, PENNARIO AND GUESTS
Jascha Heifetz, Gregor Piatigorsky, William Primrose
(RCA)

20. **BEST CLASSICAL PERFORMANCE, INSTRUMENTAL SOLOIST(S) (WITH ORCHESTRA)**
STRAVINSKY: CONCERTO IN D FOR VIOLIN
Isaac Stern (Stravinsky cond. Columbia Sym.) (Columbia)

21. **BEST CLASSICAL PERFORMANCE, INSTRUMENTAL SOLOIST OR DUO (WITHOUT ORCHESTRA)**
Columbia Records Presents VLADIMIR HOROWITZ
Vladimir Horowitz (Columbia)

22. **BEST OPERA RECORDING**
VERDI: AIDA
Georg Solti cond. Rome Opera House Orch. & Chorus
(Price, Vickers, Gorr, Merrill, Tozzi) (RCA)

23. **BEST CLASSICAL PERFORMANCE, CHORAL**
BACH: ST. MATTHEW PASSION
Philharmonia Choir, Wilhelm Pitz, choral dir./Otto Klemperer cond. Philharmonic Orch. (Angel)

24. **BEST CLASSICAL PERFORMANCE, VOCAL SOLOIST WITH OR WITHOUT ORCHESTRA**
WAGNER: GÖTTERDÄMMERUNG BRÜNNHILDE'S IMMOLATION SCENE/ WESENDONCK SONGS
Eileen Farrell (Bernstein cond. New York Philharmonic)
(Columbia)

25. **BEST CLASSICAL COMPOSITION BY CONTEMPORARY COMPOSER**
THE FLOOD
Composer: Igor Stravinsky
(Columbia)

26. **BEST ENGINEERING CONTRIBUTION, CLASSICAL**
STRAUSS: ALSO SPRACH ZARATHUSTRA OP.30
(Reiner cond. Chicago Sym.)
Engineer: Lewis W. Layton
(RCA)

27. **BEST ALBUM COVER, CLASSICAL**
THE INTIMATE BACH
(Almeida, Majewski, De Rosa)
Art Director: Marvin Schwartz
(Capitol)

28. **BEST COMEDY PERFORMANCE**
THE FIRST FAMILY
Vaughn Meader (Cadence)

29. **BEST DOCUMENTARY OR SPOKEN WORD RECORDING (OTHER THAN COMEDY)**
THE STORY-TELLER: A SESSION WITH CHARLES LAUGHTON
Charles Laughton (Capitol)

30. **BEST ENGINEERING CONTRIBUTION—OTHER THAN NOVELTY OR CLASSICAL**
HATARI! (Henry Mancini)
Engineer: Al Schmitt (RCA)

31. **BEST ENGINEERING CONTRIBUTION—NOVELTY**
THE CIVIL WAR. VOL. I (Frederick Fennell)
Engineer: Robert Fine (Mercury)

32. **BEST ALBUM COVER**
LENA . . . LOVELY AND ALIVE (Lena Horne)
Art Director: Robert Jones (RCA)

33. **BEST RECORDING FOR CHILDREN**
SAINT-SAENS: CARNIVAL OF THE ANIMALS/BRITTEN: YOUNG PERSON'S GUIDE TO THE ORCHESTRA
Leonard Bernstein (Columbia)

34. **BEST ROCK AND ROLL RECORDING**
ALLEY CAT
Bent Fabric (Atco)

35. **BEST COUNTRY AND WESTERN RECORDING**
FUNNY WAY OF LAUGHIN'
Burl Ives (Decca)

36. **BEST RHYTHM AND BLUES RECORDING**
I CAN'T STOP LOVING YOU
Ray Charles (ABC)

37. **BEST FOLK RECORDING**
IF I HAD A HAMMER
Peter, Paul and Mary
(Warner Bros.)

38. **BEST GOSPEL OR OTHER RELIGIOUS RECORDING**
GREAT SONGS OF LOVE AND FAITH
Mahalia Jackson (Columbia)

39. **BEST NEW ARTIST OF 1962**
ROBERT GOULET (Columbia)

6TH ANNUAL (1963) GRAMMY WINNERS
Announced on May 12, 1964
Eligibility Year: December 1, 1962 through November 30, 1963

1. **RECORD ON THE YEAR**
THE DAYS OF WINE AND ROSES
Henry Mancini (RCA)

2. **ALBUM OF THE YEAR**
THE BARBRA STREISAND ALBUM
Barbra Streisand (Columbia)

3. **ALBUM OF THE YEAR, CLASSICAL**
BRITTEN: WAR REQUIEM
Benjamin Britten cond. London Sym. Orch. & Chorus (London)

4. **SONG OF THE YEAR**
THE DAYS OF WINE AND ROSES
Composers: Henry Mancini and Johnny Mercer (RCA)

5. **BEST INSTRUMENTAL THEME**
MORE (THEME FROM "MONDO CANE")
Composers: Norman Newell, Nino Oliviero, and Riz Ortolani (United Artists)

6. **BEST VOCAL PERFORMANCE, FEMALE**
THE BARBRA STREISAND ALBUM
Barbra Streisand (Columbia)

7. **BEST VOCAL PERFORMANCE, MALE**
WIVES AND LOVERS (single)
Jack Jones (Kapp)

8. **BEST INSTRUMENTAL JAZZ PERFORMANCE, SOLOIST OR SMALL GROUP**
CONVERSATIONS WITH MYSELF
Bill Evans (Verve)

9. **BEST INSTRUMENTAL JAZZ PERFORMANCE, LARGE GROUP**
ENCORE: WOODY HERMAN, 1963
Woody Herman Band (Philips)

10. **BEST ORIGINAL JAZZ COMPOSITION**
GRAVY WALTZ
Composers: Steve Allen, Ray Brown

11. **BEST PERFORMANCE BY AN ORCHESTRA—FOR DANCING**
THIS TIME BY BASIE! HITS OF THE 50'S AND 60'S
Count Basie (Reprise)

12. **BEST PERFORMANCE BY AN ORCHESTRA OR INSTRUMENTALIST WITH ORCHESTRA—NOT FOR JAZZ OR DANCING**
JAVA
Al Hirt (RCA)

13. **BEST INSTRUMENTAL ARRANGEMENT**
I CAN'T STOP LOVING YOU (Count Basie)
Arranger: Quincy Jones (Reprise)

14. **BEST BACKGROUND ARRANGEMENT**
THE DAYS OF WINE AND ROSES (Mancini)
Arranger: Henry Mancini (RCA)

15. **BEST PERFORMANCE BY A VOCAL GROUP**
BLOWIN' IN THE WIND
Peter, Paul and Mary (Warner Bros.)

16. **BEST PERFORMANCE BY A CHORUS**
BACH'S GREATEST HITS
The Swingle Singers (Philips)

17. **BEST ORIGINAL SCORE FROM A MOTION PICTURE OR TELEVISION SHOW**
TOM JONES
Composer: John Addison (United Artists)

18. **BEST SCORE FROM AN ORIGINAL CAST SHOW ALBUM**
SHE LOVES ME
Composers: Jerry Bock, Sheldon Harnick (MGM)

19. **BEST CLASSICAL PERFORMANCE, ORCHESTRA**
BARTOK: CONCERTO FOR ORCHESTRA
Erich Leinsdorf, Boston Sym. Orch. (RCA)

20. **BEST CLASSICAL PERFORMANCE, CHAMBER MUSIC**
EVENING OF ELIZABETHAN MUSIC
Julian Bream Consort (RCA)

21. **BEST CLASSICAL PERFORMANCE, INSTRUMENTAL SOLOIST(S) (WITH ORCHESTRA)**
TCHAIKOVSKY: CONCERTO NO.1 IN B-FLAT MINOR FOR PIANO & ORCHESTRA
Artur Rubinstein (Leinsdorf cond. Boston Sym. Orch.) (RCA)

22. **BEST CLASSICAL PERFORMANCE, INSTRUMENTAL SOLOIST OR DUO (WITHOUT ORCH.)**
THE SOUND OF HOROWITZ
Vladimir Horowitz (Columbia)

23. **BEST OPERA RECORDING**
PUCCINI: MADAMA BUTTERFLY
Erich Leinsdorf cond. RCA Italiana Opera Orch. & Chorus (Price, Tucker, Elias) (RCA)

24. **BEST CLASSICAL PERFORMANCE, CHORAL**
BRITTEN: WAR REQUIEM
David Willcocks, dir. Bach Choir/Edward Chapman, dir. Highgate School Choir/Benjamin Britten cond. London Sym. Orch. & Chorus (London)

25. **BEST CLASSICAL PERFORMANCE, VOCAL SOLOIST (WITH OR WITHOUT ORCHESTRA)**
GREAT SCENES FROM GERSHWIN'S PORGY AND BESS
Leontyne Price (RCA)

26. **BEST CLASSICAL COMPOSITION BY A CONTEMPORARY COMPOSER**
WAR REQUIEM
Composer: Benjamin Britten (London)

27. **BEST ENGINEERED RECORDING, CLASSICAL**
PUCCINI: MADAMA BUTTERFLY (Leinsdorf)
Engineer: Lewis Layton (RCA)

28. **BEST ALBUM COVER, CLASSICAL**
PUCCINI: MADAMA BUTTERFLY (Leinsdorf)
Art Director: Robert Jones (RCA)

29. **MOST PROMISING NEW CLASSICAL RECORDING ARTIST**
ANDRE WATTS (Pianist) (Columbia)

30. **BEST COMEDY PERFORMANCE**
HELLO MUDDUH, HELLO FADDAH
Allan Sherman (Warner Bros.)

31. **BEST DOCUMENTARY, SPOKEN WORD OR DRAMA RECORDING (OTHER THAN COMEDY)**
WHO'S AFRAID OF VIRGINIA WOOLF?
Edward Albee (Warner Bros.)

32. **BEST ENGINEERED RECORDING—OTHER THAN CLASSICAL**
CHARADE (Mancini Orch. & Chorus)
Engineer: James Malloy (RCA)

33. **BEST ENGINEERED RECORDING—SPECIAL OR NOVEL EFFECTS**
CIVIL WAR VOL. II (Frederick Fennell)
Engineer: Robert Fine (Mercury)

34. **BEST ALBUM COVER— OTHER THAN CLASSICAL**
THE BARBRA STREISAND ALBUM
Art Director: John Berg (Columbia)

35. **BEST ALBUM NOTES**
THE ELLINGTON ERA
(Duke Ellington)
Stanley Dance, Leonard Feather
(Columbia)

36. **BEST RECORDING FOR CHILDREN**
BERNSTEIN CONDUCTS FOR YOUNG PEOPLE
Leonard Bernstein, New York Philharmonic (Columbia)

37. **BEST ROCK AND ROLL RECORDING**
DEEP PURPLE
Nino Tempo & April Stevens (Atco)

38. **BEST COUNTRY & WESTERN RECORDING**
DETROIT CITY
Bobby Bare (RCA)

39. **BEST RHYTHM AND BLUES RECORDING**
BUSTED
Ray Charles (ABC/Paramount)

40. **BEST FOLK RECORDING**
BLOWIN' IN THE WIND
Peter, Paul and Mary
(Warner Bros.)

41. **BEST GOSPEL OR OTHER RELIGIOUS RECORDING (MUSICAL)**
DOMINIQUE
Soeur Sourire (The Singing Nun)
(Philips)

42. **BEST NEW ARTIST OF 1963**
SWINGLE SINGERS (Philips)

7TH ANNUAL (1964) GRAMMY WINNERS
Announcement on April 13, 1965
Eligibility Year: December 1, 1963 through November 30, 1964

1. **RECORD OF THE YEAR**
THE GIRL FROM IPANEMA
Stan Getz, Astrud Gilberto
(Verve)

2. **ALBUM OF THE YEAR**
GETZ/GILBERTO
Stan Getz, Joao Gilberto (Verve)

3. **ALBUM OF THE YEAR, CLASSICAL**
BERNSTEIN: SYMPHONY NO. 3 ("KADDISH")
Leonard Bernstein cond. New York Philharmonic (Columbia)

4. **SONG OF THE YEAR**
HELLO, DOLLY!
Composer: Jerry Herman (Kapp)

5. **BEST INSTRUMENTAL COMPOSITION (OTHER THAN JAZZ)**
THE PINK PANTHER THEME
Composer: Henry Mancini (RCA)

6. **BEST VOCAL PERFORMANCE, FEMALE**
PEOPLE (single)
Barbra Streisand (Columbia)

7. **BEST VOCAL PERFORMANCE, MALE**
HELLO, DOLLY! (single)
Louis Armstrong (Kapp)

8. **BEST INSTRUMENTAL JAZZ PERFORMANCE, SMALL GROUP OR SOLOIST WITH SMALL GROUP**
GETZ/GILBERTO
Stan Getz (Verve)

9. **BEST INSTRUMENTAL JAZZ PERFORMANCE, LARGE GROUP OR SOLOIST WITH LARGE GROUP**
GUITAR FROM IPANEMA
Laurindo Almeida (Capitol)

10. **BEST ORIGINAL JAZZ COMPOSITION**
THE CAT
Composer: Lalo Schifrin (Verve)

11. **BEST INSTRUMENTAL PERFORMANCE, NON-JAZZ**
PINK PANTHER
Henry Mancini (RCA)

12. **BEST INSTRUMENTAL ARRANGEMENT**
PINK PANTHER
(Henry Mancini)
Arranger: Henry Mancini (RCA)

13. **BEST ACCOMPANIMENT ARRANGEMENT FOR VOCALIST(S) OR INSTRUMENTALIST(S)**
PEOPLE
Barbra Streisand
Arranger: Peter Matz (Columbia)

14. **BEST PERFORMANCE BY A VOCAL GROUP**
A HARD DAY'S NIGHT
The Beatles (Capitol)

15. **BEST PERFORMANCE BY A CHORUS**
THE SWINGLE SINGERS GOING BAROQUE
The Swingle Singers (Philips)

16. **BEST ORIGINAL SCORE WRITTEN FOR A MOTION PICTURE OR TV SHOW**
MARY POPPINS
Composers: Richard M. and Robert B. Sherman (Buena Vista)

17. **BEST SCORE FROM AN ORIGINAL CAST SHOW ALBUM**
FUNNY GIRL
Composers: Jule Styne and Bob Merrill (Capitol)

18. **BEST COMEDY PERFORMANCE**
I STARTED OUT AS A CHILD
Bill Cosby (Warner Bros.)

19. **BEST DOCUMENTARY, SPOKEN WORD OR DRAMA RECORDING (OTHER THAN COMEDY)**
BBC TRIBUTE TO JOHN F. KENNEDY
"That Was the Week That Was"
Cast (Decca)

20. **BEST ENGINEERED RECORDING**
GETZ/GILBERTO (Stan Getz, Joao Gilberto)
Engineer: Phil Ramone (Verve)

21. **BEST ENGINEERED RECORDING—SPECIAL OR NOVEL EFFECTS**
THE CHIPMUNKS SING THE BEATLES
Engineer: Dave Hassinger
(Liberty)

22. **BEST ALBUM COVER**
PEOPLE (Barbra Streisand)
Art Director: Robert Cato
Photographer: Don Bronstein
(Columbia)

23. **BEST RECORDING FOR CHILDREN**
MARY POPPINS
Julie Andrews, Dick Van Dyke
(Buena Vista)

24. **BEST ROCK AND ROLL RECORDING**
DOWNTOWN
Petula Clark (Warner Bros.)

25. **BEST RHYTHM AND BLUES RECORDING**
HOW GLAD I AM
Nancy Wilson (Capitol)

26. **BEST FOLK RECORDING**
WE'LL SING IN THE SUNSHINE
Gale Garnett (RCA)

27. **BEST GOSPEL OR OTHER RELIGIOUS RECORDING (MUSICAL)**
GREAT GOSPEL SONGS
Tennessee Ernie Ford (Capitol)

28. **BEST NEW ARTIST OF 1964**
THE BEATLES (Capital)

29. **BEST COUNTRY & WESTERN SINGLE**
DANG ME
Roger Miller (Smash)

30. **BEST COUNTRY & WESTERN ALBUM**
DANG ME/CHUG-A-LUG
Roger Miller (Smash)

31. **BEST COUNTRY & WESTERN VOCAL PERFORMANCE, FEMALE**
HERE COMES MY BABY (single)
Dottie West (RCA)

32. **BEST COUNTRY & WESTERN VOCAL PERFORMANCE, MALE**
DANG ME (single)
Roger Miller (Smash)

33. **BEST COUNTRY & WESTERN SONG**
DANG ME
Composer: Roger Miller (Smash)

34. **BEST NEW COUNTRY & WESTERN ARTIST OF 1964**
ROGER MILLER (Smash)

35. **BEST ALBUM NOTES**
MEXICO (LEGACY COLLECTION) (Chavez)
Stanton Catlin, Carleton Beals (Columbia)

36. **BEST PERFORMANCE, ORCHESTRA**
MAHLER: SYMPHONY NO. 5 IN C SHARP MINOR BERG: "WOZZECK" EXCERPTS
Erich Leinsdorf, Boston Sym. Orch. (RCA)

37. **BEST CHAMBER PERFORMANCE, INSTRUMENTAL**
BEETHOVEN: TRIO NO. 1 IN E FLAT, OP.1., NO. 1
(Jacob Lateiner, piano)
Jascha Heifetz, Gregor Piatigorsky (RCA)

38. **BEST CHAMBER MUSIC PERFORMANCE, VOCAL**
IT WAS A LOVER AND HIS LASS (MORLEY, BYRD)
New York Pro Musica, Noah Greenberg, cond. (Decca)

39. **BEST PERFORMANCE, INSTRUMENTAL SOLOIST(S) (WITH ORCHESTRA)**
PROKOFIEFF: CONCERTO NO. 1 IN D MAJOR FOR VIOLIN Isaac Stern (Ormandy cond. Philadelphia Orch.)
(Columbia)

40. **BEST PERFORMANCE, INSTRUMENTAL SOLOIST (WITHOUT ORCHESTRA)**
VLADIMIR HOROWITZ PLAYS BEETHOVEN, DEBUSSY, CHOPIN (BEETHOVEN: SONATA NO. 8 "PATHETIQUE"; DEBUSSY: PRELUDES; CHOPIN: ETUDES & SCHERZOS 1 THRU 4)
Vladimir Horowitz (Columbia)

41. **BEST OPERA RECORDING**
BIZET: CARMEN
Herbert von Karajan cond. Vienna Philharmonic Orch. & Chorus
(Price, Corelli, Merrill, Freni) (RCA)

42. **BEST CHORAL PERFORMANCE (OTHER THAN OPERA)**
BRITTEN: A CEREMONY OF CAROLS
Robert Shaw cond. Robert Shaw Chorale and Orch. (RCA)

43. **BEST VOCAL SOLOIST PERFORMANCE (WITH OR WITHOUT ORCHESTRA)**
BERLIOZ: NUITS D'ETE (SONG CYCLE)/FALLA: EL AMOR BRUJO
(Reiner cond. Chicago Sym.)
Leontyne Price (RCA)

44. **BEST COMPOSITION BY A CONTEMPORARY COMPOSER**
PIANO CONCERTO
Composer: Samuel Barber
(Columbia)

45. **BEST ENGINEERED RECORDING— CLASSICAL**
BRITTEN: YOUNG PERSON'S GUIDE TO THE ORCHESTRA
(Giulini, Philharmonia)
Engineer: Douglas Larter (Angel)

46. **BEST ALBUM COVER— CLASSICAL**
SAINT-SAENS: CARNIVAL OF THE ANIMALS/BRITTEN: YOUNG PERSON'S GUIDE TO THE ORCHESTRA (Fiedler, Boston Pops)
Art Director: Robert Jones, Graphic Artist: Jan Balet (RCA)

47. **MOST PROMISING NEW RECORING ARTIST**
MARILYN HORNE (London)

8TH ANNUAL (1965) GRAMMY WINNERS
Announced on March 15, 1966
Eligibility Year: December 1, 1964 through November 30, 1965

1. **RECORD OF THE YEAR**
A TASTE OF HONEY
Herb Alpert & the Tijuana Brass
A&R Producers: Herb Alpert and Jerry Moss (A&M)

2. **ALBUM OF THE YEAR**
SEPTEMBER OF MY YEARS
Frank Sinatra
A&R Producer: Sonny Burke
(Reprise)

3. **ALBUM OF THE YEAR— CLASSICAL**
HOROWITZ AT CARNEGIE HALL (A Historic Return)
Vladimir Horowitz
A&R Producer: Thomas Frost
(Columbia)

4. **SONG OF THE YEAR**
THE SHADOW OF YOUR SMILE (LOVE THEME FROM THE SANDPIPER)
Composers: Paul Francis Webster and Johnny Mandel
(Mercury)

5. **BEST VOCAL PERFORMANCE, FEMALE**
MY NAME IS BARBRA (Album)
Barbra Streisand (Columbia)

6. **BEST VOCAL PERFORMANCE, MALE**
IT WAS A VERY GOOD YEAR (Single)
Frank Sinatra (Reprise)

7. **BEST INSTRUMENTAL PERFORMANCE, NON-JAZZ**
A TASTE OF HONEY
Herb Alpert & the Tijuana Brass
(A&M)

8. **BEST PERFORMANCE BY A VOCAL GROUP**
WE DIG MANCINI
Anita Kerr Singers (RCA)

9. **BEST PERFORMANCE BY A CHORUS**
ANYONE FOR MOZART?
The Swingle Singers (Philips)

10. **BEST ORIGINAL SCORE WRITTEN FOR A MOTION PICTURE OR TV SHOW**
THE SANDPIPER
Composer: Johnny Mandel
(Mercury)

11. **BEST SCORE FROM AN ORIGINAL SHOW ALBUM**
ON A CLEAR DAY YOU CAN SEE FOREVER
Composers: Alan Lerner, Burton Lane (RCA)

12. **BEST COMEDY PERFORMANCE**
WHY IS THERE AIR?
Bill Cosby (Warner Bros.)

13. **BEST SPOKEN WORD OR DRAMA RECORDING**
JOHN F. KENNEDY—AS WE REMEMBER HIM
Producer: Goddard Lieberson,
(Columbia)

14. **BEST NEW ARTIST**
TOM JONES (Parrot)

15. **BEST RECORDING FOR CHILDREN**
DR. SEUSS PRESENTS "FOX IN SOX" AND "GREEN EGGS AND HAM"
Marvin Miller (RCA-Camden)

16. **BEST ALBUM NOTES**
SEPTEMBER OF MY YEARS
(Frank Sinatra)
Stan Cornyn (Reprise)

17. **BEST INSTRUMENTAL JAZZ PERFORMANCE, SMALL GROUP OR SOLOIST WITH SMALL GROUP**
THE "IN" CROWD
Ramsey Lewis Trio (Cadet)

18. **BEST INSTRUMENTAL JAZZ PERFORMANCE, LARGE GROUP OR SOLOIST WITH LARGE GROUP**
ELLINGTON '66
Duke Ellington Orchestra
(Reprise)

19. **BEST ORIGINAL JAZZ COMPOSITION**
JAZZ SUITE ON THE MASS TEXTS
Composer: Lalo Schifrin (RCA)

20. **BEST INSTRUMENTAL ARRANGEMENT**
A TASTE OF HONEY
(Herb Alpert & Tijuana Brass)
Arranger: Herb Alpert (A&M)

21. **BEST ARRANGEMENT ACCOMPANYING A VOCALIST OR INSTRUMENTALIST**
IT WAS A VERY GOOD YEAR
(Frank Sinatra)
Arranger: Gordon Jenkins
(Reprise)

22. **BEST CONTEMPORARY (R&R) SINGLE**
KING OF THE ROAD
Roger Miller (Smash)

23. **BEST CONTEMPORARY (R&R) VOCAL PERFORMER, FEMALE**
I KNOW A PLACE (Single)
Petula Clark (Warner Bros.)

24. **BEST CONTEMPORARY (R&R) VOCAL PERFORMER MALE**
KING OF THE ROAD
Roger Miller (Smash)

25. **BEST CONTEMPORARY (R&R) PERFORMANCE GROUP (VOCAL OR INSTRUMENTAL)**
FLOWERS ON THE WALL (Single)
The Statler Brothers (Columbia)

26. **BEST RHYTHM & BLUES RECORDING**
PAPA'S GOT A BRAND NEW BAG
James Brown (King)

27. **BEST FOLK RECORDING**
AN EVENING WITH BELAFONTE/MAKEBA
Harry Belafonte, Miriam Makeba (RCA)

28. **BEST GOSPEL OR OTHER RELIGIOUS RECORDING (MUSICAL)**
SOUTHLAND FAVORITES
George Beverly Shea and the Anita Kerr Singers (RCA)

29. **BEST COUNTRY & WESTERN SINGLE**
KING OF THE ROAD
Roger Miller (Smash)

30. **BEST COUNTRY & WESTERN ALBUM**
THE RETURN OF ROGER MILLER
Roger Miller (Smash)

31. **BEST COUNTRY & WESTERN VOCAL PERFORMANCE, FEMALE**
QUEEN OF THE HOUSE
Jody Miller (Capitol)

32. **BEST COUNTRY & WESTERN VOCAL PERFORMANCE, MALE**
KING OF THE ROAD
Roger Miller (Smash)

33. **BEST COUNTRY & WESTERN SONG**
KING OF THE ROAD
Songwriter: Roger Miller (Smash)

34. **BEST NEW COUNTRY & WESTERN ARTIST**
STATLER BROTHERS (Columbia)

35. **BEST ENGINEERED RECORDING**
A TASTE OF HONEY (Herb Albert & Tijuana Brass)
Engineer: Larry Levine (A&M)

36. **BEST ENGINEERED RECORDING, CLASSICAL**
HOROWITZ AT CARNEGIE HALL—An Historic Return
Engineer: Fred Plaut (Columbia)

37. **BEST ALBUM COVER— PHOTOGRAPHY**
JAZZ SUITE ON THE MASS TEXTS (Paul Horn)
Art Director: Bob Jones
Photographer: Ken Whitmore (RCA)

38. **BEST ALBUM COVER— GRAPHIC ARTS**
BARTOK: CONCERTO NO. 2 FOR VIOLIN/STRAVINSKY: CONCERTO FOR VIOLIN (Silverstein, Leinsdorf cond. Boston Sym.)
Art Director: George Estes
Graphic Artist: James Alexander (RCA)

39. **BEST CLASSICAL PERFORMANCE, ORCHESTRA**
IVES: SYMPHONY NO. 4
Leopold Stokowski cond. American Sym. Orch. (Columbia)

40. **BEST CLASSICAL CHAMBER MUSIC PERFORMANCE, INSTRUMENTAL OR VOCAL**
BARTOK: THE SIX STRING QUARTETS
Juilliard String Quartet
(Columbia)

41. **BEST CLASSICAL PERFORMANCE, INSTRUMENTAL SOLOIST(S) (WITH ORCHESTRA)**
BEETHOVEN: CONCERTO NO. 4 IN G MAJOR FOR PIANO AND ORCHESTRA
Artur Rubinstein (Leinsdorf cond. Boston Sym.) (RCA)

42. **BEST CLASSICAL PERFORMANCE, INSTRUMENTAL SOLOIST (WITHOUT ORCHESTRA)**
HOROWITZ AT CARNEGIE HALL—An Historic Return
Vladimir Horowitz (Columbia)

43. **BEST OPERA RECORDING**
BERG: WOZZECK
Karl Bohm cond. Orch. of German Opera, Berlin
(Fisher Dieskau, Lear, Wunderlich) (DGG)

44. **BEST CHORAL PERFORMANCE (OTHER THAN OPERA)**
STRAVINSKY: SYMPHONY OF PSALMS/POULENC: GLORIA
Robert Shaw cond. Robert Shaw Chorale, RCA Victor Sym. Orch.
(RCA)

45. **BEST VOCAL PERFORMANCE—WITH OR WITHOUT ORCHESTRA**
STRAUSS: SALOME (DANCE OF THE SEVEN VEILS, INTERLUDE, FINAL SCENE) THE EGYPTIAN HELEN (AWAKENING SCENE)
Leontyne Price (RCA)

46. **BEST COMPOSITION BY A CONTEMPORARY CLASSICAL COMPOSER**
SYMPHONY NO. 4
Composer: Charles Ives
(Columbia)

47. **MOST PROMISING NEW RECORDING ARTIST**
PETER SERKIN, Pianist (RCA)

9TH ANNUAL (1966) GRAMMY WINNERS
Announced on March 2, 1967
Eligibility Year: November 2, 1965 through November 1, 1966

1. **RECORD OF THE YEAR**
STRANGERS IN THE NIGHT
Frank Sinatra
A&R Producer: Jimmy Bowen
(Reprise)

2. **ALBUM OF THE YEAR**
SINATRA—A MAN & HIS MUSIC
Frank Sinatra
A&R Producer: Sonny Burke
(Reprise)

3. **SONG OF THE YEAR**
MICHELLE
Songwriters: John Lennon, Paul McCartney (Capitol)

4. **BEST INSTRUMENTAL THEME**
BATMAN THEME
Composer: Neal Hefti (RCA)

5. **BEST VOCAL PERFORMANCE, FEMALE**
IF HE WALKED INTO MY LIFE (Single)
Eydie Gorme (Columbia)

6. **BEST VOCAL PERFORMANCE, MALE**
STRANGERS IN THE NIGHT
Frank Sinatra (Reprise)

7. **BEST INSTRUMENTAL PERFORMANCE (OTHER THAN JAZZ)**
WHAT NOW MY LOVE
Herb Albert & the Tijuana Brass (A&M)

8. **BEST PERFORMANCE BY A VOCAL GROUP**
A MAN AND A WOMAN
Anita Kerr Singers (Warner Bros.)

9. **BEST PERFORMANCE BY A CHORUS**
SOMEWHERE, MY LOVE
(Lara's Theme from "Dr. Zhivago")
Ray Conniff Singers (Columbia)

10. **BEST ORIGINAL SCORE WRITTEN FOR A MOTION PICTURE OR TV SHOW**
DR. ZHIVAGO
Composer: Maurice Jarre (MGM)

11. **BEST SCORE FROM AN ORIGINAL CAST SHOW ALBUM**
MAME
Composer: Jerry Herman (Columbia)

12. **BEST COMEDY PERFORMANCE**
WONDERFULNESS
Bill Cosby (Warner Bros.)

13. **BEST SPOKEN WORD, DOCUMENTARY OR DRAMA RECORDING**
EDWARD R. MURROW—A REPORTER REMEMBERS VOL. 1 THE WAR YEARS
Edward R. Murrow (Columbia)

14. **BEST RECORDING FOR CHILDREN**
DR. SEUSS PRESENTS "IF I RAN THE ZOO" AND "SLEEP BOOK"
Marvin Miller (RCA-Camden)

15. **BEST ALBUM NOTES**
SINATRA AT THE SANDS
Stan Cornyn (Reprise)

16. **BEST INSTRUMENTAL JAZZ PERFORMANCE GROUP OR SOLOIST WITH GROUP**
GOIN' OUT OF MY HEAD
Wes Montgomery (Verve)

17. **BEST ORIGINAL JAZZ COMPOSITION**
IN THE BEGINNING GOD
Composer: Duke Ellington (RCA)

18. **BEST CONTEMPORARY (R&R) RECORDING**
WINCHESTER CATHEDRAL
New Vaudeville Band (Fontana)

19. **BEST CONTEMPORARY (R&R) SOLO VOCAL PERFORMANCE, MALE OR FEMALE**
ELEANOR RIGBY (single)
Paul McCartney (Capitol)

20. **BEST CONTEMPORARY (R&R) GROUP PERFORMANCE, VOCAL OR INSTRUMENTAL**
MONDAY, MONDAY (Single)
The Mamas & The Papas (Dunhill)

21. **BEST RHYTHM & BLUES RECORDING**
CRYING TIME
Ray Charles (ABC-Paramount)

22. **BEST RHYTHM & BLUES SOLO VOCAL PERFORMANCE, MALE OR FEMALE**
CRYING TIME (Single)
Ray Charles (ABC-Paramount)

23. **BEST RHYTHM & BLUES GROUP, VOCAL OR INSTRUMENTAL**
HOLD IT RIGHT THERE (Single)
Ramsey Lewis (Cadet)

24. **BEST FOLK RECORDING**
BLUES IN THE STREET
Cortelia Clark (RCA)

25. **BEST SACRED RECORDING (MUSICAL)**
GRAND OLD GOSPEL
Porter Wagoner & the Blackwood Bros. (RCA)

26. **BEST COUNTRY & WESTERN RECORDING**
ALMOST PERSUADED
David Houston (Epic)

27. **BEST COUNTRY & WESTERN VOCAL PERFORMANCE, FEMALE**
DON'T TOUCH ME (Single)
Jeannie Seely (Monument)

28. **BEST COUNTRY & WESTERN VOCAL PERFORMANCE, MALE**
ALMOST PERSUADED (Single)
David Houston (Epic)

29. **BEST COUNTRY & WESTERN SONG**
ALMOST PERSUADED
Songwriters: Billy Sherrill, Glenn Sutton (Epic)

30. **BEST INSTRUMENTAL ARRANGEMENT**
WHAT NOW MY LOVE (Herb Alpert & Tijuana Brass)
Arranger: Herb Alpert (A&M)

31. **BEST ARRANGEMENT ACCOMPANYING A VOCALIST OR INSTRUMENTALIST**
STRANGERS IN THE NIGHT (Frank Sinatra)
Arranger: Ernie Freeman (Reprise)

32. **BEST ENGINEERED RECORDING**
STRANGERS IN THE NIGHT (Frank Sinatra)
Engineers: Eddie Brackett, Lee Herschberg (Reprise)

33. **BEST ENGINEERED RECORDING, CLASSICAL**
WAGNER: LOHENGRIN (Leindorf cond. Boston Sym., Pro Musica Chorus)
Engineer: Anthony Salvatore (RCA)

34. **BEST ALBUM COVER, PHOTOGRAPHY**
CONFESSIONS OF A BROKEN MAN (Porter Wagoner)
Art Director: Robert Jones
Photographer: Les Leverette (RCA)

35. **BEST ALBUM COVER, GRAPHIC ARTS**
REVOLVER (The Beatles)
Graphic Art: Klaus Voormann (Capitol)

36. **ALBUM OF THE YEAR, CLASSICAL**
IVES: SYMPHONY NO. 1 IN D MINOR
Morton Gould cond. Chicago Sym.
A&R Producer: Howard Scott (RCA)

37. **BEST CLASSICAL PERFORMANCE, ORCHESTRA**
MAHLER: SYMPHONY NO. 6 IN A MINOR
Erich Leinsdorf cond. Boston Sym. (RCA)

38. **BEST CHAMBER MUSIC PERFORMANCE, INSTRUMENTAL OR VOCAL**
BOSTON SYMPHONY CHAMBER PLAYERS
Boston Symphony Chamber Players (RCA)

39. **BEST PERFORMANCE, INSTRUMENTAL SOLOIST(S) (WITH OR WITHOUT ORCHESTRA)**
BAROQUE GUITAR
Julian Bream (RCA)

40. **BEST OPERA RECORDING**
WAGNER— DIE WALKURE
Georg Solti cond. Vienna Philharmonic
(Nilsson, Crespin, Ludwig, King, Hotter) (London)

41. **BEST CLASSICAL CHORAL PERFORMANCE (OTHER THAN OPERA)**
HANDEL: MESSIAH
Robert Shaw cond. Robert Shaw Chorale and Orch. (RCA)

IVES: MUSIC FOR CHORUS
(Gen. William Booth Enters Into Heaven, Serenity, The Circus Band, etc.)
Gregg Smith cond. Columbia Chamber Orch., Gregg Smith Singers, Ithaca College Concert Choir/George Bragg cond. Texas Boys Choir (Columbia)

42. **BEST CLASSICAL VOCAL SOLOIST PERFORMANCE (WITH OR WITHOUT ORCHESTRA)**
PRIMA DONNA
Leontyne Price (Molinari-Pradelli cond. RCA Italiana Opera Orch.) (RCA)

10TH ANNUAL (1967) GRAMMY WINNERS
Announced on February 29, 1968
Eligibility Year: November 2, 1966 through November 1, 1967

1. **RECORD OF THE YEAR**
UP, UP AND AWAY
5th Dimension
A&R Producers: Marc Gordon, Johnny Rivers (Soul City)

2. **ALBUM OF THE YEAR**
SGT. PEPPER'S LONELY HEARTS CLUB BAND
The Beatles
A&R Producer: George Martin (Capitol)

3. **SONG OF THE YEAR**
UP, UP AND AWAY
Songwriter: Jim Webb (Soul City)

4. **BEST INSTRUMENTAL THEME**
MISSION: IMPOSSIBLE
Composer: Lalo Schifrin (Dot)

5. **BEST VOCAL PERFORMANCE, FEMALE**
ODE TO BILLIE JOE (Single)
Bobbie Gentry (Capitol)

6. **BEST VOCAL PERFORMANCE, MALE**
BY THE TIME I GET TO PHOENIX (Single)
Glen Campbell (Capitol)

7. **BEST INSTRUMENTAL PERFORMANCE**
CHET ATKINS PICKS THE BEST
Chet Atkins (RCA)

8. **BEST PERFORMANCE BY A VOCAL GROUP (Two to Six Persons)**
UP, UP AND AWAY
5th Dimension (Soul City)

9. **BEST PERFORMANCE BY A CHORUS (Seven or More Persons)**
UP, UP AND AWAY
Johnny Mann Singers (Liberty)

10. **BEST ORIGINAL SCORE WRITTEN FOR A MOTION PICTURE OR TV SHOW**
MISSION: IMPOSSIBLE
Composer: Lalo Schifrin (Dot)

11. **BEST SCORE FROM AN ORIGINAL CAST SHOW ALBUM**
CABARET
Composers: Fred Ebb and John Kander
A&R Producer: Goddard Lieberson (Columbia)

12. **BEST COMEDY RECORDING**
REVENGE
Bill Cosby (WB-7 Arts)

12. **BEST NEW ARTIST**
BOBBIE GENTRY (Capitol)

14. **BEST INSTRUMENTAL JAZZ PERFORMANCE, SMALL GROUP OR SOLOIST WITH SMALL GROUP**
MERCY, MERCY, MERCY
Cannonball Adderley Quintet (Capitol)

15. **BEST INSTRUMENTAL JAZZ PERFORMANCE, LARGE GROUP OR SOLOIST WITH LARGE GROUP**
FAR EAST SUITE
Duke Ellington (RCA)

16. **BEST CONTEMPORARY SINGLE**
UP, UP AND AWAY
5th Dimension
A&R Producers: Marc Gordon, Johnny Rivers (Soul City)

17. **BEST CONTEMPORARY ALBUM**
SGT PEPPER'S LONELY HEARTS CLUB BAND
The Beatles
A&R Producer: George Martin (Capitol)

18. **BEST CONTEMPORARY FEMALE SOLO VOCAL PERFORMANCE**
ODE TO BILLIE JOE
Bobbie Gentry (Capitol)

19. **BEST CONTEMPORARY MALE SOLO VOCAL PERFORMANCE**
BY THE TIME I GET TO PHOENIX
Glen Campbell (Capitol)

20. **BEST CONTEMPORARY GROUP PERFORMANCE, VOCAL OR INSTRUMENTAL**
UP, UP AND AWAY
5th Dimension (Soul City)

21. **BEST RHYTHM & BLUES RECORDING**
RESPECT
Aretha Franklin
A&R Producer: Jerry Wexler (Atlantic)

22. **BEST RHYTHM & BLUES SOLO VOCAL PERFORMANCE, FEMALE**
RESPECT
Aretha Franklin (Atlantic)

23. **BEST RHYTHM & BLUES SOLO VOCAL PERFORMANCE, MALE**
DEAD END STREET
Lou Rawls (Capitol)

24. **BEST RHYTHM & BLUES GROUP PERFORMANCE, VOCAL OR INSTRUMENTAL (Two or More Persons)**
SOUL MAN
Sam & Dave (Stax)

25. **BEST SACRED PERFORMANCE**
HOW GREAT THOU ART
Elvis Presley (RCA)

26. **BEST GOSPEL PERFORMANCE**
MORE GRAND OLD GOSPEL
Porter Wagoner & the
Blackwood Bros. (RCA)

27. **BEST FOLK PERFORMANCE**
GENTLE ON MY MIND
John Hartford (RCA)

28. **BEST COUNTRY & WESTERN RECORDING**
GENTLE ON MY MIND
Glen Campbell
A&R Producer: Al De Lory
(Capitol)

29. **BEST COUNTRY & WESTERN SOLO VOCAL PERFORMANCE, FEMALE**
I DON'T WANNA PLAY HOUSE
Tammy Wynette (Epic)

30. **BEST COUNTRY & WESTERN SOLO VOCAL PERFORMANCE, MALE**
GENTLE ON MY MIND
Glen Campbell (Capitol)

31. **BEST COUNTRY & WESTERN PERFORMANCE, DUET, TRIO OR GROUP (VOCAL OR INSTRUMENTAL)**
JACKSON
Johnny Cash and June Carter
(Columbia)

32. **BEST COUNTRY & WESTERN SONG**
GENTLE ON MY MIND
Songwriter: John Hartford (RCA)

33. **BEST SPOKEN WORD, DOCUMENTARY OR DRAMA RECORDING**
GALLANT MEN
Sen. Everett M. Dirksen
(Capitol)

34. **BEST RECORDING FOR CHILDREN**
DR. SEUSS: HOW THE GRINCH STOLE CHRISTMAS
Boris Karloff (MGM)

35. **BEST INSTRUMENTAL ARRANGEMENT**
ALFIE (Bacharach Orch.)
Arranger: Burt Bacharach (A&M)

36. **BEST ARRANGEMENT ACCOMPANYING VOCALIST(S) OR INSTRUMENTALIST(S)**
ODE TO BILLIE JOE
(Bobbie Gentry)
Arranger: Jimmie Haskell
(Capitol)

37. **BEST ENGINEERED RECORDING**
SGT. PEPPER'S LONELY HEARTS CLUB BAND (Beatles)
Engineer: G.E. Emerick
(Capitol)

38. **BEST ENGINEERED RECORDING, CLASSICAL**
THE GLORIOUS SOUND OF BRASS
(Philadelphia Brass Ensemble)
Engineer: Edward T. Graham
(Capitol)

39. **BEST ALBUM COVER, PHOTOGRAPHY**
BOB DYLAN'S GREATEST HITS
Art Directors: John Berg, Bob Cato
Photographer: Roland Scherman
(Columbia)

40. BEST ALBUM COVER, GRAPHIC ARTS
SGT. PEPPER'S LONELY HEARTS CLUB BAND
Art Directors: Peter Blake, Jann Haworth (Capitol)

41. BEST ALBUM NOTES
SUBURBAN ATTITUDES IN COUNTRY VERSE
John O. Loudermilk (RCA)

42. ALBUM OF THE YEAR, CLASSICAL (Tie)
BERG: WOZZECK
Pierre Boulez cond. Paris National Opera
A&R Producer: Thomas Shepard (Columbia)

MAHLER: SYMPHONY NO. 8 IN E FLAT MAJOR ("SYMPHONY OF A THOUSAND")
Leonard Bernstein, London Sym.
A&R Producer: John McClure (Columbia)

43. BEST CLASSICAL PERFORMANCE, ORCHESTRA
STRAVINSKY: FIREBIRD & PETROUCHKA SUITES
Igor Stravinsky cond. Columbia Sym. (Columbia)

44. BEST CHAMBER MUSIC PERFORMANCE
WEST MEETS EAST
Ravi Shanker & Yehudi Menuhin (Angel)

45. BEST CLASSICAL PERFORMANCE, INSTRUMENTAL SOLOIST(S) (WITH OR WITHOUT ORCHESTRA)
HOROWITZ IN CONCERT
Vladimir Horowitz (Columbia)

46. BEST OPERA RECORDING
BERG: WOZZECK
Pierre Boulez cond. Paris National Opera (Berry, Strauss, Uhl, Doench)
A&R Producer: Thomas Shepard (Columbia)

47. BEST CLASSICAL CHORAL PERFORMANCE (Tie)
MAHLER: SYMPHONY NO. 8 IN E FLAT MAJOR
Leonard Bernstein cond. London Sym. (Columbia)

ORFF: CATULLI CARMINA
Robert Page cond. Temple Univ. Chorus; Eugene Ormandy cond. Philadelphia Orch (Columbia)

48. BEST CLASSICAL VOCAL SOLOIST PERFORMANCE
PRIMA DONNA, VOLUME 2
Leontyne Price (Molinari-Pradelli cond. RCA Italiana Opera Orch.) (RCA)

11TH ANNUAL (1968) GRAMMY WINNERS
Announced on March 12, 1969
Eligibility Year: November 2, 1967 through November 1, 1968

1. RECORD OF THE YEAR
MRS. ROBINSON
Simon & Garfunkel
A&R Producers: Paul Simon, Art Garfunkel, Roy Halee (Columbia)

2. ALBUM OF THE YEAR
BY THE TIME I GET TO PHOENIX
Glen Campbell
A&R Producer: Al De Lory (Capitol)

3. **SONG OF THE YEAR**
LITTLE GREEN APPLES
Songwriter: Bobby Russell
(Columbia)

4. **BEST NEW ARTIST OF 1968**
JOSE FELICIANO (RCA)

5. **BEST INSTRUMENTAL
ARRANGEMENT**
CLASSICAL GAS (Mason
Williams)
Arranger: Mike Post (WB/7 Arts)

6. **BEST ARRANGEMENT
ACCOMPANYING
VOCALIST(S)**
MAC ARTHUR PARK (Richard
Harris)
Arranger: Jim Webb (Dunhill)

7. **BEST ENGINEERED
RECORDING**
WICHITA LINEMAN (Glen
Campbell)
Engineers: Joe Polito, Hugh
Davies (Capitol)

8. **BEST ALBUM COVER**
UNDERGROUND (Thelonius
Monk)
Art Directors: John Berg,
Richard Mantel
Photography: Horn/Griner Studio
(Columbia)

9. **BEST ALBUM NOTES**
JOHNNY CASH AT FOLSOM
PRISON
Annotator: Johnny Cash
(Columbia)

10. **BEST CONTEMPORARY–POP
VOCAL PERFORMANCE,
FEMALE**
DO YOU KNOW THE WAY TO
SAN JOSE (single)
Dionne Warwicke (Scepter)

11. **BEST CONTEMPORARY–POP
VOCAL PERFORMANCE,
MALE**
LIGHT MY FIRE (single)
Jose Feliciano (RCA)

12. **BEST CONTEMPORARY–POP
PERFORMANCE VOCAL,
DUO OR GROUP**
MRS. ROBINSON
Simon & Garfunkel (Columbia)

13. **BEST CONTEMPORARY–POP
PERFORMANCE CHORUS**
MISSION IMPOSSIBLE/
NORWEGIAN WOOD (medley)
Alan Copeland Singers (Atco)

14. **BEST CONTEMPORARY–POP
PERFORMANCE,
INSTRUMENTAL**
CLASSICAL GAS
Mason Williams (WB-7 Arts)

15. **BEST RHYTHM & BLUES
VOCAL PERFORMANCE,
FEMALE**
CHAIN OF FOOLS (single)
Aretha Franklin (Atlantic)

16. **BEST RHYTHM & BLUES
VOCAL PERFORMANCE,
MALE**
(SITTIN' ON) THE DOCK OF
THE BAY (single)
Otis Redding (Volt)

17. **BEST RHYTHM & BLUES
PERFORMANCE BY A DUO
OR GROUP, VOCAL OR
INSTRUMENTAL**
CLOUD NINE
The Temptations (Soul/Gordy)

18. **BEST RHYTHM & BLUES
SONG**
(SITTIN' ON) THE DOCK OF
THE BAY
Songwriters: Otis Redding, Steve
Cropper (Volt)

19. **BEST COUNTRY VOCAL
PERFORMANCE, FEMALE**
HARPER VALLEY P.T.A.
(single)
Jeannie C. Riley (Plantation)

20. **BEST COUNTRY VOCAL PERFORMANCE, MALE**
FOLSOM PRISON BLUES
(Single)
Johnny Cash (Columbia)

21. **BEST COUNTRY PERFORMANCE, DUO OR GROUP VOCAL OR INSTRUMENTAL**
FOGGY MOUNTAIN BREAKDOWN
Flatt & Scruggs (Columbia)

22. **BEST COUNTRY SONG**
LITTLE GREEN APPLES
Songwriter: Bobby Russell
(Smash)

23. **BEST SACRED PERFORMANCE**
BEAUTIFUL ISLE OF SOMEWHERE
Jake Hess (RCA)

24. **BEST GOSPEL PERFORMANCE**
THE HAPPY GOSPEL OF THE HAPPY GOODMANS
Happy Goodman Family (Word)

25. **BEST SOUL GOSPEL PERFORMANCE**
THE SOUL OF ME
Dottie Rambo (Heartwarming)

26. **BEST FOLK PERFORMANCE**
BOTH SIDES NOW
Judy Collins (Elektra)

27. **BEST INSTRUMENAL THEME**
CLASSICAL GAS
Composer: Mason Williams
(WB-7 Arts)

28. **BEST ORIGINAL SCORE WRITTEN FOR A MOTION PICTURE OR A TV SPECIAL**
THE GRADUATE
Songwriter: Paul Simon
Additional Music: Dave Grusin
(Columbia)

29. **BEST SCORE FROM AN ORIGINAL CAST SHOW ALBUM**
HAIR
Composers: Gerome Ragni, James Rado, Galt MacDermott
A&R Producer: Andy Wiswell
(RCA)

30. **BEST COMEDY RECORDING**
TO RUSSELL, MY BROTHER, WHOM I SLEPT WITH
Bill Cosby (WB-7 Arts)

31. **BEST SPOKEN WORD RECORDING**
LONESOME CITIES (album)
Rod McKuen (WB-7 Arts)

32. **BEST INSTRUMENTAL JAZZ PERFORMANCE, SMALL GROUP OR SOLOIST WITH SMALL GROUP**
BILL EVANS AT THE MONTREUX JAZZ FESTIVAL
Bill Evans Trio (Verve)

33. **BEST INSTRUMENTAL JAZZ PEFORMANCE, LARGE GROUP OR SOLOIST WITH LARGE GROUP**
AND HIS MOTHER CALLED HIM BILL
Duke Ellington (RCA)

34. **BEST CLASSICAL PERFORMANCE, ORCHESTRA**
BOULEZ CONDUCTS DEBUSSY
New Philharmonia, Orch., Pierre Boulez, cond. (Columbia)

35. **BEST CHAMBER MUSIC PERFORMANCE**
GABRIELI: CANZONI FOR BRASS, WINDS, STRINGS & ORGAN
E. Power Biggs with Edward Tarr Ensemble & Gabrieli Consort, Vittorio Negri, cond.
(Columbia)

36. **BEST OPERA RECORDING**
MOZART: COSI FAN TUTTE
Erich Leinsdorf cond. New
Philharmonia Orch. & Ambrosian
Opera Chorus (Price, Raskin,
Troyanos, Milnes, Shirley,
Flagello)
A&R Producer: Richard Mohr
(RCA)

37. **BEST PERFORMANCE,
INSTRUMENTAL SOLOIST(S)
(WITH OR WITHOUT
ORCHESTRA)**
HOROWITZ ON TELEVISION
Vladimir Horowitz (Columbia)

38. **BEST CHORAL
PERFORMANCE (OTHER
THAN OPERA)**
THE GLORY OF GABRIELI
Vittorio Negri cond./Gregg Smith
Singers/Texas Boys Choir,
George Bragg, dir./Edward Tarr
Ensemble (with E. Power Biggs)
(Columbia)

39. **BEST CLASSICAL VOCAL
SOLOIST PERFORMANCE**
ROSSINI RARITIES
Montserrat Caballe (Cillario
cond. RCA Italiana Opera Orch.
& Chorus) (RCA)

40. **BEST ENGINEERED
RECORDING, CLASSICAL**
MAHLER: SYMPHONY NO. 9
IN D MAJOR (Solti cond.
London Sym. Orch.)
Engineer: Gordon Parry
(London)

12TH ANNUAL (1969) GRAMMY WINNERS
Announced on March 11, 1970
Eligibility Year: November 2, 1968 through November 1, 1969

1. **RECORD OF THE YEAR**
AQUARIUS/LET THE
SUNSHINE IN
5th Dimension
A&R Producer: Bones Howe
(Soul City)

2. **ALBUM OF THE YEAR**
BLOOD, SWEAT & TEARS
Blood, Sweat & Tears
A&R Producer: James Guercio
(Columbia)

3. **SONG OF THE YEAR**
GAMES PEOPLE PLAY
Songwriter: Joe South

4. **BEST NEW ARTIST OF 1969**
CROSBY, STILLS & NASH
(Atlantic)

5. **BEST INSTRUMENTAL
ARRANGEMENT**
LOVE THEME FROM ROMEO
& JULIET
Arranger: Henry Mancini (RCA)

6. **BEST ARRANGEMENT
ACCOMPANYING
VOCALIST(S)**
SPINNING WHEEL
(Blood, Sweat & Tears)
Arranger: Fred Lipsius
(Columbia)

7. **BEST ENGINEERED RECORDING**
ABBEY ROAD (The Beatles)
Engineers: Geoff Emerick, Philip McDonald (Apple)

8. **BEST ALBUM COVER**
AMERICA THE BEAUTIFUL
(Gary McFarland)
Painting: Evelyn J. Kelbish
Graphics: David Stahlberg

9. **BEST ALBUM NOTES**
NASHVILLE SKYLINE (Bob Dylan)
Annotator: Johnny Cash
(Columbia)

10. **BEST CONTEMPORARY VOCAL PERFORMANCE, FEMALE**
IS THAT ALL THERE IS (single)
Peggy Lee (Capitol)

11. **BEST CONTEMPORARY VOCAL PERFORMANCE, MALE**
EVERYBODY'S TALKIN'
Harry Nilsson (United Artists)

12. **BEST CONTEMPORARY VOCAL PERFORMANCE BY A GROUP**
AQUARIUS/LET THE SUNSHINE IN
5th Dimension (Soul City)

13. **BEST CONTEMPORARY PERFORMANCE BY A CHORUS**
LOVE THEME FROM ROMEO & JULIET
Percy Faith Orchestra & Chorus (Columbia)

14. **BEST CONTEMPORARY INSTRUMENTAL PERFORMANCE**
VARIATIONS ON A THEME BY ERIC SATIE
Blood, Sweat & Tears (Columbia)

15. **BEST CONTEMPORARY SONG**
GAMES PEOPLE PLAY
Songwriter: Joe South

16. **BEST RHYTHM & BLUES VOCAL PERFORMANCE, FEMALE**
SHARE YOUR LOVE WITH ME (Single)
Aretha Franklin (Atlantic)

17. **BEST RHYTHM & BLUES VOCAL PERFORMANCE, MALE**
THE CHOKIN' KIND (Single)
Joe Simon (Sound Stage 7)

18. **BEST RHYTHM & BLUES VOCAL PERFORMANCE BY A GROUP OR DUO**
IT'S YOUR THING
The Isley Brothers (T-Neck)

19. **BEST RHYTHM & BLUES INSTRUMENTAL PERFORMANCE**
GAMES PEOPLE PLAY
King Curtis (Atco)

20. **BEST RHYTHM & BLUES SONG**
COLOR HIM FATHER
Songwriter: Richard Spencer

21. **BEST SOUL GOSPEL**
OH HAPPY DAY
Edwin Hawkins Singers (Buddah)

22. **BEST COUNTRY VOCAL PERFORMANCE, FEMALE**
STAND BY YOUR MAN (Album)
Tammy Wynette (Epic)

23. **BEST COUNTRY VOCAL PERFORMANCE, MALE**
A BOY NAMED SUE (single)
Johnny Cash (Columbia)

24. **BEST COUNTRY PERFORMANCE BY A DUO OR GROUP**
MACARTHUR PARK
Waylon Jennings & The Kimberleys (RCA)

25. **BEST COUNTRY INSTRUMENTAL PERFORMANCE**
THE NASHVILLE BRASS FEATURING DANNY DAVIS PLAY MORE NASHVILLE SOUNDS
Danny Davis & The Nashville Brass (RCA)

26. **BEST COUNTRY SONG**
A BOY NAMED SUE
Songwriter: Shel Silverstein

27. **BEST SACRED PERFORMANCE**
AIN'T THAT BEAUTIFUL SINGING
Jake Hess (RCA)

28. **BEST GOSPEL PERFORMANCE**
IN GOSPEL COUNTRY
Porter Wagoner & the Blackwood Bros. (RCA)

29. **BEST FOLK PERFORMANCE**
CLOUDS
Joni Mitchell (Warner Bros.)

30. **BEST INSTRUMENTAL THEME**
MIDNIGHT COWBOY
Composer: John Barry

31. **BEST ORIGINAL SCORE WRITTEN FOR A MOTION PICTURE OR TV SPECIAL**
BUTCH CASSIDY & THE SUNDANCE KID
Composer: Burt Bacharach (A&M)

32. **BEST SCORE FROM AN ORIGINAL CAST SHOW ALBUM**
PROMISES, PROMISES
Composers: Burt Bacharach and Hal David
A&R Producers: Henry Jerome, Phil Ramone (Liberty/United Artists)

33. **BEST RECORDING FOR CHILDREN**
PETER, PAUL & MOMMY
Peter, Paul and Mary (Warner Bros.)

34. **BEST COMEDY RECORDING**
BILL COSBY
Bill Cosby (Uni)

35. **BEST SPOKEN WORD RECORDING**
WE LOVE YOU, CALL COLLECT
Art Linkletter & Diane (World/Cap)

36. **BEST INSTRUMENTAL JAZZ PERFORMANCE, SMALL GROUP OR SOLOIST WITH SMALL GROUP**
WILLOW WEEP FOR ME
Wes Montgomery (Verve)

37. **BEST INSTRUMENTAL JAZZ PERFORMANCE, LARGE GROUP OR SOLOIST WITH LARGE GROUP**
WALKING IN SPACE
Quincy Jones (A&M)

38. **ALBUM OF THE YEAR, CLASSICAL**
SWITCHED-ON BACH
Walter Carlos
A&R Producer: Rachel Elkind (Columbia)

39. **BEST CLASSICAL PERFORMANCE, ORCHESTRA**
BOULEZ CONDUCTS DEBUSSY, VOL. 2 "IMAGES POUR ORCHESTRE"
Pierre Boulez, Cleveland Orch. (Columbia)

40. **BEST CHAMBER MUSIC PERFORMANCE**
GABRIELI: ANTIPHONAL MUSIC OF GABRIELI (CANZONI FOR BRASS CHOIRS)
The Philadelphia, Cleveland, and Chicago Brass Ensembles (Columbia)

41. **BEST PERFORMANCE, INSTRUMENTAL SOLOIST(S) (WITH OR WITHOUT ORCHESTRA)**
SWITCHED-ON BACH
Walter Carlos (Columbia)

42. **BEST OPERA RECORDING**
WAGNER: SIEGFRIED
Herbert von Karajan cond. Berlin Philharmonic (Thomas, Stewart, Stolze, Dernesch, Keleman, Dominguez, Gayer, Ridderbusch)
A&R Producer: Otto Gerdes (DGG)

43. **BEST CHORAL PERFORMANCE (OTHER THAN OPERA)**
BERIO: SINFONIA
Swingle Singers, Ward Swingle, Choral Master/New York Philharmonic, Luciano Berio, cond. (Columbia)

44. **BEST VOCAL SOLOIST PERFORMANCE, CLASSICAL**
BARBER: TWO SCENES FROM "ANTONY & CLEOPATRA"/KNOXVILLE: SUMMER OF 1915
Leontyne Price (Schippers cond. New Philharmonia) (RCA)

45. **BEST ENGINEERED RECORDING, CLASSICAL**
SWITCHED-ON BACH (Walter Carlos)
Engineer: Walter Carlos (Columbia)

13TH ANNUAL (1970) GRAMMY WINNERS
Announced on March 16, 1971
Eligibility Year: November 2, 1969 through October 15, 1970

1. **RECORD OF THE YEAR**
BRIDGE OVER TROUBLED WATER
Simon & Garfunkel
A&R Producers: Paul Simon, Arthur Garfunkel, Roy Halee (Columbia)

2. **ALBUM OF THE YEAR**
BRIDGE OVER TROUBLED WATER
Simon & Garfunkel
A&R Producers: Paul Simon, Arthur Garfunkel, Roy Halee (Columbia)

3. **SONG OF THE YEAR**
BRIDGE OVER TROUBLED
WATER
Songwriter: Paul Simon
(Colulmbia)

4. **BEST NEW ARTIST OF THE
YEAR**
CARPENTERS (A&M)

5. **BEST INSTRUMENTAL
ARRANGEMENT**
THEME FROM "Z" (Henry
Mancini)
Arranger: Henry Mancini (RCA)

6. **BEST ARRANGEMENT
ACCOMPANYING
VOCALIST(S)**
BRIDGE OVER TROUBLED
WATER (Simon & Garfunkel)
Arrangers: Paul Simon, Arthur
Garfunkel, Jimmie Haskell,
Ernie Freeman, Larry Knechtel
(Columbia)

7. **BEST ENGINEERED
RECORDING**
BRIDGE OVER TROUBLED
WATER
(Simon & Garfunkel)
Engineer: Roy Halee (Columbia)

8. **BEST ALBUM COVER**
INDIANOLA MISSISSIPPI
SEEDS (B.B. King)
Cover Design: Robert Lockart
Photography: Ivan Nagy (ABC)

9. **BEST ALBUM NOTES**
THE WORLD'S GREATEST
BLUES SINGER
(Bessie Smith)
Annotator: Chris Albertson
(Columbia)

10. **BEST CONTEMPORARY
VOCAL PERFORMANCE,
FEMALE**
I'LL NEVER FALL IN LOVE
AGAIN
Dionne Warwicke (Album)
(Scepter)

11. **BEST CONTEMPORARY
VOCAL PERFORMANCE,
MALE**
EVERYTHING IS BEAUTIFUL
Ray Stevens (Single) (Barnaby)

12. **BEST CONTEMPORARY
VOCAL PERFORMANCE BY A
GROUP**
CLOSE TO YOU
Carpenters (A&M)

13. **BEST CONTEMPORARY
INSTRUMENTAL
PERFORMANCE**
THEME FROM "Z" AND
OTHER FILM MUSIC
Henry Mancini (RCA)

14. **BEST CONTEMPORARY
SONG**
BRIDGE OVER TROUBLED
WATER
Songwriter: Paul Simon
(Columbia)

15. **BEST RHYTHM & BLUES
VOCAL PERFORMANCE,
FEMALE**
DON'T PLAY THAT SONG
Aretha Franklin (Single) (Atlantic)

16. **BEST RHYTHM & BLUES
VOCAL PERFORMANCE,
MALE**
THE THRILL IS GONE
B.B. King (Single) (ABC)

17. **BEST RHYTHM & BLUES
VOCAL PERFORMANCE BY A
DUO OR GROUP**
DIDN'T I (BLOW YOUR MIND
THIS TIME)
The Delfonics (Philly Groove)

18. **BEST RHYTHM & BLUES
SONG**
PATCHES
Songwriters: Ronald Dunbar and
General Johnson (Atlantic)

19. **BEST SOUL GOSPEL PERFORMANCE**
EVERY MAN WANTS TO BE FREE
Edwin Hawkins Singers (Buddah)

20. **BEST COUNTRY VOCAL PERFORMANCE, FEMALE**
ROSE GARDEN
Lynn Anderson (Single)
(Columbia)

21. **BEST COUNTRY VOCAL PERFORMANCE, MALE**
FOR THE GOOD TIMES
Ray Price (Single) (Columbia)

22. **BEST COUNTRY VOCAL PERFORMANCE BY A DUO OR GROUP**
IF I WERE A CARPENTER
Johnny Cash & June Carter
(Columbia)

23. **BEST COUNTRY INSTRUMENTAL PERFORMANCE**
ME & JERRY
Chet Atkins & Jerry Reed (RCA)

24. **BEST COUNTRY SONG**
MY WOMAN, MY WOMAN, MY WIFE
Songwriter: Marty Robbins
(Columbia)

25. **BEST SACRED PERFORMANCE**
EVERYTHING IS BEAUTIFUL
Jake Hess (RCA)

26. **BEST GOSPEL PERFORMANCE (OTHER THAN SOUL GOSPEL)**
TALK ABOUT THE GOOD TIMES
Oak Ridge Boys (Heartwarming)

27. **BEST ETHNIC OR TRADITIONAL RECORDING**
GOOD FEELIN'
T-Bone Walker (Polydor)

28. **BEST INSTRUMENTAL COMPOSITION**
"AIRPORT" LOVE THEME
Composer: Alfred Newman
(Decca)

29. **BEST ORIGINAL SCORE WRITTEN FOR A MOTION PICTURE OR TV SPECIAL**
LET IT BE
Composers: John Lennon, Paul McCartney, George Harrison, Ringo Starr (Apple)

30. **BEST SCORE FROM AN ORIGINAL CAST SHOW ALBUM**
COMPANY
Composer: Stephen Sondheim
A&R Producer: Thomas Z. Shepard (Columbia)

31. **BEST RECORDING FOR CHILDREN**
SESAME STREET
Producer: Joan Cooney
(Columbia)

32. **BEST COMEDY RECORDING**
THE DEVIL MADE MY BUY THIS DRESS
Flip Wilson (Little David)

33. **BEST SPOKEN WORD RECORDING**
WHY I OPPOSE THE WAR IN VIETNAM
Dr. Martin Luther King, Jr.
(Black Forum)

34. **BEST JAZZ PERFORMANCE, SMALL GROUP OR SOLOIST WITH SMALL GROUP**
ALONE
Bill Evans (MGM)

35. **BEST JAZZ PERFORMANCE, LARGE GROUP OR SOLOIST WITH LARGE GROUP**
BITCHES BREW
Miles Davis (Columbia)

36. **ALBUM OF THE YEAR, CLASSICAL**
BERLIOZ: LES TROYENS
Colin Davis cond. Royal Opera
House Orch.
A&R Producer: Erik Smith
(Philips)

37. **BEST CLASSICAL PERFORMANCE, ORCHESTRA**
STRAVINSKY: LE SACRE DU PRINTEMPS
Pierre Boulez cond. Cleveland
Orch. (Colulmbia)

38. **BEST CLASSICAL PERFORMANCE, INSTRUMENTAL SOLOIST(S) (WITH OR WITHOUT ORCHESTRA)**
BRAHMS: DOUBLE
CONCERTO (CONCERTO IN A
MINOR FOR VIOLIN AND
CELLO)
David Oistrakh and Mstislav
Rostropovich (Angel)

39. **BEST CHAMBER MUSIC PERFORMANCE**
BEETHOVEN: THE
COMPLETE PIANO TRIOS
Eugene Istomin, Isaac Stern,
Leonard Rose (Columbia)

40. **BEST OPERA RECORDING**
BERLIOZ: LES TROYENS
Colin Davis cond. Royal Opera
House Orch. & Chorus
(Vickers, Veasey, Lindholm)
A&R Producer: Erik Smith
(Philips)

41. **BEST VOCAL SOLOIST PERFORMANCE, CLASSICAL**
SCHUBERT: LIEDER
Dietrich Fischer-Dieskau (DGG)

42. **BEST CLASSICAL PERFORMANCE (OTHER THAN OPERA)**
(IVES) NEW MUSIC OF
CHARLES IVES
Gregg Smith cond. Gregg Smith
Singers & Columbia Chamber
Ensemble (Colulmbia)

43. **BEST ENGINEERED RECORDING, CLASSICAL**
STRAVINSKY: LE SACRE DU
PRINTEMPS
(Pierre Boulez cond. Cleveland
Orch.)
Engineers: Fred Plaut, Ray
Moore, Arthur Kendy (Columbia)

14TH ANNUAL (1971) GRAMMY WINNERS
Announced on March 14, 1972
Eligibility Year: October 16, 1970 through October 15, 1971

1. **RECORD OF THE YEAR**
IT'S TOO LATE
Carole King
Producer: Lou Adler (Ode)

2. **ALBUM OF THE YEAR**
TAPESTRY
Carole King
Producer: Lou Adler (Ode)

3. **SONG OF THE YEAR**
YOU'VE GOT A FRIEND
Songwriter: Carole King (Ode)

4. **BEST NEW ARTIST OF THE YEAR**
CARLY SIMON (Elektra)

5. **BEST INSTRUMENTAL ARRANGEMENT**
THEME FROM SHAFT
Arrangers: Isaac Hayes and Johnny Allen (Enterprise)

6. **BEST ARRANGEMENT ACCOMPANYING VOCALIST(S)**
UNCLE ALBERT/ADMIRAL HALSEY (Paul & Linda McCartney)
Arranger: Paul McCartney (Apple)

7. **BEST ENGINEERED RECORDING**
THEME FROM SHAFT (Isaac Hayes)
Engineers: Dave Purple, Ron Capone, Henry Bush (Enterprise)

8. **BEST ALBUM COVER**
POLLUTION (Pollution)
Album Design: Dean O. Torrance
Art Director: Gene Brownell (Prophesy)

9. **BEST ALBUM NOTES**
SAM, HARD AND HEAVY (Sam Samudio)
Annotator: Sam Samudio (Atlantic)

10. **BEST POP VOCAL PERFORMANCE, FEMALE**
TAPESTRY (Album)
Carole King (Ode)

11. **BEST POP VOCAL PERFORMANCE, MALE**
YOU'VE GOT A FRIEND (Single)
James Taylor (Warner Bros.)

12. **BEST POP VOCAL PERFORMANCE BY A GROUP**
CARPENTERS (Album)
Carpenters (A&M)

13. **BEST POP INSTRUMENTAL PERFORMANCE**
SMACKWATER JACK (Album)
Quincy Jones (A&M)

14. **BEST RHYTHM & BLUES VOCAL PERFORMANCE, FEMALE**
BRIDGE OVER TROUBLED WATER (single)
Aretha Franklin (Atlantic)

15. **BEST RHYTHM & BLUES VOCAL PERFORMANCE, MALE**
A NATURAL MAN (Single)
Lou Rawls (MGM)

16. **BEST RHYTHM & BLUES VOCAL PERFORMANCE BY A GROUP**
PROUD MARY (Single)
Ike & Tina Turner (United Artists)

17. **BEST RHYTHM & BLUES SONG**
AIN'T NO SUNSHINE
Songwriter: Bill Withers (Sussex)

18. **BEST SOUL GOSPEL PERFORMANCE**
PUT YOUR HAND IN THE HAND OF THE MAN FROM GALILEE
Shirley Caesar (Hob)

19. **BEST COUNTRY VOCAL PERFORMANCE, FEMALE**
HELP ME MAKE IT THROUGH THE NIGHT
Sammi Smith (Single) (Mega)

20. **BEST COUNTRY VOCAL PERFORMANCE, MALE**
WHEN YOU'RE HOT, YOU'RE HOT
Jerry Reed (Single) (RCA)

21. **BEST COUNTRY VOCAL PERFORMANCE BY A GROUP**
AFTER THE FIRE IS GONE (Single)
Conway Twitty and Loretta Lynn (Decca)

22. BEST COUNTRY
    INSTRUMENTAL
    PERFORMANCE
    SNOWBIRD (Single)
    Chet Atkins (RCA)

23. BEST COUNTRY SONG
    HELP ME MAKE IT
    THROUGH THE NIGHT
    Songwriter: Kris Kristofferson

24. BEST SACRED
    PERFORMANCE
    DID YOU THINK TO PRAY
    Charley Pride (RCA)

25. BEST GOSPEL
    PERFORMANCE (OTHER
    THAN SOUL GOSPEL)
    LET ME LIVE
    Charley Pride (RCA)

26. BEST ETHNIC OR
    TRADITIONAL RECORDING
    THEY CALL ME MUDDY
    WATERS
    Muddy Waters (Chess)

27. BEST INSTRUMENTAL
    COMPOSITION
    THEME FROM SUMMER OF
    '42
    Composer: Michael Legrand
    (Warner Bros.)

26. BEST ORIGINAL SCORE
    WRITTEN FOR A MOTION
    PICTURE
    SHAFT
    Composer: Isaac Hayes
    (Enterprise)

29. BEST SCORE FROM AN
    ORIGINAL CAST SHOW
    ALBUM
    GODSPELL
    Composer: Stephen Schwartz
    Producer: Stephen Schwartz

30. BEST RECORDING FOR
    CHILDREN
    BILL COSBY TALKS TO KIDS
    ABOUT DRUGS
    Bill Cosby (Uni)

31. BEST COMEDY RECORDING
    THIS IS A RECORDING
    Lily Tomlin (Polydor)

32. BEST SPOKEN WORD
    RECORDING
    DESIDERATA
    Les Crane (Warner Bros.)

33. BEST JAZZ PERFORMANCE
    BY A SOLOIST
    THE BILL EVANS ALBUM
    Bill Evans (Columbia)

34. BEST JAZZ PERFORMANCE
    BY A GROUP
    THE BILL EVANS ALBUM
    Bill Evans Trio (Columbia)

35. BEST JAZZ PERFORMANCE
    BY A BIG BAND
    NEW ORLEANS SUITE
    Duke Ellington (Atlantic)

36. ALBUM OF THE YEAR,
    CLASSICAL
    HOROWITZ PLAYS
    RACHMANINOFF
    Vladimir Horowitz
    Producers: Richard Killough,
    Thomas Frost (Columbia)

37. BEST CLASSICAL
    PERFORMANCE,
    ORCHESTRA
    MAHLER: SYMPHONY NO. 1
    IN D MAJOR
    Carlo Maria Giulini cond.
    Chicago Sym. (Angel)

38. BEST CLASSICAL
    PERFORMANCE,
    INSTRUMENTAL SOLOIST
    OR SOLOISTS (WITH
    ORCHESTRA)
    VILLA-LOBOS: CONCERTO
    FOR GUITAR
    Julian Bream (Previn cond.
    London Sym.) (RCA)

39. **BEST CLASSICAL PERFORMANCE, INSTRUMENTAL SOLOIST OR SOLOISTS (WITHOUT ORCHESTRA)**
HOROWITZ PLAYS RACHMANINOFF
Vladimir Horowitz (Columbia)

40. **BEST CHAMBER MUSIC PERFORMANCE**
DEBUSSY: QUARTET IN G MINOR/RAVEL: QUARTET IN F MAJOR
Juilliard Quartet (Columbia)

41. **BEST OPERA RECORDING**
VERDI: AIDA
Erich Leinsdorf cond. London Sym. (Price, Domingo, Milnes, Bumbry, Raimondi)
Producer: Richard Mohr (RCA)

42. **BEST CLASSICAL VOCAL SOLOIST PERFORMANCE**
LEONTYNE PRICE SINGS ROBERT SCHUMANN
Leontyne Price (RCA)

43. **BEST CHORAL PERFORMANCE, CLASSICAL (OTHER THAN OPERA)**
BERLIOZ: REQUIEM
Colin Davis cond. London Sym./ Russell Burgess cond. Wandsworth School Boys Choir/ Arthur Oldham cond. London Sym. Chorus (Phillips)

44. **BEST ENGINEERED RECORDING, CLASSICAL**
BERLIOZ: REQUIEM
(Davis cond. London Sym./ Burgess cond. Wandsworth School Boys Choir/ Oldham cond. London Sym. Chorus)
Engineer: Vittorio Negri (Phillips)

15TH ANNUAL (1972) GRAMMY WINNERS
Announced on March 3, 1973
Eligibility Year: October 16, 1971 through October 15, 1972

1. **RECORD OF THE YEAR**
THE FIRST TIME EVER I SAW YOUR FACE
Roberta Flack
Producer: Joel Dorn (Atlantic)

2. **ALBUM OF THE YEAR**
THE CONCERT FOR BANGLA DESH
George Harrison, Ravi Shanker, Bob Dylan, Leon Russell, Ringo Starr, Billy Preston, Eric Clapton, Klaus Voormann
Producers: George Harrison, Phil Spector (Apple)

3. **SONG OF THE YEAR**
THE FIRST TIME EVER I SAW YOUR FACE
Songwriter: Ewan MacColl

4. **BEST NEW ARTIST OF THE YEAR**
AMERICA (Warner Bros.)

5. **BEST INSTRUMENTAL ARRANGEMENT**
THEME FROM THE FRENCH CONNECTION (Don Ellis)
Arranger: Don Ellis (Columbia)

6. **BEST ARRANGEMENT ACCOMPANYING VOCALIST**
WHAT ARE YOU DOING THE REST OF YOUR LIFE (Sarah Vaughn)
Arranger: Michel Legrand (Mainstream)

7. **BEST ENGINEERED RECORDING**
MOODS (Neil Diamond)
Engineer: Armin Steiner (UNI)

8. **BEST ALBUM COVER**
THE SIEGEL SCHWALL BAND
Art Director: Acy Lehman
Artist: Harvey Dinnerstein (Wooden Nickel)

9. **BEST ALBUM NOTES**
TOM T. HALL'S GREATEST HITS
Annotator: Tom T. Hall (Mercury)

10. **BEST JAZZ PERFORMANCE BY A SOLOIST**
ALONE AT LAST
Gary Burton (Atlantic)

11. **BEST JAZZ PERFORMANCE BY A GROUP**
FIRST LIGHT
Freddie Hubbard (CTI)

12. **BEST JAZZ PERFORMANCE BY A BIG BAND**
TOGA BRAVA SUITE
Duke Ellington (United Artists)

13. **BEST POP VOCAL PERFORMANCE, FEMALE**
I AM WOMAN (Single)
Helen Reddy (Capitol)

14. **BEST POP VOCAL PERFORMANCE, MALE**
WITHOUT YOU (Single)
Nilsson (RCA)

15. **BEST POP VOCAL PERFORMANCE BY A DUO, GROUP OR CHORUS**
WHERE IS THE LOVE (Single)
Roberta Flack, Donny Hathaway (Atlantic)

16. **BEST POP INSTRUMENTAL PERFORMANCE**
OUTA-SPACE (Single)
Billy Preston (A&M)

17. **BEST POP INSTRUMENTAL PERFORMANCE BY AN ARRANGER, COMPOSER, ORCHESTRA AND/OR CHORAL LEADER**
BLACK MOSES (Album)
Isaac Hayes (Enterprise)

18. **BEST RHYTHM & BLUES VOCAL PERFORMANCE, FEMALE**
YOUNG, GIFTED & BLACK (Album)
Aretha Franklin (Atlantic)

19. **BEST RHYTHM & BLUES VOCAL PERFORMANCE, MALE**
ME & MRS. JONES (Single)
Billy Paul (Philadelphia Int.)

20. **BEST RHYTHM & BLUES VOCAL PERFORMANCE BY A DUO, GROUP OR CHORUS**
PAPA WAS A ROLLING STONE (Single)
The Temptations (Gordy Motown)

21. **BEST RHYTHM & BLUES INSTRUMENTAL PERFORMANCE**
PAPA WAS A ROLLING STONE (Single)
The Temptations
Conductor: Paul Riser (Gordy Motown)

22. **BEST RHYTHM & BLUES SONG**
PAPA WAS A ROLLING STONE
Songwriters: Barrett Strong, Norman Whitfield

23. **BEST SOUL GOSPEL PERFORMANCE**
AMAZING GRACE
Aretha Franklin (Atlantic)

24. **BEST COUNTRY VOCAL PERFORMANCE, FEMALE**
HAPPIEST GIRL IN THE WHOLE USA (Single)
Donna Fargo (Dot)

25. **BEST COUNTRY VOCAL PERFORMANCE, MALE**
CHARLEY PRIDE SINGS HEART SONGS (Album)
Charley Pride (RCA)

26. **BEST COUNTRY VOCAL PERFORMANCE BY A DUO OR GROUP**
CLASS OF '57 (Single)
The Statler Bros. (Mercury)

27. **BEST COUNTRY INSTRUMENTAL PERFORMANCE**
CHARLIE MC COY/THE REAL MC COY (Album)
Charlie McCoy (Monument)

28. **BEST COUNTRY SONG**
KISS AN ANGEL GOOD MORNIN'
Songwriter: Ben Peters

29. **BEST INSPIRATIONAL PERFORMANCE**
HE TOUCHED ME
Elvis Presley (RCA)

30. **BEST GOSPEL PERFORMANCE**
LOVE
Blackwood Bros. (RCA)

31. **BEST ETHNIC OR TRADITIONAL RECORDING**
THE LONDON MUDDY WATERS SESSION
Muddy Waters (Chess)

32. **BEST RECORDING FOR CHILDREN**
THE ELECTRIC COMPANY
Project Directors: Christopher Cerf, Lee Chamberlin, Bill Cosby, Rita Moreno; Producer and Music Director: Joe Raposo (Warner Bros.)

33. **BEST COMEDY RECORDING**
FM & AM
George Carlin (Little David)

34. **BEST SPOKEN WORD RECORDING**
LENNY
Producer: Bruce Botnick (Blue Thumb)

35. **BEST INSTRUMENTAL COMPOSITION**
BRIAN'S SONG
Michel Legrand

36. **BEST ORIGINAL SCORE WRITTEN FOR A MOTION PICTURE OR A TELEVISION SPECIAL**
THE GODFATHER
Composer: Nino Rota (Paramount)

37. **BEST SCORE FROM AN ORIGINAL CAST SHOW ALBUM**
DON'T BOTHER ME, I CAN'T COPE
Composer: Micki Grant
Producer: Jerry Ragavoy (Polydor)

38. ALBUM OF THE YEAR, CLASSICAL
MAHLER: SYMPHONY NO. 8
Georg Solti cond. Chicago Sym.
Orch. Vienna Boys Choir,
Vienna State Opera Chorus,
Vienna Singverein Chorus &
Soloists
Producer: David Harvey
(London)

39. BEST CLASSICAL PERFORMANCE, ORCHESTRA
MAHLER: SYMPHONY NO. 7
Georg Solti cond. Chicago Sym.
(London)

40. BEST OPERA RECORDING
BERLIOZ: BENVENUTO
CELLINI
Colin Davis cond. BBC
Symphony & Chorus of Covent
Garden
Producer: Erik Smith (Phillips)

41. BEST CHORAL PERFORMANCE
MAHLER: SYMPHONY NO. 8
Georg Solti cond. Chicago Sym.
Orch. & Chorus. (London)

42. BEST CHAMBER MUSIC PERFORMANCE
JULIAN & JOHN
Julian Bream, John Williams
(RCA)

43. BEST INSTRUMENTAL SOLOIST PERFORMANCE (WITH ORCHESTRA)
BRAHMS: CONCERTO NO. 2
Artur Rubinstein (RCA)

44. BEST INSTRUMENTAL SOLOIST PERFORMANCE (WITHOUT ORCHESTRA)
HOROWITZ PLAYS CHOPIN
Vladimir Horowitz (Columbia)

45. BEST VOCAL SOLOIST PERFORMANCE
BRAHMS: DIE SCHÖNE
MAGELONE
Dietrich Fischer-Dieskau (Angel)

46. BEST ALBUM NOTES
VAUGHN WILLIAMS:
SYMPHONY NO. 2
Annotator: James Lyons (RCA)

47. BEST ENGINEERED RECORDING
MAHLER: SYMPHONY NO. 8
Engineers: Gordon Parry,
Kenneth Wilkinson (London)

16TH ANNUAL (1973) GRAMMY WINNERS
Announced on March 2, 1974
Eligibility Year: October 16, 1972 through October 15, 1973

1. RECORD OF THE YEAR
KILLING ME SOFTLY WITH
HIS SONG
Roberta Flack
Producer: Joel Dorn (Atlantic)

2. ALBUM OF THE YEAR
INNERVISIONS
Stevie Wonder
Producer: Stevie Wonder (Tamla/
Motown)

3. **SONG OF THE YEAR**
KILLING ME SOFTLY WITH
HIS SONG
Songwriters: Norman Gimbel,
Charles Fox

4. **BEST NEW ARTIST OF THE
YEAR**
BETTE MIDLER (Atlantic)

5. **BEST INSTRUMENTAL
ARRANGEMENT**
SUMMER IN THE CITY
(Quincy Jones)
Arranger: Quincy Jones (A&M)

6. **BEST ARRANGEMENT
ACCOMPANYING VOCALIST**
LIVE AND LET DIE (Paul
McCartney & Wings)
Arranger: George Martin (Apple)

7. **BEST ENGINEERED
RECORDING (non-classical)**
INNERVISIONS (Stevie
Wonder)
Engineers: Robert Margouleff,
Malcolm Cecil (Tamla/Motown)

8. **BEST ALBUM PACKAGE**
TOMMY (London Sym. Orch/
Chambre Choir)
Art Director: Wilkes & Braun,
Inc. (Ode)

9. **BEST ALBUM NOTES**
GOD IS IN THE HOUSE (Art
Tatum)
Annotator: Dan Morgenstern
(Onyx)

10. **BEST JAZZ PERFORMANCE
BY A SOLOIST**
GOD IS IN THE HOUSE
(Album)
Art Tatum (Onyx)

11. **BEST JAZZ PERFORMANCE
BY A GROUP**
SUPERSAX PLAYS BIRD
(Album)
Supersax (Capitol)

12. **BEST JAZZ PERFORMANCE
BY A BIG BAND**
GIANT STEPS (Album)
Woody Herman (Fantasy)

13. **BEST POP VOCAL
PERFORMANCE, FEMALE**
KILLING ME SOFTLY WITH
HIS SONG (Single)
Roberta Flack (Atlantic)

14. **BEST POP VOCAL
PERFORMANCE, MALE**
YOU ARE THE SUNSHINE OF
MY LIFE (Single)
Stevie Wonder (Tamla/Motown)

15. **BEST POP VOCAL
PERFORMANCE BY A DUO,
GROUP OR CHORUS**
NEITHER ONE OF US
(WANTS TO BE THE FIRST
TO SAY GOODBYE) (Single)
Gladys Knight & The Pips (Soul/
Motown)

16. **BEST POP INSTRUMENTAL
PERFORMANCE**
ALSO SPRACH ZARATHUSTRA
(2001) (Single)
Eumir Deodato (CTI)

17. **BEST RHYTHM & BLUES
VOCAL PERFORMANCE,
FEMALE**
MASTER OF EYES (Single)
Aretha Franklin (Atlantic)

18. **BEST RHYTHM & BLUES
VOCAL PERFORMANCE,
MALE**
SUPERSTITION (Track)
Stevie Wonder (Tamla/Motown)

19. **BEST RHYTHM & BLUES
VOCAL PERFORMANCE BY A
DUO, GROUP OR CHORUS**
MIDNIGHT TRAIN TO
GEORGIA (Single)
Gladys Knight & The Pips
(Buddah)

20. **BEST RHYTHM & BLUES INSTRUMENTAL PERFORMANCE**
HANG ON SLOOPY (Single)
Ramsey Lewis (Columbia)

21. **BEST RHYTHM & BLUES SONG**
SUPERSTITION
Songwriter: Stevie Wonder

22. **BEST SOUL GOSPEL PERFORMANCE**
LOVES ME LIKE A ROCK (Single)
Dixie Hummingbirds (ABC)

23. **BEST COUNTRY VOCAL PERFORMANCE, FEMALE**
LET ME BE THERE (Single)
Olivia Newton-John (RCA)

24. **BEST COUNTRY VOCAL PERFORMANCE, MALE**
BEHIND CLOSED DOORS (Single)
Charlie Rich (Epic/Columbia)

25. **BEST COUNTRY VOCAL PERFORMANCE BY A DUO OR GROUP**
FROM THE BOTTLE TO THE BOTTOM (Track)
Kris Kristofferson, Rita Coolidge (A&M)

26. **BEST COUNTRY INSTRUMENTAL PERFORMANCE**
DUELING BANJOS (Track)
Eric Weissberg, Steve Mandell (Warner Bros.)

27. **BEST COUNTRY SONG**
BEHIND CLOSED DOORS
Songwriter: Kenny O'Dell

28. **BEST INSPIRATIONAL PERFORMANCE**
LETS JUST PRAISE THE LORD (Album)
Bill Gaither Trio (Impact)

29. **BEST GOSPEL PERFORMANCE**
RELEASE ME (FROM MY SIN) (Album)
Blackwood Brothers (Skylite)

30. **BEST ETHNIC OR TRADITIONAL RECORDING**
THEN AND NOW (Album)
Doc Watson (United Artists)

31. **BEST RECORDING FOR CHILDREN**
SESAME STREET LIVE (Album)
Sesame Street Cast
Producer: Joe Raposo (Columbia)

32. **BEST COMEDY RECORDING**
LOS COCHINOS (Album)
Cheech & Chong (Ode)

33. **BEST SPOKEN WORD RECORDING**
JONATHAN LIVINGSTON SEAGULL (Album)
Richard Harris (Dunhill/ABC)

34. **BEST INSTRUMENTAL COMPOSITION**
LAST TANGO IN PARIS
Composer: Gato Barbieri

35. **ALBUM OF BEST ORIGINAL SCORE WRITTEN FOR A MOTION PICTURE**
JONATHAN LIVINGSTON SEAGULL
Composer: Neil Diamond (Columbia)

36. **BEST SCORE FROM THE ORIGINAL CAST SHOW ALBUM**
A LITTLE NIGHT MUSIC
Composer: Stephen Sondheim
Producer: Goddard Lieberson (Columbia)

37. **ALBUM OF THE YEAR, CLASSICAL**
BARTOK: CONCERTO FOR ORCHESTRA
Pierre Boulez cond. New York Philharmonic
Producer: Thomas Z. Shepard (Columbia)

38. **BEST CLASSICAL PERFORMANCE, ORCHESTRA**
BARTOK: CONCERTO FOR ORCHESTRA
Pierre Boulez cond. New York Philharmonic (Columbia)

39. **BEST OPERA RECORDING**
BIZET: CARMEN
Leonard Bernstein cond. Metropolitan Opera Orchestra, Manhattan Opera Chorus (Horne, McCracken, Maliponte, Krause)
Producer: Thomas W. Mowrey (DG)

40. **BEST CHORAL PERFORMANCE, CLASSICAL**
WALTON: BELSHAZZAR'S FEAST
Andre Previn cond. London Sym. Orch.; Arthur Oldham cond. London Sym. Orch. Chorus (Angel)

41. **BEST CHAMBER MUSIC PERFORMANCE**
JOPLIN: THE RED BACK BOOK
Gunther Schuller & New England Conservatory Ragtime Ensemble (Angel)

42. **BEST CLASSICAL PERFORMANCE, INSTRUMENTAL SOLOIST (WITH ORCHESTRA)**
BEETHOVEN: CONCERTI (5) FOR PIANO & ORCHESTRA
Vladimir Ashkenazy (Solti cond. Chicago Sym.) (London)

43. **BEST CLASSICAL PERFORMANCE, INSTRUMENTAL SOLOIST (WITHOUT ORCHESTRA)**
HOROWITZ PLAYS SCRIABIN
Vladimir Horowitz (Columbia)

44. **BEST CLASSICAL VOCAL SOLOIST PERFORMANCE**
PUCCINI: HEROINES (La Boheme, Tosca, Manon Lescaut)
Leontyne Price (Downes cond. New Philharmonia) (RCA)

45. **BEST ALBUM NOTES, CLASSICAL**
HINDEMITH: SONATAS FOR PIANO (COMPLETE)
Annotator: Glenn Gould (Columbia)

46. **BEST ENGINEERED RECORDING, CLASSICAL**
BARTOK: CONCERTO FOR ORCHESTRA (Boulez cond. New York Philharmonic)
Engineers: Edward T. Graham, Raymond Moore (Columbia)

17TH ANNUAL (1974) GRAMMY WINNERS
Announced on March 1, 1975
Eligibility Year: October 16, 1973 through October 15, 1974

1. **RECORD OF THE YEAR**
I HONESTLY LOVE YOU
Olivia Newton-John
Producer: John Farrar (MCA)

2. **ALBUM OF THE YEAR**
FULFILLINGNESS' FIRST
FINALE
Stevie Wonder
Producer: Stevie Wonder (Tamla/
Motown)

3. **SONG OF THE YEAR**
THE WAY WE WERE
Songwriters: Marilyn and Alan
Bergman, Marvin Hamlisch

4. **BEST NEW ARTIST OF THE
YEAR**
MARVIN HAMLISCH (MCA)

5. **BEST INSTRUMENTAL
ARRANGEMENT**
THRESHOLD (Pat Williams)
Arranger: Pat Williams (Capitol)

6. **BEST ARRANGEMENT
ACCOMPANYING VOCALISTS**
DOWN TO YOU (Joni Mitchell)
Arrangers: Joni Mitchell and
Tom Scott (Asylum)

7. **BEST ENGINEERED
RECORDING (non-classical)**
BAND ON THE RUN (Paul
McCartney & Wings) (Album)
Engineer: Geoff Emerick (Apple/
Capitol)

8. **BEST ALBUM PACKAGE**
COME & GONE (Mason Proffit)
Art Directors: Ed Thrasher,
Christopher Whorf
(Warner Bros.)

9. **BEST ALBUM NOTES (Tie)**
FOR THE LAST TIME (Bob
Wills and His Texas Playboys)
Annotator: Charles R. Townsend
(United Artists)

THE HAWK FLIES (Coleman
Hawkins)
Annotator: Dan Morgenstern
(Milestone)

10. **BEST PRODUCER OF THE
YEAR**
THOM BELL

11. **BEST JAZZ PERFORMANCE
BY A SOLOIST**
FIRST RECORDINGS! (Album)
Charlie Parker (Onyx)

12. **BEST JAZZ PERFORMANCE
BY A GROUP**
THE TRIO (Album)
Oscar Peterson, Joe Pass, Niels
Pedersen (Pablo)

13. **BEST JAZZ PERFORMANCE
BY A BIG BAND**
THUNDERING HERD (Album)
Woody Herman (Fantasy)

14. **BEST POP VOCAL
PERFORMANCE, FEMALE**
I HONESTLY LOVE YOU
(Single)
Olivia Newton-John (MCA)

15. **BEST POP VOCAL
PERFORMANCE, MALE**
FULFILLINGNESS' FIRST
FINALE (Album)
Stevie Wonder (Tamla/Motown)

16. **BEST POP VOCAL
PERFORMANCE BY A DUO,
GROUP OR CHORUS**
BAND ON THE RUN (Single)
Paul McCartney & Wings
(Apple/Capitol)

17. **BEST POP INSTRUMENAL PERFORMANCE**
THE ENTERTAINER (Single)
Marvin Hamlisch (MCA)

18. **BEST RHYTHM & BLUES VOCAL PERFORMANCE, FEMALE**
AIN'T NOTHING LIKE THE REAL THING (Single)
Aretha Franklin (Atlantic)

19. **BEST RHYTHM & BLUES VOCAL PERFORMANCE, MALE**
BOOGIE ON REGGAE WOMAN (Track)
Stevie Wonder (Tamla/Motown)

20. **BEST RHYTHM & BLUES VOCAL PERFORMANCE BY A DUO, GROUP OR CHORUS**
TELL ME SOMETHING GOOD (Single)
Rufus (ABC)

21. **BEST RHYTHM & BLUES INSTRUMENTAL PERFORMANCE**
TSOP (THE SOUND OF PHILADELPHIA) (Single)
MFSB (Philadelphia Intl./Epic)

22. **BEST RHYTHM & BLUES SONG**
LIVING FOR THE CITY
Songwriter: Stevie Wonder

23. **BEST SOUL GOSPEL PERFORMANCE**
IN THE GHETTO (Album)
James Cleveland and Southern California Community Choir (Savoy)

24. **BEST COUNTRY VOCAL PERFORMANCE, FEMALE**
LOVE SONG (Album)
Anne Murray (Capitol)

25. **BEST COUNTRY VOCAL PERFORMANCE, MALE**
PLEASE DON'T TELL ME HOW THE STORY ENDS (Single)
Ronnie Milsap (MCA)

26. **BEST COUNTRY VOCAL PERFORMANCE BY A DUO OR GROUP**
FAIRYTALE (Track)
The Pointer Sisters (Blue Thumb)

27. **BEST COUNTRY INSTRUMENTAL PERFORMANCE**
THE ATKINS–TRAVIS TRAVELING SHOW (Album)
Chet Atkins & Merle Travis (RCA)

28. **BEST COUNTRY SONG**
A VERY SPECIAL LOVE SONG
Songwriters: Norris Wilson, Billy Sherrill

29. **BEST INSPIRATIONAL PERFORMANCE**
HOW GREAT THOU ART (Track)
Elvis Presley (RCA)

30. **BEST GOSPEL PERFORMANCE**
THE BAPTISM OF JESSE TAYLOR (Single)
Oak Ridge Boys (Columbia)

31. **BEST ETHNIC OR TRADITIONAL RECORDING**
TWO DAYS IN NOVEMBER (Album)
Doc & Merle Watson (United Artists)

32. **BEST RECORDING FOR CHILDREN**
WINNIE THE POOH & TIGGER TOO (Album)
Sebastian Cabot, Sterling Holloway, Paul Winchell (Disneyland)

33. **BEST COMEDY RECORDING**
THAT NIGGER'S CRAZY
(Album)
Richard Pryor (Partee/Stax)

34. **BEST SPOKEN WORD RECORDING**
GOOD EVENING (Album)
Peter Cook & Dudley Moore
(Island)

35. **BEST INSTRUMENTAL COMPOSITION**
TUBULAR BELLS (THEME
FROM "THE EXORCIST")
Composer: Mike Oldfield

36. **ALBUM OF BEST ORIGINAL SCORE WRITTEN FOR A MOTION PICTURE OR A TELEVISION SPECIAL**
THE WAY WE WERE
Composers: Marvin Hamlisch,
Alan & Marilyn Bergman
(Columbia)

37. **BEST SCORE FROM THE ORIGINAL CAST SHOW ALBUM**
RAISIN
Composers: Judd Woldin &
Robert Britten
Producer: Thomas Z. Shepard
(Columbia)

38. **ALBUM OF THE YEAR, CLASSICAL**
BERLIOZ: SYMPHONIE
FANTASTIQUE
Georg Solti cond. Chicago Sym.
Producer: David Harvey
(London)

39. **BEST CLASSICAL PERFORMANCE, ORCHESTRA**
BERLIOZ: SYMPHONIE
FANTASTIQUE
Georg Solti cond. Chicago Sym.
(London)

40. **BEST OPERA RECORDING**
PUCCINI: LA BOHEME
Conductor: Georg Solti
Producer: Richard Mohr (RCA)

41. **BEST CHORAL PERFORMANCE, CLASSICAL (OTHER THAN OPERA)**
BERLIOZ: THE DAMNATION
OF FAUST
Conductor: Colin Davis (Philips)

42. **BEST CHAMBER MUSIC PERFORMANCE**
BRAHMS & SCHUMANN
TRIOS
Artur Rubinstein, Henryk
Szeryng, and Pierre Fournier
(RCA)

43. **BEST CLASSICAL PERFORMANCE, INSTRUMENTAL SOLOIST OR SOLOISTS (WITH ORCHESTRA)**
SHOSTAKOVICH: VIOLIN
CONCERTO NO. 1
David Oistrakh (Angel)

44. **BEST CLASSICAL PERFORMANCE, INSTRUMENTAL SOLOIST OR SOLOISTS (WITHOUT ORCHESTRA)**
ALBENIZ: IBERIA
Alicia de Larrocha (London)

45. **BEST CLASSICAL VOCAL SOLOIST PERFORMANCE**
LEONTYNE PRICE SINGS
RICHARD STRAUSS
Leontyne Price (RCA)

46. **BEST ALBUM NOTES, CLASSICAL**
THE CLASSIC ERICH
WOLFGANG KORNGOLD
Annotator: Rory Guy (Angel)

47. **BEST ENGINEERED
RECORDING, CLASSICAL**
BERLIOZ: SYMPHONIE
FANTASTIQUE
Engineer: Kenneth Wilkinson
(London)

18TH ANNUAL (1975) GRAMMY WINNERS
Announced on February 28, 1976
Eligibility Year: October 16, 1974 through October 15, 1975

1. **RECORD OF THE YEAR**
LOVE WILL KEEP US
TOGETHER
Captain & Tennille
Producer: Daryl Dragon (A&M)

2. **ALBUM OF THE YEAR**
STILL CRAZY AFTER ALL
THESE YEARS
Paul Simon
Producers: Paul Simon, Phil
Ramone (Columbia)

3. **SONG OF THE YEAR**
SEND IN THE CLOWNS
Songwriter: Stephen Sondheim

4. **BEST NEW ARTIST OF THE
YEAR**
NATALIE COLE (Capitol)

5. **BEST INSTRUMENTAL
ARRANGEMENT**
THE ROCKFORD FILES (Mike
Post)
Arrangers: Mike Post, Pete
Carpenter (MGM)

6. **BEST ARRANGEMENT
ACCOMPANYING VOCALISTS**
MISTY (Ray Stevens)
Arranger: Ray Stevens (Barnaby)

7. **BEST ENGINEERED
RECORDING (non-classical)**
BETWEEN THE LINES (Janis
Ian)
Engineers: Brooks Arthur, Larry
Alexander, Russ Payne
(Columbia)

8. **BEST ALBUM PACKAGE**
HONEY (Ohio Players)
Art Director: Jim Ladwig
(Mercury)

9. **BEST ALBUM NOTES (non-
classical)**
BLOOD ON THE TRACKS
(Bob Dylan)
Annotator: Pete Hamill
(Columbia)

10. **BEST PRODUCER OF THE
YEAR**
Arif Mardin

11. **BEST JAZZ PERFORMANCE
BY A SOLOIST**
OSCAR PETERSON AND
DIZZY GILLESPIE (Album)
Dizzy Gillespie (solo) (Pablo)

12. **BEST JAZZ PERFORMANCE
BY A GROUP**
NO MYSTERY (Album)
Chick Corea and Return To
Forever (Polydor)

13. **BEST JAZZ PERFORMANCE
BY A BIG BAND**
IMAGES (Album)
Phil Woods with Michel Legrand
& His Orchestra (Gryphon/(RCA)

14. **BEST POP VOCAL
PERFORMANCE FEMALE**
AT SEVENTEEN (Single)
Janis Ian (Columbia)

15. **BEST POP VOCAL PERFORMANCE, MALE**
STILL CRAZY AFTER ALL THESE YEARS (Album)
Paul Simon (Columbia)

16. **BEST POP VOCAL PERFORMANCE BY A DUO, GROUP OR CHORUS**
LYIN' EYES (Single)
Eagles (Asylum)

17. **BEST POP INSTRUMENTAL PERFORMANCE**
THE HUSTLE (Single)
Van McCoy and the Soul City Symphony (AVCO)

18. **BEST RHYTHM & BLUES VOCAL PERFORMANCE, FEMALE**
THIS WILL BE (Single)
Natalie Cole (Capitol)

19. **BEST RHYTHM & BLUES VOCAL PERFORMANCE, MALE**
LIVING FOR THE CITY (Single)
Ray Charles (Crossover)

20. **BEST RHYTHM & BLUES VOCAL PERFORMANCE BY A DUO, GROUP OR CHORUS**
SHINING STAR (Single)
Earth, Wind & Fire (Columbia)

21. **BEST RHYTHM & BLUES INSTRUMENTAL PERFORMANCE**
FLY, ROBIN, FLY (Single)
Silver Convention (Midland/RCA)

22. **BEST RHYTHM & BLUES SONG**
WHERE IS THE LOVE
Songwriters: Harry Wayne Casey, Richard Finch, Willie Clarke, Betty Wright

23. **BEST SOUL GOSPEL PERFORMANCE**
TAKE ME BACK (Album)
Andrae Crouch and the Disciples (Light)

24. **BEST COUNTRY VOCAL PERFORMANCE, FEMALE**
I CAN'T HELP IT (IF I'M STILL IN LOVE WITH YOU) (Single)
Linda Ronstadt (Capitol)

25. **BEST COUNTRY VOCAL PERFORMANCE, MALE**
BLUE EYES CRYING IN THE RAIN (Single)
Willie Nelson (Columbia)

26. **BEST COUNTRY VOCAL PERFORMANCE BY A DUO OR GROUP**
LOVER PLEASE (Single)
Kris Kristofferson & Rita Coolidge (Monument)

27. **BEST COUNTRY INSTRUMENTAL PERFORMANCE**
THE ENTERTAINER (Track)
Chet Atkins (RCA)

28. **BEST COUNTRY SONG**
(HEY WON'T YOU PLAY) ANOTHER SOMEBODY DONE SOMEBODY WRONG SONG
Songwriters: Chips Moman and Larry Butler

29. **BEST INSPIRATIONAL PERFORMANCE**
JESUS, WE JUST WANT TO THANK YOU (Album)
The Bill Gaither Trio (Impact)

30. **BEST GOSPEL PERFORMANCE**
NO SHORTAGE (Album)
Imperials (Impact)

31. **BEST ETHNIC OR TRADITIONAL RECORDING**
THE MUDDY WATERS WOODSTOCK ALBUM
Muddy Waters (Chess)

32. **BEST LATIN RECORDING**
SUN OF LATIN MUSIC (Album)
Eddie Palmieri (Coco)

33. **BEST RECORDING FOR CHILDREN**
THE LITTLE PRINCE (Album)
Richard Burton, narrator (RIP)

34. **BEST COMEDY RECORDING**
IS IT SOMETHING I SAID?
(Album)
Richard Pryor (Reprise)

35. **BEST SPOKEN WORD RECORDING**
GIVE 'EM HELL HARRY
(Album)
James Whitmore (United Artists)

36. **BEST INSTRUMENTAL COMPOSITION**
IMAGES
Composer: Michel Legrand

37. **ALBUM OF BEST ORIGINAL SCORE WRITTEN FOR A MOTION PICTURE OR A TELEVISION SPECIAL**
JAWS
Composer: John Williams (MCA)

38. **BEST CAST SHOW ALBUM**
THE WIZ
Composer: Charlie Smalls
Producer: Jerry Wexler (Atlantic)

39. **ALBUM OF THE YEAR, CLASSICAL**
BEETHOVEN SYMPHONIES
(9) COMPLETE
Sir Georg Solti cond. Chicago
Sym. Orch.
Producer: Ray Minshull (London)

40. **BEST CLASSICAL PERFORMANCE, ORCHESTRA**
RAVEL: DAPHNIS ET CHLOE
(Complete Ballet)
Pierre Boulez cond. New York
Philharmonic (Columbia)

41. **BEST OPERA RECORDING**
MOZART: COSI FAN TUTTE
Colin Davis cond. Royal Opera
House, Covent Garden; Principal
Solos: Caballe, Baker, Gedda,
Ganzarolli, Van Allan, Cotrubas
Producer: Erik Smith (Philips)

42. **BEST CHORAL PERFORMANCE, CLASSICAL**
ORFF: CARMINA BURANA
Robert Page dir. Cleveland
Orch.; Chorus & Boys Choir
Michael Tilson Thomas cond.
Cleveland Orch.
Soloists: Blegen, Binder, Riegel
(Columbia)

43. **BEST CHAMBER MUSIC PERFORMANCE**
SCHUBERT: TRIOS NOS. 1 IN
B FLAT MAJOR, OP. 99, & 2
IN E FLAT MAJOR, OP. 100
(THE PIANO TRIOS)
Artur Rubinstein, Henryk
Szeryng, Pierre Fournier (RCA)

44. **BEST CLASSICAL PERFORMANCE, INSTRUMENTAL SOLOIST (WITH ORCHESTRA)**
RAVEL: CONCERTO FOR
LEFT HAND & CONCERTO
FOR PIANO IN G MAJOR/
FAURE: FANTAISIE FOR
PIANO & ORCHESTRA
Alicia de Larrocha (Dee Burgos
and Foster cond. London
Philharmonic) (London)

45. **BEST CLASSICAL PERFORMANCE, INSTRUMENTAL SOLOIST (WITHOUT ORCHESTRA)**
BACH: SONATAS & PARTITAS
FOR VIOLIN
UNACCOMPANIED
Nathan Milstein (DG)

46. BEST CLASSICAL VOCAL SOLOIST PERFORMANCE
MAHLER: KINDERTOTENLIEDER
Janet Baker (Bernstein cond. Israel Philharmonic) (Columbia)

47. BEST ALBUM NOTES, CLASSICAL
FOOTLIFTERS (Schuller cond. All-Star Band)
Annotator: Gunther Schuller (Columbia)

48. BEST ENGINEERED RECORDING, CLASSICAL
RAVEL: DAPHNIS ET CHLOE (Complete Ballet)
(Pierre Boulez cond. New York Philharmonic)
Engineers: Bud Graham, Ray Moore, and Milton Cherin (Columbia)

19TH ANNUAL (1976) GRAMMY WINNERS
Announced on February 19, 1977
Eligibility Year: October 16, 1975 through September 30, 1976

1. RECORD OF THE YEAR
THIS MASQUERADE
George Benson
Producer: Tommy LiPuma (Warner Bros)

2. ALBUM OF THE YEAR
SONGS IN THE KEY OF LIFE
Stevie Wonder
Producer: Stevie Wonder (Tamla/Motown)

3. SONG OF THE YEAR
I WRITE THE SONGS
Songwriter: Bruce Johnston

4. BEST NEW ARTIST OF THE YEAR
STARLAND VOCAL BAND (Windsong/RCA)

5. BEST INSTRUMENTAL ARRANGEMENT
LEPRECHAUN'S DREAM (Chick Corea)
Arranger: Chick Corea (Polydor)

6. BEST ARRANGEMENT ACCOMPANYING VOCALISTS
IF YOU LEAVE ME NOW (Chicago)
Arrangers: Jimmy Haskell & James William Guercio (Columbia)

7. BEST ARRANGEMENT FOR VOICES
AFTERNOON DELIGHT (Starland Vocal Band)
Arrangers: Starland Vocal Band (Windsong/RCA)

8. BEST ENGINEERED RECORDING (non-classical)
BREEZIN' (George Benson)
Engineer: Al Schmitt (Warner Bros.)

9. BEST ALBUM PACKAGE
CHICAGO X (Chicago)
Art Director: John Berg (Columbia)

10. **BEST ALBUM NOTES**
THE CHANGING FACE OF
HARLEM, THE SAVOY
SESSIONS (Various)
Annotator: Dan Morgenstern
(Savoy)

11. **BEST PRODUCER OF THE
YEAR**
STEVIE WONDER

12. **BEST JAZZ VOCAL
PERFORMANCE**
FITZGERALD & PASS AGAIN
(Album)
Ella Fitzgerald (vocal) (Pablo)

13. **BEST JAZZ PERFORMANCE
BY A SOLOIST**
BASIE & ZOOT (Album)
Count Basie (solo) (Pablo)

14. **BEST JAZZ PERFORMANCE
BY A GROUP**
THE LEPRECHAUN (Album)
Chick Corea (Polydor)

15. **BEST JAZZ PERFORMANCE
BY A BIG BAND**
THE ELLINGTON SUITES
(Album)
Duke Ellington (Pablo)

16. **BEST POP VOCAL
PERFORMANCE, FEMALE**
HASTEN DOWN THE WIND
(Album)
Linda Ronstadt (Asylum)

17. **BEST POP VOCAL
PERFORMANCE, MALE**
SONGS IN THE KEY OF LIFE
(Album)
Stevie Wonder (Tamla/Motown)

18. **BEST POP VOCAL
PERFORMANCE BY A DUO,
GROUP, OR CHORUS**
IF YOU LEAVE ME NOW
(Single)
Chicago (Columbia)

19. **BEST POP INSTRUMENTAL
PERFORMANCE**
BREEZIN' (Album)
George Benson (Warner Bros.)

20. **BEST RHYTHM & BLUES
VOCAL PERFORMANCE,
FEMALE**
SOPHISTICATED LADY
(SHE'S A DIFFERENT LADY)
(Single)
Natalie Cole (Capitol)

21. **BEST RHYTHM & BLUES
VOCAL PERFORMANCE,
MALE**
I WISH (Track)
Stevie Wonder (Tamla/Motown)

22. **BEST RHYTHM & BLUES
VOCAL PERFORMANCE BY A
DUO, GROUP, OR CHORUS**
YOU DON'T HAVE TO BE A
STAR (TO BE IN MY SHOW)
(Single)
Marilyn McCoo, Billy Davis, Jr.
(ABC)

23. **BEST RHYTHM & BLUES
INSTRUMENTAL
PERFORMANCE**
THEME FROM GOOD KING
BAD (Track)
George Benson (CTI)

24. **BEST RHYTHM & BLUES
SONG**
LOWDOWN
Songwriters: Boz Scaggs, David
Paich

25. **BEST SOUL GOSPEL
PERFORMANCE**
HOW I GOT OVER (Album)
Mahalia Jackson (Columbia)

26. **BEST COUNTRY VOCAL
PERFORMANCE, FEMALE**
ELITE HOTEL (Album)
Emmylou Harris (Reprise/Warner
Bros.)

27. **BEST COUNTRY VOCAL PERFORMANCE, MALE**
(I'M A) STAND BY MY WOMAN MAN (Single)
Ronnie Milsap (RCA)

28. **BEST COUNTRY VOCAL PERFORMANCE BY A DUO OR GROUP**
THE END IS NOT IN SIGHT (THE COWBOY TUNE) (Single)
Amazing Rhythm Aces (ABC)

29. **BEST COUNTRY INSTRUMENTAL PERFORMANCE**
CHESTER & LESTER (Album)
Chet Atkins, Les Paul (RCA)

30. **BEST COUNTRY SONG**
BROKEN LADY
Songwriter: Larry Gatlin

31. **BEST INSPIRATIONAL PERFORMANCE**
THE ASTONISHING, OUTRAGEOUS, AMAZING, INCREDIBLE, UNBELIEVABLE, DIFFERENT WORLD OF GARY S. PAXTON (Album)
Gary S. Paxton (Newpax)

32. **BEST GOSPEL PERFORMANCE**
WHERE THE SOUL NEVER DIES (Single)
Oak Ridge Boys (Columbia)

33. **BEST ETHINIC OR TRADITIONAL RECORDING**
MARK TWANG (Album)
John Hartford (Flying Fish)

34. **BEST LATIN RECORDING**
UNFINISHED MASTERPIECE (Album)
Eddie Palmieri (COCO)

35. **BEST RECORDING FOR CHILDREN**
PROKOFIEV: PETER AND THE WOLF/SAINT SAENS: CARNIVAL OF THE ANIMALS
Hermione Gingold; Karl Bohm, conductor (DG)

36. **BEST COMEDY RECORDING**
BICENTENNIAL NIGGER (Album)
Richard Pryor

37. **BEST SPOKEN WORD RECORDING**
GREAT AMERICAN DOCUMENTS (Album)
Orson Welles, Henry Fonda, Helen Hayes, James Earl Jones (CBS)

38. **BEST INSTRUMENTAL COMPOSITION**
BELLAVIA
Composer: Chuck Mangione

39. **ALBUM OF BEST ORIGINAL SCORE WRITTEN FOR A MOTION PICTURE OR A TELEVISION SPECIAL**
CAR WASH
Composer: Norman Whitfield (MCA)

40. **BEST CAST SHOW ALBUM**
BUBBLING BROWN SUGAR
Various Composers
Producers: Hugo & Luigi (H & L)

41. **ALBUM OF THE YEAR, CLASSICAL**
BEETHOVEN: FIVE PIANO CONCERTOS
Artur Rubinstein; Daniel Barenboim cond. London Philharmonic
Producer: Max Wilcox (RCA)

42. **BEST CLASSICAL ORCHESTRAL PERFORMANCE**
STRAUSS: ALSO SPRACH ZARATHUSTRA
Sir Georg Solti cond. Chicago Sym. Orch.
Producer: Ray Minshull (London)

43. **BEST OPERA RECORDING**
GERSHWIN: PORGY & BESS
Lorin Maazel cond the Cleveland Orch. & Chorus
Producer: Michael Woolcock (London)

44. **BEST CHORAL PERFORMANCE, CLASSICAL**
RACHMANINOFF: THE BELLS
Arthur Oldham, chorus master of London Symphony Chorus
Andre Previn cond. London Sym Orch. (Angel)

45. **BEST CHAMBER MUSIC PERFORMANCE**
THE ART OF COURTLY LOVE
David Munrow cond. Early Music Consort of London (Seraphim)

46. **BEST CLASSICAL PERFORMANCE, INSTRUMENTAL SOLOIST (WITH ORCHESTRA)**
BEETHOVEN: THE FIVE PIANO CONCERTOS
Artur Rubinstein (Daniel Barenboim cond. London Philhamonic) (RCA)

47. **BEST CLASSICAL PERFORMANCE, INSTRUMENTAL SOLOIST (WITHOUT ORCHESTRA)**
HOROWITZ CONCERTS 1975/76
Vladimir Horowitz (RCA)

48. **BEST CLASSICAL VOCAL SOLOIST PERFORMANCE**
(HERBERT) MUSIC OF VICTOR HERBERT
Beverly Sills (Angel)

49. **BEST ENGINEERED RECORDING, CLASSICAL**
GERSHWIN: RHAPSODY IN BLUE
(George Gershwin; Thomas cond. Columbia Jazz Band)
Engineers: Edward Graham, Ray Moore, Milton Cherin (Columbia)

20TH ANNUAL (1977) GRAMMY WINNERS
Announced on February 23, 1978
Eligibility Year: October 1, 1976 through September 30, 1977

1. **RECORD OF THE YEAR**
HOTEL CALIFORNIA
Eagles
Producer: Bill Szymczyk (Asylum)

2. **ALBUM OF THE YEAR**
RUMOURS
Fleetwood Mac
Producers: Fleetwood Mac, Richard Dashut, and Ken Caillat (Warner Bros)

3. **SONG OF THE YEAR** (Tie)
LOVE THEME FROM A STAR IS BORN (EVERGREEN)
Songwriters: Barbra Streisand and Paul Williams

YOU LIGHT UP MY LIFE
Songwriter: Joe Brooks

4. **BEST NEW ARTIST OF THE YEAR**
DEBBY BOONE (Warner Bros./ Curb)

5. **BEST INSTRUMENTAL ARRANGEMENT**
NADIA'S THEME (THE YOUNG AND THE RESTLESS) (Barry De Vorzon)
Arrangers: Harry Betts, Perry Botkin Jr., and Barry De Vorzon (Arista)

6. **BEST ARRANGEMENT ACCOMPANYING VOCALIST(S)**
LOVE THEME FROM A STAR IS BORN (EVERGREEN) (Barbra Streisand)
Arranger: Ian Freebaim-Smith (Columbia)

7. **BEST ARRANGEMENT FOR VOICES**
NEW KID IN TOWN (Eagles)
Arrangers: Eagles (Asylum)

8. **BEST ENGINEERED RECORDING (non-classical)**
AJA (Steely Dan)
Engineers: Roger Nichols, Elliot Scheiner, Bill Schnee and Al Schmitt (ABC)

9. **BEST ALBUM PACKAGE**
SIMPLE DREAMS (Linda Ronstadt)
Art Director: Kosh (Asylum)

10. **BEST ALBUM NOTES**
BING CROSBY: A LEGENDARY PERFORMER
Annotator: George T. Simon (RCA)

11. **BEST PRODUCER OF THE YEAR**
PETER ASHER

12. **BEST JAZZ VOCAL PERFORMANCE**
LOOK TO THE RAINBOW (Album)
Al Jarreau (Warner Bros.)

13. **BEST JAZZ PERFORMANCE BY A SOLOIST**
THE GIANTS (Album)
Oscar Peterson (Pablo)

14. **BEST JAZZ PERFORMANCE BY A GROUP**
THE PHIL WOODS SIX-LIVE FROM THE SHOWBOAT (Album)
Phil Woods (RCA)

15. **BEST JAZZ PERFORMANCE BY A BIG BAND**
PRIME TIME (Album)
Count Basie and his Orchestra (Pablo)

16. **BEST POP VOCAL PERFORMANCE, FEMALE**
LOVE THEME FROM A STAR IS BORN (EVERGREEEN) (Single)
Barbra Streisand (Columbia)

17. **BEST POP VOCAL PERFORMANCE, MALE**
HANDY MAN (Single)
James Taylor (Columbia)

18. **BEST POP VOCAL PERFORMANCE BY A DUO, GROUP OR CHORUS**
HOW DEEP IS YOUR LOVE (Single)
Bee Gees (RSO)

19. **BEST POP INSTRUMENTAL PERFORMANCE**
STAR WARS (Album)
John Williams cond. London Sym. Orch. (20th Century)

20. **BEST RHYTHM and BLUES VOCAL PERFORMANCE, FEMALE**
DON'T LEAVE ME THIS WAY (Single)
Thelma Houston (Motown)

21. **BEST RHYTHM and BLUES VOCAL PERFORMANCE, MALE**
UNMISTAKABLY LOU (Album)
Lou Rawls (PIR/Epic)

22. **BEST RHYTHM and BLUES VOCAL PERFORMANCE BY A DUO, GROUP OR CHORUS**
BEST OF MY LOVE (Track)
Emotions (Columbia)

23. **BEST RHYTHM and BLUES INSTRUMENTAL PERFORMANCE**
Q (Track)
Brothers Johnson (AandM)

24. **BEST RHYTHM and BLUES SONG**
YOU MAKE ME FEEL LIKE DANCING
Songwriters: Leo Sayer and Vini Poncia

25. **BEST GOSPEL PERFORMANCE, CONTEMPORARY OR INSPIRATIONAL**
SAIL ON (Album)
Imperials (Dayspring/Word)

26. **BEST GOSPEL PERFORMANCE, TRADITIONAL**
JUST A LITTLE TALK WITH JESUS (Track)
Oak Ridge Boys (Rockland Road)

27. **BEST SOUL GOSPEL PERFORMANCE, CONTEMPORARY**
WONDERFUL! (Album)
Edwin Hawkins and the Edwin Hawkins Singers (Birthright)

28. **BEST SOUL GOSPEL PERFORMANCE, TRADITIONAL**
JAMES CLEVELAND LIVE AT CARNEGIE HALL (Album)
James Cleveland (Savoy)

29. **BEST INSPIRATIONAL PERFORMANCE**
HOME WHERE I BELONG (Album)
B.J. Thomas (Myrrh/Word)

30. **BEST COUNTRY VOCAL PERFORMANCE, FEMALE**
DON'T IT MAKE MY BROWN EYES BLUE (Single)
Crystal Gayle (United Artists)

31. **BEST COUNTRY VOCAL PERFORMANCE, MALE**
LUCILLE (Single)
Kenny Rogers (United Artists)

32. **BEST COUNTRY VOCAL PERFORMANCE BY A DUO OR GROUP**
HEAVEN'S JUST A SIN AWAY (Single)
The Kendalls (Ovation)

33. **BEST COUNTRY INSTRUMENTAL PERFORMANCE**
COUNTRY INSTRUMENTALIST OF THE YEAR (Album)
Hargus "Pig" Robbins (Elektra)

34. **BEST COUNTRY SONG**
DON'T IT MAKE MY BROWN EYES BLUE
Songwriter: Richard Leigh

35. **BEST ETHNIC OR TRADITIONAL RECORDING**
HARD AGAIN (Album)
Muddy Waters (Blue Sky/CBS)

36. **BEST LATIN RECORDING**
DAWN (Album)
Mongo Santamaria (Vaya)

37. **BEST RECORDING FOR CHILDREN**
AREN'T YOU GLAD YOU'RE YOU (Album)
Christopher Cerf and Jim Timmens (Sesame Street)

38. **BEST COMEDY RECORDING**
LET'S GET SMALL (Album)
Steve Martin (Warner Bros.)

39. **BEST SPOKEN WORD RECORDING**
THE BELLE OF AMHERST
(Album)
Julie Harris (Credo)

40. **BEST INSTRUMENTAL COMPOSITION**
MAIN TITLE FROM "STAR WARS"
Composer: John Williams

41. **BEST ORIGINAL SCORE WRITTEN FOR A MOTION PICTURE OR A TELEVISION SPECIAL**
STAR WARS
Composer: John Williams (20th Century)

42. **BEST CAST SHOW ALBUM**
ANNIE
Composers: Charles Strouse and Martin Charnin
Producers: Larry Morton, Charles Strouse (Columbia)

43. **ALBUM OF THE YEAR, CLASSICAL**
CONCERT OF THE CENTURY
Bernstein, Horowitz, Stern, Rostropovich, Fischer-Dieskau, Menuhin and Woodside.
Producer: Thomas Frost (Columbia)

44. **BEST CLASSICAL ORCHESTRAL PERFORMANCE**
MAHLER: SYMPHONY NO. 9
Carlo Maria Giulini cond.
Chicago Sym. Orch.
Producer: Gunther Breest (DG)

45. **BEST OPERA RECORDING**
GERSHWIN: PORGY and BESS
John De Main cond. Sherwin M. Goldman/Houston Grand Opera production. (Albert, Dale, Smith, Shakesnider, Lane, Brice, Smalls)
Producer: Thomas Z. Shepard (RCA)

46. **BEST CHORAL PERFORMANCE, CLASSICAL (OTHER THAN OPERA)**
VERDI: REQUIEM
Sir Georg Solti cond. Chicago Sym. Margaret Hillis, choral director of the Chicago Symphony Chorus (RCA)

47. **BEST CHAMBER MUSIC PERFORMANCE**
SCHOENBERG: QUARTETS FOR STRINGS
Juilliard Quartet (Columbia)

48. **BEST CLASSICAL PERFORMANCE, INSTRUMENTAL SOLOIST OR SOLOISTS (WITH ORCHESTRA)**
VIVALDI: THE FOUR SEASONS
Itzhak Perlman, Violin (Perlman cond. London Philharmonic) (Angel)

49. **BEST CLASSICAL PERFORMANCE, INSTRUMENTAL SOLOIST OR SOLOISTS (WITHOUT ORCHESTRA)**
BEETHOVEN: SONATA FOR PIANO NO. 18 SCHUMANN: FANTASIESTUCKE
Artur Rubinstein, Piano (RCA)

50. **BEST CLASSICAL VOCAL SOLOIST PERFORMANCE**
BACH: ARIAS
Janet Baker (Marriner cond. Academy of St. Martin-in-the-Fields) (Angel)

51. **BEST ENGINEERED RECORDING, CLASSICAL**
RAVEL: BOLERO
Solti cond. Chicago Sym.
Engineer: Kenneth Wilkinson (London)

21ST ANNUAL (1978) GRAMMY WINNERS
Announced on February 15, 1979
Eligibility Year: October 1, 1977 through September 30, 1978

1. **RECORD OF THE YEAR**
JUST THE WAY YOU ARE
Billy Joel
Producer: Phil Ramone
(Columbia)

2. **ALBUM OF THE YEAR**
SATURDAY NIGHT FEVER
Bee Gees, David Shire, Yvonne
Elliman, Tevares, Kool and The
Gang, K.C. and The Sunshine
Band, MFSB, Trammps, Walter
Murphy, Ralph MacDonald.
Producers: Bee Gees, Karl
Richardson, Alghy Galuten,
Freddie Perren, Bill Oakes,
David Shire, Arif Mardin,
Thomas J. Valentino, Ralph
MacDonald, W. Salter, K. G.
Productions, H.W. Casey,
Richard Finch, Bobby Martin,
Broadway Eddie, Ron Kersey
(RSO)

3. **SONG OF THE YEAR**
JUST THE WAY YOU ARE
Songwriter: Billy Joel

4. **BEST NEW ARTIST OF THE YEAR**
A TASTE OF HONEY (Capitol)

5. **BEST POP VOCAL PERFORMANCE, FEMALE**
YOU NEEDED ME (Single)
Anne Murray (Capital)

6. **BEST POP VOCAL PERFORMANCE, MALE**
COPACABANA (AT THE COPA) (Single)
Barry Manilow (Arista)

7. **BEST POP VOCAL PERFORMANCE BY A DUO, GROUP OR CHORUS**
SATURDAY NIGHT FEVER
(Album)
Bee Gees (RSO)

8. **BEST POP INSTRUMENTAL PERFORMANCE**
CHILDREN OF SANCHEZ
(Album)
Chuck Mangione Group (AandM)

9. **BEST R and B VOCAL PERFORMANCE, FEMALE**
LAST DANCE (Single)
Donna Summer (Casablanca)

10. **BEST R and B VOCAL PERFORMANCE, MALE**
ON BROADWAY (Single)
George Benson (Warner Bros.)

11. **BEST R and B VOCAL PERFORMANCE BY A DUO, GROUP OR CHORUS**
ALL 'N ALL (Album)
Earth, Wind and Fire (Columbia)

12. **BEST R and B INSTRUMENTAL PERFORMANCE**
RUNNIN' (Track)
Earth, Wind and Fire (Columbia)

13. **BEST RHYTHM and BLUES SONG**
LAST DANCE
Songwriter: Paul Jabara

14. **BEST COUNTRY VOCAL PERFORMANCE, FEMALE**
HERE YOU COME AGAIN
(Album)
Dolly Parton (RCA)

15. **BEST COUNTRY VOCAL PERFORMANCE, MALE**
GEORGIA ON MY MIND
(Single)
Willie Nelson (Columbia)

16. **BEST COUNTRY VOCAL PERFORMANCE BY A DUO OR GROUP**
MAMAS DON'T LET YOUR BABIES GROW UP TO BE COWBOYS (Single)
Waylon Jennings and Willie Nelson (RCA)

17. **BEST COUNTRY INSTRUMENTALIST PERFORMANCE**
ONE O'CLOCK JUMP (Track)
Asleep at the Wheel (Capitol)

18. **BEST COUNTRY SONG**
THE GAMBLER
Songwriter: Don Schlitz

19. **BEST GOSPEL PERFORMANCE, CONTEMPORARY OR INSPIRATIONAL**
WHAT A FRIEND (Track)
Larry Hart (Genesis)

20. **BEST GOSPEL PERFORMANCE, TRADITIONAL**
REFRESHING (Album)
The Happy Goodman Family (Canaan)

21. **BEST SOUL GOSPEL PERFORMANCE, CONTEMPORARY**
LIVE IN LONDON (Album)
Andrae Crouch and The Disciples (Light)

22. **BEST SOUL GOSPEL PERFORMANCE, TRADITIONAL**
LIVE AND DIRECT (Album)
Mighty Clouds of Joy (ABC)

23. **BEST INSPIRATIONAL PERFORMANCE**
HAPPY MAN (Album)
B.J. Thomas (Myrrh)

24. **BEST ETHNIC OR TRADITIONAL RECORDING**
I'M READY (Album)
Muddy Waters (Blue Sky)

25. **BEST LATIN RECORDING**
HOMENAJE A BENY MORE (Album)
Tito Puente (Tico)

26. **BEST RECORDING FOR CHILDREN**
THE MUPPET SHOW (Album)
Jim Henson (Arista)

27. **BEST COMEDY RECORDING**
A WILD AND CRAZY GUY (Album)
Steve Martin (Warner Bros.)

28. **BEST SPOKEN WORD RECORDING**
CITIZEN KANE (Motion Picture Soundtrack)
Orson Welles (Mark 56)

29. **BEST INSTRUMENTAL COMPOSITION**
THEME FROM "CLOSE ENCOUNTERS OF THE THIRD KIND"
Composer: John Williams

30. **BEST ALBUM OF ORIGINAL SCORE WRITTEN FOR A MOTION PICTURE OR A TELEVISION SPECIAL**
CLOSE ENCOUNTERS OF THE THIRD KIND
Composer: John Williams (Arista)

31. **BEST CAST SHOW ALBUM**
AIN'T MISBEHAVIN'
Producer: Thomas Z. Shepard (RCA)

32. **BEST JAZZ VOCAL PERFORMANCE**
ALL FLY HOME (Album)
Al Jarreau (Warner Bros.)

33. **BEST JAZZ INSTRUMENTAL PERFORMANCE, SOLOIST**
MONTREUX '77 OSCAR PETERSON JAM (Album)
Oscar Peterson (Pablo)

34. **BEST JAZZ INSTRUMENTAL PERFORMANCE, GROUP**
FRIENDS (Album)
Chick Corea (Polydor)

35. **BEST JAZZ INSTRUMENTAL PERFORMANCE, BIG BAND**
LIVE IN MUNICH (Album)
Thad Jones and Mel Lewis
(Horizon/A&M)

36. **BEST INSTRUMENTAL ARRANGEMENT**
MAIN TITLE (OVERTURE PART ONE) ("The Wiz" Original Soundtrack)
Arrangers: Quincy Jones, Robert Freedman (MCA)

37. **BEST ARRANGEMENT ACCOMPANYING VOCALIST(S)**
GOT TO GET YOU INTO MY LIFE (Earth, Wind and Fire)
Arranger: Maurice White (RSO)

38. **BEST ARRANGEMENT FOR VOICES**
STAYIN' ALIVE (The Bee Gees)
Arranger: The Bee Gees (RSO)

39. **BEST ALBUM PACKAGE**
BOYS IN THE TREES (Carly Simon)
Art Directors: Johnny Lee, Tony Lane (Elektra)

40. **BEST ALBUM NOTES**
A BING CROSBY COLLECTION, VOLS. I and II
Annotator: Michael Brooks (Columbia)

41. **BEST HISTORICAL REPACKAGE ALBUM**
LESTER YOUNG STORY VOL. 3
Producer: Michael Brooks (Columbia)

42. **BEST ENGINEERED RECORDING**
FM (NO STATIC AT ALL)
(Steely Dan) (Track)
Engineers: Roger Nichols and Al Schmitt (MCA)

43. **BEST PRODUCERS OF THE YEAR**
BEE GEES, ALBHY GALUTEN, and KARL RICHARDSON

44. **ALBUM OF THE YEAR CLASSICAL**
BRAHMS: CONCERTO FOR VIOLIN IN D MAJOR
Itzhak Perlman; Carlo Maria Giulini cond. Chicago Sym.
Producer: Christopher Bishop (Angel)

45. **BEST CLASSICAL ORCHESTRAL PERFORMANCE**
BEETHOVEN: SYMPHONIES (9) (Complete)
Herbert von Karajan cond. Berlin Philharmonic
Producer: Michel Glotz (DG)

46. **BEST OPERA RECORDING**
LEHAR: THE MERRY WIDOW
Julius Rudel cond. New York City Opera Orchestra and Chorus/Principal Solos: Sills, Titus
Producers: George Sponhaltz and John Coveney (Angel)

47. **BEST CHORAL PERFORMANCE, CLASSICAL (OTHER THAN OPERA)**
BEETHOVEN: MISSA SOLEMNIS
Sir Georg Solti, conductor; Margaret Hillis, choral director (Chicago Sym. Orch. & Chorus) (London)

48. **BEST CHAMBER MUSIC PERFORMANCE**
BEETHOVEN: SONATAS FOR VIOLIN and PIANO (COMPLETE) Itzhak Perlman and Vladimir Ashkenazy (London)

49. **BEST CLASSICAL PERFORMANCE, INSTRUMENTAL SOLOIST(S) (WITH ORCHESTRA)**
RACHMANINOFF: CONCERTO NO. 3 IN D MINOR FOR PIANO (HOROWITZ GOLDEN JUBILEE)
Vladimir Horowitz (Eugene Ormandy cond. Philadelphia Orch.) (RCA)

50. **BEST CLASSICAL PERFORMANCE, INSTRUMENTAL SOLOIST(S) (WITHOUT ORCHESTRA)**
THE HOROWITZ CONCERTS 1977/78
Vladimir Horowitz (RCA)

51. **BEST CLASSICAL VOCAL SOLOIST PERFORMANCE**
LUCIANO PAVAROTTI—HITS FROM LINCOLN CENTER
Luciano Pavarotti (London)

52. **BEST ENGINEERED RECORDING, CLASSICAL**
VARESE: AMERIQUES/ ARCANA/IONISATION (BOULEZ CONDUCTS VARESE)
Pierre Boulez cond. New York Philharmonic
Engineers: Bud Graham, Arthur Kendy, and Ray Moore (Columbia)

22ND ANNUAL (1979) GRAMMY WINNERS
Announced on February 27, 1980
Eligibility Year: October 1, 1978 through September 30, 1979

1. **RECORD OF THE YEAR**
WHAT A FOOL BELIEVES
The Doobie Brothers
Producer: Ted Templeman (Warner Bros.)

2. **ALBUM OF THE YEAR**
52ND STREET
Billy Joel
Producer: Phil Ramone (Columbia)

3. **SONG OF THE YEAR**
WHAT A FOOL BELIEVES
Songwriters: Kenny Loggins, Michael McDonald

4. **BEST NEW ARTIST**
RICKIE LEE JONES (Warner Bros.)

5. **BEST POP VOCAL PERFORMANCE, FEMALE**
I'LL NEVER LOVE THIS WAY AGAIN (Single)
Dionne Warwick (Arista)

6. **BEST POP VOCAL PERFORMANCE, MALE**
52ND STREET ALBUM
Billy Joel (Columbia)

7. **BEST POP VOCAL PERFORMANCE BY A DUO, GROUP OR CHORUS**
MINUTE BY MINUTE
The Doobie Brothers (Warner Bros.)

8. **BEST POP INSTRUMENTAL PERFORMANCE**
RISE (Single)
Herb Alpert (A&M)

9. **BEST ROCK VOCAL PERFORMANCE, FEMALE**
HOT STUFF (Single)
Donna Summer (Casablanca)

10. **BEST ROCK VOCAL PERFORMANCE, MALE**
GOTTA SERVE SOMEBODY (Single)
Bob Dylan (Columbia)

11. **BEST ROCK VOCAL PERFORMANCE BY A DUO OR GROUP**
HEARTACHE TONIGHT (Single)
Eagles (Asylum)

12. **BEST ROCK INSTRUMENTAL PERFORMANCE**
ROCKESTRA THEME (Track)
Wings (Columbia)

13. **BEST R and B VOCAL PERFORMANCE, FEMALE**
DEJA VU (Track)
Dionne Warwick (Arista)

14. **BEST R and B VOCAL PERFORMANCE, MALE**
DON'T STOP 'TIL YOU GET ENOUGH (Single)
Michael Jackson (Epic)

15. **BEST R and B VOCAL PERFORMANCE BY A DUO, GROUP OR CHORUS**
AFTER THE LOVE HAS GONE (Track)
Earth, Wind and Fire (ARC/CBS)

16. **BEST R and B INSTRUMENTAL PERFORMANCE**
BOOGIE WONDERLAND (Single)
Earth, Wind and Fire (ARC/CBS)

17. **BEST RHYTHM and BLUES SONG**
AFTER THE LOVE HAS GONE
Songwriters: David Foster, Jay Graydon, Bill Champlin

18. **BEST DISCO RECORDING**
I WILL SURVIVE (Single)
Gloria Gaynor
Producers: Dino Fekaris, Freddie Perren (Polydor)

19. **BEST COUNTRY VOCAL PERFORMANCE, FEMALE**
BLUE KENTUCKY GIRL (Album)
Emmylou Harris (Warner Bros.)

20. **BEST COUNTRY VOCAL PERFORMANCE, MALE**
THE GAMBLER (Single)
Kenny Rogers (United Artists)

21. **BEST COUNTRY VOCAL PERFORMANCE BY A DUO OR GROUP**
THE DEVIL WENT DOWN TO GEORGIA (Single)
Charlie Daniels Band (Epic)

22. **BEST COUNTRY INSTRUMENTAL PERFORMANCE**
BIG SANDY/LEATHER BRITCHES (Track)
Doc and Merle Watson (United Artists)

23. **BEST COUNTRY SONG**
YOU DECORATED MY LIFE
Songwriters: Debbie Hupp, Bob Morrison

24. **BEST GOSPEL PERFORMANCE CONTEMPORARY OR INSPIRATIONAL**
HEED THE CALL (Album)
Imperials (Dayspring)

25. **BEST GOSPEL PERFORMANCE, TRADITIONAL**
LIFT UP THE NAME OF JESUS (Album)
The Blackwood Brothers (Skylite)

26. **BEST SOUL GOSPEL PERFORMANCE, CONTEMPORARY**
I'LL BE THINKING OF YOU (Album)
Andrae Crouch (Light)

27. **BEST SOUL GOSPEL PERFORMANCE, TRADITIONAL**
CHANGING TIMES (Album)
Mighty Clouds of Joy (Epic)

28. **BEST INSPIRATIONAL PERFORMANCE**
YOU GAVE ME LOVE (WHEN NOBODY GAVE ME A PRAYER) (Album)
B.J. Thomas (Myrrh)

29. **BEST ETHNIC OR TRADITIONAL RECORDING**
MUDDY "MISSISSIPPI" WATERS LIVE (Album)
Muddy Waters (Sky/CBS)

30. **BEST LATIN RECORDING**
IRAKERE (Album)
Irakere (Columbia)

31. **BEST RECORDING FOR CHILDREN**
THE MUPPET MOVIE (Album)
Jim Henson, creator: Paul Williams, producer (Atlantic)

32. **BEST COMEDY RECORDING**
REALITY . . . WHAT A CONCEPT (Album)
Robin Williams (Casablanca)

33. **BEST SPOKEN WORD, DOCUMENTARY OR DRAMA RECORDING**
AGES OF MAN (READINGS FROM SHAKESPEARE) (Album)
Sir John Gielgud (Caedmon)

34. **BEST INSTRUMENTAL COMPOSITION**
MAIN TITLE THEME FROM SUPERMAN
Composer: John Williams

35. **BEST ALBUM OF ORIGINAL SCORE WRITTEN FOR A MOTION PICTURE OR A TELEVISION SPECIAL**
SUPERMAN
Composer: John Williams (Warner Bros.)

36. **BEST CAST SHOW ALBUM**
SWEENEY TODD
Composer/Lyricist: Stephen Sondheim
Producer: Thomas Z. Shepard (RCA)

37. **BEST JAZZ FUSION PERFORMANCE, VOCAL OR INSTRUMENTAL**
8:30 (Album)
Weather Report (ARC/CBS)

38. **BEST JAZZ VOCAL PERFORMANCE**
FINE AND MELLOW (Album)
Ella Fitzgerald (Pablo)

39. **BEST JAZZ INSTRUMENTAL PERFORMANCE, SOLOIST**
JOUSTS (Album)
Oscar Peterson (Pablo)

40. **BEST JAZZ INSTRUMENTAL PERFORMANCE, GROUP**
DUET (Album)
Gary Burton and Chick Corea (ECM/Warner Bros.)

41. BEST JAZZ INSTRUMENTAL PERFORMANCE, BIG BAND
AT FARGO, 1940 LIVE (Album)
Duke Ellington (Book of the Month Records)

42. BEST INSTRUMENTAL ARRANGEMENT
SOULFUL STRUT
Arranger: Claus Ogerman (Warner Bros.)

43. BEST ARRANGEMENT ACCOMPANYING VOCALIST(S)
WHAT A FOOL BELIEVES
Arranger: Michael McDonald (Warner Bros.)

44. BEST ALBUM PACKAGE
BREAKFAST IN AMERICA
Art Directors: Mike Doud, Mick Haggerty (A&M)

45. BEST ALBUM NOTES
CHARLIE PARKER: THE COMPLETE SAVOY SESSIONS
Annotators: Bob Porter, James Patrick (Savoy)

46. BEST HISTORICAL REISSUE
BILLIE HOLIDAY (GIANTS OF JAZZ)
Producers: Michael Brooks, Jerry Kom (Time-Life)

47. BEST ENGINEERED RECORDING (Non-Classical)
BREAKFAST IN AMERICA (Album)
Engineer: Peter Henderson (A&M)

48. PRODUCER OF THE YEAR (Non-Classical)
Larry Butler

49. BEST CLASSICAL ALBUM
BRAHMS: SYMPHONIES COMPLETE
Sir Georg Solti cond. Chicago Sym.
Producer: James Mallinson (London)

50. BEST CLASSICAL ORCHESTRAL RECORDING
BRAHMS: SYMPHONIES COMPLETE
Sir Georg Solti cond. Chicago Sym.
Producer: James Mallinson (London)

51. BEST OPERA RECORDING
BRITTEN: PETER GRIMES
Colin Davis cond. Orchestra and Chorus of the Royal Opera House, Covent Garden. Principal Solos: Vickers, Harper, Summers
Producer: Vittorio Negri (Philips)

52. BEST CHORAL PERFORMANCE, CLASSICAL (OTHER THAN OPERA)
BRAHMS: A GERMAN REQUIEM
Sir Georg Solti, cond./Margaret Hillis, choral director (Chicago Sym. Orch. & Chorus) (London)

53. BEST CHAMBER MUSIC PERFORMANCE
COPLAND: APPALACHIAN SPRING
Dennis Russell Davies cond. St. Paul Chamber Orch. (Sound 80)

54. BEST CLASSICAL PERFORMANCE, INSTRUMENTAL SOLOIST OR SOLOISTS (WITH ORCHESTRA)
BARTOK: CONCERTOS FOR PIANO NOS. 1 and 2
Maurizio Pollini (Abbado cond. Chicago Sym.) (DG)

55. BEST CLASSICAL PERFORMANCE, INSTRUMENTAL SOLOIST OR SOLOISTS (WITHOUT ORCHESTRA)
THE HOROWITZ CONCERTS 1978/79
Vladimir Horowitz (RCA)

56. BEST CLASSICAL VOCAL SOLOIST PERFORMANCE
O SOLE MIO
Luciano Pavarotti (Bologna Orchestra) (London)

57. BEST ENGINEERED RECORDING, CLASSICAL
SONDHEIM: SWEENEY TODD
Engineer: Anthony Salvatore (RCA)

58. CLASSICAL PRODUCER OF THE YEAR
JAMES MALLINSON

23RD ANNUAL (1980) GRAMMY WINNERS
Announced on February 25, 1981
Eligibility Year: October 1, 1979 through September 30, 1980

1. RECORD OF THE YEAR
SAILING
Christopher Cross
Producer: Michael Omartian
(Warner Bros.)

2. ALBUM OF THE YEAR
CHRISTOPHER CROSS
Christopher Cross
Producer: Michael Omartian
(Warner Bros.)

3. SONG OF THE YEAR
SAILING
Songwriter: Christopher Cross

4. BEST NEW ARTIST
CHRISTOPHER CROSS

5. BEST POP VOCAL PERFORMANCE, FEMALE
THE ROSE (Single)
Bette Midler (Atlantic)

6. BEST POP VOCAL PERFORMANCE, MALE
THIS IS IT (Track)
Kenny Loggins (Columbia)

7. BEST POP PERFORMANCE BY A DUO OR GROUP WITH VOCAL
GUILTY (Track)
Barbra Streisand and Barry Gibb
(Columbia)

8. BEST POP INSTRUMENTAL PERFORMANCE
ONE ON ONE (Album)
Bob James and Earl Klugh
(Columbia)

9. BEST ROCK VOCAL PERFORMANCE, FEMALE
CRIMES OF PASSION (Album)
Pat Benatar (Chrysalis)

10. BEST ROCK VOCAL PERFORMANCE, MALE
GLASS HOUSES (Album)
Billy Joel (Columbia)

11. BEST ROCK PERFORMANCE BY A DUO OR GROUP WITH VOCAL
AGAINST THE WIND (Album)
Bob Seger and The Silver Bullet Band (Capitol)

12. **BEST ROCK INSTRUMENTAL PERFORMANCE**
REGGATTA DE BLANC (Track)
Police (A&M)

13. **BEST R and B VOCAL PERFORMANCE, FEMALE**
NEVER KNEW LOVE LIKE THIS BEFORE (Single)
Stephanie Mills (Century)

14. **BEST R and B VOCAL PERFORMANCE, MALE**
GIVE ME THE NIGHT (Album)
George Benson (QWest/Warner Bros.)

15. **BEST R and B PERFORMANCE BY A DUO OR GROUP WITH VOCAL**
SHINING STAR (Single)
Manhattans (Columbia)

16. **BEST R and B INSTRUMENTAL PERFORMANCE**
OFF BROADWAY (Track)
George Benson (QWest/Warner Bros.)

17. **BEST RHYTHM & BLUES SONG**
NEVER KNEW LOVE LIKE THIS BEFORE
Songwriters: Reggie Lucas, James Mtume

18. **BEST JAZZ FUSION PERFORMANCE, VOCAL OR INSTRUMENTAL**
BIRDLAND (Single)
Manhattan Transfer (Atlantic)

19. **BEST COUNTRY VOCAL PERFORMANCE, FEMALE**
COULD I HAVE THIS DANCE (Single)
Anne Murray (Capitol)

20. **BEST COUNTRY VOCAL PERFORMANCE, MALE**
HE STOPPED LOVING HER TODAY (Single)
George Jones (Epic)

21. **BEST COUNTRY PERFORMANCE BY A DUO OR GROUP WITH VOCAL**
THAT LOVIN' YOU FEELIN' AGAIN (Single)
Roy Orbison, Emmylou Harris (Warner Bros.)

22. **BEST COUNTRY INSTRUMENTALIST PERFORMANCE**
ORANGE BLOSSOM SPECIAL/ HOEDOWN (Track)
Gilley's "Urban Cowboy" Band (Full Moon/Asylum)

23. **BEST COUNTRY SONG**
ON THE ROAD AGAIN
Songwriter: Willie Nelson

24. **BEST GOSPEL PERFORMANCE, CONTEMPORARY OR INSPIRATIONAL**
THE LORD'S PRAYER (Album)
Reba Rambo, Dony McGuire, B.J. Thomas, Andrae Crouch, The Archers, Walter and Tramaine Hawkins, Cynthia Clawson (Light)

25. **BEST GOSPEL PERFORMANCE, TRADITIONAL**
WE COME TO WORSHIP (Album)
Blackwood Brothers (Voice Box)

26. **BEST SOUL GOSPEL PERFORMANCE, CONTEMPORARY**
REJOICE (Album)
Shirley Caesar (Myrrh)

27. **BEST SOUL GOSPEL PERFORMANCE, TRADITIONAL**
LORD, LET ME BE AN INSTRUMENT (Album)
James Cleveland & The Charles Fold Singers (Savoy)

28. **BEST INSPIRATIONAL PERFORMANCE**
WITH MY SONG I WILL PRAISE HIM (Album)
Debby Boone (Lamb & Lion)

29. **BEST ETHNIC OR TRADITIONAL RECORDING**
RARE BLUES (Album)
Dr. Isaiah Ross, Maxwell Street Jimmy, Big Joe Williams, Son House, Rev. Robin Wilkins, Little Brother Montgomery, Sunnyland Slim
Producer: Norman Dayron (Takoma)

30. **BEST LATIN RECORDING**
LA ONDA VA BIEN (Album)
Cal Tjader (Concord Jazz)

31. **BEST RECORDING FOR CHILDREN**
IN HARMONY/A SESAME STREET RECORD (Album)
The Doobie Brothers, James Taylor, Carly Simon, Bette Midler, Muppets, Al Jarreau, Linda Ronstadt, Wendy Waldman, Libby Titus & Dr. John, Livingston Taylor, George Benson & Pauline Wilson, Lucy Simon, Kate Taylor & The Simon/Taylor Family
Producers: Lucy Simon and David Levine (Sesame Street/ Warner Bros.)

32. **BEST COMEDY RECORDING**
NO RESPECT (Album)
Rodney Dangerfield (Casablanca)

33. **BEST SPOKEN WORD, DOCUMENTARY OR DRAMA RECORDING**
GERTRUDE STEIN, GERTRUDE STEIN, GERTRUDE STEIN
Pat Carroll (Caedmon)

34. **BEST INSTRUMENTAL COMPOSITION**
THE EMPIRE STRIKES BACK
Composer: John Williams

35. **BEST ALBUM OF ORIGINAL SCORE WRITTEN FOR A MOTION PICTURE OR A TELEVISION SPECIAL**
THE EMPIRE STRIKES BACK
Composer: John Williams (RSO)

36. **BEST CAST SHOW ALBUM**
EVITA—PREMIER AMERICAN RECORDING
Composer: Andrew Lloyd Webber; Lyrics: Tim Rice
Producers: Andrew Lloyd Webber, Tim Rice (MCA)

37. **PLEASE NOTE THERE IS NO CATEGORY #37**

38. **BEST JAZZ VOCAL PERFORMANCE, FEMALE**
A PERFECT MATCH/ELLA & BASIE (Album)
Ella Fitzgerald (Pablo)

39. **BEST JAZZ VOCAL PERFORMANCE, MALE**
MOODY'S MOOD (Track)
George Benson (QWest/Warner Bros.)

40. **BEST JAZZ INSTRUMENTAL PERFORMANCE, SOLOIST**
I WILL SAY GOODBYE (Album)
Bill Evans (Warner Bros.)

41. **BEST JAZZ INSTRUMENTAL PERFORMANCE, GROUP**
WE WILL MEET AGAIN (Album)
Bill Evans (Warner Bros.)

42. **BEST JAZZ INSTRUMENTAL PERFORMANCE, BIG BAND**
ON THE ROAD (Album)
Count Basie and Orchestra (Pablo)

43. **BEST INSTRUMENTAL ARRANGEMENT**
DINORAH, DINORAH (George Benson)
Arrangers: Quincy Jones, Jerry Hey (Warner Bros.)

44. **BEST ARRANGEMENT ACCOMPANYING VOCALIST(S)**
SAILING (Christopher Cross)
Arrangers: Michael Omartian, and Christopher Cross (Warner Bros.)

45. **BEST ARRANGEMENT FOR VOICES**
BIRDLAND (Manhattan Transfer)
Arranger: Janis Siegel (Atlantic)

46. **BEST ALBUM PACKAGE**
AGAINST THE WIND (Bob Seger & The Silver Bullet Band)
Art Director: Roy Kohara (Capitol)

47. **BEST ALBUM NOTES**
TRILOGY: PAST, PRESENT, & FUTURE (Frank Sinatra)
Annotator: David McClintick (Reprise/Warner Bros.)

48. **BEST HISTORICAL REISSUE ALBUM**
SEGOVIA—THE EMI RECORDINGS 1927–39
Producer: Keith Hardwick (Angel)

49. **BEST ENGINEERED RECORDING (Non-Classical)**
THE WALL (Pink Floyd) (Album)
Engineer: James Guthrie (Columbia)

50. **PRODUCER OF THE YEAR (Non-Classical)**
PHIL RAMONE

51. **BEST CLASSICAL ALBUM**
BERG; LULU (COMPLETE VERSION)
Pierre Boulez cond. Orchestre de l'Opera de Paris, Principal Solos: Stratas, Minion, Mazura, Blankenheim
Producers: Guenther Breest, Michael Horwath (DG)

52. **BEST CLASSICAL ORCHESTRAL RECORDING**
BRUCKNER: SYMPHONY NO. 6 IN A MAJOR
Sir Georg Solti cond. Chicago Sym.
Producer: Ray Minshull (London)

53. **BEST OPERA RECORDING**
BERG: LULU (COMPLETE VERSION)
Pierre Boulez cond. Orchestre de l'Opera de Paris; Principal Solos: Stratas, Minton, Mazura, Blankenheim
Producers: Guenther Breest, Michael Horwath (DG)

54. **BEST CHORAL PERFORMANCE, CLASSICAL (OTHER THAN OPERA)**
MOZART: REQUIEM
Carlo Maria Giulini, cond./ Norbert Balatsch, chorus master, Philharmonia Chorus and Orch. (Angel)

55. **BEST CHAMBER MUSIC PERFORMANCE**
MUSIC FOR TWO VIOLINS (MOSZKOWSKI: SUITE FOR TWO VIOLINS/ SHOSTAKOVICH: DUETS/ PROKOFIEV: SONATA FOR TWO VIOLINS)
Itzhak Perlman and Pinchas Zukerman (Angel)

56. BEST CLASSICAL PERFORMANCE, INSTRUMENTAL SOLOIST OR SOLOISTS (WITH ORCHESTRA) (Tie)
BERG: CONCERTO FOR VIOLIN & ORCHESTRA
STRAVINSKY: CONCERTO IN D MAJOR FOR VIOLIN & ORCHESTRA
Itzhak Perlman (Seiji Ozawa cond. Boston Sym.) (DG)

BRAHMS: CONCERTO IN A MINOR FOR VIOLIN & CELLO (DOUBLE CONCERTO)
Itzhak Perlman and Mstislav Rostropovich (Haitink cond. Concertgebouw Orch.) (Angel)

57. BEST CLASSICAL PERFORMANCE, INSTRUMENTAL SOLOIST OR SOLOISTS (WITHOUT ORCHESTRA)
THE SPANISH ALBUM
Itzhak Perlman (Angel)

58. BEST CLASSICAL VOCAL SOLOIST PERFORMANCE
PRIMA DONNA, VOLUME 5— GREAT SOPRANO ARIAS FROM HANDEL TO BRITTEN
Leontyne Price
(Henry Lewis cond. Philharmonia Orch.) (RCA)

59. BEST ENGINEERED RECORDING, CLASSICAL
BERG: LULU (COMPLETE VERSION)
Engineer: Karl-August Naegler (DG)

60. CLASSICAL PRODUCER OF THE YEAR
ROBERT WOODS

24TH ANNUAL (1981) GRAMMY WINNERS
Announced on February 24, 1982
Eligibility Year: October 1, 1980 through September 30, 1981

1. RECORD OF THE YEAR
BETTE DAVIS EYES
Kim Carnes
Producer: Val Garay (EMI-America)

2. ALBUM OF THE YEAR
DOUBLE FANTASY
John Lennon/Yoko Ono
Producers: John Lennon, Yoko Ono, Jack Douglas (Warner Bros./Geffen)

3. SONG OF THE YEAR
BETTE DAVIS EYES
Songwriters: Donna Weiss, Jackie DeShannon

4. BEST NEW ARTIST
SHEENA EASTON (EMI-America)

5. BEST POP VOCAL PERFORMANCE, FEMALE
LENA HORNE—THE LADY AND HER MUSIC LIVE ON BROADWAY (Album)
Lena Horne (QWest/Warner Bros.)

6. **BEST POP VOCAL PERFORMANCE, MALE**
BREAKIN' AWAY (Album)
Al Jarreau (Warner Bros.)

7. **BEST POP PERFORMANCE BY A DUO OR GROUP WITH VOCAL**
BOY FROM NEW YORK CITY (Single)
The Manhattan Transfer (Atlantic)

8. **BEST POP INSTRUMENTAL PERFORMANCE**
THE THEME FROM HILL STREET BLUES (Single)
Mike Post featuring Larry Carlton (Elektra/Asylum)

9. **BEST ROCK VOCAL PERFORMANCE, FEMALE**
FIRE AND ICE (Single)
Pat Benatar (Chrysalis)

10. **BEST ROCK VOCAL PERFORMANCE, MALE**
JESSIE'S GIRL (Single)
Rick Springfield (RCA)

11. **BEST ROCK PERFORMANCE BY A DUO OR GROUP WITH VOCAL**
DON'T STAND SO CLOSE TO ME (Single)
The Police (A&M)

12. **BEST ROCK INSTRUMENTAL PERFORMANCE**
BEHIND MY CAMEL (Track)
The Police (A&M)

13. **BEST R & B VOCAL PERFORMANCE, FEMALE**
HOLD ON I'M COMIN' (Track)
Aretha Franklin (Arista)

14. **BEST R & B VOCAL PERFORMANCE, MALE**
ONE HUNDRED WAYS (Track from Quincy Jones's "The Dude")
James Ingram (A&M)

15. **BEST R & B PERFORMANCE BY A DUO OR GROUP WITH VOCAL**
THE DUDE (Album)
Quincy Jones (A&M)

16. **BEST R & B INSTRUMENTAL PERFORMANCE**
ALL I NEED IS YOU (Single)
David Sanborn (Warner Bros.)

17. **BEST RHYTHM & BLUES SONG**
JUST THE TWO OF US
Songwriters: Bill Withers, William Salter, Ralph MacDonald

18. **BEST JAZZ FUSION PERFORMANCE, VOCAL OR INSTRUMENTAL**
WINELIGHT (Album)
Grover Washington, Jr. (Elektra/Asylum)

19. **BEST COUNTRY VOCAL PERFORMANCE, FEMALE**
9 TO 5 (Single)
Dolly Parton (RCA)

20. **BEST COUNTRY VOCAL PERFORMANCE, MALE**
(THERE'S) NO GETTIN' OVER ME (Single)
Ronnie Milsap (RCA)

21. **BEST COUNTRY PERFORMANCE BY A DUO OR GROUP WITH VOCAL**
ELVIRA (Single)
Oak Ridge Boys (MCA)

22. **BEST COUNTRY INSTRUMENTAL PERFORMANCE**
COUNTRY—AFTER ALL THESE YEARS
Chet Atkins (RCA)

23. **BEST COUNTRY SONG**
9 TO 5
Songwriter: Dolly Parton

24. **BEST GOSPEL PERFORMANCE, CONTEMPORARY OR INSPIRATIONAL**
PRIORITY (Album)
Imperials (Dayspring/Word)

25. **BEST GOSPEL PERFORMANCE, TRADITIONAL**
THE MASTERS V (Album)
J.D. Sumner/James Blackwood/
Hovie Lister/Rosie Rozell/Jake
Hess (Skylite)

26. **BEST SOUL GOSPEL PERFORMANCE, CONTEMPORARY**
DON'T GIVE UP (Album)
Andrae Crouch (Warner Bros.)

27. **BEST SOUL GOSPEL PERFORMANCE, TRADITIONAL**
THE LORD WILL MAKE A WAY (Album)
Al Green (Hi-Myrrh/Word)

28. **BEST INSPIRATIONAL PERFORMANCE**
AMAZING GRACE (Album)
B.J. Thomas (Myrrh/Word)

29. **BEST ETHNIC OR TRADITIONAL RECORDING**
THERE MUST BE A BETTER WORLD SOMEWHERE (Album)
B.B. King (MCA)

30. **BEST LATIN RECORDING**
GUAJIRA PA LA JEVA (Track)
Clare Fischer (Pausa)

31. **BEST RECORDING FOR CHILDREN**
SESAME COUNTRY (Album)
(The Muppets, Glen Campbell,
Crystal Gayle, Loretta Lynn,
Tanya Tucker) Jim Henson,
Muppets creator; Dennis Scott,
album producer (Sesame Street)

32. **BEST COMEDY RECORDING**
REV. DU RITE (Album)
Richard Pryor (Laff)

33. **BEST SPOKEN WORD, DOCUMENTARY, OR DRAMA RECORDING**
DONOVAN'S BRAIN (Album)
Orson Welles (Radiola)

34. **BEST INSTRUMENTAL COMPOSITION**
THEME FROM HILL STREET BLUES
Composer: Mike Post

35. **BEST ALBUM OF ORIGINAL SCORE WRITTEN FOR A MOTION PICTURE OR A TELEVISION SPECIAL**
RAIDERS OF THE LOST ARK
Composer: John Williams
(Columbia)

36. **BEST CAST SHOW ALBUM**
LENA HORNE—THE LADY AND HER MUSIC LIVE ON BROADWAY
Composers & Lyricists: Various
Producer: Quincy Jones (QWest/
Warner Bros.)

37. **VIDEO OF THE YEAR**
MICHAEL NESMITH IN ELEPHANT PARTS
Michael Nesmith (Pacific Arts
Video)

38. **BEST JAZZ VOCAL PERFORMANCE, FEMALE**
DIGITAL III AT MONTREUX (Album)
Ella Fitzgerald (Pablo Live)

39. **BEST JAZZ VOCAL PERFORMANCE, MALE**
BLUE RONDO A LA TURK (Track)
Al Jarreau (Warner Bros.)

40. BEST JAZZ VOCAL PERFORMANCE, DUO OR GROUP
UNTIL I MET YOU (CORNER POCKET) (Track)
The Manhattan Transfer (Atlantic)

41. BEST JAZZ INSTRUMENTAL PERFORMANCE, SOLOIST
BYE BYE BLACKBIRD (Album)
John Coltrane (Pablo)

42. BEST JAZZ INSTRUMENTAL PERFORMANCE, GROUP
CHICK COREA AND GARY BURTON IN CONCERT, ZURICH, OCTOBER 28, 1979 (Album)
Chick Corea and Gary Burton (ECM)

43. BEST JAZZ INSTRUMENTAL PERFORMANCE, BIG BAND
WALK ON THE WATER (Album)
Gerry Mulligan and his Orchestra (DRG)

44. BEST ARRANGEMENT ON AN INSTRUMENTAL RECORDING
VELAS (Quincy Jones)
Arrangers: Quincy Jones, Johnny Mandel (A&M)

45. BEST INSTRUMENTAL ARRANGEMENT ACCOMPANYING VOCAL(S)
AI NO CORRIDA (Quincy Jones)
Arrangers: Quincy Jones, Jerry Hey (A&M)

46. BEST VOCAL ARRANGEMENT FOR TWO OR MORE VOICES
A NIGHTINGALE SANG IN BERKELEY SQUARE (The Manhattan Transfer)
Arranger: Gene Puerling (Atlantic)

47. BEST ALBUM PACKAGE
TATOO YOU (Rolling Stones)
Art Director: Peter Corriston (Rolling Stones/Atlantic)

48. BEST ALBUM NOTES
ERROLL GARNER: MASTER OF THE KEYBOARD
Annotator: Dan Morgenstern (Book-of-the-Month Records)

49. BEST HISTORICAL ALBUM
HOAGY CARMICHAEL: FROM "STAR DUST" TO "OLE BUTTERMILK SKY"
Producers: George Spitzer, Michael Brooks (Book-of-the-Month Records)

50. BEST ENGINEERED RECORDING
GAUCHO (Steely Dan) (Album)
Engineers: Roger Nichols, Elliot Scheiner, Bill Schnee, Jerry Garszva (MCA)

51. PRODUCER OF THE YEAR
QUINCY JONES

52. BEST CLASSICAL ALBUM
MAHLER: SYMPHONY NO. 2 IN C MINOR
Sir Georg Solti cond. Chicago Sym. Orch. Chorus
Producer: James Mallinson (London)

53. BEST CLASSICAL ORCHESTRAL RECORDING
MAHLER: SYMPHONY NO. 2 IN C MINOR
Sir Georg Solti cond. Chicago Sym. Orch. Chorus
Producer: James Mallinson (London)

54. BEST OPERA RECORDING
JANACEK: FROM THE HOUSE OF THE DEAD
Sir Charles Mackerras cond. Vienna Philharmonic; Principal Soloists Jiri Zahradnicek, Vaclaz Zitek, Ivo Zidek
Producer: James Mallinson (London)

55. BEST CHORAL PERFORMANCE (OTHER THAN OPERA)
HAYDN: THE CREATION
Neville Marriner, cond. Chorus of Academy of St. Martin-in-the-Fields & Academy of St. Martin-in-the-Fields (Philips)

56. BEST CHAMBER MUSIC PERFORMANCE
TCHAIKOVSKY: PIANO TRIO IN A MINOR
Itzhak Perlman, Lynn Harrell, Vladimir Ashkenazy (Angel)

57. BEST CLASSICAL PERFORMANCE, INSTRUMENTAL SOLOIST OR SOLOISTS (WITH ORCHESTRA)
ISAAC STERN 60TH ANNIVERSARY CELEBRATION
Isaac Stern, Itzhak Perlman, Pinchas Zukerman (Zubin Mehta cond. New York Philharmonic) (CBS)

58. BEST CLASSICAL PERFORMANCE, INSTRUMENTAL SOLOIST OR SOLOISTS (WITHOUT ORCHESTRA)
THE HOROWITZ CONCERTS 1979/80
Vladimir Horowitz (RCA)

59. BEST CLASSICAL VOCAL SOLOIST PERFORMANCE
LIVE FROM LINCOLN CENTER: SUTHERLAND, HORNE, PAVAROTTI
Joan Sutherland, Marilyn Horne, Luciano Pavarotti (London)

60. BEST ENGINEERED RECORDING, CLASSICAL
ISAAC STERN 60TH ANNIVERSARY CELEBRATION
(Isaac Stern, Itzhak Perlman, Pinchas Zukerman; Zubin Mehta cond. New York Philharmonic)
Engineers: Bud Graham, Ray Moore, Andre Kazdin (CBS)

61. CLASSICAL PRODUCER OF THE YEAR
JAMES MALLINSON

25TH ANNUAL (1982) GRAMMY WINNERS
Announced on February 23, 1983
Eligibility Year: October 1, 1981 through September 30, 1982

1. RECORD OF THE YEAR
ROSANNA
Toto
Producer: Toto (Columbia)

2. ALBUM OF THE YEAR
TOTO IV
Toto
Producer: Toto (Columbia)

3. SONG OF THE YEAR
ALWAYS ON MY MIND
Songwriters: Johnny Christopher, Mark James, Wayne Carson

4. BEST NEW ARTIST
MEN AT WORK (Columbia)

5. BEST POP VOCAL PERFORMANCE, FEMALE
YOU SHOULD HEAR HOW SHE TALKS ABOUT YOU (Single)
Melissa Manchester (Arista)

6. BEST POP VOCAL PERFORMANCE, MALE
TRULY (Single)
Lionel Richie (Motown)

7. **BEST POP PERFORMANCE BY A DUO OR GROUP WITH VOCAL**
UP WHERE WE BELONG (Single)
Joe Cocker & Jennifer Warnes (Island)

8. **BEST POP INSTRUMENTAL PERFORMANCE**
CHARIOTS OF FIRE (THEME) (Dance Version) (Track)
Ernie Watts (QWest/Warner Bros.)

9. **BEST ROCK VOCAL PERFORMANCE, FEMALE**
SHADOWS OF THE NIGHT (Single)
Pat Benatar (Chrysalis)

10. **BEST ROCK VOCAL PERFORMANCE, MALE**
HURTS SO GOOD (Single)
John Cougar (Riva/Polygram)

11. **BEST ROCK PERFORMANCE BY A DUO OR GROUP WITH VOCAL**
EYE OF THE TIGER (Single)
Survivor (Scotti Brothers/CBS)

12. **BEST ROCK INSTRUMENTAL PERFORMANCE**
D.N.A. (Track)
A Flock of Seagulls (Jive/Arista)

13. **BEST R & B VOCAL PERFORMANCE, FEMALE**
AND I AM TELLING YOU I'M NOT GOING (Single)
Jennifer Holliday (Geffen/Warner Bros.)

14. **BEST R & B VOCAL PERFORMANCE, MALE**
SEXUAL HEALING (Single)
Marvin Gaye (Columbia)

15. **BEST R & B PERFORMANCE BY A DUO OR GROUP WITH VOCAL**
LET IT WHIP (Single)
Dazz Band (Motown)
WANNA BE WITH YOU (Single)
Earth, Wind & Fire (ARC/CBS)

16. **BEST R & B INSTRUMENTAL PERFORMANCE**
SEXUAL HEALING (Single) (instrumental version)
Marvin Gaye (Columbia)

17. **BEST RHYTHM & BLUES SONG**
TURN YOUR LOVE AROUND
Songwriters: Jay Graydon, Steve Lukather, Bill Champlin

18. **BEST JAZZ FUSION PERFORMANCE, VOCAL OR INSTRUMENTAL**
OFFRAMP (Album)
Pat Metheny Group (ECM/Warner Bros.)

19. **BEST COUNTRY VOCAL PERFORMANCE, FEMALE**
BREAK IT TO ME GENTLY (Single)
Juice Newton (Capitol)

20. **BEST COUNTRY VOCAL PERFORMANCE, MALE**
ALWAYS ON MY MIND (Single)
Willie Nelson (Columbia)

21. **BEST COUNTRY PERFORMANCE BY A DUO OR GROUP WITH VOCAL**
MOUNTAIN MUSIC (Album)
Alabama (RCA)

22. **BEST COUNTRY INSTRUMENTAL PERFORMANCE**
ALABAMA JUBILEE (Track)
Roy Clark (Churchill)

23. **BEST COUNTRY SONG**
ALWAYS ON MY MIND
Songwriters: Johnny Christopher,
Mark James, Wayne Carson

24. **BEST GOSPEL
PERFORMANCE,
CONTEMPORARY**
AGE TO AGE (Album)
Amy Grant (Myrrh/Word)

25. **BEST GOSPEL
PERFORMANCE,
TRADITIONAL**
I'M FOLLOWING YOU (Album)
Blackwood Brothers (Voice Box)

26. **BEST SOUL GOSPEL
PERFORMANCE,
CONTEMPORARY**
HIGHER PLANE (Album)
Al Green (Myrrh/Word)

27. **BEST SOUL GOSPEL
PERFORMANCE,
TRADITIONAL**
PRECIOUS LORD (Album)
Al Green (Myrrh/Word)

28. **BEST INSPIRATIONAL
PERFORMANCE**
HE SET MY LIFE TO MUSIC
(Album)
Barbara Mandrell (Songbird/
MCA)

29. **BEST TRADITIONAL BLUES
RECORDING**
ALRIGHT AGAIN (Album)
Clarence Gatemouth Brown
(Rounder)

30. **BEST ETHNIC OR
TRADITIONAL FOLK
RECORDING**
QUEEN IDA AND THE BON
TEMPS ZYDECO BAND ON
TOUR (Album)
Queen Ida (GNR/Crescendo)

31. **BEST LATIN RECORDING**
MACHITO AND HIS SALSA
BIG BAND '82 (Album)
Machito (Timeless)

32. **BEST RECORDING FOR
CHILDREN**
IN HARMONY 2 (Album)
Billy Joel, Bruce Springsteen,
James Taylor, Kenny Loggins,
Carly and Lucy Simon, Teddy
Pendergrass, Crystal Gayle, Lou
Rawls, Deniece Williams, Janis
Ian, Dr. John
Producers: Lucy Simon, David
Levine (CBS)

33. **BEST COMEDY RECORDING**
LIVE ON THE SUNSET STRIP
(Album)
Richard Pryor (Warner Bros.)

34. **BEST SPOKEN WORD,
DOCUMENTARY, OR DRAMA
RECORDING**
RAIDERS OF THE LOST ARK:
THE MOVIE ON RECORD
(Album)
Album Producer: Tom Voegeli
(Columbia)

35. **BEST INSTRUMENTAL
COMPOSITION**
FLYING (THEME FROM E.T.
THE EXTRA-TERRESTRIAL)
Composer: John Williams

36. **BEST ALBUM OF ORIGINAL
SCORE WRITTEN FOR A
MOTION PICTURE OR A
TELEVISION SPECIAL**
E.T. THE EXTRA
TERRESTRIAL (MUSIC FROM
THE ORIGINAL MOTION
PICTURE SOUNDTRACK)
Composer: John Williams (MCA)

37. **BEST CAST SHOW ALBUM**
DREAMGIRLS
Composer: Henry Krieger
Lyricist: Tom Eyen
Producer: David Foster (Geffen/
Warner Bros.)

38. **VIDEO OF THE YEAR**
OLIVIA PHYSICAL
Olivia Newton-John (MCA Video)

39. **BEST VOCAL JAZZ PERFORMANCE, FEMALE**
GERSHWIN LIVE! (Album)
Sarah Vaughan (CBS)

40. **BEST JAZZ VOCAL PERFORMANCE, MALE**
AN EVENING WITH GEORGE SHEARING & MEL TORME (Album)
Mel Torme (Concord Jazz)

41. **BEST JAZZ VOCAL PERFORMANCE DUO OR GROUP**
ROUTE 66 (Single)
The Manhattan Transfer (Atlantic)

42. **BEST JAZZ INSTRUMENTAL PERFORMANCE, SOLOIST**
WE WANT MILES (Album)
Miles Davis (Columbia)

43. **BEST JAZZ INSTRUMENTAL PERFORMANCE, GROUP**
"MORE" LIVE (Album)
Miles Davis (Columbia)

44. **BEST JAZZ INSTRUMENTAL PERFORMANCE, BIG BAND**
WARM BREEZE (Album)
Count Basie & His Orchestra (Pablo Today)

45. **BEST ARRANGEMENT ON AN INSTRUMENTAL RECORDING**
FLYING (John Williams)
Arranger: John Williams (MCA)

46. **BEST INSTRUMENTAL ARRANGEMENT ACCOMPANYING VOCAL(S)**
ROSANNA (Toto)
Arrangers: Jerry Hey, David Paich, Jeff Porcaro (Columbia)

47. **BEST VOCAL ARRANGEMENT FOR TWO OR MORE VOICES**
ROSANNA (Toto)
Arranger: David Paich (Columbia)

48. **BEST ALBUM PACKAGE**
GET CLOSER (Linda Ronstadt)
Art Directors: Kosh with Ron Larson (Elektra/Asylum)

49. **BEST ALBUM NOTES**
BUNNY BERIGAN ("GIANTS OF JAZZ") (Bunny Berigan)
Annotators: John Chilton and Richard Sudhalter (Time Life)

50. **BEST HISTORIC ALBUM**
THE TOMMY DORSEY/FRANK SINATRA SESSIONS VOLS. 1, 2 & 3
Producers: Alan Dell, Ethel Gabriel, Don Wardell

51. **BEST ENGINEERED RECORDING**
TOTO (Toto) (Album)
Engineers: Al Schmitt, Tom Knox, Greg Ladanyi, David Leonard (Columbia)

52. **PRODUCER OF THE YEAR**
TOTO

53. **BEST CLASSICAL ALBUM**
BACH: THE GOLDBERG VARIATIONS
Glenn Gould
Producers: Glenn Gould & Samuel Carter (CBS)

54. **BEST CLASSICAL ORCHESTRAL RECORDING**
MAHLER: SYMPHONY NO. 7 IN E MINOR
James Levine cond. Chicago Sym.
Producers: Thomas Z. Shepard, Jay David Saks (RCA)

55. **BEST OPERA RECORDING**
WAGNER: DER RING DES NIBELUNGEN
Pierre Boulez cond. Bayreuth Festival Orch.; Principal Solos: Jones, Altmeyer, Wenkel, Hofmann, Jung, Jerusalem, Zednik, McIntryre, Salminen, Becht
Producer: Andrew Kazdin (Phillips)

56. BEST CHORAL PERFORMANCE (OTHER THAN OPERA)
BERLIOZ: LA DAMNATION DE FAUST
Sir Georg Solti cond. Chicago Sym. Margaret Hillis, choral director, Chicago Sym. Chorus (London)

57. BEST CHAMBER MUSIC PERFORMANCE
BRAHMS: THE SONATAS FOR CLARINET & PIANO OP. 120
Richard Stoltzman & Richard Goode (RCA)

58. BEST CLASSICAL PERFORMANCE, INSTRUMENTAL SOLOIST OR SOLOISTS (WITH ORCHESTRA)
ELGAR: CONCERTO FOR VIOLIN IN B MINOR
Itzhak Perlman (Daniel Barenboim cond. Chicago Sym.) (DG)

59. BEST CLASSICAL PERFORMANCE, INSTRUMENTAL SOLOIST OR SOLOISTS (WITHOUT ORCHESTRA)
BACH: THE GOLDBERG VARIATIONS
Glenn Gould (CBS)

60. BEST CLASSICAL VOCAL SOLOIST PERFORMANCE
LEONTYNE PRICE SINGS VERDI
Leontyne Price (Zubin Mehta cond. Israel Philharmonic Orch.) (London)

61. BEST ENGINEERED RECORDING, CLASSICAL
MAHLER: SYMPHONY NO. 7 IN E MINOR
Engineer: Paul Goodman (RCA)

62. CLASSICAL PRODUCER OF THE YEAR
ROBERT WOODS

26TH ANNUAL (1983) GRAMMY WINNERS
Announced on February 28, 1984
Eligibility Year: October 1, 1982 through September 30, 1983

1. RECORD OF THE YEAR
BEAT IT
Michael Jackson
Producers: Quincy Jones, Michael Jackson (Epic/CBS)

2. ALBUM OF THE YEAR
THRILLER
Michael Jackson
Producer: Quincy Jones (Epic/CBS)

3. NEW SONG OF THE YEAR
EVERY BREATH YOU TAKE
Songwriter: Sting

4. BEST NEW ARTIST
CULTURE CLUB (Epic/CBS)

5. BEST POP VOCAL PERFORMANCE, FEMALE
FLASHDANCE—WHAT A FEELING (Single)
Irene Cara (Casablanca/Polygram)

6. BEST POP VOCAL PERFORMANCE, MALE
THRILLER (Album)
Michael Jackson (Epic/CBS)

7. BEST POP PERFORMANCE BY A DUO OR GROUP WITH VOCAL
EVERY BREATH YOU TAKE (Single)
The Police (A&M)

8. **BEST POP INSTRUMENTAL PERFORMANCE**
BEING WITH YOU (Track)
George Benson (Warner Bros.)

9. **BEST ROCK VOCAL PERFORMANCE, FEMALE**
LOVE IS A BATTLEFIELD (Single)
Pat Benatar (Chrysalis)

10. **BEST ROCK VOCAL PERFORMANCE, MALE**
BEAT IT (Single)
Michael Jackson (Epic/CBS)

11. **BEST ROCK PERFORMANCE BY A DUO OR GROUP WITH VOCAL**
SYNCHRONICITY (Album)
The Police (A&M)

12. **BEST ROCK INSTRUMENTAL PERFORMANCE**
BRIMSTONE & TREACLE (Track)
Sting (A&M)

13. **BEST R & B VOCAL PERFORMANCE, FEMALE**
CHAKA KHAN (Album)
Chaka Khan (Warner Bros.)

14. **BEST R & B VOCAL PERFORMANCE, MALE**
BILLIE JEAN (Single)
Michael Jackson (Epic/CBS)

15. **BEST R & B PERFORMANCE BY A DUO OR GROUP WITH VOCAL**
AIN'T NOBODY (Single)
Rufus & Chaka Khan (Warner Bros.)

16. **BEST R & B INSTRUMENTAL PERFORMANCE**
ROCKIT (Single)
Herbie Hancock (Columbia)

17. **BEST NEW RHYTHM & BLUES SONG**
BILLIE JEAN
Songwriter: Michael Jackson

18. **BEST JAZZ FUSION PERFORMANCE, VOCAL OR INSTRUMENTAL**
TRAVELS (Album)
Pat Metheny Group (ECM/ Warner Bros.)

19. **BEST COUNTRY VOCAL PERFORMANCE, FEMALE**
A LITTLE GOOD NEWS (Single)
Anne Murray (Capitol)

20. **BEST COUNTRY VOCAL PERFORMANCE, MALE**
I.O.U. (Single)
Lee Greenwood (MCA)

21. **BEST COUNTRY PERFORMANCE BY A DUO OR GROUP WITH VOCAL**
THE CLOSER YOU GET (Album)
Alabama (RCA)

22. **BEST COUNTRY INSTRUMENTAL PERFORMANCE**
FIREBALL (Track)
The New South (Ricky Skaggs, Jerry Douglas, Tony Rice, J.D. Crowe, Todd Phillips) (Sugar Hill)

23. **BEST NEW COUNTRY SONG**
STRANGER IN MY HOUSE
Songwriter: Mike Reid

24. **BEST GOSPEL PERFORMANCE, FEMALE**
AGELESS MEDLEY (Single)
Amy Grant (Myrrh/Word)

25. **BEST GOSPEL PERFORMANCE, MALE**
WALLS OF GLASS (Album)
Russ Taff (Myrrh/Word)

26. **BEST GOSPEL PERFORMANCE BY A DUO OR GROUP**
MORE THAN WONDERFUL (Track)
Sandi Patti & Larnelle Harris (Impact/Benson)

27. **BEST SOUL GOSPEL PERFORMANCE, FEMALE**
WE SING PRAISES (Album)
Sandra Crouch (Light/Lexicon)

28. **BEST SOUL GOSPEL PERFORMANCE, MALE**
I'LL RISE AGAIN (Album)
Al Green (Myrrh/Word)

29. **BEST SOUL GOSPEL PERFORMANCE BY A DUO OR GROUP**
I'M SO GLAD I'M STANDING HERE TODAY (Track)
Bobby Jones with Barbara Mandrell (Myrrh/Word)

30. **BEST INSPIRATIONAL PERFORMANCE**
HE'S A REBEL (Track)
Donna Summer (Mercury/Polygram)

31. **BEST LATIN POP PERFORMANCE**
ME ENAMORE (Album)
Jose Feliciano (Profono/TPL)

32. **BEST TROPICAL LATIN PERFORMANCE**
ON BROADWAY (Album)
Tito Puente and His Latin Ensemble (Concord Picante)

33. **BEST MEXICAN/AMERICAN PERFORMANCE**
ANSELMA (Track)
Los Lobos (Slash/Warner Bros.)

34. **BEST TRADITIONAL BLUES RECORDING**
BLUES 'N JAZZ (Album)
B.B. King (MCA)

35. **BEST ETHNIC OR TRADITIONAL FOLK RECORDING**
I'M HERE (Album)
Clifton Chenier and His Red Hot Louisiana Band (Alligator)

36. **BEST RECORDING FOR CHILDREN**
E.T. THE EXTRA-TERRESTRIAL (Album)
Michael Jackson, narration and vocals
Producer: Quincy Jones (MCA)

37. **BEST COMEDY RECORDING**
EDDIE MURPHY COMEDIAN (Album)
Eddie Murphy (The Entertainment Co./Columbia)

38. **BEST SPOKEN WORD OR NON-MUSICAL RECORDING**
COPLAND: LINCOLN PORTRAIT (Album)
William Warfield (Mercury/Phillips)

39. **BEST INSTRUMENTAL COMPOSITION**
LOVE THEME FROM FLASHDANCE
Composer: Giorgio Moroder

40. **BEST ALBUM OF ORIGINAL SCORE WRITTEN FOR A MOTION PICTURE OR A TELEVISION SPECIAL**
FLASHDANCE
Songwriters & Composers:
Giorgio Moroder, Keith Forley, Irene Cara, Shandi Sinnamon, Ronald Magness, Douglas Cotler, Richard Gilbert, Michael Boddicker, Jerry Hey, Phil Ramone, Michael Sembello, Kim Carnes, Duane Hitchings, Craig Krampf, Dennis Matkosky (Casablanca/Polygram)

41. **BEST CAST SHOW ALBUM**
CATS (COMPLETE ORIGINAL BROADWAY CAST RECORDING)
Producer: Andrew Lloyd Webber (Geffen/Warner Bros.)

42. **BEST VIDEO, SHORT FORM**
GIRLS ON FILM/HUNGRY
LIKE THE WOLF
Duran Duran (Picture Music
International/Sony)

43. **BEST VIDEO ALBUM**
DURAN DURAN
Duran Duran (Picture Music
International/Thorne EMI/
Pioneer Artists)

44. **BEST JAZZ VOCAL
PERFORMANCE, FEMALE**
THE BEST IS YET TO COME
(Album)
Ella Fitzgerald (Pablo Today)

45. **BEST JAZZ VOCAL
PERFORMANCE, MALE**
TOP DRAWER (Album)
Mel Torme (Concord Jazz)

46. **BEST JAZZ VOCAL
PERFORMANCE, DUO OR
GROUP**
WHY NOT! (Track)
The Manhattan Transfer
(Atlantic)

47. **BEST JAZZ INSTRUMENTAL
PERFORMANCE, SOLOIST**
THINK OF ONE (Album)
Wynton Marsalis (Columbia)

48. **BEST JAZZ INSTRUMENTAL
PERFORMANCE, GROUP**
AT THE VANGUARD (Album)
The Phil Woods Quartet
(Antilles/Island)

49. **BEST JAZZ INSTRUMENTAL
PERFORMANCE, BIG BAND**
ALL IN GOOD TIME (Album)
Rob McConnell and the Boss
Brass (Dark Orchid)

50. **BEST ARRANGEMENT ON
AN INSTRUMENTAL**
SUMMER SKETCHES '82
(Dave Grusin & N.Y./L.A.
Dream Band)
Arranger: Dave Grusin (GRP)

51. **BEST INSTRUMENTAL
ARRANGEMENT
ACCOMPANYING VOCAL(S)**
WHAT'S NEW (Linda Ronstadt)
Arranger: Nelson Riddle
(Asylum/EA)

52. **BEST VOCAL
ARRANGEMENT FOR TWO
OR MORE VOICES**
BE BOP MEDLEY (Chaka
Khan)
Vocal Arrangers: Arif Mardin,
Chaka Khan (Warner Bros.)

53. **BEST ALBUM PACKAGE**
SPEAKING IN TONGUES
(Talking Heads)
Art Director: Robert
Rauschenberg (Sire/Warner
Bros.)

54. **BEST ALBUM NOTES**
THE "INTERPLAY" SESSIONS
(Bill Evans)
Annotator: Orrin Keepnews
(Milestone)

55. **BEST HISTORICAL ALBUM**
THE GREATEST
RECORDINGS OF ARTURO
TOSCANINI, SYMPHONIES
VOL. 1 (Arturo Toscanini)
Producers: Stanley Walker, Allan
Steckler (Franklin Mint)

56. **BEST ENGINEERED
RECORDING (Non-Classical)**
THRILLER (Michael Jackson)
(Album)
Engineer: Bruce Swedien (Epic/
CBS)

57. **PRODUCER OF THE YEAR
(Non-Classical)**
QUINCY JONES & MICHAEL
JACKSON

58. **BEST CLASSICAL ALBUM**
MAHLER: SYMPHONY NO 9
IN D MAJOR
Sir Georg Solti cond. Chicago
Sym. Orch. & Chorus
Producer: James Mallinson
(Londton)

59. **BEST CLASSICAL ORCHESTRAL RECORDING**
MAHLER: SYMPHONY NO 9 IN D MAJOR
Sir Georg Solti cond. Chicago Sym.
Producer: James Mallinson (London)

60. **BEST OPERA RECORDING (TIE)**
MOZART: LE NOZZI DE FIGARO
Sir Georg Solti cond. London Philharmonic; Principal Solos: Kanawa, Popp, Ramey, Allen, Moll, von Stade
Producer: Christopher Raeburn (London)

VERDI: LA TRAVIATA (Original Soundtrack)
James Levine cond. Metropolitan Opera Orch. & Chorus; Principal Solos: Stratas, Domingo, MacNeil
Producers: Max Wilcox, Jay David Saks (Elektra)

61. **BEST CHORAL PERFORMANCE (OTHER THAN OPERA)**
HAYDN: THE CREATION
Sir Georg Solti cond. Chicago Sym. Orch.; Margaret Hillis, choral director, Chicago Sym. Chorus (London)

62. **BEST CHAMBER MUSIC PERFORMANCE**
BRAHMS: SONATA FOR CELLO & PIANO IN E MINOR, OP. 38 & SONATA IN F MAJOR, OP. 99
Mstislav Rostropovich and Rudolf Serkin (DG)

63. **BEST CLASSICAL PERFORMANCE, INSTRUMENTAL SOLOIST OR SOLOISTS (WITH ORCHESTRA)**
HAYDN: CONCERTO FOR TRUMPET & ORCHESTRA IN E-FLAT MAJOR/L. MOZART: CONCERTO FOR TRUMPET & ORCHESTRA IN D MAJOR/ HUMMEL: CONCERTO FOR TRUMPET & ORCHESTRA IN E-FLAT MAJOR
Wynton Marsalis (Raymond Leppard cond. National Philharmonic) (CBS)

64. **BEST CLASSICAL PERFORMANCE, INSTRUMENTAL SOLOIST OR SOLOISTS (WITHOUT ORCHESTRA)**
BEETHOVEN: SONATA FOR PIANO NO. 12 IN A-FLAT MAJOR, OP. 26 & NO. 13 IN E-FLAT MAJOR, OP. 27. NO. 1
Glenn Gould (CBS)

65. **BEST CLASSICAL VOCAL SOLOIST PERFORMANCE**
LEONTYNE PRICE & MARILYN HORNE IN CONCERT AT THE MET
Leontyne Price & Marilyn Horne (James Levine cond. the Metropolitan Opera Orch.) (RCA)

66. **BEST ENGINEERED RECORDING, CLASSICAL**
MAHLER: SYMPHONY NO. 9 IN D MAJOR
Sir Georg Solti cond. Chicago Sym. Orch. & Chorus
Engineer: James Lock (London)

67. **CLASSICAL PRODUCER OF THE YEAR**
MARC J. AUBORT AND JOANNA NICKRENZ

27TH ANNUAL (1984) GRAMMY WINNERS
Announced on February 26, 1985
Eligibility Year: October 1, 1983 through September 30, 1984

1. **RECORD OF THE YEAR**
WHAT'S LOVE GOT TO DO
WITH IT
Tina Turner
Producer: Terry Britten (Capitol)

2. **ALBUM OF THE YEAR**
CAN'T SLOW DOWN
Lionel Richie
Producers: Lionel Richie and
James Anthony Carmichael
(Motown)

3. **SONG OF THE YEAR**
WHAT'S LOVE GOT TO DO
WITH IT
Songwriters: Graham Lyle and
Terry Britten

4. **BEST NEW ARTIST**
CYNDI LAUPER (Portrait/CBS)

5. **BEST POP VOCAL
PERFORMANCE, FEMALE**
WHAT'S LOVE GOT TO DO
WITH IT (Single)
Tina Turner (Capitol)

6. **BEST POP VOCAL
PERFORMANCE, MALE**
AGAINST ALL ODDS (TAKE A
LOOK AT ME NOW) (Single)
Phil Collins (Atlantic)

7. **BEST POP PERFORMANCE
BY A DUO OR GROUP WITH
VOCAL**
JUMP (FOR MY LOVE) (Single)
Pointer Sisters (Planet/RCA)

8. **BEST POP INSTRUMENTAL
PERFORMANCE**
GHOSTBUSTERS (instrumental
version) (Track from
"Ghostbusters")
Ray Parker Jr. (Arista)

9. **BEST ROCK VOCAL
PERFORMANCE, FEMALE**
BETTER BE GOOD TO ME
(Single)
Tina Turner (Capitol)

10. **BEST ROCK VOCAL
PERFORMANCE, MALE**
DANCING IN THE DARK
(single)
Bruce Springsteen (Columbia)

11. **BEST ROCK PERFORMANCE
BY A DUO OR GROUP WITH
VOCAL**
PURPLE RAIN—MUSIC FROM
THE MOTION PICTURE
(Album)
Prince and the Revolution
(Warner Bros.)

12. **BEST ROCK INSTRUMENTAL
PERFORMANCE**
CINEMA (Track from "90125")
Yes (Atco/Atlantic)

13. **BEST R & B VOCAL
PERFORMANCE, FEMALE**
I FEEL FOR YOU (Single)
Chaka Khan (Warner Bros.)

14. **BEST R & B VOCAL
PERFORMANCE, MALE**
CARIBBEAN QUEEN (NO
MORE LOVE ON THE RUN)
(Single)
Billy Ocean (Jive/Arista)

15. **BEST R & B PERFORMANCE
BY A DUO OR GROUP WITH
VOCAL**
YAH MO B THERE (Single)
James Ingram and Michael
McDonald (QWest/Warner Bros.)

16. **BEST R & B INSTRUMENTAL PERFORMANCE**
SOUND-SYSTEM (Album)
Herbie Hancock (Columbia)

17. **BEST NEW RHYTHM & BLUES SONG**
I FEEL FOR YOU
Songwriter: Prince

18. **BEST JAZZ FUSION PERFORMANCE, VOCAL OR INSTRUMENTAL**
FIRST CIRCLE (Album)
Pat Metheny Group (ECM/Warner Bros.)

19. **BEST COUNTRY VOCAL PERFORMANCE, FEMALE**
IN MY DREAMS (Single)
Emmylou Harris (Warner Bros.)

20. **BEST COUNTRY VOCAL PERFORMANCE, MALE**
THAT'S THE WAY LOVE GOES (Single)
Merle Haggard (Epic/CBS)

21. **BEST COUNTRY PERFORMANCE BY A DUO OR GROUP WITH VOCAL**
MAMA HE'S CRAZY (Single)
The Judds (RCA)

22. **BEST COUNTRY INSTRUMENTAL PERFORMANCE**
WHEEL HOSS (Track from "Country Boy")
Ricky Skaggs (Columbia)

23. **BEST COUNTRY SONG**
CITY OF NEW ORLEANS
Songwriter: Steve Goodman

24. **BEST GOSPEL PERFORMANCE, FEMALE**
ANGELS (Track from "Straight Ahead")
Amy Grant (Myrrh/Word)

25. **BEST GOSPEL PERFORMANCE, MALE**
MICHAEL W. SMITH (Album)
Michael W. Smith (Reunion/Word)

26. **BEST GOSPEL PERFORMANCE BY A DUO OR GROUP**
KEEP THE FLAME BURNING (Track from Debby Boone "Surrender")
Debby Boone and Phil Driscoll (Lamb & Lion/Sparrow)

27. **BEST SOUL GOSPEL PERFORMANCE, FEMALE**
SAILIN' (Album)
Shirley Caesar (Myrrh/Word)

28. **BEST SOUL GOSPEL PERFORMANCE, MALE**
ALWAYS REMEMBER (Track from "No Time to Lose")
Andrae Crouch (Light/Lexicon)

29. **BEST SOUL GOSPEL PERFORMANCE BY A DUO OR GROUP**
SAILIN' ON THE SEA OF YOUR LOVE (Track from Shirley Caesar "Sailin")
Shirley Caesar and Al Green (Myrrh/Word)

30. **BEST INSPIRATIONAL PERFORMANCE**
FORGIVE ME (Track from "Cats Without Claws")
Donna Summer (Geffen/Warner Bros.)

31. **BEST LATIN POP PERFORMANCE**
ALWAYS IN MY HEART (SIEMPRE EN MI CORAZON) (Album)
Placido Domingo (CBS Masterworks)

32. **BEST TROPICAL LATIN PERFORMANCE**
PALO PA RUMBA (Album)
Eddie Palmieri (Musica Latina)

33. **BEST MEXICAN/AMERICAN PERFORMANCE**
ME GUSTAS TAL COMO ERES (Single)
Sheena Easton and Luis Miguel (Top Hits)

34. **BEST TRADITIONAL BLUES RECORDING**
BLUES EXPLOSION (Album)
John Hammond, Stevie Ray Vaughan & Double Trouble, Sugar Blue, Koko Taylor & The Blues Machine, Luther "Guitar Junior" Johnson, J.B. Hutto & The New Hawks (Atlantic)

35. **BEST ETHNIC OR TRADITIONAL FOLK RECORDING**
ELIZABETH COTTEN LIVE! (Album)
Elizabeth Cotten (Arhoolie)

36. **BEST REGGAE RECORDING**
ANTHEM (Album)
Black Uhuru (Island)

37. **BEST RECORDING FOR CHILDREN**
WHERE THE SIDEWALK ENDS (Album)
Shel Silverstein
Album Producer: Ron Haffkine (Columbia)

38. **BEST COMEDY RECORDING**
EAT IT (Track from "Weird Al Yankovic in 3-D")
"Weird Al" Yankovic (Rock N Roll)

39. **BEST SPOKEN WORD OR NON-MUSICAL RECORDING**
THE WORDS OF GANDHI (Album)
Ben Kingsley (Caedmon)

40. **BEST INSTRUMENTAL COMPOSITION (Tie)**
THE NATURAL (Track from "The Natural")
Composer: Randy Newman (Warner Bros.)

OLYMPIC FANFARE AND THEME (Track from "The Official Music of the XXIIIrd Olympiad at Los Angeles")
Composer: John Williams (Columbia)

41. **BEST ALBUM OF ORIGINAL SCORE WRITTEN FOR A MOTION PICTURE OR A TELEVISION SPECIAL**
PURPLE RAIN
Songwriters: Prince, John L. Nelson, Lisa & Wendy (Warner Bros.)

42. **BEST CAST SHOW ALBUM**
SUNDAY IN THE PARK WITH GEORGE
Composer & Lyricist: Stephen Sondheim
Producer: Thomas Z. Shepard (RCA)

43. **BEST VIDEO, SHORT FORM**
DAVID BOWIE (Beta)
David Bowie (Sony/Picture Music)

44. **BEST VIDEO ALBUM**
MAKING MICHAEL JACKSON'S THRILLER (VHS)
Michael Jackson (Vestron Music Video)

45. **BEST JAZZ VOCAL PERFORMANCE**
NOTHIN' BUT THE BLUES (Album)
Joe Williams (Delos)

(Jazz Vocal Categories 45, 46, 47 were combined)

48. **BEST JAZZ INSTRUMENTAL PERFORMANCE, SOLOIST**
HOT HOUSE FLOWERS (Album)
Wynton Marsalis (Columbia)

49. **BEST JAZZ INSTRUMENTAL PERFORMANCE, GROUP**
NEW YORK SCENE (Track)
Art Blakey (Concord Jazz)

50. **BEST JAZZ INSTRUMENTAL PERFORMANCE, BIG BAND**
88 BASIE STREET (Album)
Count Basie and His Orchestra (Pablo)

51. **BEST ARRANGEMENTS ON AN INSTRUMENTAL**
GRACE (GYMNASTICS THEME) (Quincy Jones) (Track from "Official Music of XXIIIrd Olympiad in Los Angeles")
Arrangers: Quincy Jones and Jeremy Lubbock (Columbia)

52. **BEST INSTRUMENTAL ARRANGEMENT ACCOMPANYING VOCAL(S)**
HARD HABIT TO BREAK (Chicago) (Single)
Arrangers: David Frost and Jeremy Lubbock (Full Moon/ Warner Bros.)

53. **BEST VOCAL ARRANGEMENT FOR TWO OR MORE VOICES**
AUTOMATIC (Pointer Sisters) (Track from "Break Out")
Arrangers: Pointer Sisters (Planet/RCA)

54. **BEST ALBUM PACKAGE**
SHE'S SO UNUSUAL (Cyndi Lauper)
Art Director: Janet Perr (Portrait/ CBS)

55. **BEST ALBUM NOTES**
BIG BAND JAZZ (Paul Whiteman, Fletcher Henderson, Chick Webb, Tommy Dorsey, Count Basie, Benny Goodman and Others)
Annotators: Gunther Schuller, ·Martin Williams (Smithsonian)

56. **BEST HISTORICAL ALBUM**
BIG BAND JAZZ (Paul Whiteman, Fletcher Henderson, Chick Webb, Tommy Dorsey, Count Basie, Benny Goodman and others)
Producer: J.R. Taylor (Smithsonian)

57. **BEST ENGINEERED RECORDING (Non-Classical)**
17 (Chicago) (Album)
Engineer: Humberto Gatica (FullMoon/Warner Bros.)

58. **PRODUCER OF THE YEAR (Non-Classical) (Tie)**
DAVID FOSTER

LIONEL RICHIE and JAMES ANTHONY CARMICHAEL

59. **BEST CLASSICAL ALBUM**
AMADEUS (Original Soundtrack)
Neville Marriner cond. the Academy of St. Martin-in-the-Fields/Ambrosian Opera Chorus. Choristers of Westminster Abbey/Soloists
Producer: John Strauss (Fantasy)

60. **BEST CLASSICAL ORCHESTRAL RECORDING**
PROKOFIEV: SYMPHONY NO. 5 IN B FLAT, OP. 100
Leonard Slatkin cond. the Saint Louis Symphony
Producer: Jay David Saks (RCA)

61. **BEST OPERA RECORDING**
BIZET: CARMEN (Original
Soundtrack)
Lorin Maazel cond. Orchestre
National de France/Choeurs et
Maitrise de Radio France/
Principal Soloists: Julia Migenes
Johnson, Faith Esham, Placido
Domingo, Ruggero Raimondi
Producer: Michel Glotz (Erato)

62. **BEST CHORAL
PERFORMANCE (OTHER
THAN OPERA)**
BRAHMS: A GERMAN
REQUIEM
James Levine cond. Chicago
Sym. Orch.; Margaret Hillis,
choral director of the Chicago
Sym. Chorus (RCA)

63. **BEST CLASSICAL
PERFORMANCE,
INSTRUMENTAL SOLOIST
OR SOLOISTS (WITH
ORCHESTRA)**
WYNTON MARSALIS, EDITA
GRUBEROVA: HANDEL,
PURCELL, TORELLI, FASCH,
MOLTER
Wynton Marsalis (Raymond
Leppard conducting the English
Chamber Orchestra) (CBS
Masterworks)

64. **BEST CLASSICAL
PERFORMANCE,
INSTRUMENTAL SOLOIST
OR SOLOISTS (WITHOUT
ORCHESTRA)**
BACH: THE
UNACCOMPANIED CELLO
SUITES
Yo-Yo Ma (CBS Masterworks)

65. **BEST CHAMBER MUSIC
PERFORMANCE**
BEETHOVEN THE LATE
STRING QUARTETS
The Juilliard String Quartet (CBS
Masterworks)

66. **BEST CLASSICAL VOCAL
SOLIST PERFORMANCE**
RAVEL: SONGS OF MAURICE
RAVEL
Jessye Norman, Jose Van Dam,
Heather Harper (Pierre Boulez
conducting the Members of
Ensemble Intercomtemporian &
BBC Sym. Orch.) (CBS
Masterworks)

67. **BEST NEW CLASSICAL
COMPOSITION**
ANTONY AND CLEOPATRA
Composer: Samuel Barber (New
World)

68. **BEST ENGINEERED
RECORDING, CLASSICAL**
PROKOFIEV: SYMPHONY NO.
5 IN B FLAT, OP 100 (Leonard
Slatkin cond. the Saint Louis
Symphony)
Engineer: Paul Goodman (RCA)

69. **CLASSICAL PRODUCER OF
THE YEAR**
STEVEN EPSTEIN

28TH ANNUAL (1985) GRAMMY WINNERS
Announced on February 25, 1986
Eligibility Year: October 1, 1984 through September 30, 1985

1. **RECORD OF THE YEAR**
   WE ARE THE WORLD
   USA For Africa
   Producer: Quincy Jones
   (Columbia/CBS)

2. **ALBUM OF THE YEAR**
   NO JACKET REQUIRED
   Phil Collins
   Producers: Phil Collins, Hugh
   Padgham (Atlantic)

3. **SONG OF THE YEAR**
   WE ARE THE WORLD
   Songwriters: Michael Jackson,
   Lionel Richie

4. **BEST NEW ARTIST**
   SADE (Portrait/CBS)

5. **BEST POP VOCAL
   PERFORMANCE, FEMALE**
   SAVING ALL MY LOVE FOR
   YOU (Single)
   Whitney Houston (Arista)

6. **BEST POP VOCAL
   PERFORMANCE, MALE**
   NO JACKET REQUIRED
   (Album)
   Phil Collins (Atlantic)

7. **BEST POP PERFORMANCE
   BY A DUO OR GROUP WITH
   VOCAL**
   WE ARE THE WORLD (Single)
   USA for Africa (Columbia/CBS)

8. **BEST POP INSTRUMENTAL
   PERFORMANCE**
   MIAMI VICE THEME (Single)
   Jan Hammer (MCA)

9. **BEST ROCK VOCAL
   PERFORMANCE, FEMALE**
   ONE OF THE LIVING
   Tina Turner (Capitol)

10. **BEST ROCK VOCAL
    PERFORMANCE, MALE**
    THE BOYS OF SUMMER
    (Single)
    Don Henley (Geffen)

11. **BEST ROCK PERFORMANCE
    BY A DUO OR GROUP WITH
    VOCAL**
    MONEY FOR NOTHING
    (Single)
    Dire Straits (Warner Bros)

12. **BEST ROCK INSTRUMENTAL
    PERFORMANCE**
    ESCAPE (Track from "Flash")
    Jeff Beck (Epic/CBS)

13. **BEST R & B VOCAL
    PERFORMANCE, FEMALE**
    FREEWAY OF LOVE (Single)
    Aretha Franklin (Arista)

14. **BEST R & B VOCAL
    PERFORMANCE, MALE**
    IN SQUARE CIRCLE (Album)
    Stevie Wonder (Tamla/Motown)

15. **BEST R & B PERFORMANCE
    BY A DUO OR GROUP WITH
    VOCAL**
    NIGHTSHIFT (Single)
    Commodores (Gordy/Motown)

16. **BEST R & B INSTRUMENTAL
    PERFORMANCE**
    MUSICIAN (Album)
    Ernie Watts (Quest)

17. **BEST RHYTHM & BLUES
    SONG**
    FREEWAY OF LOVE
    Songwriters: Narada Michael
    Walden, Jeffrey Cohen

18. **BEST JAZZ FUSION PERFORMANCE, VOCAL OR INSTRUMENTAL**
STRAIGHT TO THE HEART (Album)
David Sanborn (Warner Bros.)

19. **BEST JAZZ VOCAL PERFORMANCE, FEMALE**
CLEO AT CARNEGIE (THE 10TH ANNIVERSARY CONCERT) (Album)
Cleo Lane (DRG)

20. **BEST JAZZ VOCAL PERFORMANCE, MALE**
ANOTHER NIGHT IN TUNISIA (Track from "Vocalese")
Jon Hendricks & Bobby McFerrin (Atlantic)

21. **BEST JAZZ VOCAL PERFORMANCE, DUO OR GROUP**
VOCALESE (Album)
The Manhattan Transfer (Atlantic)

22. **BEST JAZZ INSTRUMENTAL PERFORMANCE, SOLOIST**
BLACK CODES FROM THE UNDERGROUND (Album)
Wynton Marsalis (Columbia/CBS)

23. **BEST JAZZ INSTRUMENTAL PERFORMANCE, GROUP**
BLACK CODES FROM THE UNDERGROUND (Album)
Wynton Marsalis Group (Columbia/CBS)

24. **BEST JAZZ INSTRUMENTAL PERFORMANCE, BIG BAND**
THE COTTON CLUB/ ORIGINAL MOTION PICTURE SOUNDTRACK (Album)
John Barry & Bob Wilber (Geffen)

25. **BEST COUNTRY VOCAL PERFORMANCE, FEMALE**
I DON'T KNOW WHY YOU DON'T WANT ME (Single)
Rosanne Cash (CBS)

26. **BEST COUNTRY VOCAL PERFORMANCE, MALE**
LOST IN THE FIFTIES TONIGHT (IN THE STILL OF THE NIGHT) (Single)
Ronnie Milsap (RCA)

27. **BEST COUNTRY PERFORMANCE BY A DUO OR GROUP WITH VOCAL**
WHY NOT ME (Album)
The Judds (RCA)

28. **BEST COUNTRY INSTRUMENTAL PERFORMANCE**
COSMIC SQUARE DANCE (Track from "Stay Tuned")
Chet Atkins & Mark Knopfler (Columbia/CBS)

29. **BEST COUNTRY SONG**
HIGHWAYMAN
Songwriter: Jimmy L. Webb

30. **BEST GOSPEL PERFORMANCE, FEMALE**
UNGUARDED (Album)
Amy Grant (Myrrh/Word)

31. **BEST GOSPEL PERFORMANCE, MALE**
HOW EXCELLENT IS THY NAME (Track from "I've Just Seen Jesus")
Larnelle Harris (Impact/Benson)

32. **BEST GOSPEL PERFORMANCE BY A DUO OR GROUP**
I'VE JUST SEEN JESUS (Track from "I've Just Seen Jesus")
Larnelle Harris & Sandi Patti (Impact/Benson)

33. **BEST SOUL GOSPEL PERFORMANCE, FEMALE**
MARTIN (Single)
Shirley Caesar (Rejoice/Word)

34. **BEST SOUL GOSPEL PERFORMANCE, MALE**
BRING BACK THE DAYS OF YEA AND NAY (Track from "Tomorrow")
Marvin Winans (Light)

35. **BEST SOUL GOSPEL PERFORMANCE BY A DUO OR GROUP**
TOMORROW (Album)
The Winans (Light)

36. **BEST INSPIRATIONAL PERFORMANCE**
COME SUNDAY (Track from "Say You Love Me")
Jennifer Holliday (Geffen)

37. **BEST LATIN PERFORMANCE**
ES FACIL AMAR (Album)
Lani Hall (A&M)

38. **BEST TROPICAL LATIN PERFORMANCE (Tie)**
MAMBO DIABLO (Album)
Tito Puente and His Latin Ensemble (Concord Jazz)

SOLITO (Album)
Eddie Palmieri (Musica Latina Int'l)

39. **BEST MEXICAN/AMERICAN PERFORMANCE**
SIMPLEMENTE MUJER (Album)
Vikki Carr (Discos CBS Int'l)

40. **BEST TRADITIONAL BLUES RECORDING**
MY GUITAR SINGS THE BLUES (Track from "Six Silver Strings")
B.B. King (MCA)

41. **BEST ETHNIC OR TRADITIONAL FOLK RECORDING**
MY TOOT TOOT (Single)
Rockin Sidney (Maison De Soul)

42. **BEST POLKA RECORDING**
70 YEARS OF HITS (Album)
Frank Yankovic (Cleveland Int'l/CBS)

43. **BEST REGGAE RECORDING**
CLIFF HANGER (Album)
Jimmy Cliff (Columbia/CBS)

44. **BEST RECORDING FOR CHILDREN**
FOLLOW THAT BIRD (THE ORIGINAL MOTION PICTURE SOUNDTRACK) (Jim Henson's Muppets and the Sesame Street Cast)
Muppets Creator: Jim Henson
Producer: Steve Buckingham (RCA)

45. **BEST COMEDY RECORDING**
WHOOPI GOLDBERG (ORIGINAL BROADWAY SHOW RECORDING) (Album)
Whoopi Goldberg (Geffen)

46. **BEST SPOKEN WORD OR NON-MUSICAL RECORDING**
MA RAINEY'S BLACK BOTTOM (Original Broadway Cast)
Producer: Mike Berniker (Manhattan)

47. **BEST MUSIC VIDEO, SHORT FORM**
WE ARE THE WORLD—THE VIDEO EVENT (VHS) (Beta) (USA For Africa)
Video Director: Tom Tribovich
Record Producer: Quincy Jones (RCA/Columbia Pictures Home Video)

48. **BEST MUSIC VIDEO, LONG FORM**
HUEY LEWIS AND THE NEWS: THE HEART OF ROCK 'N' ROLL
(VHS) (Beta)
Huey Lewis and the News
Video Director: Bruce Gowers
(Warner Home Video)

49. **BEST INSTRUMENTAL COMPOSITION**
MIAMI VICE THEME
Composer: Jan Hammer (MCA)

50. **BEST ALBUM OF ORIGINAL SCORE WRITTEN FOR A MOTION PICTURE OR TELEVISION SPECIAL**
BEVERLY HILLS COP
Composers & Songwriters: Sharon Robinson, Jon Gilutin, Bunny Hull, Hawk, Howard Hewett, Micki Free, Sue Sheridan, Howie Rice, Keith Forsey, Harold Faltermeyer, Allee Willis, Dan Sembello, Marc Benno, Richard Theisen (MCA)

51. **BEST CAST SHOW ALBUM**
WEST SIDE STORY
Producer: John McClure (D.G.)

52. **BEST ARRANGEMENT ON AN INSTRUMENTAL**
EARLY A.M. ATTITUDE (Track from "Harlequin") (Dave Grusin and Lee Ritenour)
Arrangers: Dave Grusin, Lee Ritenour (GRP)

53. **INSTRUMENTAL ARRANGEMENT ACCOMPANYING VOCAL(S)**
LUSH LIFE (Track from "Lush Life") (Linda Ronstadt)
Arranger: Nelson Riddle (Asylum)

54. **BEST VOCAL ARRANGEMENT FOR TWO OR MORE VOICES**
ANOTHER NIGHT IN TUNISIA (Single)
(The Manhattan Transfer)
Arrangers: Cheryl Bentyne, Bobby McFerrin (Atlantic)

55. **BEST ALBUM PACKAGE**
LUSH LIFE (Linda Ronstadt)
Art Director: Kosh, Ron Larson (Asylum)

56. **BEST ALBUM NOTES**
SAM COOKE LIVE AT THE HARLEM SQUARE CLUB, 1963 (Sam Cooke)
Album Notes Writer: Peter Guralnick (RCA)

57. **BEST HISTORICAL ALBUM**
RCA/MET—100 SINGERS—100 YEARS
(From Melba, Schumann-Heink, Caruso through Price, Verrett, Domingo and 94 others)
Producer: John Pfeiffer (RCA Red Seal)

58. **BEST ENGINEERED RECORDING (Non-Classical)**
BROTHERS IN ARMS (Album) (Dire Straits)
Engineer: Neil Dorfsman (Warner Bros.)

59. **PRODUCER OF THE YEAR (Non-Classical)**
Phil Collins & Hugh Padgham

60. **BEST CLASSICAL ALBUM**
BERLIOZ: REQUIEM
Robert Shaw cond. the Atlanta Sym. Orch. & Chorus/John Aler
Producer: Robert E. Woods (Telarc)

61. **BEST CLASSICAL ORCHESTRAL RECORDING**
FAURE: PELLEAS ET MELISANDE
Robert Shaw cond. the Atlanta Sym. Orch.
Album Producer: Robert E. Woods (Telarc)

62. **BEST OPERA RECORDING**
SCHOENBERG: MOSES UND ARON
Sir Georg Solti cond. Chicago Sym. Orch. & Chorus; Principal Soloists: Franz Mazura, Philip Langridge
Producer: James Mallinson (London)

63. **BEST CHORAL PERFORMANCE (OTHER THAN OPERA)**
BERLIOZ: REQUIEM
Robert Shaw cond. Atlanta Sym. Orch. & Chorus (Telarc)

64. **BEST CLASSICAL PERFORMANCE, INSTRUMENTAL SOLOIST OR SOLOISTS (WITH ORCHESTRA)**
ELGAR: CELLO CONCERTO OP. 85/WALTON: CONCERTO FOR CELLO & ORCHESTRA
Yo-Yo Ma
(Andre Previn cond. London Sym. Orch.) (CBS Masterworks)

65. **BEST CLASSICAL PERFORMANCE, INSTRUMENTAL SOLOIST OR SOLOISTS (WITHOUT ORCHESTRA)**
RAVEL: GASPARD DE LA NUIT, PAVANE POUR UNE INFANTE DEFUNTE, VALSES NOBLES ET SENTIMENTALES
Vladimir Ashkenazy (London)

66. **BEST CHAMBER MUSIC PERFORMANCE**
BRAHMS: CELLO AND PIANO SONATAS IN E MINOR & F MAJOR
Emanuel Ax & Yo-Yo Ma (RCA)

67. **BEST CLASSICAL VOCAL SOLOIST PERFORMANCE**
BERLIOZ: REQUIEM
John Aler
(Robert Shaw cond. Atlanta Sym. Orch. & Chorus (Telarc)

68. **BEST NEW CLASSICAL ARTIST**
Chicago Pro Musica (Reference)

69. **BEST CONTEMPORARY COMPOSITION**
LLOYD WEBBER: REQUIEM
Composer: Andrew Lloyd Webber (Angel)

70. **BEST ENGINEERED RECORDING, CLASSICAL**
BERLIOZ: REQUIEM
(Robert Shaw cond. Atlanta Sym. Orch. & Chorus/John Aler)
Engineer: Jack Renner (Telarc)

71. **CLASSICAL PRODUCER OF THE YEAR**
ROBERT WOODS

29TH ANNUAL (1986) GRAMMY WINNERS
Announced on February 24, 1987
Eligibility Year: October 1, 1985 through September 30, 1986

1. **RECORD OF THE YEAR**
HIGHER LOVE
Steve Winwood
Producers: Russ Titelman, Steve
Winwood (Island)

2. **ALBUM OF THE YEAR**
GRACELAND
Paul Simon
Producer: Paul Simon (Warner
Bros.)

3. **SONG OF THE YEAR**
THAT'S WHAT FRIENDS ARE
FOR
Dionne & Friends featuring
Elton John, Gladys Knight, and
Stevie Wonder
Songwriters: Burt Bacharach &
Carole Bayer Sager

4. **BEST NEW ARTIST**
BRUCE HORNSBY AND THE
RANGE (RCA)

5. **BEST POP VOCAL
PERFORMANCE, FEMALE**
THE BROADWAY ALBUM
(Album)
Barbra Streisand (Columbia/CBS)

6. **BEST POP VOCAL
PERFORMANCE, MALE**
HIGHER LOVE (Single)
Steve Winwood (Island)

7. **BEST POP PERFORMANCE
BY A DUO OR GROUP WITH
VOCAL**
THAT'S WHAT FRIENDS ARE
FOR (Single)
Dionne & Friends featuring
Elton John, Gladys Knight, and
Stevie Wonder (Columbia/CBS)

8. **BEST POP INSTRUMENTAL
PERFORMANCE
(ORCHESTRA, GROUP OR
SOLOIST)**
TOP GUN ANTHEM (Track
from "Top Gun" soundtrack)
Harold Faltermeyer & Steve
Stevens (Columbia/CBS)

9. **BEST NEW AGE
RECORDING**
DOWN TO THE MOON
(Album)
Andreas Vollenweider (FM/CBS)

10. **BEST ROCK VOCAL
PERFORMANCE, FEMALE**
BACK WHERE YOU STARTED
(Track from "Break Every Rule")
Tina Turner (Capitol)

11. **BEST ROCK VOCAL
PERFORMANCE, MALE**
ADDICTED TO LOVE (Single)
Robert Palmer (Island)

12. **BEST ROCK PERFORMANCE
BY A DUO OR GROUP WITH
VOCAL**
MISSIONARY MAN (Single)
Eurythmics (Island)

13. **BEST ROCK INSTRUMENTAL
PERFORMANCE
(ORCHESTRA, GROUP OR
SOLOIST)**
PETER GUNN (Track from "In
Visible Silence")
The Art of Noise featuring
Duane Eddy (China/Chrysalis)

14. **BEST R&B PERFORMANCE,
FEMALE**
RAPTURE (Album)
Anita Baker (Elektra)

15. **BEST R&B PERFORMANCE, MALE**
LIVING IN AMERICA (Single)
James Brown (Scotti Bros./CBS)

16. **BEST R&B PERFORMANCE BY A DUO OR GROUP WITH VOCAL**
KISS (Single)
Prince and The Revolution
(Paisley Park)

17. **BEST R&B INSTRUMENTAL PERFORMANCE (ORCHESTRA, GROUP OR SOLOIST)**
AND YOU KNOW THAT (Track
from "Shades")
Yellowjackets (MCA)

18. **BEST RHYTHM & BLUES SONG**
SWEET LOVE
Songwriters: Anita Baker, Louis
A. Johnson, Gary Bias (Elektra)

19. **BEST JAZZ FUSION PERFORMANCE, VOCAL OR INSTRUMENTAL**
DOUBLE VISION (Album)
Bob James & David Sanborn
(Warner Bros.)

20. **BEST JAZZ VOCAL PERFORMANCE, FEMALE**
TIMELESS (Album)
Diane Schuur (GRP)

21. **BEST JAZZ VOCAL PERFORMANCE, MALE**
ROUND MIDNIGHT (Track
from "Round Midnight"
soundtrack)
Bobby McFerrin (Columbia/CBS)

22. **BEST JAZZ VOCAL PERFORMANCE, DUO OR GROUP**
FREE FALL (Album)
2 + 2 Plus (Clare Fischer & His
Latin Jazz Sextet) (Discovery)

23. **BEST JAZZ INSTRUMENTAL PERFORMANCE, SOLOIST**
TUTU (Album)
Miles Davis (Warner Bros.)

24. **BEST JAZZ INSTRUMENTAL PERFORMANCE, GROUP**
J MOOD (Album)
Wynton Marsalis (Columbia/CBS)

25. **BEST JAZZ INSTRUMENTAL PERFORMANCE, BIG BAND**
THE TONIGHT SHOW BAND
WITH DOC SEVERINSEN
(Album)
The Tonight Show Band with
Doc Severinsen (Amherst)

26. **BEST COUNTRY VOCAL PERFORMANCE, FEMALE**
WHOEVER'S IN NEW
ENGLAND (Single)
Reba McEntire (MCA)

27. **BEST COUNTRY VOCAL PERFORMANCE, MALE**
LOST IN THE FIFTIES
TONIGHT (Album)
Ronnie Milsap (RCA)

28. **BEST COUNTRY PERFORMANCE BY A DUO OR GROUP WITH VOCAL**
GRANDPA (TELL ME 'BOUT
THE GOOD OLD DAYS)
(Single)
The Judds (Wynonna & Naomi)
(RCA)

29. **BEST COUNTRY INSTRUMENTAL PERFORMANCE (ORCHESTRA, GROUP OR SOLOIST)**
RAISIN' THE DICKENS (Track
from "Love's Gonna Get Ya")
Ricky Skaggs (Epic/CBS)

30. **BEST COUNTRY SONG**
GRANDPA (TELL ME 'BOUT
THE GOOD OLD DAYS)
Songwriter: Jamie O'Hara (RCA)

31. **BEST GOSPEL PERFORMANCE, FEMALE**
MORNING LIKE THIS (Album)
Sandi Patti (Word)

32. **BEST GOSPEL PERFORMANCE, MALE**
TRIUMPH (Album)
Philip Bailey (Myrrh/Word)

33. **BEST GOSPEL PERFORMANCE BY A DUO OR GROUP, CHOIR OR CHORUS**
THEY SAY (Track from "So Glad I Know")
Sandi Patti & Deniece Williams (Sparrow)

34. **BEST SOUL GOSPEL PERFORMANCE, FEMALE**
I SURRENDER ALL (Track from "So Glad I Know")
Deniece Williams (Sparrow)

35. **BEST SOUL PERFORMANCE, MALE**
GOING AWAY (Single)
Al Green (A&M)

36. **BEST SOUL GOSPEL PERFORMANCE BY A DUO OR GROUP, CHOIR OR CHORUS**
LET MY PEOPLE GO (Album)
The Winans (QWest)

37. **BEST LATIN POP PERFORMANCE**
LELOLAI (Track from "Te Amare")
Jose Feliciano (RCA)

38. **BEST TROPICAL LATIN PERFORMANCE**
ESCENAS (Album)
Ruben Blades (Elektra)

39. **BEST MEXICAN/AMERICAN PERFORMANCE**
AY TE DEJO EN SAN ANTONIO (Album)
Flaco Jimenez (Arhoolie)

40. **BEST TRADITIONAL BLUES RECORDING**
SHOWDOWN! (Album)
Albert Collins, Robert Cray, and Johnny Copeland (Alligator)

41. **BEST TRADITIONAL FOLK RECORDING**
RIDING THE MIDNIGHT TRAIN (Album)
Doc Watson (SugarHill)

42. **BEST CONTEMPORARY FOLK RECORDING**
TRIBUTE TO STEVE GOODMAN (Album)
(Arlo Guthrie, John Hartford, Richie Havens, Bonnie Koloc, Nitty Gritty Dirt Band, John Prine, and others)
Producers: Hank Neuberger, Al Bunetta, Dan Einstein (Red Pajamas)

43. **BEST POLKA RECORDING (Tie)**
ANOTHER POLKA CELEBRATION (Album)
Eddie Blazonczyk's Versatones (Bel Aire)

I REMEMBER WARSAW (Album)
Jimmy Sturr & His Orchestra (Starr)

44. **BEST REGGAE RECORDING**
BABYLON THE BANDIT (Album)
Steel Pulse (Elektra)

45. **BEST RECORDING FOR CHILDREN**
THE ALPHABET (Cassette)
(The Sesame Street Muppets)
Muppets Creator: Jim Henson
Producers: Kathryn King, Geri Van Rees (Golden Books)

46. **BEST COMEDY RECORDING**
THOSE OF YOU WITH OR
WITHOUT CHILDREN,
YOU'LL UNDERSTAND
(Album)
Bill Cosby (Geffen)

47. **BEST SPOKEN WORD OR
NON-MUSICAL RECORDING**
INTERVIEWS FROM THE
CLASS OF '55 RECORDING
SESSIONS (Album)
Carl Perkins, Jerry Lee Lewis,
Rob Orbison, Johnny Cash, Sam
Phillips, Rick Nelson, and Chips
Moman (America Record Corp.)

48. **BEST MUSICAL CAST SHOW
ALBUM**
FOLLIES IN CONCERT
Composer & lyricist: Stephen
Sondheim
Producer: Thomas Z. Shepard
(RCA)

49. **BEST INSTRUMENTAL
COMPOSITION**
OUT OF AFRICA (MUSIC
FROM THE MOTION
PICTURE SOUNDTRACK)
(Album)
Composer: John Barry (MCA)

50. **BEST MUSIC VIDEO, SHORT
FORM (VHS)**
DIRE STRAITS: BROTHERS IN
ARMS
Dire Straits (Warner Reprise
Video)

51. **BEST MUSIC VIDEO, LONG
FORM (VHS) (Beta) (Disc)**
BRING ON THE NIGHT
Sting
Video Director: Michael Apted
(Karl-Lorimar Home Video)

52. **BEST ARRANGEMENT ON
AN INSTRUMENTAL**
SUITE MEMORIES (Track from
"Someplace Else")
(Bill Watrous with Patrick
Williams and His Orchestra)
Arranger: Patrick Williams
(Soundwings)

53. **BEST INSTRUMENTAL
ARRANGEMENT
ACCOMPANYING VOCAL(S)**
SOMEWHERE (Track from
"The Broadway Album")
(Barbra Streisand)
Arranger: David Foster
(Columbia/CBS)

54. **BEST ALBUM PACKAGE**
TUTU (Miles Davis)
Art Director: Eiko Ishioka
(Warner Bros.)

55. **BEST ALBUM NOTES**
THE VOICE, THE COLUMBIA
YEARS 1943–1952 (Frank
Sinatra)
Annotators: Gary Giddins,
Wilfrid Sheed, Jonathan
Schwartz, Murray Kempton,
Andrew Sarris, Stephen Holden,
and Frank Conroy (Columbia/
CBS)

56. **BEST HISTORICAL ALBUM**
ATLANTIC RHYTHM AND
BLUES 1947–1974 VOLS. 1-7
(Brook Benton, Ray Charles, The
Coasters, The Drifters, Roberta
Flack, Aretha Franklin, Otis
Redding, and many others)
Producers: Bob Porter, Aziz
Goksel (Atlantic)

57. **BEST ENGINEERED
RECORDING (Non-Classical)**
BACK IN THE HIGH LIFE
(Album)
(Steve Winwood)
Engineers: Tom Lord Alge &
Jason Corsaro (Island)

58. **PRODUCER OF THE YEAR**
(Non-Classical)
Jimmy Jam & Terry Lewis

59. **BEST CLASSICAL ALBUM**
HOROWITZ: THE STUDIO
RECORDINGS, NEW YORK
1985
Vladimir Horowitz
Producer: Thomas Frost (DG)

60. **BEST CLASSICAL
ORCHESTRAL RECORDING**
LISZT: A FAUST SYMPHONY
Sir Georg Solti cond. Chicago
Sym. Orch.
Producer: Michael Haas (London)

61. **BEST OPERA RECORDING**
BERNSTEIN: CANDIDE
John Mauceri cond. the New
York City Opera Chorus &
Orch.; Principal Soloists: Erie
Mills, David Eisler, John
Lankston, Joyce Castle, Scott
Reeve, Jack Harrold, James
Billings, Maris Clement
Producer: Elizabeth Ostrow
(New World)

62. **BEST CHORAL
PERFORMANCE (OTHER
THAN OPERA)**
ORFF: CARMINA BURANA
James Levine cond. Chicago
Sym. Orch. & Chorus; Margaret
Hillis, choral director (DG)

63. **BEST CLASSICAL
PERFORMANCE,
INSTRUMENTAL SOLOIST
OR SOLOISTS (WITH OR
WITHOUT ORCHESTRA)**
HOROWITZ: THE STUDIO
RECORDINGS, NEW YORK
1985
Vladimir Horowitz (DG)

64. **BEST CHAMBER MUSIC
PERFORMANCE
(INSTRUMENTAL OR VOCAL)**
BEETHOVEN: CELLO &
PIANO SONATA NO. 4 IN C
MAJOR/ AND VARIATIONS
Yo-Yo Ma & Emanuel Ax (CBS
Masterworks)

65. **BEST CLASSICAL VOCAL
SOLOIST PERFORMANCE**
MOZART: KATHLEEN
BATTLE SINGS MOZART
Kathleen Battle (Angel)

66. **BEST CONTEMPORARY
COMPOSITION**
LUTOSLAWSKI: SYMPHONY
NO. 3
Composer: Witold Lutoslawski
(CBS/Masterworks)

67. **BEST ENGINEERED
RECORDING, CLASSICAL**
HOROWITZ: THE STUDIO
RECORDINGS, NEW YORK
1985
Vladimir Horowitz
Engineer: Paul Goodman (DG)

66. **BEST PRODUCER OF THE
YEAR**
THOMAS FROST

30TH ANNUAL (1987) GRAMMY WINNERS
Announced on March 2, 1988
Eligibility Year: October 1, 1986 through September 30, 1987

1. **RECORD OF THE YEAR**
GRACELAND
Paul Simon
Producer: Paul Simon (Warner Bros.)

2. **ALBUM OF THE YEAR**
JOSHUA TREE
U2
Producers: Daniel Lanois, Brian Eno (Island)

3. **SONG OF THE YEAR**
SOMEWHERE OUT THERE
Linda Ronstadt & James Ingram
Songwriters: James Horner, Barry Mann, Cynthia Weil (MCA)

4. **BEST NEW ARTIST**
Jody Watley (MCA)

5. **BEST POP VOCAL PERFORMANCE, FEMALE**
I WANNA DANCE WITH SOMEBODY (WHO LOVES ME) (Single)
Whitney Houston (Arista)

6. **BEST POP VOCAL PERFORMANCE, MALE**
BRING ON THE NIGHT (Album)
Sting (A&M)

7. **BEST POP PERFORMANCE BY A DUO OR GROUP WITH VOCAL**
(I'VE HAD) THE TIME OF MY LIFE (Track from "Dirty Dancing" Original Soundtrack)
Bill Medley & Jennifer Warnes (BMG Music/RCA)

8. **BEST POP INSTRUMENTAL PERFORMANCE (ORCHESTRA, GROUP OR SOLOIST)**
MINUTE BY MINUTE (Single)
Larry Carlton (MCA)

9. **BEST NEW AGE PERFORMANCE**
YUSEF LATEEF'S LITTLE SYMPHONY (Album)
Yusef Lateef (Atlantic)

10. No Category

11. **BEST ROCK VOCAL PERFORMANCE, SOLO**
TUNNEL OF LOVE (Album)
Bruce Springstein (Columbia/CBS)

12. **BEST ROCK PERFORMANCE BY A DUO OR GROUP WITH VOCAL**
THE JOSHUA TREE (Album)
U2 (Island)

13. **BEST ROCK INSTRUMENTAL PERFORMANCE (ORCHESTRA GROUP OR SOLOIST)**
JAZZ FROM HELL (Album)
Frank Zappa (Barking Pumpkin/Rykodisc)

14. **BEST R&B VOCAL PERFORMANCE, FEMALE**
ARETHA (Album)
Aretha Franklin (Arista)

15. **BEST R&B VOCAL PERFORMANCE, MALE**
JUST TO SEE HER (Single)
Smokey Robinson (Motown)

16. **BEST R&B PERFORMANCE BY A DUO OR GROUP WITH VOCAL**
I KNEW YOU WERE WAITING (FOR ME) (Track from "Aretha")
Aretha Franklin & George Michael (Arista)

17. **BEST R&B INSTRUMENTAL PERFORMANCE (ORCHESTRA, GROUP, OR SOLOIST)**
CHICAGO SONG (Single)
David Sanborn (Warner Bros.)

18. **BEST RHYTHM & BLUES SONG**
LEAN ON ME (Club Nouveau)
Songwriter: Bill Withers (King Jay/Warner Bros.)

19. **BEST JAZZ FUSION PERFORMANCE, VOCAL OR INSTRUMENTAL**
STILL LIFE (TALKING) (Album)
Pat Metheny Group (Geffen)

20. **BEST JAZZ VOCAL PERFORMANCE, FEMALE**
DIANE SCHUUR AND THE COUNT BASIE ORCHESTRA (Album)
Diane Schuur (GRP)

21. **BEST JAZZ VOCAL PERFORMANCE, MALE**
WHAT IS THIS THING CALLED LOVE (Track from "The Other Side of Round Midnight—Dexter Gordon")
Bobby McFerrin (Blue Note)

22. No Category

23. **BEST JAZZ INSTRUMENTAL PERFORMANCE, SOLOIST**
THE OTHER SIDE OF ROUND MIDNIGHT (Album)
Dexter Gordon (Blue Note)

24. **BEST JAZZ INSTRUMENTAL PERFORMANCE, GROUP**
MARSALIS STANDARD TIME—VOLUME 1 (Album)
Wynton Marsalis (Columbia/CBS)

25. **BEST JAZZ INSTRUMENTAL PERFORMANCE, BIG BAND**
DIGITAL DUKE (Album)
The Duke Ellington Orch.
Mercer Ellington cond. (GRP)

26. **BEST COUNTRY VOCAL PERFORMANCE, FEMALE**
50'S LADIES (Track from "50's Ladies")
K.T. Oslin (BMG Music/RCA)

27. **BEST COUNTRY VOCAL PERFORMANCE, MALE**
ALWAYS & FOREVER (Album)
Randy Travis (Warner Bros.)

28. **BEST COUNTRY PERFORMANCE BY A DUO OR GROUP WITH VOCAL**
TRIO (Album)
Dolly Parton, Linda Ronstadt & Emmylou Harris (Warner Bros.)

29. **BEST COUNTRY VOCAL PERFORMANCE, DUET**
MAKE NO MISTAKE, SHE'S MINE (Single)
Ronnie Milsap & Kenny Rogers (BMG Music/RCA)

30. **BEST COUNTRY INSTRUMENTAL PERFORMANCE (ORCHESTRA, GROUP OR SOLOIST)**
STRING OF PARS (Track from "Asleep at the Wheel")
Asleep at the Wheel (Epic)

31. **BEST COUNTRY SONG**
FOREVER AND EVER, AMEN
Randy Travis
Songwriters: Paul Overstreet, Don Schlitz (Warner Bros.)

32. **BEST GOSPEL PERFORMANCE, FEMALE**
I BELIEVE IN YOU (Track from "Water Under the Bridge") Deniece Williams (Columbia/CBS)

33. **BEST GOSPEL PERFORMANCE, MALE**
THE FATHER HATH PROVIDED (Album) Larnelle Harris (Benson)

34. **BEST GOSPEL PERFORMANCE BY A DUO, GROUP, CHOIR OR CHORUS**
CRACK THE SKY (Album) Mylon LeFevre & Broken Heart (Myrrh/Word)

35. **BEST SOUL GOSPEL PERFORMANCE, FEMALE**
FOR ALWAYS (Track from "Bebe & CeCe Winans") CeCe Winans (Sparrow)

36. **BEST SOUL GOSPEL PERFORMANCE, MALE**
EVERYTHING'S GONNA BE ALRIGHT (Track from "Soul Survivor") Al Green (A&M)

37. **BEST SOUL GOSPEL PERFORMANCE BY A DUO, GROUP, CHOIR OR CHORUS**
AIN'T NO NEED TO WORRY (Single) The Winans & Anita Baker (QWest)

38. **BEST LATIN POP PERFORMANCE**
UN HOMBRE SOLO (Album) Julio Iglesias (Discos CBS Intl.)

39. **BEST TROPICAL LATIN PERFORMANCE**
LA VERDAD—THE TRUTH (Album) Eddie Palmieri (Fania/Musica Latina Intl.)

40. **BEST MEXICAN/AMERICAN PERFORMANCE**
GRACIAS! AMERICA SIN FRONTERAS (Album) Los Tigres Del Norte (Profono Intl.)

41. **BEST TRADITIONAL BLUES RECORDING**
HOUSEPARTY NEW ORLEANS STYLE (Album) Professor Longhair (Rounder)

42. **BEST CONTEMPORARY BLUES RECORDING**
STRONG PERSUADER (Album) The Robert Cray Band (Mercury/Hightone)

43. **BEST TRADITIONAL FOLK RECORDING**
SHAKA ZULU (Album) Ladysmith Black Mambazo (Warner Bros.)

44. **BEST CONTEMPORARY FOLK RECORDING**
UNFINISHED BUSINESS (Album) Steve Goodman (Red Pajamas)

45. **BEST POLKA RECORDING**
A POLKA JUST FOR ME (Album) Jimmy Sturr & His Orchestra (Starr)

46. **BEST REGGAE RECORDING**
NO NUCLEAR WAR (Album) Peter Tosh (EMI-America)

47. **BEST RECORDING FOR CHILDREN**
THE ELEPHANT'S CHILD (Album) Jack Nicholson, narration; Bobby McFerrin, music; Producers: Bobby McFerrin, Tom Bradshaw, Mark Sottnick (Windham Hill)

48. BEST COMEDY RECORDING
A NIGHT AT THE MET
(Album)
Robin Williams (Columbia/CBS)

49. BEST SPOKEN WORD OR NON-MUSICAL RECORDING
LAKE WOBEGON DAYS
(Cassette)
Garrison Keillor (PHC)

50. BEST MUSICAL CAST SHOW ALBUM
LES MISERABLES (ORIGINAL BROADWAY CAST RECORDING)
Lyricist: Herbert Kretzmer
Composer: Claude-Michel Schonberg
Producers: Alain Boublil & Claude-Michel Schonberg
(Geffen)

51. BEST INSTRUMENTAL COMPOSITION
CALL SHEET BLUES (Track from "The Other Side of Round Midnight—Dexter Gordon")
(Wayne Shorter, Herbie Hancock, Ron Carter, Billy Higgins)
Composers: Wayne Shorter, Herbie Hancock, Ron Carter, Billy Higgins (Blue Note)

52. BEST ALBUM OF ORIGINAL INSTRUMENTAL BACKGROUND SCORE WRITTEN FOR A MOTION PICTURE OR TELEVISION
THE UNTOUCHABLES
(Original Motion Picture Soundtrack) (Album)
Composer: Ennio Morricone
(A&M)

53. BEST SONG WRITTEN SPECIFICALLY FOR A MOTION PICTURE OR TELEVISION
SOMEWHERE OUT THERE
(Linda Ronstadt & James Ingram)
Songwriters: James Horner, Barry Mann, Cynthia Weil
(MCA)

54. BEST PERFORMANCE MUSIC VIDEO
THE PRINCE'S TRUST ALL-STAR ROCK CONCERT (VHS)
(Elton John, Tina Turner, Sting, and others)
Video Producer: Anthony Eaton
(MGM Home Video)

55. BEST CONCEPT MUSIC VIDEO
LAND OF CONFUSION (VHS)
Genesis
Video Directors: John Lloyd, Jim Yurich
Video Producer: Jon Blair
(Atlantic Video)

56. BEST ARRANGEMENT ON AN INSTRUMENTAL
TAKE THE "A" TRAIN (Track from "The Tonight Show Band with Doc Severinsen, Vol. II")
(The Tonight Show Band with Doc Severinsen)
Instrumental Arranger: Bill Holman (Amherst)

57. BEST INSTRUMENTAL ARRANGEMENT ACCOMPANYING VOCAL(S)
DEEDLES' BLUES (Track from "Diane Schuur & The Count Basie Orchestra") (Diane Schuur & The Count Basie Orch.)
Instrumental Arranger: Frank Foster (GRP)

58. BEST ALBUM PACKAGE
KING'S RECORD SHOP
(Roseanne Cash)
Art Director: Bill Johnson
(Columbia/CBS)

59. **BEST ALBUM NOTES**
THELONIOUS MONK—THE
COMPLETE RIVERSIDE
RECORDINGS
(Thelonious Monk)
Annotator: Orrin Keepnews
(Riverside)

60. **BEST HISTORICAL ALBUM**
THELONIOUS MONK—THE
COMPLETE RIVERSIDE
RECORDINGS
(Thelonious Monk)
Producer: Orrin Keepnews
(Riverside)

61. **BEST ENGINEERED
RECORDING (Non-Classical)**
BAD (Album) (Michael Jackson)
Engineers: Bruce Swedien,
Humberto Gatica (Epic)

62. **PRODUCER OF THE YEAR
(Non-Classical)**
NARADA MICHAEL WALDEN

63. **BEST CLASSICAL ALBUM**
HOROWITZ IN MOSCOW
Vladimir Horowitz
Producer: Thomas Frost
(Deutsche Grammophon)

64. **BEST ORCHESTRAL
RECORDING**
BEETHOVEN: SYMPHONY
NO. 9 IN D MINOR (CHORAL)
Sir Georg Solti cond. Chicago
Sym. Orch.
Producer: Michael Haas (London)

65. **BEST OPERA RECORDING**
(R.) STRAUSS: ARIADNE AUF
NAXOS
James Levine cond. the Vienna
Philharmonic; Principal Soloists:
Anna Tomowa-Sintow, Kathleen
Battle, Agnes Baltsa, Gary
Lakes, Hermann Prey
Producer: Cord Garben
(Deutsche Grammophon)

66. **BEST CHORAL
PERFORMANCE (OTHER
THAN OPERA)**
HINDEMITH: WHEN LILACS
LAST IN THE DOORYARD
BLOOM'D (A REQUIEM FOR
THOSE WE LOVE)
Robert Shaw cond. Atlanta Sym.
Chorus & Orch. (Telarc)

67. **BEST CLASSICAL
PERFORMANCE,
INSTRUMENTAL SOLOIST
OR SOLOISTS (WITH
ORCHESTRA)**
MOZART: VIOLIN CONS.
NOS. 2 & 4 IN D
Itzhak Perlman (James Levine
cond. Vienna Philharmonic) (DG)

68. **BEST CLASSICAL
PERFORMANCE,
INSTRUMENTAL SOLOIST
OR SOLOISTS (WITHOUT
ORCHESTRA)**
HOROWITZ IN MOSCOW
Vladimir Horowitz, piano (DG)

69. **BEST CHAMBER MUSIC
PERFORMANCE,
INSTRUMENTAL OR VOCAL**
BEETHOVEN: THE
COMPLETE PIANO TRIOS
Itzhak Perlman, Lynn Harrell &
Vladimir Ashkenazy (Angel)

70. **BEST CLASSICAL VOCAL
SOLOIST PERFORMANCE**
KATHLEEN BATTLE—
SALZBURG RECITAL
Kathleen Battle (James Levine,
accomp.) (DG)

71. **BEST CONTEMPORARY
COMPOSITION**
PENDERECKI: CELLO
CONCERTO NO. 2
Composer: Krzysztof Penderecki
(Erato-Editions)

**72. BEST ENGINEERED
RECORDING, CLASSICAL**
FAURE: REQUIEM, OP. 48/
DURUFLE: REQUIEM, OP. 9
(Robert Shaw cond. Atlanta Sym.
Chorus & Orch.)
Engineer: Jack Renner (Telarc)

**73. CLASSICAL PRODUCER OF
THE YEAR**
ROBERT WOODS

31ST ANNUAL (1988) GRAMMY WINNERS
Announced on February 22, 1989
Eligibility Year: October 1, 1987 through September 30, 1988

1. RECORD OF THE YEAR
DON'T WORRY BE HAPPY
Bobby McFerrin
Producer: Linda Goldstein (EMI/
USA)

2. ALBUM OF THE YEAR
FAITH
George Michael
Producer: George Michael
(Columbia/CBS)

3. SONG OF THE YEAR
DON'T WORRY BE HAPPY
Bobby McFerrin
Songwriter: Bobby McFerrin
(EMI/USA)

4. BEST NEW ARTIST
TRACY CHAPMAN (Elektra)

**5. BEST POP VOCAL
PERFORMANCE, FEMALE**
FAST CAR (Single)
Tracy Chapman (Elektra)

**6. BEST POP VOCAL
PERFORMANCE, MALE**
DON'T WORRY BE HAPPY
(Single)
Bobby McFerrin (EMI/USA)

**7. BEST POP VOCAL
PERFORMANCE BY A DUO
OR GROUP WITH VOCAL**
BRASIL (Album)
The Manhattan Transfer
(Atlantic)

**8. BEST POP INSTRUMENTAL
PERFORMANCE
(ORCHESTRA, GROUP OR
SOLOIST)**
CLOSE-UP (Album)
David Sanborn (Reprise)

**9. BEST ROCK VOCAL
PERFORMANCE, FEMALE**
TINA LIVE IN EUROPE
(Album)
Tina Turner (Capitol)

**10. BEST ROCK VOCAL
PERFORMANCE, MALE**
SIMPLY IRRESISTIBLE
(Album)
Robert Palmer (EMI/Manhattan)

**11. BEST ROCK PERFORMANCE
BY A DUO OR GROUP WITH
VOCAL**
DESIRE (Single)
U2 (Island)

**12. BEST ROCK INSTRUMENTAL
PERFORMANCE
(ORCHESTRA, GROUP, OR
SOLOIST)**
BLUES FOR SALVADOR
(Album)
Carlos Santana (Columbia/CBS)

**13. BEST HARD ROCK/METAL
PERFORMANCE VOCAL OR
INSTRUMENTAL**
CREST OF A KNAVE (Album)
Jethro Tull (Chrysalis)

14. **BEST R&B VOCAL PERFORMANCE, FEMALE**
GIVING YOU THE BEST THAT I GOT (Single)
Anita Baker (Elektra)

15. **BEST R&B VOCAL PERFORMANCE, MALE**
INTRODUCING THE HARDLINE ACCORDING TO TERENCE TRENT D'ARBY (Album)
Terence Trent D'Arby (Columbia/CBS)

16. **BEST R&B PERFORMANCE BY A DUO OR GROUP WITH VOCAL**
LOVE OVERBOARD (Single)
Gladys Knight & The Pips (MCA)

17. **BEST R&B INSTRUMENTAL PERFORMANCE (ORCHESTRA, GROUP, OR SOLOIST)**
LIGHT YEARS (Track from "GRP Super Live in Concert, Vols. 1 & 2")
Chick Corea (GRP)

18. **BEST RHYTHM & BLUES SONG**
GIVING YOU THE BEST THAT I GOT (Anita Baker)
Songwriters: Anita Baker, Skip Scarborough, Randy Holland (Elektra)

19. **BEST RAP PERFORMANCE**
PARENTS JUST DON'T UNDERSTAND (Track from "He's the DJ I'm the Rapper")
D.J. Jazzy Jeff & The Fresh Prince

20. **BEST NEW AGE PERFORMANCE**
FOLKSONGS FOR A NUCLEAR VILLAGE (Album)
Shadowfax (Capitol)

21. **BEST JAZZ FUSION PERFORMANCE**
POLITICS (Album)
Yellowjackets (MCA)

22. **BEST JAZZ VOCAL PERFORMANCE, FEMALE**
LOOK WHAT I GOT! (Album)
Betty Carter (Verve)

23. **BEST JAZZ VOCAL PERFORMANCE, MALE**
BROTHERS (Track from "Rob Wasserman's Duets")
Bobby McFerrin (MCA)

24. **BEST JAZZ VOCAL PERFORMANCE, DUO, OR GROUP**
SPREAD LOVE (Single)
Take 6 (Reprise)

25. **BEST JAZZ INSTRUMENTAL PERFORMANCE, SOLOIST (ON A JAZZ RECORDING)**
DON'T TRY THIS AT HOME (Album)
Michael Brecker (MCA Impulse)

26. **BEST JAZZ INSTRUMENTAL PERFORMANCE, GROUP**
BLUES FOR COLTRANE, A TRIBUTE TO JOHN COLTRANE (Album)
McCoy Tyner, Pharaoh Sanders, David Murray, Cecil McBee, and Roy Haynes (MCA Impulse)

27. **BEST JAZZ INSTRUMENTAL PERFORMANCE, BIG BAND**
BUD & BIRD (Album)
Gil Evans & The Monday Night Orchestra (Intersound)

28. **BEST COUNTRY VOCAL PERFORMANCE, FEMALE**
HOLD ME (Track from "This Woman")
K.T. Oslin (RCA)

29. **BEST COUNTRY VOCAL PERFORMANCE, MALE**
OLD 8X10 (Album)
Randy Travis (Warner Bros.)

30. **BEST COUNTRY PERFORMANCE BY A DUO OR GROUP WITH VOCAL**
GIVE A LITTLE LOVE (Track from "Greatest Hits")
The Judds (RCA)

31. **BEST COUNTRY VOCAL COLLABORATION**
CRYING (Single)
Roy Orbison & k.d. lang (Virgin)

32. **BEST COUNTRY INSTRUMENTAL PERFORMANCE (ORCHESTRA, GROUP OR SOLOIST)**
SUGARFOOT RAG (Track from "Western Standard Time")
Asleep at the Wheel (Epic)

33. **BEST BLUEGRASS RECORDING (VOCAL OR INSTRUMENTAL)**
SOUTHERN FLAVOR (Album)
Bill Monroe (MCA)

34. **BEST COUNTRY SONG**
HOLD ME
(K.T. Oslin)
Songwriter: K.T. Oslin

35. **BEST GOSPEL PERFORMANCE, FEMALE**
LEAD ME ON (Album)
Amy Grant (A&M)

36. **BEST GOSPEL PERFORMANCE, MALE**
CHRISTMAS (Album)
Larnelle Harris (Benson)

37. **BEST GOSPEL PERFORMANCE BY A DUO OR GROUP, CHOIR OR CHORUS**
THE WINANS LIVE AT CARNEGIE HALL (Album)
The Winans (QWest)

38. **BEST SOUL GOSPEL PERFORMANCE, FEMALE**
ONE LORD, ONE FAITH, ONE BAPTISM (Album)
Aretha Franklin (Arista)

39. **BEST SOUL GOSPEL PERFORMANCE, MALE**
ABUNDANT LIFE (Track from "Ron Winans Family & Friends Choir")
BeBe Winans (Selah)

40. **BEST SOUL GOSPEL PERFORMANCE BY A DUO OR GROUP, CHOIR OR CHORUS**
TAKE SIX (Album)
Take 6 (Reprise)

41. **BEST LATIN POP PERFORMANCE**
ROBERTO CARLOS (Album)
Roberto Carlos (Discos CBS Int'l)

42. **BEST TROPICAL LATIN PERFORMANCE**
ANTECEDENTE (Album)
Ruben Blades (Elektra)

43. **BEST MEXICAN/AMERICAN PERFORMANCE**
CANCIONES DE MI PADRE (Album)
Linda Ronstadt (Elektra)

44. **BEST TRADITIONAL BLUES RECORDING**
HIDDEN CHARMS (Album)
Willie Dixon (Bug/Capitol)

45. **BEST CONTEMPORARY BLUES RECORDING**
DON'T BE AFRAID OF THE DARK (Single)
The Robert Cray Band (Mercury)

46. **BEST TRADITIONAL FOLK RECORDING**
FOLKWAYS: A VISION SHARED—A TRIBUTE TO WOODY GUTHRIE AND LEADBELLY (Album)
Producers: Don DeVito, Joe McEwen, Harold Leventhal, Ralph Rinzler (Columbia/CBS)

47. **BEST CONTEMPORARY FOLK RECORDING**
TRACY CHAPMAN (Album)
Tracy Chapman (Elektra)

48. **BEST POLKA RECORDING**
BORN TO POLKA (Album)
Jimmy Sturr & His Orchestra
(Starr)

49. **BEST REGGAE RECORDING**
CONSCIOUS PARTY (Album)
Ziggy Marley and the Melody
Makers (Virgin)

50. **BEST RECORDING FOR
CHILDREN**
PECOS BILL (Album)
Robin Williams, narrator: Ry
Cooder, music; Producers: Mark
Scottnick, Ry Cooder (Windham-
Hill)

51. **BEST COMEDY RECORDING**
GOOD MORNING VIETNAM
(Album)
Robin Williams (A&M)

52. **BEST SPOKEN WORD OR
NON-MUSICAL RECORDING**
SPEECH BY REV. JESSE
JACKSON (JULY 27) (Track from
"Arethan Franklin's One Lord,
One Faith, One Baptism")
Rev. Jesse Jackson (Arista)

53. **BEST MUSICAL CAST SHOW
ALBUM**
INTO THE WOODS
Composer & Lyricist: Stephen
Sondheim
Producer: Jay David Saks (RCA)

54. **BEST INSTRUMENTAL
COMPOSITION**
THE THEME FROM L.A.
LAW (Track from "Music from
L.A. Law & Otherwise")
Composer: Mike Post (Polydor)

55. **BEST ALBUM OF ORIGINAL
INSTRUMENTAL
BACKGROUND SCORE
WRITTEN FOR A MOTION
PICTURE OR TELEVISION**
THE LAST EMPEROR
Composers: Ryuichi Sakamoto,
David Byrne, Cong Su (Virgin)

56. **BEST SONG WRITTEN
SPECIFICALLY FOR A
MOTION PICTURE OR
TELEVISION**
TWO HEARTS (Track from
"Buster") (Phil Collins)
Songwriters: Phil Collins,
Lamont Dozier (Atlantic)

57. **BEST PERFORMANCE MUSIC
VIDEO**
WHERE THE STREETS HAVE
NO NAME
U2
Director: Meiert Avis
Producers: Michael Hamlyn, Ben
Dossett (Island)

58. **BEST CONCEPT MUSIC
VIDEO**
FAT
"Weird Al" Yankovic
Director: Jay Levey
Producer: Susan Zwerman
(Rock'n'Roll/Epic)

59. **BEST ARRANGEMENT ON
AN INSTRUMENTAL**
MEMOS FROM PARADISE
(Track from "Memos from
Paradise")
(Eddie Daniels)
Arranger: Roger Kellaway (GRP)

60. **BEST INSTRUMENTAL
ARRANGEMENT
ACCOMPANYING VOCAL(S)**
NO ONE IS ALONE (Track
from "Cleo Sings Sondheim")
(Cleo Laine)
Arranger: Jonathan Tunick (RCA)

61. **BEST ALBUM PACKAGE**
TIRED OF RUNNIN'
(O'Kanes)
Art Director: Bill Johnson

62. **BEST ALBUM NOTES**
CROSSROADS
(Eric Clapton)
Annotator: Anthony DeCurtis
(Polydor)

63. **BEST HISTORICAL ALBUM**
CROSSROADS
(Eric Clapton)
Producer: Bill Levenson
(Polydor)

64. **BEST ENGINEERED RECORDING (NON-CLASSICAL)**
ROLL WITH IT (Album)
(Steve Winwood)
Engineer: Tom Lord Alge
(Virgin)

65. **PRODUCER OF THE YEAR** (Non-Classical)
NEIL DORFSMAN

66. **BEST CLASSICAL ALBUM**
VERDI: REQUIEM AND OPERATIC CHORUSES
Robert Shaw cond. Atlanta Sym. Orch. & Chorus
Producer: Robert Woods (Telarc)

67. **BEST ORCHESTRAL RECORDING**
ROREM: STRING SYMPHONY; SUNDAY MORNING; EAGLES
Robert Shaw cond. Atlanta Sym. Orch. "String Symphony"/Louis Lane cond. Atlanta Sym. Orch. "Sunday Morning" & "Eagles"
Producer: Robert Woods (New World)

68. **BEST OPERA RECORDING**
WAGNER: LOHENGRIN
Sir Georg Solti cond. Vienna State Opera Choir & Vienna Philharmonic (Placido Domingo, Jessye Norman, Eva Randova, Siegmund Nimsgern, Hans Sotin, Dietrick Fischer-Dieskau)
Producer: Christopher Raeburn (London)

69. **BEST CHORAL PERFORMANCE (OTHER THAN OPERA)**
VERDI: REQUIEM & OPERATIC CHORUSES
Robert Shaw cond. Atlanta Sym. Chorus & Orch. (Telarc)

70. **BEST CLASSICAL PERFORMANCE, INSTRUMENTAL SOLOIST OR SOLOISTS (WITH ORCHESTRA)**
MOZART: PIANO CONCERTO NO. 23 IN A
Vladimir Horowitz
(Giulini cond. La Scala Opera Orchestra) (DG)

71. **BEST CLASSICAL PERFORMANCE, INSTRUMENTAL SOLOIST OR SOLOISTS (WITHOUT ORCHESTRA)**
ALBENIZ: IBERIA; NAVARRA; SUITE ESPAGNOLA
Alicia de Larrocha (London)

72. **BEST CHAMBER MUSIC PERFORMANCE (INSTRUMENTAL OR VOCAL)**
BARTOK: SONATA FOR TWO PIANOS & PERCUSSION/ BRAHMS: VARIATIONS ON A THEME BY JOSEPH HAYDN FOR TWO PIANOS
Murray Perahia and Sir Georg Solti, pianos, with David Corkhill and Evelyn Glennie, percussion (CBS Masterworks)

73. **BEST CLASSICAL VOCAL SOLOIST PERFORMANCE**
LUCIANO PAVAROTTI IN CONCERT
Luciano Pavarotti (CBS Masterworks)

74. **BEST CONTEMPORARY COMPOSITION**
ADAMS: NIXON IN CHINA
Composer: John Adams (Elektra/ Nonesuch)

75. **BEST ENGINEERED RECORDING, CLASSICAL**
VERDI: REQUIEM & OPERATIC CHORUSES
(Robert Shaw cond. Atlanta Sym. Orch. & Chorus)
Engineer: Jack Renner (Telarc)

76. **CLASSICAL PRODUCER OF
THE YEAR**
ROBERT WOODS

32ND ANNUAL (1989) GRAMMY WINNERS
Announced on February 21, 1990
Eligibility Year: October 1, 1988 through September 30, 1989

1. **RECORD OF THE YEAR**
WIND BENEATH MY WINGS
Bette Midler
Producer: Arif Mardin (Atlantic)

2. **ALBUM OF THE YEAR**
NICK OF TIME
Bonnie Raitt
Producer: Don Was (Capitol)

3. **SONG OF THE YEAR**
WIND BENEATH MY WINGS
Songwriters: Larry Henley, Jeff
Silbar (Atlantic)

4. **NEW ARTIST**
MILLI VANILLI (Arista)*

5. **POP VOCAL PERFORMANCE,
FEMALE**
NICK OF TIME
(Track from "Nick of Time")
Bonnie Raitt (Capitol)

6. **POP VOCAL PERFORMANCE,
MALE**
HOW AM I SUPPOSED TO
LIVE WITHOUT YOU
Michael Bolton (Columbia/CBS)

7. **POP PERFORMANCE
BY DUO OR GROUP VOCAL**
DON'T KNOW MUCH
Linda Ronstadt, Aaron Neville
(Elektra)

8. **POP INSTRUMENTAL
PERFORMANCE**
HEALING CHANT
(Track from "Yellow Moon")
Neville Brothers (A&M)

9. **ROCK VOCAL
PERFORMANCE, FEMALE**
NICK OF TIME
Bonnie Raitt (Capitol)

10. **ROCK VOCAL
PERFORMANCE, MALE**
END OF THE INNOCENCE
Don Henley (Geffen)

11. **ROCK PERFORMANCE
BY DUO OR GROUP
WITH VOCAL**
TRAVELING WILBURYS
VOLUME ONE
Traveling Wilburys (Wilbury/
Warner Bros.)

12. **ROCK INSTRUMENTAL
PERFORMANCE**
JEFF BECK'S GUITAR SHOP
WITH TERRY BOZZIO
AND TONY HYMAS
Jeff Beck with Terry Bozzio,
Tony Hymas (Epic)

13. **HARD ROCK PERFORMANCE
(VOCAL OR INSTRUMENTAL)**
CULT OF PERSONALITY
Living Colour (Epic)

14. **METAL PERFORMANCE
(VOCAL OR INSTRUMENTAL)**
ONE
Metallica (Electra)

15. **R&B VOCAL PERFORMANCE,
FEMALE**
GIVING YOU THE BEST
THAT I GOT
Anita Baker (Elektra)

*Award later withdrawn.

16. **R&B VOCAL PERFORMANCE, MALE**
EVERY LITTLE STEP
Bobby Brown (MCA)

17. **R&B PERFORMANCE BY A DUO OR GROUP WITH VOCAL**
BACK TO LIFE
Soul II Soul (Virgin)

18. **R&B INSTRUMENTAL PERFORMANCE**
AFRICAN DANCE
(track from Keep on Movin')
Soul II Soul (Virgin)

19. **RHYTHM & BLUES SONG**
IF YOU DON'T KNOW ME BY NOW
Songwriters: Kenny Gamble, Leon Huff (Elektra)

20. **RAP PERFORMANCE**
BUST A MOVE
Young MC (Delicious Vinyl)

21. **NEW AGE PERFORMANCE**
PASSION—MUSIC FOR "THE LAST TEMPTATION OF CHRIST"
Peter Garbiel (Geffen)

22. **JAZZ FUSION PERFORMANCE**
LETTER FROM HOME
Pat Metheny Group (Geffen)

23. **JAZZ VOCAL PERFORMANCE, FEMALE**
BLUES ON BROADWAY
Ruth Brown (Fantasy)

24. **JAZZ VOCAL PERFORMANCE, MALE**
WHEN HARRY MET SALLY. . .
Harry Connick Jr. (Columbia/CBS)

25. **JAZZ VOCAL PERFORMANCE, DUO OR GROUP**
MAKIN' WHOOPEE
Dr. John, Rickie Lee Jones (Warner Bros.)

26. **JAZZ INSTRUMENTAL PERFORMANCE, SOLOIST**
AURA
Miles Davis (Columbia/CBS)

27. **JAZZ INSTRUMENTAL PERFORMANCE, GROUP**
CHICK COREA AKOUSTIC BAND
Chick Corea Akoustic Band (GRP)

28. **JAZZ INSTRUMENTAL PERFORMANCE, BIG BAND**
AURA
Miles Davis (Columbia/CBS)

29. **COUNTRY VOCAL PERFORMANCE, FEMALE**
ABSOLUTE TORCH AND TWANG
k.d. lang (Sire)

30. **COUNRY VOCAL PERFORMANCE, MALE**
LYLE LOVETT AND HIS LARGE BAND
Lyle Lovett (MCA)

31. **COUNTRY PERFORMANCE BY A DUO OR GROUP WITH VOCAL**
WILL THE CIRCLE BE UNBROKEN VOL. 2
The Nitty Gritty Dirt Band (Universal)

32. **COUNTRY VOCAL COLLABORATION**
THERE'S A TEAR IN MY BEER
Hank Williams Jr., Hank Williams Sr. (Curb)

33. **COUNTRY INSTRUMENTAL PERFORMANCE**
AMAZING GRACE
(Track from "Will The Circle
Be Unbroken Vol. 2")
Randy Scruggs (Universal)

34. **BLUEGRASS RECORDING**
THE VALLEY ROAD
(Track from "Will the Circle
Be Unbroken Vol. 2")
Bruce Hornsby & The Nitty
Gritty Dirt Band (Universal)

35. **COUNTRY SONG**
AFTER ALL THIS TIME
Songwriter: Rodney Crowell
(Columbia)

36. **GOSPEL VOCAL PERFORMANCE, FEMALE**
DON'T CRY (Track from
"Heaven")
CeCe Winans (Capitol/Sparrow)

37. **GOSPEL VOCAL PERFORMANCE, MALE**
MEANTIME
(Track from "Heaven")
BeBe Winans (Capitol)

38. **GOSPEL VOCAL PERFORMANCE BY A DUO OR GROUP, CHOIR OR CHORUS**
THE SAVIOR IS WAITING
(Track from "Our Hymns")
Take 6 (Word)

39. **SOUL GOSPEL VOCAL PERFORMANCE, FEMALE, MALE**
AS LONG AS WE'RE
TOGETHER
Al Green (A&M)

40. **SOUL GOSPEL VOCAL PERFORMANCE BY A DUO, GROUP, CHOIR OR CHORUS**
LET BROTHERLY LOVE
CONTINUE
(Track from "Brotherly Love")
Daniel Winans & Choir (Rejoice)

41. **LATIN POP PERFORMANCE**
CIELITO LINDO
Jose Feliciano (EMI)

42. **TROPICAL LATIN PERFORMANCE**
RITMO EN EL CORAZON
Celia Cruz & Ray Barretto
(Fania)

43. **MEXICAN/AMERICAN PERFORMANCE**
LA PISTOLA Y EL CORAZON
Los Lobos (Warner Bros./Slash)

44. **TRADITIONAL BLUES RECORDING**
I'M IN THE MOOD
(Track from "The Healer")
John Lee Hooker & Bonnie Raitt
(Chameleon Music Group)

45. **CONTEMPORARY BLUES RECORDING**
IN STEP
Stevie Ray Vaughan, Double
Trouble (Epic)

46. **TRADITIONAL FOLK RECORDING**
LE MYSTERE DES VOIX
BULGARES, VOL. II
Bulgarian State Female Vocal
Choir (Elektra/Noncsuch)

47. **CONTEMPORARY FOLK RECORDING**
INDIGO GIRLS
Indigo Girls (Epic)

48. **POLKA RECORDING**
ALL IN MY LOVE FOR YOU
Jimmy Sturr and His Orchestra
(Starr)

49. **REGGAE RECORDING**
ONE BRIGHT DAY
Ziggy Marley and The Melody
Makers (Virign)

50. **RECORDING FOR CHILDREN**
THE ROCKA-A-BYE
COLLECTION, VOL. I
Tanya Goodman (Jaba Records)

51. COMEDY RECORDING
P.D.Q. BACH: 1712
OVERTURE & OTHER
MUSICAL ASSAULTS
Professor Peter Schickele: The
Greater Hoople Area Off-Season
Philharmonic (Telarc)

**52. SPOKEN WORD OR NON-
MUSICAL RECORDING**
IT'S ALWAYS SOMETHING
Gilda Radner
(Simon & Schuster Audio)

**53. MUSICAL CAST
SHOW ALBUM**
JEROME ROBBINS'
BROADWAY
(Jason Alexander, Debbie
Shapiro, Robert La Fosse
and others)
Producer: Jay David Saks
(RCA Victor)

**54. INSTRUMENTAL
COMPOSITION**
THE BATMAN THEME
Composer: Danny Elfman
(Warner Bros.)

**55. ALBUM OF ORIGINAL
INSTRUMENTAL
BACKGROUND SCORE
WRITTEN FOR MOTION
PICTURE OR TELEVISION**
THE FABULOUS BAKER
BOYS
Composer: Dave Grusin (GRP)

**56. SONG WRITTEN
SPECIFICALLY FOR MOTION
PICTURE OR TELEVISION**
LET THE RIVER RUN (from
the motion picture "Working
Girl")
Songwriter: Carly Simon (Arista)

57. MUSICVIDEO—SHORT FORM
LEAVE ME ALONE
Michael Jackson; Jim Blashfield,
director; Frank Dileo, Michael
Jackson, Jim Blashfield, Jerry
Kramer, producers (Epic)

58. MUSICVIDEO—LONG FORM
RHYTHM NATION
Janet Jackson; Dominic Sena,
Johathan Dayton, Valerie Faris,
directors; Aris McGarry,
Johathan Dayton, Valerie Faris,
producers (A&M)

**59. INSTRUMENTAL
ARRANGEMENT**
SUITE FROM THE MILAGRO
BEANFIELD WAR
(Track from "Migration")
Arranger: Dave Grusin (GRP)

**60. INSTRUMENTAL
ARRANGEMENT
ACCOMPANYING VOCALISTS**
MY FUNNY VALENTINE
(Track from "The Fabulous Baker
Boys" soundtrack)
Dave Grusin, instrumental
arranger (GRP)

61. ALBUM PACKAGE
SOUND & VISION
Art Director: Roger Gorman
(Rykodisk Inc.)

62. ALBUM NOTES
BIRD: THE COMPLETE
CHARLIE PARKER
ON VERVE
Annotator: Phil Schaap (Verve)

63. HISTORICAL ALBUM
CHUCK BERRY—
THE CHESS BOX
Andy McKane, album producer
(Chess/MCA)

64. ENGINEERED RECORDING
CRY LIKE A RAINSTORM—
HOWL LIKE THE WIND
Engineer: George Massenburg
(Elektra)

65. PRODUCER OF THE YEAR
(Non-Classical)
PETER ASHER

66. CLASSICAL ALBUM
BARTOK: 6 STRING
QUARTETS
Emerson String Quartet
Producer: Wolf Erichson (DG)

67. ORCHESTRAL PERFORMANCE
MAHLER: SYMPHONY NO. 3
IN D MINOR
Leonard Bernstein cond. New
York Philharmonic (DG)

68. OPERA RECORDING
WAGNER: DIE WALKUERE
James Levine cond. Metropolitan
Opera Orch. (Lakes, Moll,
Morris, Norman Behrens,
Ludwig)
Producer: Cord Garben (DG)

69. CHORAL PERFORMANCE (OTHER THAN OPERA)
BRITTEN: WAR REQUIEM
Robert Shaw cond. Atlanta Sym.
Orch. & Chorus and Atlanta Boy
Choir (Telarc)

70. CLASSICAL PERFORMANCE, INSTRUMENTAL SOLOIST(S) WITH ORCHESTRA
BARBER: CELLO CONCERTO,
OP. 22/BRITTEN: SYMPHONY
FOR CELLO & ORCHESTRA,
OP. 68
Yo-Yo Ma, cello; David Zinman
cond. Baltimore Sym. Orch.
(CBS Masterworks)

71. CLASSICAL PERFORMANCE, INSTRUMENTAL SOLOIST (WITHOUT ORCHESTRA)
BACH: ENGLISH SUITES,
BWV 806-11
Andras Schiff, piano (London)

72. CHAMBER MUSIC PERFORMANCE
BARTOK: 6 STRING
QUARTETS
Emerson String Quartet (DG)

73. CLASSICAL VOCAL SOLOIST PERFORMANCE
KNOXVILLE—SUMMER OF
1915 (Music of Barber, Menotti,
Harbison, Stravinsky)
Dawn Upshaw (David Zinman
cond. Orchestra of St. Luke's)
(Elektra/Nonesuch)

74. CONTEMPORARY COMPOSITION
REICH: DIFFERENT TRAINS
(Kronos Quartet)
Composer: Steve Reich (Elektra/
Nonesuch)

75. ENGINEERED RECORDING, CLASSICAL
BRITTEN: WAR REQUIEM
Robert Shaw cond. Atlanta Sym.
Orch & Chorus & Atlanta Boy
Choir & Solos
Engineer: Jack Renner (Telarc)

76. CLASSICAL PRODUCER OF THE YEAR
ROBERT WOODS

33RD ANNUAL (1990) GRAMMY WINNERS
Announced on February 20, 1991
Eligibility Year: October 1, 1989 through September 30, 1990

1. RECORD OF THE YEAR
ANOTHER DAY IN PARADISE
Phil Collins
Producers: Phil Collins, Hugh
Padgham (Atlantic)

2. ALBUM OF THE YEAR
BACK ON THE BLOCK
Qunicy Jones
Producer: Quincy Jones (QWest/
Warner Bros.)

3. **SONG OF THE YEAR**
FROM A DISTANCE
Songwriter: Julie Gold (Atlantic)

4. **NEW ARTIST**
MARIAH CAREY (Columbia/
CBS)

5. **POP VOCAL PERFORMANCE,
FEMALE**
VISION OF LOVE
Mariah Carey (Columbia/CBS)

6. **POP VOCAL PERFORMANCE,
MALE**
OH PRETTY WOMAN
(Track from "A Black & White
Night Live")
Roy Orbison (Virgin)

7. **POP PERFORMANCE
BY A DUO OR GROUP
WITH VOCAL**
ALL MY LIFE
Linda Ronstadt with Aaron
Neville (Elektra Entertainment)

8. **POP INSTRUMENTAL
PERFORMANCE**
TWIN PEAKS THEME (Track
from "Twin Peaks" soundtrack)
Angelo Badalamenti
(Warner Bros.)

9. **ROCK VOCAL
PERFORMANCE, FEMALE**
BLACK VELVET
Alannah Myles (Atlantic)

10. **ROCK VOCAL
PERFORMANCE, MALE**
BAD LOVE
Eric Clapton (Reprise/Duck)

11. **ROCK PERFORMANCE
BY A DUO OR GROUP
WITH VOCAL**
JANIE'S GOT A GUN
Aerosmith (Geffen)

12. **ROCK INSTRUMENTAL
PERFORMANCE**
D/FW (Track from "Family
Style")
The Vaughan Brothers (Epic
Associated)

13. **HARD ROCK PERFORMANCE
(VOCAL OR INSTRUMENTAL)**
TIME'S UP
Living Colour (Epic)

14. **METAL PERFORMANCE
(VOCAL OR INSTRUMENTAL)**
STONE COLD CRAZY (Track
from "Rubaiyat"/various artists)
Metallica (Elektra Entertainment)

15. **ALTERNATIVE MUSIC
PERFORMANCE
(VOCAL OR INSTRUMENTAL)**
I DO NOT WANT WHAT
I HAVEN'T GOT
Sinead O'Connor
(Ensign/Chrysalis)

16. **R&B VOCAL PERFORMANCE,
FEMALE**
COMPOSITIONS
Anita Baker
(Elektra Entertainment)

17. **R&B VOCAL PERFORMANCE,
MALE**
HERE AND NOW
Luther Vandross (Epic)

18. **R&B PERFORMANCE
BY A DUO OR GROUP
WITH VOCAL**
I'LL BE GOOD TO YOU
Ray Charles, Chaka Khan
(QWest)

19. **RHYTHM & BLUES SONG**
U CAN'T TOUCH THIS
Songwriters: Rick James, James
Miller, M.C. Hammer (Capitol)

20. **RAP SOLO PERFORMANCE**
U CAN'T TOUCH THIS
M.C. Hammer (Capitol)

21. **RAP PERFORMANCE BY A DUO OR GROUP**
BACK ON THE BLOCK (Track from "Back on the Block")
Ice-T, Melle Mel, Big Daddy Kane, Kool Moe Dee (Warner Bros.)

22. **NEW AGE PERFORMANCE**
Mark Ishman
Mark Ishman (Virgin)

23. **JAZZ FUSION PERFORMANCE**
BIRDLAND
(Track from "Back on the Block")
Quincy Jones (various artists)
(QWest/Warner Bros.)

24. **JAZZ VOCAL PERFORMANCE, FEMALE**
ALL THAT JAZZ
Ella Fitzgerald (Pablo)

25. **JAZZ VOCAL PERFORMANCE, MALE**
WE ARE IN LOVE
Harry Connick Jr.
(Columbia/CBS)

26. **JAZZ INSTRUMENTAL PERFORMANCE, SOLOIST**
THE LEGENDARY OSCAR PETERSON TRIO LIVE AT THE BLUE NOTE
Oscar Peterson (Telarc)

27. **JAZZ INSTRUMENTAL PERFORMANCE, GROUP**
THE LEGENDARY OSCAR PETERSON TRIO LIVE AT THE BLUE NOTE
The Oscar Peterson Trio (Telarc)

28. **JAZZ INSTRUMENTAL PERFORMANCE, BIG BAND**
BASIE'S BAG
(Track from "Big Boss Band")
George Benson featuring the Count Basie Orchestra
(Warner Bros.)

29. **COUNTRY VOCAL PERFORMANCE, FEMALE**
WHERE'VE YOU BEEN
Kathy Mattea (Mercury)

30. **COUNRY VOCAL PERFORMANCE, MALE**
WHEN I CALL YOUR NAME
Vince Gill (MCA)

31. **COUNTRY PERFORMANCE BY A DUO OR GROUP WITH VOCAL**
PICKIN' ON NASHVILLE
The Kentucky Headhunters
(Mercury)

32. **COUNTRY LOCAL COLLABORATION**
POOR BOY BLUES
Chet Atkins & Mark Knopfler
(Columbia/CBS)

33. **COUNTRY INSTRUMENTAL PERFORMANCE**
SO SOFT, YOUR GOODBYE
(Track from "Neck and Neck")
Chet Atkins & Mark Knopfler
(Columbia/CBS)

34. **BLUEGRASS RECORDING**
I'VE GOT THAT OLD FEELING
Alison Kraus (Rounder)

35. **COUNTRY SONG**
WHERE'VE YOU BEEN
Songwriters: Jon Vezner, Don Henry (Mercury)

36. **ROCK/CONTEMORARY GOSPEL ALBUM**
BEYOND BELIEF
Petra (Dayspring/Word)

37. **POP GOSPEL ALBUM**
ANOTHER TIME . . . ANOTHER PLACE
Sandi Patti (A&M/Word Inc.)

38. **SOUTHERN GOSPEL ALBUM**
THE GREAT EXCHANGE
Bruce Carroll (Word)

39. TRADITIONAL SOUL GOSPEL ALBUM
TRAMAINE HAWKINS LIVE
Tramaine Hawkins
(Sparrow Corporation)

40. CONTEMPORARY SOUL GOSPEL ALBUM
SO MUCH 2 SAY
Take 6 (Reprise)

41. GOSPEL ALBUM BY A CHOIR OR CHORUS
HAVING CHURCH
Rev. James Cleveland & the
Southern California Community
Choir; Rev. James Cleveland,
choir director (Savoy)

42. LATIN POP PERFORMANCE
POR QUE TE TENGO QUE
OLVIDAR? (Track from "Nina")
Jose Feliciano
(Capitol/EMI Latin)

43. TROPICAL LATIN PERFORMANCE
TITO PUENTE PRESENTS
MILLIE P.
Tito Puente & Millie P.

44. MEXICAN/AMERICAN PERFORMANCE
SOY DE SAN LUIS
(Track from "Texas Tornados")
Texas Tornados (Reprise)

45. TRADITIONAL BLUES RECORDING
LIVE AT SAN QUENTIN
B.B. King (MCA)

46. CONTEMPORARY BLUES RECORDING
FAMILY STYLE
The Vaughan Brothers
(Epic Associated)

47. TRADITIONAL FOLK RECORDING
ON PRAYING GROUND
Doc Watson (Sugar Hill)

48. CONTEMPORARY FOLK RECORDING
STEADY ON
Shawn Colvin (Columbia/CBS)

49. REGGAE RECORDING
TIME WILL TELL—A
TRIBUTE TO BOB MARLEY
Bunny Wailer (Shanachie)

50. POLKA RECORDING
WHEN IT'S POLKA TIME AT
YOUR HOUSE
Jimmy Sturr & His Orchestra
(Starr)

51. RECORDING FOR CHILDREN
THE LITTLE MERMAID—
ORIGINAL MOTION PICTURE
SOUNDTRACK
Composers (songs and
instrumental score): Howard
Ashman, Alan Menken
(Disneyland Records)

52. COMEDY RECORDING
P.D.Q. BACH:
OEDIPUS TEX & OTHER
CHORAL CALAMITIES
Professor Peter Schickele (Telarc)

53. SPOKEN WORD OR NON-MUSICAL RECORDING
GRACIE: A LOVE STORY
George Burns (Simon & Schuster
Audio)

54. MUSICAL CAST SHOW ALBUM
LES MISERABLES, THE
COMPLETE SYMPHONIC
RECORDING
(Gary Morris, Philip Quast, Kaho
Shimada, Tracey Shayne and
various casts) Alain Boublil,
Herbert Kretzmer, lyricists:
Claude Michel Schonberg,
composer
Producer: David Caddick
(Relativity Records)

55. **INSTRUMENTAL COMPOSITION**
CHANGE OF HEART (Track from "Question and Answer")
Composer: Pat Metheny (Geffen)

56. **INSTRUMENTAL COMPOSITION WRITTEN FOR A MOTION PICTURE OR FOR TELEVISION**
GLORY
Composer: James Horner (Virgin)

57. **SONG WRITTEN SPECIFICALLY FOR A MOTION PICTURE OR FOR TELEVISION**
UNDER THE SEA
(Track from "The Little Mermaid" original soundtrack)
Songwriters: Alan Menken, Howard Ashman
(Disneyland Records)

58. **MUSICVIDEO—SHORT FORM**
OPPOSITES ATTRACT
Paula Abdul;
Michael Patterson, Candice Reckinger, video directors;
Sharon Oreck, video producer
(Virgin)

59. **MUSICVIDEO—LONG FORM**
PLEASE HAMMER DON'T HURT 'EM THE MOVIE
M.C. Hammer; Ruppert Wainwright, video director; John Oetjen, video producer
(Fragile Films)

60. **ARRANGEMENT ON AN INSTRUMENTAL**
BIRDLAND
(Track from "Back on the Block")
Arrangers: Quincy Jones, Ian Prince, Rod Temperton, Jerry Hey (QWest/Warner Bros.)

61. **INSTRUMENTAL ARRANGEMENT ACCOMPANYING VOCAL(S)**
THE PLACES YOU FIND LOVE
(Track from "Back on the Block")
Arrangers: Jerry Hey, Glen Ballard, Clif Magness, Quincy Jones (QWest/Warner Bros.)

62. **ENGINEERED RECORDING (NON-CLASSICAL)**
BACK ON THE BLOCK
Engineer: Bruce Swedien
(QWest/Warner Bros.)

63. **PRODUCER OF THE YEAR (Non-Classical)**
QUINCY JONES

64. **ALBUM PACKAGE**
DAYS OF OPEN HAND
(special edition hologram cover)
Art Directors: Len Peltier, Jeffrey Gold, Suzanne Vega (A&M)

65. **ALBUM NOTES**
BROWNIE: THE COMPLETE EMARCY RECORDINGS OF CLIFFORD BROWN
Annotator: Dan Morgenstern
(Emarcy)

66. **HISTORICAL ALBUM**
ROBERT JOHNSON: THE COMPLETE RECORDINGS
Producer: Lawrence Cohn
(Columbia/CBS)

67. **CLASSICAL ALBUM**
IVES: SYMPHONY NO. 2; THE GONG ON THE HOOK AND LADDER (FIREMAN'S PARADE ON MAIN STREET); CENTRAL PARK IN THE DARK; THE UNANSWERED QUESTION
Leonard Bernstein cond. New York Philharmonic
Producer: Hans Weber (DG)

68. **ORCHESTRAL
PERFORMANCE**
SHOSTAKOVICH:
SYMPHONIES NOS. 1, OP. 10,
& 7 (LENINGRAD) OP. 60
Leonard Bernstein cond. Chicago
Sym. Orch. (DG)

69. **OPERA RECORDING**
WAGNER: DAS RHEINGOLD
James Levine cond. Metropolitan
Opera Orchestra; Principal solos:
Morris, Ludwig, Jerusalem,
Wlaschiha, Moll, Zednik,
Rootering
Producer: Cord Garben (DG)

70. **CHORAL PERFORMANCE
(OTHER THAN OPERA)**
WALTON: BELSHAZZAR'S
FEAST/BERNSTEIN:
CHICHESTER PSALMS;
MISSA BREVIS
Robert Shaw cond. Atlanta Sym.
Chorus & Orch. (Telarc)

71. **CLASSICAL PERFORMANCE,
INSTRUMENTAL SOLOIST(S)
(WITH ORCHESTRA)**
SHOSTAKOVICH: VIOLIN
CONCERTO NO. 1 IN A
MINOR/GLAZUNOV: VIOLIN
CONCERTO IN A MINOR, OP.
82
Itzhak Perlman, violin (Zubin
Mehta cond. Israel Philharmonic)
(Angel)

72. **CLASSICAL PERFORMANCE,
INSTRUMENTAL SOLOIST(S)
(WITHOUT ORCHESTRA)**
THE LAST RECORDING
(CHOPIN, HAYDN, LISZT,
WAGNER)
Vladimir Horowitz, piano
(Sony Classical)

73. **CHAMBER MUSIC OR
OTHER SMALL ENSEMBLE
PERFORMANCE**
BRAHMS: THE THREE
VIOLIN SONATAS (NOS. 1,
OP. 78; 2, OP. 100; 3, OP. 108)
Itzhak Perlman, violin; Daniel
Barenboim, piano
(Sony Classical)

74. **CLASSICAL VOCAL
PERFORMANCE**
CARRERAS, DOMINGO,
PAVAROTTI IN CONCERT
Jose Carreras, Placido Domingo,
Luciano Pavarotti, tenors (Zubin
Mehta cond. Orchestra del
Maggio Musicale Fiorentino &
Orchestra del Teatro dell' Opera
di Roma) (London)

75. **CONTEMPORARY
COMPOSITION**
BERNSTEIN: ARIAS &
BARCAROLLES
William Sharp, baritone; Judy
Kaye, mezzo-soprano; Michael
Barrett & Steven Blier, pianos
(Koch International)

76. **ENGINEERED RECORDING,
CLASSICAL**
RACHMANINOFF: VESPERS
Robert Shaw cond. Robert Shaw
Festival Singers
Engineer: Jack Renner (Telarc)

77. **CLASSICAL PRODUCER
OF THE YEAR**
ADAM STERN

34th ANNUAL (1991) GRAMMY WINNERS*
Announced on February 25, 1992
Eligibility Year: October 1, 1990 through September 30, 1991

1. **RECORD OF THE YEAR**
UNFORGETTABLE
Natalie Cole (with Nat King
Cole)
Producer: David Foster (Elektra)

2. **ALBUM OF THE YEAR**
UNFORGETTABLE
Natalie Cole
Producers: Andre Fischer, David
Foster, Tommy Lipuma (Elektra)

3. **SONG OF THE YEAR**
UNFORGETTABLE
Songwriter: Irving Gordon

4. **NEW ARTIST**
MARC COHN (Atlantic)

5. **POP VOCAL PERFORMANCE,
FEMALE**
SOMETHING TO TALK
ABOUT (single)
Bonnie Raitt (Capitol)

6. **POP VOCAL PERFORMANCE,
MALE**
WHEN A MAN LOVES A
WOMAN (single)
Michael Bolton (Columbia)

7. **POP PERFORMANCE BY A
DUO OR GROUP WITH
VOCAL**
LOSING MY RELIGION
(single)
R.E.M. (Warner Bros.)

8. **TRADITIONAL POP
PERFORMANCE**
UNFORGETTABLE (single)
Natalie Cole (with Nat King
Cole) (Elektra)

9. **POP INSTRUMENTAL
PERFORMANCE**
ROBIN HOOD: PRINCE
OF THIEVES (soundtrack)
Michael Kamen cond. Greater
Los Angeles Orch. (Morgan
Creek)

10. **ROCK VOCAL
PERFORMANCE, SOLO**
LUCK OF THE DRAW (album)
Bonnie Raitt (Capitol)

11. **ROCK PERFORMANCE BY A
DUO OR GROUP WITH
VOCAL**
LOSING MY RELIGION
(single)
R.E.M. (Warner Bros.)

12. **HARD ROCK VOCAL
PERFORMANCE**
FOR UNLAWFUL CARNAL
KNOWLEDGE (album)
Van Halen (Warner Bros.)

13. **METAL PERFORMANCE
WITH VOCAL**
METALLICA (album)
Metallica (Elektra)

14. **ROCK INSTRUMENTAL
PERFORMANCE**
CLIFFS OF DOVER (single)
Eric Johnson (Capitol)

15. **ROCK SONG**
SOUL CAGE
(Sting)
Songwriter: Sting

16. **ALTERNATIVE MUSIC
ALBUM**
OUT OF TIME
R.E.M. (Warner Bros.)

* Winners for 1991 were announced as *Broken Record* went to press. Text
references to the number of awards won by an artist or a group should be
increased by the number of awards listed here.

17. **R&B VOCAL PERFORMANCE, FEMALE (Tie)**
BURNIN' (album)
Patti LaBelle (MCA)

HOW CAN I EASE THE PAIN (single)
Lisa Fischer (Elektra)

18. **R&B VOCAL PERFORMANCE, MALE**
POWER OF LOVE (album)
Luther Vandross (Epic)

19. **R&B PERFORMANCE BY A DUO OR VOCAL GROUP**
COOLEY HIGH HARMONY (album)
Boyz II Men (Motown)

20. **R&B INSTRUMENTAL PERFORMANCE**
(no nominations because of insufficient eligible entries)

21. **RHYTHM & BLUES SONG**
POWER OF LOVE
(Luther Vandross)
Songwriters: Luther Vandross, Marcus Miller, Teddy Vann

22. **RAP SOLO PERFORMANCE**
MAMA SAID KNOCK YOU OUT (single)
L. L. Cool J (Columbia)

23. **RAP PERFORMANCE BY A DUO OR GROUP**
SUMMERTIME (single)
D. J. Jazzy Bell & The Fresh Prince

24. **NEW AGE ALBUM, VOCAL OR INSTRUMENTAL**
FRESH AIRE 7
Mannheim Steamroller (American Gramaphone)

25. **CONTEMPORARY JAZZ PERFORMANCE, VOCAL OR INSTRUMENTAL**
SASSY (Track from "The Offbeat of 'Avenues")
Manhattan Transfer

26. **JAZZ VOCAL PERFORMANCE**
HE IS CHRISTMAS (album)
Take 6 (Reprise)

27. **JAZZ INSTRUMENTAL SOLO**
I REMEMBER YOU (Track from "Serenity")
Stan Getz (Emarcy)

28. **JAZZ INSTRUMENTAL PERFORMANCE GROUP**
SATURDAY NIGHT AT THE BLUE NOTE (album)
Oscar Peterson Trio (Telarc)

29. **LARGE JAZZ ENSEMBLE PERFORMANCE**
LIVE AT ROYAL FESTIVAL HALL (album)
Dizzy Gillespie and the United Nations Orchestra (Enja)

30. **COUNTRY VOCAL PERFORMANCE, FEMALE**
DOWN AT THE TWIST AND SHOUT (single)
Mary-Chapin Carpenter (Columbia)

31. **COUNTRY VOCAL PERFORMANCE, MALE**
ROPIN' THE WIND (album)
Garth Brooks (Capitol)

32. **COUNTRY PERFORMANCE BY A DUO OR GROUP WITH VOCAL**
LOVE CAN BUILD A BRIDGE (single)
The Judds (RCA)

33. **COUNTRY VOCAL COLLABORATION**
RESTLESS (single from "Mark O'Connor & the New Nashville Cats" album)
Steve Wariner, Ricky Scaggs, Vince Gill (Warner Bros.)

34. **COUNTRY INSTRUMENTAL PERFORMANCE**
THE NEW NASHVILLE CATS (album)
Mark O'Connor (Warner Bros.)

35. **BLUEGRASS ALBUM**
SPRING TRAINING
Carl Jackson, John Starling, The
Nashville Ramblers (Sugar Hill)

36. **COUNTRY SONG**
LOVE CAN BUILD A BRIDGE
(The Judds)
Songwriters: Naomi Judd, John
Jarvis, Paul Overstreet

37. **ROCK/CONTEMPORARY
GOSPEL ALBUM**
UNDER THE INFLUENCE
Russ Taff (Myrrh)

38. **POP GOSPEL ALBUM**
FOR THE SAKE OF THE
CALL
Steven Curtis Chapman
(Sparrow)

39. **SOUTHERN GOSPEL ALBUM**
HOMECOMING
The Gaither Vocal Band (Star
Song)

40. **TRADITIONAL SOUL
GOSPEL ALBUM**
PRAY FOR ME
The Mighty Clouds of Joy
(Word)

41. **CONTEMPORARY SOUL
GOSPEL ALBUM**
DIFFERENT LIFESTYLES
BeBe and CeCe Winans
(Sparrow)

42. **GOSPEL ALBUM BY A
CHOIR OR CHORUS**
THE EVOLUTION
OF GOSPEL
Sounds of Blackness, Gary
Hines, Choir Director
(Perspective/A&M)

43. **LATIN POP ALBUM**
COSAS DEL AMOR
Vikki Carr (Sony Discos
International)

44. **TROPICAL LATIN ALBUM**
BACHATA ROSA
Juan Luis Guerra (Karen)

45. **MEXICAN-AMERICAN
ALBUM**
16 DE SEPTIEMBRE
Little Joe (Sony Discos
International)

46. **TRADITIONAL BLUES
ALBUM**
LIVE AT THE APOLLO
B. B. King (GRP)

47. **CONTEMPORARY BLUES
ALBUM**
DAMN RIGHT, I'VE GOT
THE BLUES
Buddy Guy (Silvertone)

48. **TRADITIONAL FOLK ALBUM**
THE CIVIL WAR (Original
Soundtrack Recording)
Various Artists (Elektra/
Nonesuch)

49. **CONTEMPORARY FOLK
ALBUM**
THE MISSING YEARS
John Prine (Oh Boy)

50. **REGGAE ALBUM, VOCAL
OR INSTRUMENTAL**
AS RAW AS EVER
Shabba Ranks (Epic)

51. **WORLD MUSIC ALBUM,
VOCAL OR INSTRUMENTAL**
PLANET DRUM
Mickey Hart (Rykodisc)

52. **POLKA ALBUM, VOCAL
OR INSTRUMENTAL**
LIVE! AT GILLEY'S
Jimmy Shurr and His Orchestra
(Starr)

53. **ALBUM FOR CHILDREN**
A CAPELLA KIDS
The Maranatha! Kids (Maranatha)

54. **COMEDY ALBUM, SPOKEN
OR MUSICAL**
P.D.Q. BACH: WTWP
CLASSICAL TALKITY-TALK
RADIO
Professor Peter Schickele (Telarc)

55. SPOKEN WORD OR NON-MUSICAL ALBUM
THE CIVIL WAR
Ken Burns (Sound Edition)

56. MUSICAL SHOW ALBUM
THE WILL ROGERS FOLLIES
(Original Broadway Cast)
Composer: Cy Coleman
Lyricists: Betty Comden, Adolph Green
Producers: Cy Coleman, Mike Berniker (Columbia)

57. INSTRUMENTAL COMPOSITION
BASQUE (Track from "The Wind Beneath My Wings")
Composer: Elton John

58. INSTRUMENTAL COMPOSITION WRITTEN FOR A MOTION PICTURE OR TV
DANCES WITH WOLVES
Composer: John Barry

59. SONG WRITTEN FOR A MOTION PICTURE OR TV
(EVERYTHING I DO) I DO IT FOR YOU (from "Robin Hood: Prince of Thieves") (single)
Songwriters: Bryan Adams, Robert John "Mutt" Lange, Michael Kamen

60. MUSICVIDEO—SHORT FORM
LOSING MY RELIGION
R.E.M.
Tarsem, video director; Dave Ramser, video line producer (Warner Bros.)

61. MUSICVIDEO—LONG FORM
MADONNA: BLONDE AMBITION WORLD TOUR LIVE
Madonna
David Mallet and Mark "Aldo" Miceli, video directors; Tony Eaton, video line producer (Pioneer LDCA Inc.)

62. ARRANGEMENT ON AN INSTRUMENTAL
BESS, YOU IS MY WOMAN / I LOVES YOU PORGY (MEDLEY) (Track from "The Gershwin Connection")
Arranger: Dave Grusin (GRP)

63. INSTRUMENTAL ARRANGEMENT ACCOMPANYING VOCALS
UNFORGETTABLE (single)
Arranger: Johnny Mandel (Elektra)

64. ENGINEERED RECORDING (NON-CLASSICAL)
UNFORGETTABLE (album)
Engineers: Al Schmitt, Woody Woodruff, Arman Steiner (Elektra)

65. PRODUCER OF THE YEAR
(Non-Classical)
DAVID FOSTER

66. ALBUM PACKAGE
BILLIE HOLIDAY: THE COMPLETE DECCA RECORDINGS
Art director: Vartan (GRP)

67. ALBUM NOTES
STAR TIME
Annotators: James Brown (intro), Cliff White, Harry Weinger, Nelson George, Alan M. Leeds (Polydor)

68. HISTORICAL ALBUM
BILLIE HOLIDAY: THE COMPLETE DECCA RECORDINGS
Producers: Steven Lasker, Andy McKaie (GRP)

69. CLASSICAL ALBUM
BERNSTEIN: CANDIDE
Leonard Bernstein cond. London Sym. Orch.; Principal soloists: Hadley, Anderson, Ludwig, Green, Gebba, Jones, Ollmann
Producer: Hans Weber (DG)

70. **ORCHESTRAL PERFORMANCE**
CORIGLIANO: SYMPHONY NO. 1
Daniel Barenboim cond. Chicago Sym. Orch. (Erato/Elektra International Classics)

71. **OPERA RECORDING**
WAGNER: GÖTTERDÄMMERUNG
James Levine cond. Metropolitan Opera Orch. & Chorus; Principal soloists: Behrens, Studer, Schwarz, Goldberg, Weikl, Wlaschiha, Salminen
Producer: Cord Garben (DG)

72. **PERFORMANCE OF A CHORAL WORK**
BACH: MASS IN B MINOR
Sir Georg Solti cond. Chicago Sym. Chorus & Orch.; Margaret Hillis, choral dir. (London)

73. **CLASSICAL PERFORMANCE, INSTRUMENTAL SOLOIST(S) (WITH ORCHESTRA)**
BARBER: PIANO CONCERTO, OP. 38
John Browning, piano (Leonard Slatkin cond. St. Louis Sym. Orch.)

74. **CLASSICAL PERFORMANCE, INSTRUMENTAL SOLOIST (WITHOUT ORCHESTRA)**
GRANADOS: GOYESCAS; ALLEGRO DE CONCIERTO; DANZA LENTA
Alicia de Larrocha, piano (RCA)

75. **CHAMBER MUSIC PERFORMANCE**
BRAHMS: PIANO QUARTETS (OPP. 25–26)
Isaac Stern and Jaime Laredo, violins; Yo-Yo Ma, cello; Emanuel Ax, piano (Sony Classical)

76. **CLASSICAL VOCAL PERFORMANCE**
THE GIRL WITH ORANGE LIPS (De Falla, Ravel, Kim, Stravinsky, DeLage)
Dawn Upshaw, soprano (ensemble accompanist) (Elektra/Nonesuch)

77. **CONTEMPORARY COMPOSITION**
CORIGLIANO: SYMPHONY NO. 1
Daniel Barenboim cond. Chicago Sym. Orch. (Erato/Elektra International Classics)

78. **ENGINEERED CLASSICAL RECORDING**
BARBER: SYMPHONY NO. 1, OP. 9; PIANO CONCERTO, OP. 38; SOUVENIRS, OP. 38
John Browning, piano; Leonard Slatkin cond. St. Louis Sym. Orch.
Engineer: William Hoekstra (RCA)

79. **CLASSICAL PRODUCER OF THE YEAR**
JAMES MALLINSON